Literary Ar Memorials Of London (Volume II)

J. Heneage Jesse

Alpha Editions

This Edition Published in 2021

ISBN: 9789354505720

Design and Setting By
Alpha Editions
www.alphaedis.com
Email – info@alphaedis.com

LITERARY AND HISTORICAL

MEMORIALS OF LONDON.

VOL. II.

THE TOWER OF LONDON IN THE REIGN OF HENRY THE FIFTH.

Illustrating the Captivity of Charles, Duke of Orleans.

LITERARY

AND HISTORICAL

By J. HENEAGE JESSE.

AUTHOR OF " MEMOIRS OF THE COURT OF ENGLAND," " GEORGE SELWYN
AND HIS CONTEMPORARIES," " THE PRETENDERS AND THEIR
ADHERENTS," ETC.

IN TWO VOLUMES.

VOL. II.

LONDON:
RICHARD BENTLEY, NEW BURLINGTON STREET,

1847.

.

LONDON:
Printed by S. & J. BENTLEY, WILSON, and FLEY,
Bangor House, Shoe Lane.

CONTENTS

OF

THE SECOND VOLUME.

THE HAYMARKET, LEICESTER SQUARE, AND ST. MARTIN'S IN THE FIELDS.

PAGE

COVENT GARDEN.

DRURY LANE AND CONTIGUOUS STREETS.

ILLUSTRATIONS.

—

LITERARY AND HISTORICAL

MEMORIALS OF LONDON.

THE HAYMARKET, LEICESTER SQUARE, AND ST. MARTIN'S IN THE FIELDS.

HAYMARKET.—HAYMARKET THEATRE.—SUFFOLK HOUSE.—LEICESTER SQUARE.—ANECDOTE OF GOLDSMITH.—ST. MARTIN'S LANE, CHURCH, AND CHURCHYARD. — SOHO SQUARE.—WARDOUR, AND OXFORD STREETS.—RATHBONE PLACE.

As late as the last days of the Protectorate, the tract of ground to the north, between Pall Mall and the villages of Hampstead and Highgate, consisted almost entirely of open country. St. Martin's Church stood literally in the fields; Whitcombe Street was then Hedge Lane; St. Martin's Lane and the Haymarket were really shady lanes with hedges on each side of them; the small village of St. Giles stood in the fields a little to the east; a windmill, surrounded by one or two scattered dwelling-houses, was to be seen where the present Windmill Street now stands; Leicester Square was occupied by

Leicester House and its pleasure-grounds; while the only other object, worthy of notice, was a building on the rising ground at the upper end of the Haymarket then known as the "Gaming House." Shortly after the Restoration, this latter building was pulled down, and Coventry House, from which the present Coventry Street derives its name, was erected on its site. This house appears to have been built by the Right Honourable Henry Coventry, Ambassador to Sweden and Secretary of State in the reign of Charles the Second, who retired here from the cares of public employment in 1679; and who died here in December 1686.*

In 1711, the celebrated statesman, Sir William Wyndham, then a young man of five-and-twenty, was residing in the Haymarket. He had only recently become a husband, and still more recently a father, when a fire broke out in his house, by which his young wife (a daughter of the "proud" Duke of Somerset), and his infant child, very nearly lost their lives. Swift writes on the day on which the accident occurred, "I was awaked at three this morning, my man and the people of the house telling me of a great fire in the Haymarket. I slept again, and two hours after my man came in again, and told me it was Sir William Wyndham's house burnt, and that two maids, leaping out of an upper room to avoid the fire, both fell on their heads, one of them upon the iron spikes before the door, and both lay dead in the streets. It is supposed to have

* Granger's " Biog. Hist."

been some carelessness of one or both those maids. The Duke of Ormond was there helping to put out the fire. Wyndham gave 6000*l.* but a few months ago for that house, as he told me, and it was very richly furnished. His young child escaped very narrowly; Lady Catherine escaped barefoot; they all went to Northumberland House. Wyndham has lost 10,000*l.* by this accident; his lady 1000*l.* worth of clothes; it was a terrible accident."*

In a miserable lodging in the Haymarket, Addison composed his celebrated poem, the "Campaign," written, as is well known, at the express desire of Lords Godolphin and Halifax to celebrate the recent victory of Blenheim. "Pope," says Mr. D'Israeli, "was one day taking his usual walk with Harte in the Haymarket, when he desired him to enter a little shop, where going up three pair of stairs into a small room, Pope said, ' In this garret Addison wrote his ' Campaign !' To the feelings of the poet this garret had become a consecrated spot; genius seemed more itself, placed in contrast with its miserable locality." †

It was in the Haymarket that Baretti (whose name is so intimately associated with the literary annals of the last century,) had the misfortune to take away the life of a fellow-creature in a street quarrel, for which he was subsequently arraigned for murder at the bar of the Old Bailey on the 20th of October, 1769. It is remarkable, that, among

* " Journal to Stella," 2nd March, 1711–12.
† D'Israeli's " Literary Character."

the witnesses who spoke to his character for humanity at his trial, he should have numbered so many celebrated men as Burke, Garrick, Goldsmith, Reynolds, Topham Beauclerk, and Dr. Johnson.   Baretti, it seems, was hurrying up the Haymarket, when he was accosted by a woman, who behaved with such rude indecency, that he was provoked to give her a blow on the arm.   Three men, who were her companions, immediately made a rush at him, and pushing him off the pavement, attempted to thrust him into the mud.   Alarmed for his safety, Baretti stabbed one of the men with a knife which he was in the habit of carrying for the purpose of carving fruit.   On this the man pursued and collared him, when Baretti, still more alarmed for his safety, stabbed him repeatedly with the knife, of which wounds he died the following day.   Baretti was acquitted at his trial, on the ground that he had acted in self-defence.*

As late as the year 1755, according to a map printed for " Stow's Survey," the spot of ground, on which the Italian Opera House now stands, was occupied by such places as Market Lane, Whitehorse Yard, and the Phœnix and Unicorn Inns: the latter standing at the south-east corner facing Cockspur Street and Pall Mall East.   The next object of interest in the Haymarket is the Haymarket Theatre.   The first stone of Sir John Vanbrugh's theatre, as it was then occasionally styled from his

* See Boswell's " Life of Johnson," vol. iii. p. 98; and " European Magazine," vol. xvi. p. 91.

having been the original projector of it, was laid by
Anne, Countess of Sunderland, the most beautiful
of the four charming daughters of the great Duke of
Marlborough. She was usually styled the "Little
Whig," from the smallness of her stature and the
interest which she took in party politics, and Colley
Cibber informs us that this remarkable title was
actually engraved on the foundation-stone. The
theatre was opened on the 9th of April, 1705,
with an Italian Opera, which met with but indifferent success, and about half a century since was
burnt to the ground.* The patent by which it is
now held was granted to the celebrated Foote, and
was afterwards purchased, and successively held, by
the two Colmans, father and son.

Close to the Haymarket Theatre, on the site of
the present Suffolk Street and Suffolk Place, stood
Suffolk House, the residence, in the days of James
the First, of Thomas, first Earl of Suffolk and his
beautiful and unprincipled Countess, whose names
so frequently occur in the profligate annals of that
reign. In the old street, which was erected on its
site, lived the charming actress, Mary Davis, who is
said to have captivated the heart of Charles the
Second, by singing, in the character of Celania,
in "The Mad Shepherdess," the song,—

My lodging is on the cold ground.

Pepys informs us, that, in 1667, Charles publicly
acknowledged the beautiful girl as his mistress;—

* Cibber's " Apology for his Life," " Biographia Dramatica,"
Introduction.

that he presented her with a ring valued at *seven hundred* pounds, and furnished a house for her in Suffolk Street. Pepys further informs us that he happened one day to be passing by when she was stepping into her coach, in Suffolk Street, and he tells us a "mighty fine coach" it was. Little else is known of Mary Davis, but that her picture was painted by Lely, and that a daughter which she had by Charles became the mother of the ill-fated Francis Ratcliffe, Earl of Derwentwater.

In Suffolk Street, lived Miss Van Homrigh, the celebrated Vanessa of Swift's poetry, and the victim of his eccentric brutality. It was at her mother's house, in Suffolk Street, that we find him keeping his best cassock and wig, ready to put them on when he paid visits to the House of Lords, and it was here that,—

> Vanessa held Montaigne and read,
> While Mrs. Susan combed her head.

Running parallel with Suffolk Place, is James Street, with its well-known tennis-court, in which Charles the Second and his brother, the Duke of York, used frequently to indulge in their favourite game. The house, No. 17, at the south-west corner of the Haymarket and James Street, is said to be that, through which the royal brothers used to pass on their way to the tennis-court.

Passing through Panton Street, (so called from a Colonel Thomas Panton who obtained authority to build houses here, in 1671,) we come to Leicester Square, or, as it is still occasionally styled, Leicester

Fields. It appears by "Faithorne's Plan of London," printed in 1658, that Leicester House, the residence of the Sidneys, Earls of Leicester, was then the only house on the site of the present Square. Here, on the 13th of February, 1662, died the amiable and interesting daughter of James the First, Elizabeth, Queen of Bohemia, whose melancholy story is still seldom read without a tear. In this house,—at the time when the recent magnificent victories of Blenheim, Oudenarde, and Malplaquet, had rendered his name a household word with the English people,—Prince Eugene was lodged during his visit to England, in 1711.* In the course of the same century, Leicester House, to use the words of Pennant, became "successively the pouting-place of Princes." When George the Second, then Prince of Wales, quarrelled with his father, in 1717, he took up his residence with his family, in Leicester House. At length, on St. George's day, 1720, an interview took place between the father and son, and we are told that the first intimation which the public had that it was satisfactory, was the fact that, when the Prince returned to Leicester House, he was attended, as formerly, by the royal guards.

Here Frederick, Prince of Wales, resided with his Princess and her children, during the many years that he was on bad terms with his father, George the Second. On the 4th of January, 1749, we find the royal children, (including George the

* Swift's "Journal to Stella," 6th January, 1711-12.

Third, then a boy of eleven years old,) performing
the play of "Cato," before their parents at Leicester
House : the following is the *dramatis personæ* :—

Cato .	.	.	Master Nugent.
Portius .	.	.	Prince George (afterwards George III).
Juba	.	.	Prince Edward (afterwards Duke of York).
Sempronius	.	.	Master Evelyn,
Lucius	.	.	Master Montague.
Decius .	.	.	Lord Milsington.
Syphax	.	.	Master North.
Marcus .	.	.	Master Madden.
Marcia	.	.	Princess Augusta (afterwards Duchess of Brunswick).
Lucia .	.	.	Princess Elizabeth.*

In Leicester House, Frederick, Prince of Wales,
breathed his last. He had been ill for some days,
but so little did his family apprehend any fatal result, that almost at the moment of his decease they
were amusing themselves with cards in the outer
room. Between nine and ten o'clock in the evening,
he was seized with a fit of coughing. It had continued for some time, when the Prince laid his
hand on his stomach and said, "*Je sens la mort.*"
His favourite German page, who was supporting
him, suddenly felt him shiver, and exclaimed, " The
Prince is going !" The Princess, who was at the
foot of the bed, immediately caught up a candle
and ran towards him, but before she could reach
him he was dead. According to Wraxall, the person in whose arms the Prince expired, was Des-
noyèrs, a celebrated dancing-master of the period,
who, at the moment of the fatal seizure, was en-

* Lady Hervey's " Letters."

gaged in playing the violin for the amusement of the dying man.[*]

Leicester House, which is described in 1773, as a "large old brick building with a court-yard before it,"[†] was pulled down in 1806. It stood on the north side of the square, on the site of the present Leicester Place. Adjoining it, to the west, stood Saville House, the residence of Sir George Saville, ancestor of the Earls and Marquesses of Halifax. George the Third resided here during the life-time of his father, Frederick Prince of Wales, and on his accession to the throne we find his brother, the young Duke of York, keeping his court here. This house was the scene of one of the famous riots fomented by Lord George Gordon, in 1780; the interior being completely pillaged and destroyed by the mob. Some of the apartments, we believe, of old Saville House still remain, and are now chiefly occupied by a shooting-gallery, and what was recently Miss Linwood's well-known exhibition of needle-work.

In Leicester Square lived at different periods three of the greatest painters which this country has produced; Sir James Thornhill, Sir Joshua Reynolds, and Hogarth. Thornhill breathed his last in this square, on the 25th of October, 1764. In the course of the day he had been brought from Chiswick, in rather a weak state of health, but with his accustomed cheerfulness unimpaired. He ap-

[*] Wraxall's "Memoirs of His Own Time."
[†] Noorthouck's "Hist. of London," 1773.

peared much gratified by a letter which was handed
to him from a friend in Pennsylvania, and having
drawn up a rough draught of an answer to it, he
retired to rest. Shortly afterwards he was seized
with an attack of vomiting, and having rung his
bell, he was found in a hopeless condition, and
expired about two hours afterwards.

The residence of Sir Joshua Reynolds, and the
house in which he died, was No. 47, on the West
side of the Square, which is now occupied by a
Literary and Scientific Institution. How changed
from the days when Burke, Goldsmith, Garrick,
Topham Beauclerk, Dr. Johnson, and Boswell, were
feasted at Sir Joshua's hospitable board ! I seldom
pass by this house without calling to mind a curious
passage in the life of Oliver Goldsmith, of which
Leicester square was the scene, and in which the
mingled vanity and simplicity of this remarkable
man were singularly exemplified. The story was
thus related to Mr. Croker by an eye-witness.
" One afternoon, as Colonel O'Moore and Mr. Burke
were going to dine with Sir Joshua Reynolds, they
observed Goldsmith (also on his way to Sir Joshua's)
standing near a crowd of people, who were staring
and shouting at some foreign women at the windows
of one of the houses in Leicester Square. ' Observe
Goldsmith,' said Mr. Burke to O'Moore, ' and mark
what passes between him and me by-and-bye at Sir
Joshua's.' They passed on, and arrived before
Goldsmith, who came soon after, and Mr. Burke
affected to receive him very coolly. This seemed

to vex poor Goldsmith, who begged Mr. Burke would tell him how he had had the misfortune to offend him. Burke appeared very reluctant to speak ; but, after a good deal of pressing, said that ' he was really ashamed to keep up an intimacy with one who could be guilty of such monstrous indiscretions as Goldsmith had just exhibited in the square.' Goldsmith, with great earnestness, protested he was unconscious of what was meant. ' Why,' said Burke, did you not exclaim, as you were looking up at those women, what stupid beasts the crowd must be for staring with such admiration at those *painted jezebels*; while a man of your talents passed by unnoticed?' Goldsmith was horror-struck, and said, ' Surely, surely, my dear friend, I did not say so?' ' Nay,' replied Burke, ' if you had not said so, how should I have known it?' ' That's true,' answered Goldsmith, with great humility. ' I am very sorry—it was very foolish : *I do recollect that something of the kind passed through my mind, but I did not think I had uttered it.*' "*

Hogarth, the great artist of human nature, lived and died at the south-east corner of Leicester Square, now well known as Sabloniere's Hotel. It is remarkable that both Thornhill and his son-in-law Hogarth should have died in the same month, in the same year, and in the same square, and that both should have been buried at Chiswick. The house in which Hogarth breathed his last is in

* Boswell's " Life of Johnson," note by Croker.

other respects of great interest. Here, during a
visit which he paid to England, lived the great
Polish patriot, formerly the aide-de-camp of Wash-
ington, Thaddeus Kosciusko :—

> ————————————— Ye who dwell
> Where Kosciusko dwelt, remembering yet
> The unpaid amount of Catherine's bloody debt!
> Poland! o'er which the avenging angel past,
> But left thee as he found thee still a waste;
> Forgetting all thy still enduring claim,
> Thy lotted people and extinguished name;
> Thy sigh for freedom, thy long-flowing tear,
> That sound that crushes in the tyrant's ear,—
> Kosciusko! on—on—on—the thirst of war,
> Gasps for the blood of serfs and of their Czar, &c.*

There may be those persons to whom it may be
interesting to be informed, that the Countess Guic-
cioli, whose changeless affection soothed the closing
years of the author of the above beautiful lines,
and whose name will descend to posterity connected with the love and the poetry of Lord Byron,
resided, during a visit which she paid to England,
in the same house in which Kosciusko lived and
Hogarth died.   There are other persons, less
poetically constituted, to whom it may be no less
interesting to be informed that, in the adjoining
house lived the celebrated surgeon, John Hunter,
during the last years of his valuable life, and that
here he formed his extensive museum of anatomical
preparations for the illustration of physiological
science.†

Our   remaining   notices   of   Leicester   square,

* " The Age of Bronze."
† See Foote's " Life of John Hunter," and " Gentleman's
Magazine," vol. lxiv.

though not without interest, may be summed up in a few words. In 1698, we find the Marquis of Carmarthen residing in Leicester Square, and giving a ball here to Peter the Great, whom he had been selected to attend during his visit to England. Swift informs us that he lodged here in 1711,* and here, on the 29th of December, 1765, died "at his house in Leicester Square," Prince Frederick William, youngest brother of George the Third, at the age of sixteen. In Leicester Square stood formerly the "Feathers" public-house; the favourite resort of Grose, the antiquarian, of Henderson, the actor, and of "Athenian" Stuart.

Behind Leicester House stood, in 1658, the Military Yard, founded by Henry Prince of Wales, the interesting and high-spirited son of James the First. In the days of Charles the Second it was converted by a M. Foubert into an academy for riding and other manly exercises, and even as late as the days of Pennant continued to be a noted riding-school.† In Orange Court, Leicester Square, lived John Opie, the celebrated painter, who died in 1807.

In the centre of the north side of Leicester Square is a small and dirty outlet, called St. Martin's Street. In this miserable place, at the corner of Long's Court, in a house of good size, and formerly perhaps of some pretensions, lived Sir Isaac Newton. The house will be easily dis-

* "Journal to Stella," 28th Nov. 1711.
† Pennant's "London."

cernible by a small wooden erection on the roof,
which is said to have been the private observatory
of the immortal philosopher. He seems to have
removed to this street from Jermyn Street.

From St. Martin's Street we easily pass into
St. Martin's Lane, which was converted from a
country lane into a populous street about the
middle of the seventeenth century. Here, in 1660,
at the residence of her father, Dr. Killegrew,—the
witty and well-known favourite of Charles the
Second,—was born, the pious and gifted, Anne
Killegrew, the poetess and the painter, unspoiled
by being a beauty and unsophisticated by being
a maid of honour! Her name is celebrated by
Antony Wood, Ballard, Vertue, and Horace Walpole, but it is Dryden who has immortalized her
beauty, her genius, and her worth :—

> Art she had none, yet wanted none ;
>   For nature did that want supply ;
> So rich in treasures of her own,
>   She might our boasted stores defy ;
> Such noble vigour did her verse adorn,
> That it seemed borrowed where 'twas only born.

Anne Killegrew, as we have already mentioned,
died in the apartments of her father, in the cloisters
of Westminster Abbey, at the age of twenty-four,
and was buried in the Savoy Chapel, in the Strand.

At No. 103, St. Martin's Lane, lived Sir James
Thornhill, the painter, previous to his removal to
Leicester Square, and at the back of this house
he founded, to his credit, one of the earliest schools
for the study of the antique. This house is con-

nected with an interesting anecdote. Hogarth,
then unknown to fame, had formed a clandestine
marriage with the daughter of Sir James Thornhill,
which the decorator of Windsor Castle and Greenwich Hospital was little inclined either to overlook
or to forgive. They were living on bad terms together, — the son-in-law in his poverty and the
father-in-law in his pride,—when one morning, on
his entering his breakfast-room, he was struck by
some drawings which he perceived on the table.
They were the first pencil sketches of Hogarth's
immortal series of pictures, "The Harlot's Progress." To the credit of Thornhill he forgot the
poverty of his son-in-law in his admiration of his
genius, and from henceforward they were reconciled.
It is remarkable, that the house in which this scene
occurred should afterwards have been the residence
of Sir Joshua Reynolds.

We descend, by way of St. Martin's Lane, to
that famous and beautiful structure, St. Martin's
Church, rendered, perhaps, the more striking from
its contrast with the disgraceful deformities with
which modern barbarism has been permitted to
desecrate one of the finest sites in any capital in
Europe. In any other country public indignation
would long since have swept its absurdities to the
ground ; and it is still to be hoped that something
may be done to remedy this grievous desecration.

St. Martin's Church, so deservedly celebrated for
the elegance of its steeple and the extreme beauty
of its portico, stands on a spot of ground which

appears to have been bestowed at a very early
period on the abbot and convent of St. Peter's
Westminster. That a church existed here in very
early times is proved from a dispute which took
place in 1222, between William, Abbot of Westminster, and Eustace, Bishop of London, concerning
the dependence upon, or exemption of, St. Martin's-
in-the-Fields, from the jurisdiction of the latter
prelate. In the reign of Henry the Eighth, a small
church was built here at the expense of the King,
and since that period St. Martin's has continued to
be an appropriation in the gift of the sovereign·
In consequence of the increase of the neighbouring
population, the church built by Henry was enlarged
in 1607, James the First and his son Henry defray-
ing a part of the expense, and the parish the other
part. Finally, this church was pulled down in 1721,
and between that year and 1726 the present beautiful building was erected by Gibbs, at the expense
of 37,000*l.*

St. Martin's Church is associated with the names
of many individuals, to whose history is attached a
deep and lasting interest. The immortal Ben Jonson, whose parents lived close by in Hartshorn
Lane, was first sent, we are told, to "a private
school in the church of St. Martin's-in-the-Fields ;*"
and it was in this church that the unfortunate
Prince Charles Edward is stated to have formally
abjured the religion of his forefathers.†

* Sir Thomas Pope Blunt's " Censura Authorum."
† Walpole's " Letters to Sir Horace Mann."

25

In the burial-ground of St. Martin's lie the remains of Mrs. Anne Turner, so celebrated as the
agent of the Countess of Somerset in effecting the
tragical murder of Sir Thomas Overbury. She was
the widow of a physician, who left her young,
beautiful and penniless; when, preferring crime to
poverty, she was easily enlisted in the dark designs
of her patroness. In the world of fashion, in the
days of James the First, she was remarkable for
having introduced yellow starch into ruffs. When
Coke, the Lord Chief Justice, passed sentence of
death on her, he added the singular order, that,
" as she was the person who had brought yellow
starched ruffs into vogue, she should be hanged in
that dress, that the same might end in shame and
detestation." It is remarkable that the hangman
who executed this wretched woman appeared decorated with yellow ruffs on the scaffold. Anne
Turner was hung at Tyburn on the 15th of November, 1615, and, according to Camden, died a
" true penitent." There were many, indeed, who
seem to have forgotten the fact of her detestable
crime, in the interest excited by her youth and
beauty, and her becoming demeanour on the scaffold. A Mr. John Castle writes to one of his
correspondents, on the 28th of November, 1615,
" Since I saw you, I saw Mrs. Turner die. If
detestation of painted pride, lust, malice, powdered
hair, yellow bands, and the rest of the wardrobe of
court vanities, — if deep sighs, tears, confessions,
ejaculations of the soul, admonitions to all sorts of

people to make God and an unspotted conscience
always our friends,—if the protestation of faith and
hope to be washed by the same Saviour and the
like mercies that Mary Magdalen was, be signs and
demonstrations of a blessed penitent, then I will tell
you that this poor broken woman went *à cruce ad
gloriam,* and now enjoys the presence of her and our
Redeemer.   Her body being taken down by her
brother, one Norton, servant to the Prince, was,
in a coach, conveyed to St. Martin's-in-the-Fields,
where, in the evening of the same day, she had an
honest and a decent burial."*   Another of her
admirers has celebrated the beautiful murderess in
some lines but little known, in which, if the sentiment is misplaced, the verses at least have considerable merit.

> The roses on her lovely cheek were dead ;
> The earth's pale colour had all overspread
> Her sometime lively look ; and cruel Death,
> Coming untimely with his wintry breath,
> Blasted the fruit, which, cherry-like, in show,
> Upon her dainty lips did whilom grow.
> O how the cruel cord did misbecome
> Her comely neck ! and yet by law's just doom
> Had been her death.   Those locks, like golden thread,
> That used in youth to enshrine her globe-like head,
> Hung careless down ; and that delightful limb,
> Her snow-white nimble hand, that used to trim
> Those tresses up, now spitefully did tear
> And rend the same ; nor did she now forbear
> To beat the breast of more than lily white,
> Which sometime was the bed of sweet delight.
> From those two springs where joy did whilom dwell,
> Grief's pearly drops upon her pale cheek fell.†

The celebrated John Lacy, the dancing-master,

---

* Bishop Goodman's " Memoirs."   † " Harleian Miscellany."

the soldier, the actor, and the dramatic writer,—the man of varied fortunes and of varied talents,—sleeps in the burial-ground of St. Martin's. In the days when our sovereigns mingled with their people; when they connected themselves with their amusements and patronized the stage, so delighted was Charles the Second with Lacy's theatrical performances that he caused his picture to be taken in three different characters. This picture was at Windsor within the last few years, and is doubtless still in existence. Near the grave of Lacy is that of Nell Gwynne,— one who acted, and laughed, and coquetted on the boards of the same theatre, and who charmed the same audience. Her remains were brought here from her house in Pall Mall, and her funeral sermon was preached by Dr. Tenison, Vicar of St. Martin's, and afterwards Archbishop of Canterbury. In his discourse he spoke almost enthusiastically of her charities, her benevolence, her sincere repentance and pious end. The encomiums which he heaped on the frail but repentant actress were afterwards maliciously dwelt upon to the Queen of William the Third, but the reply of Mary was creditable to her heart; " I have heard as much," she said : " it is a sign that the poor unfortunate woman died penitent ; for if I can read a man's heart through his looks, had she not made a pious and Christian end, the doctor would never have been induced to speak well of her."* To the ringers of St. Martin-in-the-Fields Nell Gwynne bequeathed a small sum annually, which they still

* " Biog. Brit."

continue to enjoy. Probably she may have wished
that their merry chimes should peal over her grave
when she was no more; but few have listened to
their exhilarating sounds as they burst forth on a
summer evening, without thinking of the merry days
and the chequered fortunes of the kind-hearted and
charitable Nell Gwynne.

In the vaults under the church lie the remains of
the well-known dramatic writer, Mrs. Centlivre,*
whose history is quite as extraordinary, and even
more romantic than that of Nell Gwynne; and in
the church-yard, after a life of misery and privation, was buried another celebrated dramatic
writer, George Farquhar, the author of the "Beaux'
Stratagem."† He died before he had completed
his thirtieth year, and it is difficult to pass by
St. Martin's church-yard without reflecting on the
melancholy end of one so gifted and so young.
"Dear Bob," (was his last letter to Wilks,
and perhaps the last he ever wrote,) "I have not
anything to leave thee to perpetuate my memory,
but two helpless girls; look upon them sometimes,
and think of him that was, to the last moment
of his life, thine, GEORGE FARQUHAR." It is but
due to Wilks to record that he punctually obeyed
the dying injunctions of his unfortunate friend.

At St. Martin's-in-the-Fields was buried Sir
Winston Churchill, formerly of some note as an
historian, but now principally remembered from his

* See " Biog. Dram." v. i. p. 97.
† " Farquhar's Works," Memoir by Leigh Hunt.

having been the father of the great Duke of Marlborough.* In the days of his wealth and grandeur,
it might have been expected that his fortunate and
illustrious son would have raised some monument to
his father's memory ; but unfortunately it was not in
the nature of the Duke of Marlborough to spend a
guinea unnecessarily, even though demanded by
common decency and prompted by filial affection.
Lastly, in the churchyard rest the remains of the
great sculpter, Roubiliac, who died in 1762, and
whose remains were followed to the grave by
Hogarth and Sir Joshua Reynolds.

From the fact of the greater number of the
children of Charles the First having been born at
the neighbouring palace of Whitehall, it might have
been expected that their births would have been
registered at the parish church of St. Martin's.
With one single exception, however, this is not the
case. There is no doubt that the King invariably
gave orders for the usual insertion in the parish
register, and that he sent a sum of money for the
purpose. The persons, however, whom he entrusted with the payment, are said to have appropriated the money to their own use.†

Soho Square, which we readily reach by way
of Prince's Street and Wardour Street, was commenced in the reign of Charles the Second, and
was originally called King's Square. "The Duke
of Monmouth," says Pennant, "lived in the centre
house facing the statue. Originally, the square

* " Athenæ Oxonienses."   † Fuller's " Worthies."

was called, in honour of him, Monmouth Square; and afterwards changed to that of King's Square. I have a tradition, that, on his death the admirers of that unfortunate man changed it to *Soho*, being the word of the day at the field of Sedgmoor." That the ill-fated Duke of Monmouth resided on the spot mentioned by Pennant there can be no question; and, as regards the popular fiction that Soho Square derived its name from the watch-word at the battle of Sedgmoor, it is remarkable that every subsequent historian of London should have followed his authority. It is sufficient, however, to upset the "tradition" of Pennant, to remark that in the "Present State of England," published in 1683, more than four years before the battle of Sedgmoor, the London residence of the Duke of Monmouth is distinctly stated to be *Soho Square*.

In addition to the Duke of Monmouth, Soho Square, as late as the last century, contained the London residences of the Bellasyses earls of Fauconberg, and the Howards, Earls of Carlisle. The last of the Fauconberg family who resided in Soho Square, was Mary Cromwell, third daughter of the great Protector, and wife of Thomas, first Earl of Fauconberg. At the back of the east side of the square, are still retained the names of Fauconberg Street and Fauconberg Mews, denoting that Fauconberg House must have stood in the immediate vicinity.

At what period the Howards deserted Carlisle

House in Soho Square, we have no record. However, in the middle of the last century, we find it occupied by the famous Mrs. Cornely, whose public balls, masquerades, and admirable suppers attracted to her assemblies all the rank and beauty of the day. Carlisle House stood at the north-east corner of the square.

The well-known admiral, Sir Cloudesley Shovel, lived in what has been notorious in our time as the " White House," on the east side of Soho Square. After his melancholy death, his body, having been thrown on shore on the island of Scilly, was brought from thence to his house in London, and subsequently was conveyed from Soho Square with considerable state to Westminster Abbey.* In 1726, we find the celebrated Spanish minister, Ripperda, living with great splendour in Soho Square ; † and lastly, at Nos. 20 and 21, formerly one house, lived Sir Joseph Banks.

With the exception of Gerard Street, the streets in the neighbourhood of Soho Square present no particular feature of interest. Dean Street, and Compton Street, derive their names from Bishop Compton, then Dean of St. Paul's, who at one period held the living of St. Ann's Soho ; and Monmouth Street, as is well-known, is indebted for its name to the unfortunate Duke. This street is now principally celebrated as an emporium for worn out articles of wearing apparel, a purpose to

* Biog. Brit. Art. " Shovel."
† Lord Mahon's " Hist. of England."

which it has been adapted for at least the last
century.   Gay says in his " Trivia,"—

> Shall the huge mutton smoke upon your boards ?
> Such Newgate's copious market best affords ;
> Wouldst thou with mighty beef augment thy meal ?
> Seek Leadenhall : St. James's sends thee veal !
> Thames Street gives cheeses ; Covent Garden fruits ;
> Moorfields old books ; and Monmouth Street old suits.

In Wardour Street lived the great sculptor, Flaxman, but Gerard Street is especially endeared to us
as containing the house in which Dryden lived and
died.   In his dedication of " Don Sebastian " to
Lord Leicester, he speaks of himself as " a poor
inhabitant of his lordship's suburbs, whose best prospect is on the garden of Leicester House ;" and in a
letter to Elmes Steward he writes, " My house is
the fifth door, on the left hand, coming from Newport Street."   From Malone we learn, that the
house so consecrated by genius is No. 43, and we
learn still further from Spence, on the authority of
Pope, that the apartment in which the great poet
" used most commonly to write " was in the ground-
room next the street.   The extraordinary and disgraceful scene which took place at this house, on the
occasion of Dryden's funeral, is too well known to
require a repetition of the particulars.*

There are other interesting associations attached
to Gerard Street.   Here Edmund Burke lived for
many years ; from this street, in 1777, we find
Hannah More dating her letters ; and here, in 1764,
at the sign of the " Turk's Head," Dr. Johnson and

* See Johnson's " Life of Dryden."

Sir Joshua Reynolds founded the celebrated " Literary Club."   Besides these two illustrious men, here
used to assemble Burke, Bennet Langton, Topham
Beauclerk, Oliver Goldsmith, George Colman. Garrick, Sir William Jones, Boswell, Charles James
Fox, George Stevens, Gibbon, Adam Smith, the
Wartons, Richard Brinsley Sheridan, Sir Joseph
Banks, William Windham, Malone, and other celebrated persons.   The club continued to be held at
the Turk's Head till 1783, when their landlord died,
and the house was shortly afterwards shut up. They
then removed to " Prince's " in Sackville Street, and
subsequently to " Baxter's," afterwards " Thomas's "
in Dover Street. In 1792, they removed to Parsloe's,
in St. James's Street ; and, in 1799, to the Thatched
House in the same street, where the club still continues to be held.

Gerard Street derives its name from its having
been erected on the site of the house and gardens of
Charles Gerard, first Earl of Macclesfield, so distinguished for his loyalty to Charles the First, and for
his gallantry during the civil wars. Pennant says,
" The profligate Lord Mohun lived in this street,
and was brought there after he was killed in the
duel with the Duke of Hamilton : I have heard
that his good lady was vastly displeased at the
bloody corpse being flung upon the best bed." Pennant seems to have been in ignorance, that Lord
Mohun's " good lady " was the grand-daughter
of the gallant Earl of Macclesfield, and that the
circumstance of the second Earl bequeathing to

Lord Mohun the greater portion of his estates led to his unfortunate law-suit and duel with the Duke of Hamilton, in which both lost their lives in November, 1712. Pennant, moreover, is wrong in his assertion, that Lord Mohun's "bloody corpse" was carried to his house in Gerard Street, inasmuch as, at the time of his death, he was unquestionably residing in Great Marlborough Street. From the circumstance of Lord Mohun having resided at one period in Gerard Street, it is reasonable to presume that the site on which it now stands was part of the property bequeathed to him by the Earl of Macclesfield. Previous to its falling into the hands of the Gerards, this ground was walled in by order of Henry Prince of Wales, son of James the First, for the purpose of being used for "the exercise of arms."

In Newport Market, within a short distance of Gerard Street, was the chapel of the famous Orator Henley, whom Pope has immortalized in the Dunciad :—

> High on a gorgeous seat, that far out-shone
> Henley's gilt tub, and Flecknoe's Irish throne.

And again,—

> Imbrowned with native bronze, lo ! Henley stands,
> Tuning his voice, and balancing his hands,
> How fluent nonsense trickles from his tongue !
> How sweet the periods, neither said nor sung !
> Still break the benches, Henley, with thy strain,
> While Sherlock, Howe, and Gibson, preach in vain.

Oxford Street, which was built at different periods during the last century, was originally called the "road to Oxford." As regards historical or literary associations, this street, though perhaps the largest in Europe, is singularly deficient in interest, and the few objects or names of any importance with which it is connected, may be summed up in a few words.

Not the least interesting spot is the once fashionable place of amusement, the " Pantheon," now converted into the purposes of a bazaar. The original building was erected in 1771, after a design by Wyatt, and was opened to the public, as a kind of " town Ranelagh," on the 27th of January, 1772. " Near two thousand persons," we are told, " of the highest rank and fashion assembled on this occasion to admire the splendid structure, which contained fourteen rooms, exclusive of the Rotunda." Boswell mentions his visiting it with Dr. Johnson shortly after it was opened. " We walked," he says, " to the Pantheon. The first view of it did not strike us as much as Ranelagh, of which he said, the coup d'œil was the finest thing he had ever seen. However, as Johnson said, we saw the Pantheon in a time of mourning, when there was a dull uniformity; whereas we had seen Ranelagh, when the view was enlivened with a gay profusion of colours." The original building was burnt down, and being rebuilt on a smaller scale, was again used for masquerades and concerts, but being deserted by persons of fashion, it remained closed for several years, when it was converted to its present purpose.

At No. 64, Wells Street, Oxford Street, within a short distance from Berners Street, lived at one

time Dr. James Beattie, the author of " The Min-
strel." Newman Street, a little to the east, is also
interesting from having contained the residence of
several eminent artists, by which class of persons it
has long been colonized. Among the most distinguished persons who have lived here may be mentioned West, the painter, and the younger Bacon,
the sculptor.

Running parallel with Newman Street is Rathbone Place, apparently, in former days, a favourite
resort of the Scottish nobility and gentry, for we
find it, at different times, the place of residence of
the unfortunate Lords Lovat, Balmerino, and Kilmarnock, who suffered on the scaffold for their share
in the Rebellion of 1745. In Hanway Street, close
by, is a public-house, known as the " Blue Posts,"
which was kept by the once celebrated chess-player,
Sturges, the author of a treatise on the game; and,
lastly, in Tottenham Court Road, stands the taber-
nacle built by the famous preacher, George Whit-
field, in 1756.

COVENT GARDEN.

COVENT GARDEN, or rather Convent Garden, derives its name from occupying the site of what was
anciently a vast garden, belonging to the Abbey
and Convent of Westminster, and which extended
as far west as St. Martin's Church.   Behind the
houses on the north side of York Street, stone
coffins, and other relics of the dead, have from time
to time been discovered, which would lead us to
presume that on this spot was the cemetery of
the ancient monks.   After the dissolution of the
monasteries, Convent Garden was bestowed by Edward the Sixth on his uncle, the great Protector,
Edward, Duke of Somerset, and on his attainder was
transferred to John, Earl of Bedford.   It is almost
needless to remark, that from this family,—in whom
the valuable property, once the site of the fair
gardens of the monks of Westminster, is still vest-
ed,—Bedford Street, Bedfordbury, Russell Street,
and Tavistock Street, derive their names.

It appears by a plan of London, printed in 1560,
that Covent Garden was then an open area sur-

rounded by meadows and lanes, with the exception
of the south side where it was bounded by the
gardens of Bedford House. A market appears to
have been first established here in 1634, about
which time Francis, fourth Earl of Bedford, employed Inigo Jones to erect the present piazzas on the
north and east sides. It was originally intended to
continue them round the whole square; and, indeed,
it appears by a print of Hollar's now before me, that
the piazza formerly extended along the east side,
where the "Hummums" now stand: this part,
however, was burnt down, not many years after its
erection. At the close of the seventeenth century
we find the 'prentices of London resorting here to
play at cricket under the porticos, and from Gray's
"Trivia" we learn, that, at a somewhat later period,
the manly game of foot-ball used to be played in
the area where the market now stands :—

> Where Covent Garden's famous temple stands,
> That boasts the work of Jones' immortal hands ;
> Here oft my course I bend, when lo ! from far
> I spy the furies of the foot-ball war ;
> The 'prentice quits his shop to join the crew,
> Increasing crowds the flying game pursue, &c.

To those who are intimate with, and delight in,
the literary history of their country ; — to those to
whom the haunts of departed genius are as hallowed
ground, there is no spot in London replete with
associations of such deep interest as Covent Garden
and the streets with which it is intersected. It is
remarkable, that Sir Peter Lely, Sir Godfrey Kneller, and the celebrated landscape painter, Richard
Wilson, should have been occupants, at different

times, of the same apartments, on the north side
of Covent Garden. In 1716, I find Nicholas Rowe,
the dramatic poet, dating his letters from Covent
Garden, and close by lived Thomas Southern, the
author of "Oroonoko," and of the "Fatal Marriage." Oldys tells us in his MS. notes to Langbaine;—"I remember him a grave and venerable
old gentleman. He lived near Covent Garden, and
used often to frequent the evening prayers there, always neat and decently dressed, commonly in black,
with his silver sword and silver locks; but latterly, it
seems, he resided at Westminster." In Covent
Garden, died, in 1702, John Zachary Kneller, the
elder brother of Sir Godfrey, and himself a painter
of some merit.

The "Old Hummums," Covent Garden, was the
scene of what Dr. Johnson called the "best accredited ghost-story" he had ever heard. The person,
whose ghost was supposed to have appeared here,
was Ford, a relation of Johnson's, and said to
be the riotous parson of Hogarth's "Midnight
modern Conversation." The story, as related by
Johnson to Boswell, is as follows:—"A waiter at
the Hummums, in which Ford died, had been absent for some time, and returned, not knowing that
Ford was dead. Going down to the cellar, according to the story, he met him; going down again, he
met him a second time. When he came up, he
asked some of the people of the house what Ford
could be doing there? They told him Ford was dead.
The waiter took a fever, in which he lay for some

time. When he recovered, he said he had a message to deliver to some women from Ford; but he
was not to tell what, or to whom. He walked out;
he was followed, but somewhere about St. Paul's
they lost him. He came back, and said he had
delivered the message, and the women exclaimed,
'Then we are all undone.' Dr. Pallet, who was a
credulous man, inquired into the truth of this story,
and he said the evidence was irresistible." Dr. Johnson further informs us, that Mrs. Johnson went to
the Hummums, on purpose to inquire into the truth
of this strange story, and came away perfectly satisfied that there was no imposition.

The large house, now Evans's Hotel, at the north-
west corner of Covent Garden, was originally the
residence of Admiral Russell, afterwards Earl of
Orford, celebrated for his brilliant victory over
the French off La Hogue in 1692. It afterwards
became the residence of the Lords Archer, of whom
the last baron died in 1778.

We find Covent Garden the scene of more
than one adventure in the works of Congreve and
Fielding, and its hotels and taverns, more especially, continued to be the resort of wits, poets,
actors, and men of fashion, for nearly two centuries. The "Piazza" hotel was the favourite
retreat of Richard Brinsley Sheridan, and of the
men of wit and rank with whom he associated;
and in the parlour of the "Bedford" met the
shilling-rubber club, of which Fielding, Hogarth,
Goldsmith, and Churchill were members. It was

at one of their meetings at the " Bedford," that the
quarrel took place between Hogarth and Churchill,
which induced the latter to satirize his friend, and
the former to retaliate with his unrivalled pencil.
The " Epistle to Hogarth," is comparatively forgotten, but Churchill will still live as " Bruin," when
his verse shall have passed into oblivion.

Unquestionably the most interesting spot in
Covent Garden is the church, dedicated to St.
Paul. Few perhaps there are, who are in the
habit of passing by this heavy looking building, who
are aware that, with the exception of Westminster
Abbey, it contains the remains of more men of
genius and celebrity than any other church in
London. We search in vain, however, for any
memorials to the illustrious dead ; indeed, with
the exception of a small tablet to the memory
of Macklin the actor, there is not a monument
within the walls of the church to point out the
name or the resting-place of a single person of
genius or celebrity.

St. Paul's, Covent Garden, was built by Inigo
Jones, at the expense of the Earl of Bedford.
According to Horace Walpole, who speaks on the
authority of Speaker Onslow, the Earl sent for the
great architect, and, telling him that he required a
chapel for the parishioners who resided on his
property, added, that he intended to put himself
to no considerable expense ; "in fact," he said, " I
would not have it much better than a barn."
" Then," said Inigo Jones, " you shall have the

handsomest barn in England." The truth of this story has sometimes been called in question, but we believe without sufficient reason. The building has occasionally found its admirers, but most persons probably will agree with Walpole, who tells us he could see no beauty in it. "The barn-roof over the portico," he says, "strikes my eye with as little idea of dignity or beauty as it could do if it covered nothing but a barn." In 1795, only seven years after it had been restored at an expense of 11,000l., the interior of the church,—including the monuments to the dead and the entire wood-work,—was destroyed by fire. It was shortly afterwards, however, restored at the expense of the parishioners.

We will now proceed to name a few of the more remarkable persons, whose remains lie either in the church or church-yard of St. Paul's, Covent Garden. In the church-yard was buried the celebrated favourite of James the First, Robert Carr, Earl of Somerset; the union of whose daughter with William, first Duke of Bedford, doubtless led to his being interred on this, the property of the Russells. We stand, too, on the ground which covers the dust of Sir Peter Lely. His monument, which was of white marble, and which was destroyed by the fire of 1795, was adorned with a bust of the great artist, between two cupids, and was ornamented with fruit, foliage, and other devices. The inscription alone has been preserved.*

In the vaults of the church lies the body of the

* See " The New View of London," 1708.

handsome and gallant William Wycherley, the author of the "Plain Dealer," whose beauty of person and graceful address no less endeared him to the ladies, than his conversation and wit rendered him acceptable to Charles the Second and his gay courtiers. Here, too, either in the church or church-yard, rest the remains of another eminent dramatic writer, Thomas Southern.

Let us pause for a moment on the grave of Samuel Butler, the author of "Hudibras." Fortunately, Anthony Wood has enabled us to point out the spot where rest the remains of the most humorous of poets. "This Sam. Butler," he says, "who was a boon and witty companion, especially among the company he knew well, died of a consumption, 25th of September, 1680, and was, according to his desire, buried six foot deep in the yard belonging to the church of St. Paul, in Covent Garden, within the liberty of Westminster, viz., at the west end of the said yard, on the north side, and under the wall, of the church ; and under that wall which parts the yard from the common highway."* He was buried, we are told, at the expense

---

* "Athenæ Oxonienses," vol. ii. p. 453. Aubrey, however, who followed Butler's remains to the grave, places the burial-place of the poet at the *east* end, and not the *west*, of the north side of the church-yard. "He died of a consumption," says Aubrey, "Sept. 25 (A. D. 1680, 70 circiter), and was buried 27th, according to his own appointment in the church-yard of Covent Garden ; sc. in the north part next the church at the east end. His feet touch the wall. His grave, two yards distant from the pilaster of the dore (by his desire), six foot deepe. About twenty-five of his old acquaintance at his funerall, I myself being one." " Letters of Eminent Men," vol. ii. p. 263.

of "his good friend" Mr. Longueville, of the
Temple. According to the authors of the Biographia Britannica, " That gentleman would fain have
buried him in Westminster Abbey, and spoke,
with that view, to several persons, who had been
his admirers, offering to pay his part; but none of
them would contribute: whereupon Mr. Longueville
buried him very privately at St. Paul's, Covent
Garden; himself, and seven or eight more, following him to the grave." The monument to the
memory of Butler, in Westminster Abbey, was
erected at the expense of a meritorious citizen of
London, Alderman Barber. Subsequently some
persons, unknown to fame, erected a monument
to the memory of the poet, in the church-yard in
which he was interred, but I could not discover
that any trace of it now remains. The inscription
on the latter possessed but little merit, but it at
least informs us that—

> A few plain men, to pomp and pride unknown,
> O'er a poor bard have raised this humble stone, &c.

Adverting to the London churches in general, we
shall perceive, in our future rambles over the metropolis, that it is not in St. Paul's Covent Garden
alone, that the wise, the witty, and the gifted,
moulder without a memorial, and consequently that
the resting-place of their hallowed remains is left to
be pointed out in such ephemeral pages as are now
presented to the reader. From the government of
our country,—differing widely in taste and policy
from that of every other country in Europe,—genius

has little to expect in its life-time, and has still less hope of being honoured with a tribute after death. We are still, however, sanguine enough to believe that, from individual liberality, from individual respect for the illustrious dead, or, it may be, from a romantic and enthusiastic admiration for departed genius, there may be persons forthcoming, ready to take their share in raising memorials, however simple, in the various London churches, to the memory of the children of genius,—and most of them were the children of misfortune,—whose resting-places are at present unrecorded, and, comparatively speaking, unknown.

Who is there has not been interested in the history of John Taylor, the "water-poet," and yet we search through the church-yard of St. Paul's, Covent Garden, in which he sleeps, and there is no record of his grave. Here was buried by torch-light, Wilks, the great actor of the reign of King William and of Queen Anne. Here, too, was carried to his last home in the church-yard,—followed to the grave by the most eminent persons of his profession,—the most gifted of comic actors, the "Lord Ogleby" and the "Sir Peter Teazle" of the last century, Thomas King. There is, however, no monument to his memory, neither is there a record of the resting-place of Dr. Wolcot, the memorable Peter Pindar, who sleeps beneath the floor of the vestry-room. The admirable actor, Charles Macklin, has been more fortunate, for the affection of his survivors has raised a tribute to his genius. He

was buried under a vault in the chancel. On the
26th of November, 1788, he was representing at
Covent Garden Theatre the part of Sir Pertinax
Mac Sycophant, in his own comedy of "The Man of
the World," when he felt himself suddenly overtaken by disease, and his memory failed him. He
had strength of mind enough, however, to address
himself to the audience; and, in a painful farewell,
he told them that, unless he felt himself more
capable of administering to their amusement, he
should never again present himself before them.
Six months afterwards, he reappeared on the stage
for his own benefit, in the character of Shylock,
but his memory again failed him, and another
actor was called upon to continue the part.
Disease, however, though it drove him from
the stage, and deprived him of the excitement
he had derived from his favourite pursuit, appears
to have had no effect in shortening his life.
He survived till the 11th of July, 1797, when
he died at the age, it is said, of 107.

Either in the vaults of the church, or in the
church-yard, rest the remains of more than one
other actor or actress of celebrity. In the church-
yard lie the remains of " Joe Haines," and of
the admirable actress, Mrs. Davenport; and in
one corner sleep Michael Kelly, Edwin, and
Estcourt. Nor are these the only remarkable
persons who are interred in the precincts of St.
Paul's, Covent Garden. Dr. Arne, the celebrated
musical composer, and John Zachary Kneller, the

brother of the great artist, were buried within the
walls of the church; and either in the church or
church-yard lie the remains of the well-known Sir
Robert Strange, the engraver.

The names of the streets in the vicinity
of Covent Garden bespeak, within a few years,
the date of their erection. King Street, Charles
Street, and Henrietta Street, derive their names
from King Charles the First and his Queen,
Henrietta Maria; as also do James Street and York
Street, from James, Duke of York; and Catherine
Street, from the consort of Charles the Second.
Bedford Street, Russell Street, and Tavistock Street,
derive their names from the noble family on whose
property they were built. We will now endeavour
to extract as much interest as possible, from a ramble through these gloomy but interesting streets.

In Russell Street, running from Covent Garden
towards Drury Lane Theatre, were situated three of
the most celebrated and once fashionable coffee-
houses in London, "Button's," "Will's," and
"Tom's." Will's coffee-house, so conspicuous in the
literary history of a former age, stood on the north
side of Russell Street. Here used to assemble the
wits and men of fashion of the reign of William the
Third, and of the earlier part of the reign of Queen
Anne; and here, for many years, the immortal
Dryden sat and was reverentially listened to as the
great oracle of the place. "It was Dryden," says
Spence, on the authority of Pope, "who made Will's
coffee-house the great resort for the wits of his

time." In the winter, we are told, his acknowledged place of honour was by the fire-side, and
in summer his chair was removed to the corner
of the balcony on the first floor, overlooking the
street. This was in the days when men of fashion
were somewhat better informed than they are in
our own time; when discussions on literature and
the drama were the agreeable topic of every-day
conversation, and supplied the vacuum in society
which is now supplied by French novels and an
Italian opera. In any literary dispute, the great poet
was invariably made the referee; those who were
unknown to fame never dreamed of being admitted
to the principal table at which Dryden presided;
and the young men of rank and fashion, we are told,
considered it the highest honour to be allowed to
take a pinch out of his snuff-box. It was to Will's,
that Pope, then a mere child, (for he could not
have completed his twelfth year,) induced his friends
to carry him in order to feast his eyes with the
sight of the great poet, in whose path of fame and
genius he was destined hereafter so worthily to
follow " *Tantum Virgilium vidit.*" " Who does
not wish," says Dr. Johnson, " that Dryden could
have known the value of the homage that was paid
him, and foreseen the greatness of his young admirer?"* Pope himself became afterwards a
constant frequenter of Will's, though it was not
till the illustrious Dryden was no more. " He
had now," says Dr. Johnson, " declared himself a

* Johnson's " Life of Pope."

poet; and thinking himself entitled to a poetical
conversation, began at seventeen to frequent Will's,
a coffee-house on the north side of Russell Street, in
Covent Garden, where the wits of that time used to
assemble, and where Dryden had, when he lived,
been accustomed to preside."

Another frequenter of Will's, Dean Lockyer, has
left us an interesting account of Dryden, as he
appeared at his favourite coffee-house. " I was
about seventeen," he says, " when I first came up
to town, and was an odd-looking boy, with short
rough hair, and that sort of awkwardness which
one always brings up at first out of the country
with one. However, in spite of my bashfulness and
appearance, I used now and then to thrust myself
into Will's to have the pleasure of seeing the most
celebrated wits of that time, who then resorted
thither. The second time that ever I was there
Mr. Dryden was speaking of his own things, as he
frequently did, especially of such as had been lately
published. ' If anything of mine is good,' says he,
' it is " Mac Flecnoe ;" and I value myself the more
upon it, as it is the first piece of ridicule written in
heroics.' On hearing this, I plucked up my spirits
so far as to say, in a voice but just loud enough to
be heard, ' that "Mac Flecnoe" was a very fine poem,
but that I had not imagined it to be the first that
was ever writ that way.' On this Dryden turned
short upon me, as surprised at my interposing ; asked
me how long I had been a dabbler in poetry ; and
added, with a smile, ' Pray, sir, what is it that you

did imagine to have been writ so before?'   I
named Boileau's "Lutrin," and Tassoni's "Sec-
chia Rapita," which I had read, and knew Dryden
had borrowed some strokes from each.   ' 'Tis true,'
said Dryden, ' I had forgotten them.'   A little after,
Dryden went out, and in going spoke to me again,
and desired me to come and see him the next day.
I was highly delighted with the invitation, went to
see him accordingly, and was well acquainted with
him ever after as long as he lived."*

Button's coffee-house stood also in Russell Street,
on the south side, about two doors from Covent
Garden Market.   Here assembled Pope, Swift,
Addison, Garth, Arbuthnot, Steele, Ambrose Phillips, and all the most celebrated men of the Augustan age of England.   Button's, as is well known,
was the favourite resort of Addison.   According to
Spence, on the authority of Pope, Button was an
old servant of Addison, who, after the death of
Dryden, had influence enough to transfer the wits
from Will's to the house of his *protégé*.   Dr. Johnson has entered further into particulars.   "Button,"
he says, "had been a servant in the Countess of
Warwick's family, who, under the patronage of
Addison, kept a coffee-house on the south side of
Russell Street, about two doors from Covent Garden.   Here it was that the wits of that time used
to assemble.   It is said that when Addison 'had
suffered any vexation from the Countess, he withdrew the company from Button's house.   From the

* Spence's " Anecdotes."

coffee-house he went again to a tavern, where he often sat late, and drank too much wine."* "Addison," says Pope, " usually studied all the morning, then met his party at Button's, dined there, and stayed for five or six hours, and sometimes far into the night. I was of the company for about a year, but found it too much for me. It hurt my health, and so I quitted it."†

It was at Button's, according to Pope, that Addison took him aside, "after their long coldness, to explain the circumstances under which he had patronized Tickell's translation of the Iliad in opposition to that of Pope; but the particulars of their misunderstanding are too well known to require repetition. It was here, too, that Ambrose Phillips hung the rod over the seat which was usually occupied by Pope. Phillips, while a young student at St. John's College, Cambridge, had published his "Six Pastorals," the intrinsic merit of which is said to have excited the jealousy of Pope, who certainly lashed them severely and with great humour in the "Guardian." It was under these circumstances that Phillips suspended the rod over Pope's seat at Button's. The insult fell harmless on the great poet, who retaliated by his well-known lines in the "Prologue to the Satires,"

> The bard whom pilfered pastorals renown,
> Who turns a Persian tale for half-a-crown,
> Just writes to make his barrenness appear,
> And strains, from hard-bound brains, eight lines a-year.

---

* Johnson's " Life of Addison."
† Spence's " Anecdotes."

After the death of Addison, Button's fell into disrepute, and a few years afterwards it is known that Addison's old servant was receiving relief from the parish of St. Paul's, Covent Garden.

In the "Guardian," Button's coffee-house is spoken of as being "over against Tom's, in Covent Garden." This house (No. 17, Russell Street), memorable from the days of Queen Anne to the reign of George the Third, is still standing. In the preface to a work, entitled, "Descriptive Particulars of English Coronation Medals," the author, Mr. Till, thus writes:—"The room in which I conduct my business, as a coin dealer, is that which, in 1764,—by a general subscription among nearly seven hundred of the nobility, foreign ministers, gentry, and geniuses of the age,—became the card-room and place of meeting for many of the now illustrious dead, till 1768, when a voluntary subscription among its members induced Mr. Haines, the proprietor, to take in the next room westward as a coffee-room; and the whole floor, *en suite*, was converted into card and conversation rooms. Here assembled Dr. Johnson, Garrick, Murphy, Dr. Dodd, Dr. Goldsmith, Sir Joshua Reynolds, Foote, Moody, Count Bruhl, Sir Philip Francis, George Colman, the elder, the Dukes of Northumberland and Montague, Lord Rodney, George Steevens, Warner, and many others, all of whom have long since passed to that 'bourne from whence no traveller returns.'"

In connection with Russell Street, Covent Garden, there is a very curious passage in Gibbon's

" Memoirs of his Life and Writings," in which the
great historian, then a student of Magdalen College, Oxford, describes the circumstances attending his abjuration of the Protestant faith.   They
were still the days when, in the words of Blackstone,
" where a person is reconciled to the See of Rome, or
procures others to be reconciled, the offence amounts
to high-treason." There were other laws, too, which
condemned the priest to perpetual banishment, and
transferred the proselyte's estate to his nearest relation: the visit, therefore, to Russell Street, was one
of danger, and was paid with great secrecy. " In my
last excursion to London," says Gibbon, "I addressed
myself to Mr. Lewis, a Roman Catholic bookseller
in Russell Street, Covent Garden, who recommended me to a priest, of whose name and order I
am at present ignorant.   In our first interview he
soon discovered that persuasion was needless. After
sounding the motives and merits of my conversion,
he consented to admit me into the pale of the
church; and at his feet, on the eighth of June,
1753, I solemnly, though privately, abjured the
errors of heresy. The seduction of an English
youth of family and fortune was an act of as much
danger as glory; but he bravely overlooked the
danger, of which I was not then sufficiently informed.   An elaborate controversial epistle, approved by my direction and addressed to my father,
announced and justified the step which I had taken.
My father was neither a bigot nor a philosopher;
but his affection deplored the loss of an only son;

and his good sense was astonished at my strange departure from the religion of my country. In the first sally of passion he divulged a secret which prudence might have suppressed, and the gates of Magdalen College were for ever shut against my return."

At No. 8, Russell Street, now the "Caledonian Coffee House," lived the well-known "Tom Davies," the bookseller and actor. To the admirers of Dr. Johnson, and especially of Boswell's inimitable biography, this house will always be interesting as that which witnessed the introduction of these two remarkable men to each other.* Boswell, it seems, had more than once been disappointed in his eager desire to be introduced to Dr. Johnson, but at length fortune threw him in the way of the great mammoth of literature. "At last," says Boswell, and with Boswell the day was one indeed *notanda cretâ;* "on Monday, the 16th of May, when I was sitting in Mr. Davies's back-parlour, after having drunk tea with him and Mrs. Davies, Johnson unexpectedly came into the shop; and Mr. Davies having perceived him, through the glass door in the room in which we were sitting, advancing towards us, he rumoured his awful approach to me, somewhat in the manner of an actor in the part of Horatio, when he addresses Hamlet on the appearance of his father's ghost,—' Look, my lord, it comes.' I

* " No. 8," says Boswell, " the very place where I was fortunate enough to be introduced to the illustrious subject of this work, deserves to be particularly marked. I never pass by it without feeling reverence and regret." Boswell's " Life of Johnson," note.

found that I had a very perfect idea of Johnson's
figure, from the portrait of him painted by Sir
Joshua Reynolds, soon after he had published his
"Dictionary," in the attitude of sitting in his easy
chair in deep meditation. Mr. Davies mentioned
my name, and respectfully introduced me to him.
I was much agitated; and recollecting his prejudice
against the Scotch, of which I had heard much, I
said to Davies, " Don't tell where I come from.'—
'From Scotland,' cried Davies, roguishly.—'Mr.
Johnson,' said I, 'I do, indeed, come from Scotland,
but I cannot help it.'—I am willing to flatter myself
that I meant this as light pleasantry, to soothe and
conciliate him, and not as an humiliating abasement
at the expense of my country. But however that
might be, this speech was somewhat unlucky; for
with that quickness of wit for which he was remarkable, he seized the expression 'come from Scotland,' which I used in the sense of being of that
country: and as if I had said that I had come
away from it, or left it, retorted, 'That, sir, I find, is
what a good many of your country cannot help.'
This stroke stunned me a good deal; and when we
had sat down, I felt myself not a little embarrassed,
and apprehensive of what might come next. He
then addressed himself to Davies. 'What do you
think of Garrick? He has refused me an order for
the play for Miss Williams, because he knows the
house will be full, and that an order will be worth
three shillings!' Eager to take any opening to get
into conversation with him, I ventured to say, ' O,

sir, I cannot think Mr. Garrick would grudge such a
trifle to you.'—'Sir,' said he, with a stern look, 'I
have known David Garrick longer than you have
done; and I know no right you have to talk to me
on the subject!' Perhaps I deserved this check;
for it was rather presumptuous in me, an entire
stranger, to express any doubt of the justice of his
animadversion upon his old acquaintance and pupil.
I now felt myself much mortified, and began to
think that the hope which I had long indulged of
obtaining his acquaintance was blasted. And, in
truth, had not my ardour been uncommonly strong,
and my resolution uncommonly persevering, so
rough a reception might have deterred me for ever
from making any further attempts." Boswell, however, "sat out" the great man, satisfied that though
there was a roughness in his manner, there was no
innate ill-nature in his composition. "Davies," he
says, "followed me to the door, and when I com-
plained to him a little of the hard blows which the
great man had given me, he kindly took upon him
to console me by saying, 'Don't be uneasy; I can
see he likes you very well." * Like Boswell, the
author has ever felt that No. 8, Russell Street,
deserves to be "particularly marked," and seldom
has he passed through this street without glancing
his eye through the window to where stood
Tom Davies's back-parlour, in which commenced

* Those who may wish to be better informed as to the nature
of the outrage, will find the particulars in the "Biographia Britannica," vol. vi. p. 3604; the "Athenæ Oxonienses," vol. ii.
col. 1100; and Anthony Wood's "Life of Himself," p. 187.

thati ntimacy, to which we are indebted for the most charming and instructive biographical work which exists in the literature of any country.

From Russell Street we pass into Bow Street, once one of the most fashionable streets in London. Dryden writes,—

I've had to-day a dozen billet-doux,
From fops, and wits, and cits, and Bow Street beaux.

In this street was born, on the 5th of December, 1661, the great minister, Robert Harley Earl of Oxford; here the celebrated sculptor, Grinlin Gibbons, died on the 3rd of August 1721; and here also was the shop of the famous publisher, Jacob Tonson.

Another remarkable person who was an inhabitant of this street, was William Wycherley, and here it was that the great dramatic poet was visited in his sickness by King Charles the Second, who seems to have taken a great delight in his society. " Mr. Wycherley," we are told, " happened to fall sick at his lodgings in Bow Street, Covent Garden, during which period the King did him the honour to visit him. Finding his body extremely weakened, and his spirits miserably shattered, he commanded him, as soon as he should be able to take a journey, to go to the south of France, believing that the air of Montpelier would contribute to restore him as much as anything, and assured him, at the same time, that, as soon as he was capable of taking the journey, he would order him five hundred pounds to defray the charges of it. Mr. Wycherley accordingly went to France, and having spent the winter

there, returned to England in the spring, entirely
restored to his former vigour both of body and
mind." *

It was immediately after his return from Montpelier, that Wycherley met with his well-known
adventure with the young and beautiful Countess of
Drogheda. " He went down to Tunbridge," we are
told, " either to take the benefit of the waters, or the
diversions of the place ; when, walking one day upon
the Wells' Walk with his friend Mr. Fairbeard, of
Gray's Inn, just as he came up to the bookseller's
shop, the Countess of Drogheda,† a young widow,
rich, noble, and beautiful, came to the bookseller,
and inquired for the " Plain Dealer." ' Madam,'
says Mr. Fairbeard, ' since you are for the " Plain
Dealer," there he is for you;' pushing Mr. Wycherley towards her. ' Yes,' says Mr. Wycherley,
' this lady can bear *plain* dealing, for she appears
to be so accomplished, that what would be a compliment to others, spoken to her would *be plain dealing.*'
' No, truly, Sir,' said the Countess, ' I am not
without my faults any more than the rest of my
sex, but, notwithstanding, I love *plain dealing,* and
am never more fond of it than when it tells me
of them.' — ' Then, madam,' says Mr. Fairbeard,
' you and the " Plain Dealer" seem designed by
heaven for each other.' In short, Mr. Wycherley
walked with the Countess upon the walks, waited

---

* " Life of Wycherley," in Biog. Brit.
† Letitia Isabella, daughter of John Robartes, Earl of Radnor,
and widow of Charles, second Earl of Drogheda.

upon her home, visited her daily at her lodgings while she continued at Tunbridge, and at her apartments in Hatton Garden after she went to London, where in a little time he got her consent to marry her." It is almost needless to add, that the jealous disposition of Lady Drogheda rendered their marriage almost as an unhappy a one, as was that of Wycherley's contemporary, Addison, with the Countess of Warwick.

At the Cock Tavern, in Bow Street,—a favourite resort of men of fashion in the days of Charles the Second,—took place, in 1633, the disreputable frolic, in which the accomplished Charles Sackville Earl of Dorset, then Lord Buckhurst,—

" The best good man, with the worst-natured muse,"

Sir Charles Sedley, the poet, and Sir Thomas Ogle, were the actors. The story is much too indecent for repetition; and so enraged was the populace at the nature of the frolic, that they endeavoured to break open the tavern-doors, and, in the riot which ensued, Lord Buckhurst and his companions nearly lost their lives. They were carried before the Court of Common Pleas, where a heavy fine was inflicted upon them, the penalty imposed on Sir Charles Sedley being five hundred pounds. When placed at the bar, Sir Robert Hyde, the Lord Chief Justice, in commenting upon the offence, inquired sarcastically of Sedley if he had ever read the "Complete Gentleman?" "I believe," was the reply, "that I have read more

E 2

books than your Lordship." Sedley and his fellow culprits employed Killegrew, and another courtier, to intercede with the King for a mitigation of their fine. Instead, however, of exerting themselves in the cause of their friends, they are said to have begged the amount for their own use, and actually to have extorted it to the last penny.

In Bow Street lived the eminent and eccentric physician, Dr. John Radcliffe, now principally remembered as the founder of the Radcliffe Library at Oxford. He is one of those men, of whose history the little we know is so full of interest, that it leaves us deeply to regret that we can discover no more. One anecdote connected with his residence in Bow Street is well known. The garden of his house adjoined that of Sir Godfrey Kneller, behind the Piazza, in Covent Garden, and, being intimate friends, they agreed that a door-way should be broken through the wall, to admit of their enjoying a free intercourse with each other. Some misunderstanding, however, having arisen between them, Kneller sent a message to Radcliffe that he intended to close up the door. "Tell him," said the witty physician, "that he may do anything with it but paint it." Sir Godfrey's reply to the messenger was equally pointed. "Tell Dr. Radcliffe," he said, "with my compliments, that I will take anything from him but his physic."

Dr. Radcliffe, on his first establishing himself in London, appears to have fixed upon Bow Street, as his residence, as being then one of the most fashionable streets of the metropolis. How little suited, however, he was, to be a courtier;—how little fitted to pander to the sickly fancies of princes and fine ladies,—is proved by the manner in which he conducted himself, on two different occasions, when summoned into the sick chambers of William the Third and Queen Anne. A year or two before his death, King William sent for Radcliffe, and among other symptoms of disease, mentioned that while his body was becoming emaciated, his legs had swollen far beyond their natural size. Radcliffe made the necessary examination. "I would not," he said, "have your Majesty's *two* legs for your *three* kingdoms." King William never forgave him for this unseasonable speech, and though he continued to make use of Radcliffe's prescriptions till within three days of his death, he could never again be persuaded to admit him into his presence. His speech to Queen Anne, shewed a no less want of reverence for a crowned head. A messenger arriving at his residence, with the intelligence that the Queen, then Princess of Denmark, was alarmingly ill, he not only delayed obeying the summons till after a considerable interval had elapsed, but on being admitted into the presence of the royal sufferer, treated her malady with undisguised scorn. "She has only the vapours," he said, and added with a characteristic oath, — "She is as well as any woman breathing, if she could only be persuaded to believe it." His imprudence, however, sealed his fate as a courtier. On his next appearance at court, he was stopped by an officer in the antichamber, and informed that the princess had no longer any occasion for his services. However, in the last illness of Prince George of Denmark, the Queen's affection for her husband so far overcame the indignation which she felt at the conduct of her former medical attendant, that she ordered him to be immediately summoned. When she herself, too, lay on her death-bed, he was also sent for to attend her. The summons was disobeyed, and the circumstance aroused a general and indignant outcry against the eccentric physician. Radcliffe pleaded indisposition, and, after a full investigation of such evidence as has been handed down to us, we cannot but come to the conclusion that this was the true cause which detained him from the bedside of his expiring sovereign. In one of his letters he writes,—"I know the nature of attending crowned heads in their last moments too well, to be fond of waiting upon them, without being sent for by a proper authority. You have heard of pardons being signed for physicians, before a sovereign's demise: however, ill as I was, I would have gone to the Queen in a horse-litter, had either her Majesty, or those in commission, next to her, commanded me so to do."

We may be accused, perhaps, in our notice of Bow Street and Dr. Radcliffe, of having entered too much into extraneous matter, but the wit and eccentricities of a remarkable man,—especially of one whose name is perhaps but little familiar to the

general reader,—tempted us into a passing digression. We would willingly relate further anecdotes
of Dr. Radcliffe, and especially his witty retorts to
Madame D'Orsley, which are familiar alone to
those who delight in old books, and which formed
the subject of a Latin poem, in the "Anthologia."
They might, however, offend the morbid prudery of
the present age ; an age in which, by some strange
anomaly, it is a stigma *not* to have read Shakspeare, and yet a crime to have read Fielding; an
age in which, by some still stranger anomaly, the
daily newspapers, with all their gross details of
debauchery and incest, are laid freely before the
young and uninitiated, while it is a crime to insert,
in a *book*, a witty,—and that which time, perhaps,
has rendered a classical anecdote, — to which our
grandmothers listened with delight, and which they
repeated without a blush.

Before taking our leave of Bow Street, let us
mention that it was apparently in this street that
the celebrated Prince Eugene dined with Dr. Radcliffe. The entertainment which the physician provided for the hero was plain beef and a pudding.
The Prince thanked him for the compliment, "You
have considered me," he said, "not as a courtier,
but as a soldier."

Of James Street, which runs out of Covent Garden, parallel with Bow Street, nothing remarkable
is known, except that David Garrick resided here
in 1747, the year in which the great actor became
manager of Drury Lane, and when the Theatre

opened with the celebrated prologue of Dr. Johnson. In the "General Advertiser" for the 7th of
April, 1747, is the following advertisement:—
"Mr. Garrick hopes the gentlemen and ladies
who had taken places for his benefit, the 16th of
last month, will excuse his deferring it to the
30th of this, his illness not permitting him to have
it sooner. Tickets and places to be had at Mr.
Garrick's lodgings in James Street, Covent Garden,
and of Mr. Page, at the stage-door of the
Theatre."

King Street leads from Covent Garden into St.
Martin's lane. Here, at the house of their father,
who kept an upholsterer's shop, called the "Two
Crowns and Cushions," were born the celebrated
Dr. Thomas Arne, the composer, and his sister, Mrs.
Cibber. But the most interesting spot is Rose
Street, a small and wretched-looking street, at the
north-west of King Street. Here, Samuel Butler,
the author of "Hudibras," lived for many years,
and here he is supposed to have died; here, apparently, stood the Rose Tavern, at which the famous
"Treason Club" was held in 1688; * and here
the celebrated bookseller, Edmund Curll, had his
shop; the sign of which was "Pope's Head." But
the circumstance which has rendered Rose Street
classic ground, is the fact of its having been the
spot where Dryden received his memorable cudgel-
ing. The "Essay on Satire" had recently been
published, in which, besides being accused of

* See Macpherson's "Orig. Papers," vol. i. p. 289.

cowardice, there was every indignity offered to the Earl of Rochester, which could reflect on his character as a wit, a rake, or a poet :

> He, while he mischief means to all mankind,
> Himself alone the ill effects does find ;
> False are his words, affected is his wit,
> So often he does aim, so seldom hit ;
> To every face he cringes while he speaks,
> But when the back is turned, the head he breaks :
> Mean in each action, lewd in every limb,
> Manners themselves are mischievous in him ;
> A proof that chance alone makes every creature,
> A very Killegrew without good-nature.

And again—

> Falsely he falls into some dangerous noose,
> And then as meanly labours to get loose ;
> A life so infamous is better quitting,
> Spent in base injury and low submitting.
> I'd like to have left out his poetry,
> Forgot by all almost as well as me.
> Sometimes he has some humour ; never wit
> And if it rarely,—very rarely,—hit,
> 'Tis under so much nasty rubbish laid,
> To find it out 's the cinderwoman's trade,
> Who for the wretched remnants of a fire,
> Must toil all day in ashes and in mire.

The " Essay on Satire " was supposed to be the joint production of Dryden, and of John Sheffield, Earl of Mulgrave, afterwards Duke of Buckingham. There can be little doubt, however, that, with the exception of a few clumsy lines, Dryden was the author of the whole poem. According, indeed, to Dean Lockier, the Duke merely made a few alterations in the poem, and these were, generally speaking, for the worse.* At all events, Rochester chose to look upon Dryden as the author, and,

* Spence's " Anecdotes of Men and Books."

adopting a mode of revenge, which was not un-
common in the days of Charles the Second, he
hired some ruffians, who waylaid the great poet, in
Rose Street, (on his way from Wills's Coffee-house
to his own house, in Gerard Street,) and inflicted on
him a severe personal chastisement.

The name of Dryden occurs in connection with
another *fracas*, which took place in Covent
Garden, in the days of Charles the Second.   The
principals in the quarrel were Sir H. Bellasys
and another courtier, Thomas Porter, and the circumstances, as related by Pepys, throw a curious
light on the manners of the time. "They two
dined yesterday at Sir Robert Carr's, where, it
seems, people do drink high, all that come. It
happened that these two, the greatest friends in the
world, were talking together, and Sir H. Bellasys
talked a little louder than ordinary to Tom Porter,
giving of him some advice. Some of the company
standing by said, ' What are they quarrelling, that
they talk so high ? ' Sir H. Bellasys hearing it,
said, ' No,' says he, I would have you know that I
never quarrel, but I strike ; and take that as a rule
of mine.' ' How,' says Tom Porter, 'strike? I
would I could see the man in England that durst
give me a blow.'   With that, Sir H. Bellasys did
give him a box of the ear; and so they were going to
fight there, but were hindered. And by-and-bye
Tom Porter went out, and, meeting Dryden the
poet, told him of the business, and that he was
resolved to fight Sir H. Bellasys presently ; for he

knew that, if he did not, they should be friends
to-morrow, and then the blow would rest upon him,
which he would prevent; and desired Dryden to let
him have his boy to bring him notice which way
Sir H. Bellasys goes. By-and-bye he is informed
that Sir H. Bellasys' coach was coming: so Tom
Porter went down out of the coffee-house, where
he stayed for the tidings, and stopped the coach,
and bade Sir H. Bellasys come out. 'Why,' says
H. Bellasys, 'you will not hurt me coming out, will
you?' 'No,' says Tom Porter. So, out he went,
and both drew; and H. Bellasys having drawn, and
flung away his scabbard, Tom Porter asked him
whether he was ready. The other answering him
he was, they fell to fight, some of their acquaintance by. They wounded one another, and Bellasys
so much, that it is feared he will die: and, finding
himself severely wounded, he called to Tom Porter,
and kissed him, and bade him shift for himself;
'for,' says he, 'Tom, thou hast hurt me, but I will
make shift to stand upon my legs till thou mayest
withdraw, and the world will not take notice of you,
for I would not have thee troubled for what thou
hast done.' And so, whether he did fly or not I
cannot tell; but Tom Porter shewed H. Bellasys
that he was wounded too: and they are both ill,
but Sir H. Bellasys to fear of life." Bellasys survived his wounds only ten days.

At the West end of King Street is Bedford
Street, which connects this part of Covent Garden
with the Strand. Whyte, in his " Miscellanea

Nova," relates an anecdote connected with this
street, which throws a light on the well-known
personal peculiarities of Dr. Johnson. " Mrs. Sheridan," he says, " at one time lived in Bedford Street,
opposite Henrietta Street, which ranges with the
south side of Covent Garden, so that the prospect
lies open the whole way, free of interruption. We
were standing together in the drawing-room, expecting Johnson, who was to dine there. Mr.
Sheridan asked me, "could I see the length of the
garden ?' ' No, sir.' ' Take your opera-glass, Johnson is coming, you may know him by his gait.'
I perceived him at a good distance, working along
with a peculiar solemnity of deportment, and an
awkward sort of measured step. At that time the
broad flagging at each side of the streets was not
universally adopted, and stone posts were in fashion,
to prevent the annoyance of carriages. Upon every
post, as he passed along, I could observe he de-
liberately laid his hand; but missing one of them
when he had got at some distance, he seemed
suddenly to recollect himself, and immediately
returning back, carefully performed the accustomed
ceremony, and resumed his former course, not
omitting one till he gained the crossing. This,
Mr. Sheridan assured me, however odd it may
appear, was his constant practice; but why or
wherefore he could not inform me." " Sir Joshua
Reynolds," says Boswell, " has observed Johnson to
go a good way about, rather than pass a particular
alley in Leicester Fields; but this Sir Joshua

imputed to his having had some disagreeable
recollection associated with it."

Running parallel with King Street, to the south
of Covent Garden, is Henrietta Street. It was
from a house in this street, that the beautiful
Georgiana, Duchess of Devonshire, and the other fair
and high-born women who canvassed for Charles
James Fox, used to watch the humours of the
Westminster election.   Pitt writes to Wilberforce
on the 8th of April, 1784, " Westminster goes on
well, in spite of the Duchess of Devonshire, and the
other women of the people ; but when the poll will
close is uncertain."   Hannah More, as appears
from the date of her letters, resided at one period in
Henrietta Street, and in one of them we find an
amusing account of an adventure which she met with
during the Westminster election.   To one of her
sisters she writes,—" I had like to have got into
a fine scrape the other night.   I was going to pass
the evening at Mrs. Coles's, in Lincoln's Inn Fields.
I went in a chair.   They carried me through Covent
Garden.   A number of people, as I went along,
desired the men not to go through the Garden,
as there were an hundred armed men, who suspected
every chairman belonged to Brookes's, and would fall
upon us.   In spite of my entreaties the men would
have persisted, but a stranger, out of humanity,
made them set me down, and the shrieks of the
wounded, for there was a terrible battle, intimidated
the chairmen, who were at last prevailed upon to
carry me another way.   A vast number of people

followed me, crying out, "It is Mrs. Fox: none but
Mr. Fox's wife would dare to come into Covent
Garden in a chair: she is going to canvas in the
dark!' Though not a little frightened I laughed
heartily at this, but shall stir out no more in a chair
for some time."

In Henrietta Street was the shop of the mounte-
bank almanac-maker, Partridge, and here at one
period resided the charming actress, Mrs. Clive.
Here, too, died a poet, formerly of some celebrity,
Paul Whitehead. As a poet he has ceased to be
read, and almost to be remembered; but those who
are curious in literary history still remember him
as having been the social companion of Frederick
Prince of Wales, — as one whose poetical squibs
had a considerable influence over the politics of the
day,—and as one of the mysterious brotherhood
who assembled at Medmenham Abbey, and whose
sensual orgies were afterwards in revenge exposed
by Wilkes, when prosecuted on account of his
"Essay on Woman." By his last will, Paul Whitehead bequeathed his heart, enclosed in a marble
urn, to his friend, Lord Le Despencer, with a request that it might be placed in his Lordship's
mausoleum at High Wycombe. The fantastic wish
was complied with, but what has since become of
the heart and the urn we know not.

Between Covent Garden and the Strand, running
parallel with Henrietta Street, is Maiden Lane,
which, according to Mr. D'Israeli, takes its name
from an image of the Virgin, which formerly

stood here.* It was here that Voltaire resided
during his visit to England in 1727, and, as appears
by one of his letters to Swift dated the 14th of
December in that year, the sign of the house in
which he lodged was the " White Peruke." In this
street also are the once famous " Cyder Cellars,"
now, we believe, frequented principally by those
who delight in late hours, ribaldry and song, but
formerly the favourite resort of no less remarkable
men than Porson and Parr.

At the eastern end of Maiden Lane is Southampton Street, once the residence of the charming actress
Mrs. Oldfield ; and adjoining it is Exeter Street,
where Dr. Johnson, unfriended and almost penniless, first took up his abode when he arrived in
London, in 1737, with David Garrick. " His first
lodgings," says Boswell, " were at the house of Mr.
Norris, in Exeter Street, adjoining Catherine Street,
in the Strand. 'I dined,' said he, ' very well for
eightpence, with very good company, at the Pine
Apple, in New Street, just by. Several of them
had travelled. They expected to meet every day,
but did not know one another's names. It used to
cost the rest a shilling, for they drank wine ; but I
had a cut of meat for sixpence and bread for a
penny, and gave the waiter a penny, so that I was
quite well served, nay, better than the rest, for they
gave the waiter nothing.'" " Painful as it is to
relate," says Cumberland, " I have heard Dr. Johnson assert, that he subsisted himself for a consider-

* " Curiosities of Literature."

able space of time upon the scanty pittance of four-
pence halfpenny per day."

The last of the streets which we shall mention, in
immediate connection with Covent Garden, is Tavistock Street, which is almost a continuation of
Maiden Lane. At the south-eastern corner of this
street lived the unfortunate Miss Ray, the beautiful
mistress of Lord Sandwich, who was shot by her
lover, the Rev. James Hackman, on the 7th of
April, 1779. Hackman had been formerly a lieutenant in the 68th regiment of foot, and, while in
command of a recruiting party at Huntingdon, had
been invited to Lord Huntingdon's seat at Hinchin-
brooke, where he fell violently in love with his
future victim. Failing in his repeated endeavours to
prevail upon her to become his wife, he determined,
while under the influence of a maddening jealousy,
to put an end to her life and his own. Accordingly, having posted himself under the piazza of
Covent Garden, as she was quitting the theatre, he
discharged the contents of a pistol at her head, and
immediately afterwards fired another pistol at himself.
The following account of the transaction appeared
in one of the journals of the succeeding day :—
" Last night the following melancholy fate terminated the existence of the beautiful, the favoured,
and yet the unfortunate Miss Ray. As she was
stepping into her carriage from Covent Garden, a
clergyman, whose name we hear is Hackman, came
up and lodged the contents of a pistol in her head,
which done he instantly shot himself, and they fell

together. They were carried into the Shakspeare, and the ablest assistance called for, but Miss Ray expired in a few minutes. The desperate assassin still lives to account for the horrid act, and, it is hoped, to suffer for it, his wound being on the temple, and supposed not to be dangerous. An express was instantly sent for Lord Sandwich. He came about twelve o'clock in the most lamentable agonies, and expressed a sorrow that certainly did infinite honour to his feelings."

The " Morning Post " of the following day (April the 9th) contains further particulars connected with this celebrated tragedy. " On Wednesday night Miss Ray was coming out of the playhouse, accompanied by Signora Galli, and a gentleman who had politely offered to see her to her carriage, when she was followed by the resolute assassin who committed the act. He stepped up to her just as she had her foot on the step of the coach, pulled her by her sleeve, which occasioned her to turn round, when, without the smallest previous menace or address, he put a pistol to her forehead, and shot her instantly dead. He then fired another at himself, which, however, did not prove equally effectual. The ball grazed upon the upper part of the head, but did not penetrate sufficiently to produce any fatal effect; he fell, however, and so firmly was he bent upon the entire completion of the fatal business he had meditated, that he was found beating his head with the utmost violence with the but-end of the pistol, by Mr. Mahon,

apothecary, of Covent Garden, who wrenched the
instrument from his hand. He was carried to the
Shakspeare tavern, where his wound was dressed.
The body of the lovely victim was likewise carried
to the same place." Hackman was tried for murder
on the 17th of April, and, being found guilty, was
hanged a few days afterwards at Tyburn. Miss Ray
was originally a milliner's apprentice in St. George's
Court, St. John's Lane, Clerkenwell; and Hackman,
at the time when he deprived her of life, was residing in Craven Street, in the Strand. Next door to
Miss Ray, in Tavistock Street, lived Macklin, the
actor.

To give an account of Covent Garden Theatre
would amount to little less than a history of the
stage during upwards of a century. It is sufficient
to observe, that the original theatre was built in
1733; that it was rebuilt in 1787, enlarged in
1792, and on the night of the 20th September,
1808, was burnt to the ground, when upwards of
107,000l. worth of property is said to have been
destroyed. The present theatre, which rose rapidly
on its ruins, was opened on the 18th of September,
1809.

DRURY LANE AND CONTIGUOUS STREETS.

DRURY LANE. —DRURY HOUSE. — WYCH STREET. — DRURY LANE
THEATRE.—LONG ACRE.—PHŒNIX ALLEY. —QUEEN STREET.—
LINCOLN'S INN FIELDS.—PORTUGAL STREET.—DUKE STREET.—ST.
GILES'S CHURCH AND CHURCHYARD.

DRURY LANE derives its name from having been
built nearly on the site of Drury House, the residence of the once powerful family of the Druries.
"It is singular," says Pennant, "that this lane, of
later times so notorious for intrigues, should derive
its title from a family name, which, in the language
of Chaucer, had an amorous signification :—

" Of bataille and of chevalrie,
Of ladies love and *druerie*,
Anon I wool you tell."

Drury House, which stood where Craven Buildings and the Olympic Theatre now stand, is said to
have been built by the gallant and courtly Sir William Drury,—Lord Deputy of Ireland in the reign of
Queen Elizabeth and a Knight of the Garter,—who
was killed in a duel with Sir John Burroughs, on
account of a quarrel between them on an absurd
question of precedency.*   He was succeeded by his

* Camden's " Life of Queen Elizabeth."

F 2

son, Sir Robert Drury, in whose life-time the celebrated Dr. Donne found a welcome refuge in Drury House during the days of his poverty.* Here, too, it was, that the unfortunate Earl of Essex and his friends met secretly to plan the rash conspiracy, which ended in as fatal a catastrophe.

Some time after the death of Sir Robert Drury, this property came into the possession of William, Lord Craven, the gay courtier of the reign of James the Second, the hero of the "tremendous breach of Creutznach," and the presumed husband of the charming Elizabeth, Queen of Bohemia. Lord Craven pulled down the old mansion of the Druries, and built on its site a large brick pile, in which we find the Queen of Bohemia residing shortly after the Restoration of her brother, Charles the Second. Part of Craven House was taken down in 1723, but the remaining portion continued to be used as an inn till the commencement of the present century, when, with other buildings, it was pulled down to make room for the Olympic Theatre. Pennant tells us, that, in searching after old Craven House, he discovered a public-house, the sign of which was a head of the Queen of Bohemia, Lord Craven's "admired mistress," which proved its identity. Within little more than half a century, there was to be seen, in the court in Craven Buildings, a fresco painting of Lord Craven, seated, in full armour, on a white horse, with a truncheon in his hand.

* Walton's " Life of Dr. Donne."

In the reign of Charles the Second, we find Drury Lane one of the most fashionable situations in London. Besides Craven House, here stood Clare House, the residence of the Earl of Clare, and Anglesea House, the residence of the Earl-of Anglesea.* In Craven Buildings lived, at different periods, the celebrated actresses Mrs. Bracegirdle and Mrs. Pritchard.

In Drury Lane lived Anne Clarges, who became the mistress, and afterwards the wife, of the celebrated George Monk, Duke of Albemarle. "Monk," says Lord Clarendon, in his "History of the Rebellion," "was cursed, after a long familiarity, to marry a woman of the lowest extraction, the least wit, and less beauty." Clarendon afterwards speaks of her as a "woman with nothing feminine about her but her make;" and Burnet styles her a "ravenous, mean, and contemptible creature, who thought of nothing but getting and spending." She was the daughter of a blacksmith, who lived in Drury Lane, and was bred a milliner. "When Monk was a prisoner in the Tower," says Aubrey, "his sempstress, Anne Clarges, a blacksmith's daughter, was kind to him in a double capacity. It must be remembered that he was then in want, and that she assisted him. Here she was got with child. She was not at all handsome, nor cleanly. Her mother was one of the five women-barbers, and a woman of ill-fame. A ballad was made on her and the other four; the burden of it was—

* "Present State of England," 1683.

Did you ever hear the like,
   Or ever hear the fame,
Of five women barbers,
   Who lived in Drury Lane."*

In a curious memoir, in the British Museum, of one Mul-Sack, a noted highwayman, I found the following notice of these ladies ;—" There were five noted Amazons in Drury Lane, who were called women-shavers, and whose actions were then talked of about town, till being apprehended for a riot, and one or two of them severely punished, the rest fled to Barbadoes." The author of the " Memoir of Mul-Sack" mentions a brutal and disgusting act of cruelty which was perpetrated by these wretches on another woman, the particulars of which are too gross for publication, but which sufficiently attest how detestable was the character of the " five women-shavers" of Drury Lane.

Drury Lane was one of the first places in London which was visited by that terrible calamity, the great Plague, in 1665. Pepys mentions his being at " the coffee-house" on the 24th of May, when he says all the conversation was " of the plague growing upon us in this town, and of remedies against it, some saying one thing, and some another." On the 7th of June,— which he speaks of as " the hottest day that ever I felt in my life," he says in his " Diary," " This day, much against my will, I did in Drury Lane see two or three houses marked with a red cross upon the doors, and ' Lord have mercy upon us ' writ there." Two years

---

* Aubrey's " Letters of Eminent Men."

NELL GWYNNE IN DRURY LANE. 71

afterward, when Pepys was passing through Drury
Lane, on his way to Westminster, the street presented a very different appearance. It was on
May-day, 1677, and the passage in his "Diary"
shews that the beautiful and warm-hearted Nell
Gwynne was at this period an inhabitant of Drury
Lane. "To Westminster, in the way, many milk-
maids, with their garlands upon their pails, dancing
with a fiddler before them; and saw pretty Nelly
stand at her lodgings-door, in Drury Lane, in her
smock sleeves and bodice, looking upon one; she
seemed a mighty pretty creature."

After Drury Lane had ceased to bear the fashionable reputation which it enjoyed in the seventeenth
century, it became in the reign of Queen Anne,
and up to a much later period, notorious as a colony
for those unfortunate off-shoots of genius, who may
perhaps be best designated as "poor authors." In
the wittiest satirical poem of modern times, the
"Epistle to Dr. Arbuthnot," Pope, speaking of the
disagreeable manner in which he was pestered by
authors to read their MSS., writes:—

> I sit with sad civility; I read
> With honest anguish, and an aching head;
> And drop at last, but in unwilling ears,
> This saving counsel, "Keep your piece nine years."
> "Nine years!" cries he, who high in Drury Lane,
> Lulled by soft zephyrs through the window-pane,
> Rhymes ere he wakes, and prints before Term ends,
> Obliged by hunger, and request of friends, &c.

Goldsmith also writes, in his "Description of an
author's bed-chamber," by which was probably intended his own :—

Where the Red Lion staring o'er the way,
Invites each passing stranger that can pay ;
Where Calvert's butt, and Parson's black champagne
Regale the drabs and bloods of Drury Lane ;
There, in a lonely room, from bailiffs snug,
The Muse found Scroggen stretched beneath a rug ;
A window, patched with paper, lent a ray,
That dimly shewed the state in which he lay, &c.

In Wych Street, corrupted from Witch Street,* — a continuation of Drury Lane, running into the Strand, — is NEW INN, an inn of Chancery, under the government of the Middle Temple. It was anciently a common inn or hostelry, known by the sign of the "Blessed Virgin," and, in the reign of Richard the Third, was obtained from Sir John Fineux, Lord Chief Justice of England, for the rent of six pounds a year. It is principally interesting from Sir Thomas More having studied here before he became a member of Lincoln's Inn. On the south side of Wych Street is LYON'S INN, which dates as far back as the reign of Henry the Fifth, and which is said to have been also anciently a common inn for travellers, with the sign of the Lion.

Drury Lane Theatre,—from its numerous classical associations, from its antiquity as a place of public amusement, from the memory of the eminent actors and actresses who have "fretted their hour" upon its stage, and from its scenic representations having excited, for more than two centuries, the tears or the laughter of the gay, the gallant, the beautiful, and the learned,—will always be regarded as a most

* " New View of London," 1708.

interesting spot. The present theatre stands on the site of a playhouse, which appears to have been erected here in the reign of Queen Elizabeth, under the name of the Phœnix, and which was destroyed by the mob in 1617, and the stage-property torn to pieces.* It had originally been a cock-pit, and from these names Phœnix Alley, on the southeast side of Long Acre, and Cock-pit Alley, in Great Wyld Street, apparently derive their designations. In the reign of James the First, the actors at the Phœnix were called the Queen's servants, till the death of Anne of Denmark, when they were called the Lady Elizabeth's servants, from the Princess Elizabeth, afterwards Queen of Bohemia. On the marriage of Charles the First with Henrietta Maria, in 1625, they resumed their old name of the Queen's servants.

Of the character of the performances, and the names of the plays which were acted on the boards of the Phœnix, we have no record till 1629, when Shirley's comedy of the "Wedding,"—a play of considerable merit, and which has since twice been revived,—is recorded to have been represented there.† This was followed, in 1633, by Massinger's admirable play, the "New Way to Pay Old Debts." The fashionable fanaticism, which prevailed during

* Kennet's " Complete History."
† Such is the fact usually stated in the accounts of Drury Lane Theatre, but I find Webster's tragedy of the " White Devil," acted by the " Queen's servants" at the Phœnix, as early as 1612. The curious in such matters would probably, on investigation, discover many other plays, of merit and celebrity, acted here at this early period.

the Commonwealth, closed the doors of the Phœnix, and it was not till 1658 that it was reopened by Sir William Davenant, with such pieces, chiefly consisting of declamation and music, as were calculated to suit the yielding, but still fastidious prudery of the age.

At the restoration of Charles the Second, the revolution which took place in manners was scarcely less remarkable than that which had been effected in politics, and the Phœnix, or, as it was still indifferently styled, the Cock-pit, was taken possession of by a meritorious bookseller, of the name of Rhodes, who acted there with two of his apprentices, afterwards the celebrated Betterton and Kynaston. Not long afterwards, the well-known Thomas Killegrew had influence enough with his easy sovereign to obtain a patent for opening a royal theatre, the actors at which,—and the name is still familiar to us on the playbills of the present day,—were designated "His Majesty's servants." At the same time, Sir William Davenant obtained a patent to open another theatre, under the name of the "Duke of York's Company," while that of Killegrew was distinguished as the "King's."

The two rival companies being thus formed, Davenant, with Rhodes, Betterton, and Kynaston, established himself, in the first instance, at the Phœnix, from whence he removed, in 1662, to the new-built theatre in Lincoln's Inn Fields, and subsequently, in 1671, to a far more magnificent one in Dorset Garden, probably where the old playhouse in Salisbury Court had formerly stood. In the meantime, Killegrew, with the King's company, had established himself at the Red Bull, in St. John's Street, where he continued but a short time, when he removed to Gibbon's Tennis Court, near Clare Market. This theatre, however, being but ill adapted to theatrical representations, he erected a more convenient one on the site of the old Phœnix, which was opened on the 8th of April, 1663, with Beaumont and Fletcher's comedy of the "Humourous Lieutenant." From this period, the Phœnix,— with continued success, though with diminished talent,—has continued to be familiarly known as Drury Lane Theatre to the present time. "About ten of the King's company," says Colley Cibber, "were on the royal household establishment, having each ten yards of scarlet cloth, with a proper quantity of lace, allowed them for liveries; and in their warrants from the Lord Chamberlain were styled Gentlemen of the Great Chamber. Whether the like appointments were extended to the Duke's company, I am not certain."

We must not omit to mention, that it was at the theatre in Drury Lane that Charles the Second first became enamoured of Nell Gwynne, when she appeared in the character of Valeria, in Dryden's tragedy of "Tyrannic Love." Dryden, it is said, selected her for this character, from the circumstance of its being necessary that she should die on the stage, in order to admit of her speaking his lively epilogue:—

O, poet, damned dull poet ! who could prove
So senseless, to make Nelly die for love ?
Nay, what 's yet worse, to kill me in the prime
Of Easter-term, in tart and cheesecake-time !

The great poet had been partial to the beautiful
actress from the commencement of her career, and
is said to have composed this particular epilogue,—
and, indeed, at other times, to have selected her
for particularly striking parts,—in order that she
might attract the notice of Charles.

Pepys, although a married man, had no objection
to being admitted into the dressing-rooms of the
actresses, at the " King's House " in Drury Lane.
Here it was that he was first introduced to Nell
Gwynne behind the scenes, after she had been acting Cælia, in Beaumont and Fletcher's play of the
" Humourous Lieutenant." Speaking of another
actress of some celebrity, he says, " Knipp took us
all in, and introduced us to Nelly, a most pretty
woman, who acted the great part of Cælia to-day,
very fine, and did it very well : I kissed her, and so
did my wife, *and a mighty pretty soul she is.*" On a
subsequent occasion Pepys writes, " After dinner,
with my wife, to the King's house, to see the
" Maiden Queen," a new play of Dryden's, mightily
commended for the regularity of it, and the strain
and wit, and the truth ; for there is a comical part
done by Nell, which is Florimel, that I never can
hope ever to see the like done again by man or
woman. The King and Duke of York were at the
play. So great performance of a comical part was
never, I believe, in the world before as Nell do

this, both as a mad girl, then most and best of all when she comes in like a young gallant; and hath the motions and carriage of a spark, the most that ever I saw any man have. It makes me, I confess, admire her."

The new theatre lasted but a short time, being burnt to the ground, with fifty or sixty of the adjoining houses, in the month of January, 1672. It was rebuilt after a plan by Sir Christopher Wren, and reopened, with a prologue and epilogue by Dryden, on the 26th of March, 1674. In 1741, having fallen into a ruinous state, it was almost entirely rebuilt, and again, in 1794, every vestige of Wren's building was razed to the ground, and a theatre, somewhat larger than the present one, was erected on its site. This building was entirely destroyed by the fire which took place on the 24th of February, 1809. The present theatre was commenced in 1811, and, on the 10th of October, 1812, it was opened to the public, with the well-known poetical address of Lord Byron.

From Drury Lane let us stroll into Long Acre, certainly not the least interesting ground which we have yet traversed. In the reign of Edward the Sixth, this spot consisted of a large field, styled indifferently the Seven Acres, or the Long Acre, and was granted, together with Covent Garden, to John Earl of Bedford. It was sometimes styled the Elms, from a row of trees which grew upon it, and was first built upon in the reign of Charles the First.

In a " cellar " in Long Acre, lived, at one period,

in a miserable state of destitution, one of the
sweetest of lyrical poets, the once gay and gallant Richard Lovelace, the favourite of courts, and
the darling of the Muses and the ladies. "He
was accounted," says Anthony Wood, "the most
amiable and beautiful person that ever eye beheld;
a person also of minute modesty, virtue, and courtly
deportment, which made him, especially when he
retired to the great city, much admired and adored
by the female sex." Faithful to his unfortunate
sovereign, Charles the First, he was committed to
the Gatehouse, by the House of Commons, for his
boldness in presenting a petition from the County
of Kent, in which they prayed the House to settle
the government, and restore the King to his rights.

Anthony Wood tells us, that it was during his
imprisonment in the Gatehouse that Lovelace
composed his beautiful verses, "To Althea from
Prison :"—

> Stone walls do not a prison make,
>   Nor iron bars a cage;
> Minds innocent and quiet take
>   That for an hermitage.
> If I have freedom in my love,
>   And in my soul am free,—
> Angels alone, that soar above,
>   Enjoy such liberty.

Lovelace spent his fortune in the royal cause, and
it was not till all further hope of assisting his sovereign was at an end, that he went over to the Continent and raised a regiment for the French King.
He was wounded at Dunkirk, and it was long believed in England that he had died of his wounds.
It was under this false impression, that Miss Lucy

Sacheverel, a young and beautiful girl, the Lucasta
of his poetry, gave her hand to another. The poet
some time afterwards returned to England, and was
again imprisoned till the death of Charles the First.
When he obtained his release, liberty could scarcely
have been a boon to him, for, according to Wood,
he found himself in the most miserable state of
destitution. He died in 1658, in "a very mean
lodging," in Gunpowder Alley, near Shoe Lane,
Holborn.

In yon dark alley, where the wintry day
Sheds through the dingy pane its sickliest ray;
Where childhood's merry laughter never sounds,
But crime skulks forth, and penury abounds;
There, racked with anguish on his tattered bed,
Young, gifted Lovelace drooped his dying head!
How changed from him, who poured in happier days
His courtly verse in fair Althea's praise;
Or, doomed to share his captive monarch's fate,
Sang just as sweetly through his prison grate;
The courtier, soldier, poet; he who threw
O'er pleasure's flowery path a brighter hue;
He who eclipsed the titled and the vain,
In royal Henrietta's laughing train;
Whose graceful form, and whose enchanting song,
Woke the warm wish in that enamoured throng;
The world caressing, by the world carest,
The star of genius sparkling on his breast;
First in the foray, lightest in the dance,
Lord of the song, of pleasure, and the lance;
Now, with no friend to close his glazing eye,
But left in want and solitude to die;
By strangers' hands his feverish wants supplied,
Each loved one absent, and each prayer denied.
And where is she who roused his early lay?
The young, the gay, the lovely,—where are they?
Where are the laughing queen and courtly train,
Who hung enamoured on the poet's strain?
Some share their murdered monarch's bloody tomb,
And some in want and exile mourn their doom;
Nor deem what anguish marks the mournful end,
Of him they loved, the poet and the friend!—J. H. J.

In Phœnix Alley, Long Acre, the celebrated John Taylor, the "Water Poet," kept his public-house during the days of the Civil Wars and the Commonwealth. Adored by the poor, and by those of his own station in life, he was not unfrequently visited by persons of high rank, who came to amuse themselves either with the oddities of genius, or with his really instructive and entertaining conversation. Though displayed in a different manner, his veneration for the unfortunate house of Stuart was not less deep than that of his courtly contemporary, Richard Lovelace. After the execution of Charles the First, he had courage enough to change the sign of his house for that of the "Mourning Crown," till the offence which it gave to the ruling powers compelled him to remove it. He then hung up his own picture, to which he affixed the following lines,—

> There 's many a King's head hanged up for a sign,
> And many a Saint's head, too,—then why not mine ?

Every one remembers the rebuke which Dr. Johnson gave to Boswell, when, after the former had repeated to the company after dinner, in his "forcible melodious manner," the concluding lines of the Dunciad, Boswell, perhaps somewhat flippantly, observed, that the poem was far too fine for such a subject,—"a poem on what ? "—" Why on *dunces;*" said Johnson. "It was worth while being a dunce then: ah! sir, hadst *thou* lived in those days! but it is not worth while being a dunce now, when there are no wits." Among those to whom

it was "worth while" to live in the days of Pope,
and whom he has immortalized in the Dunciad, was
Edward Ward, a voluminous, but now forgotten poet,
in Hudibrastic verse, who, at one period of his life,
like Taylor, the Water Poet, kept a house of entertainment in Long Acre. He is twice honoured by
a mention in the Dunciad :—

> Not sail with Ward to ape-and-monkey climes,
> Where vile Mundungus trucks for viler rhymes !

And again,—

> As thick as bees o'er vernal blossoms fly,
> As thick as eggs at Ward in pillory.

Ward is, perhaps, best known as the author of
the "London Spy." In the notes to the Dunciad
he is mentioned as the mere keeper of a "public-
house," but he is known to have been a man of original humour; his ale was famous; and his parlour
was especially frequented by persons of the high-
church party. He subsequently kept a public-house
in Moorfields.

We have already mentioned the names of
three poets as connected with Long Acre ; but
we must not forget that of Matthew Prior, whose
name is associated, though somewhat disreput-
ably, with this particular spot. To the world in
general, Prior is sufficiently familiar as the friend
and correspondent of Pope, Swift, Bolingbroke,
all the wits and statesmen of the Augustan age
of England ; — as having written familiar verses
on the Duchess of Queensberry ; — as being the
author of poems whose merit has continued to

render them popular even in our own times;—as the secret negotiator of the famous Treaty of Utrecht, and afterwards as the accredited Ambassador from the Court of England to that of Versailles. But when we are admitted behind the scenes,—when we search into the secret history of the poet and politician,—it is not a little curious to find him hurrying from the society of Pope, and Swift, and St. John, to enjoy unrestrained freedom with a common soldier and his wife, in Long Acre. " I have been assured," says the younger Richardson, "that having spent the evening with Oxford, Bolingbroke, Pope, and Swift, Prior would go and smoke a pipe, and drink a bottle of ale, with a common soldier and his wife, in Long Acre, before he went to bed." The wife of the soldier, here alluded to, has been supposed to be the original of the Chloe of Prior's poetry: at all events the latter was one of the lowest cast of society. " His Chloe," says Dr. Johnson, " was probably sometimes ideal; but the woman with whom he cohabited was a despicable drab of the lowest species. One of his wenches, perhaps Chloe, while he was absent from his house, stole his plate, and ran away; as was related by a woman who had been his servant."—" Prior," said Pope to Spence, " used to bury himself for whole days and nights together with a poor mean creature; and often drank hard. He left most of his effects to the poor woman he kept company with, his Chloe. Every body knows what a wretch she was. I think she had been a little alehouse-keeper's wife." *   Such is the connection of Prior with Long Acre!

Long Acre and Drury Lane were the first streets which were visited by the giant pestilence which devastated London in 1665. According to Defoe, in his "History of the Plague," the first victim was a person who had been infected by a parcel of silks from Holland, which were opened in the house in which he died. "At the latter end of November, or the beginning of December, 1664," writes Defoe, "two men, said to be Frenchmen, died of the plague in Long Acre, or rather, at the upper end of Drury Lane. The family they were in endeavoured to conceal it as much as possible; but, as it had gotten some vent in the discourse of the neighbourhood, the Secretaries of State got knowledge of it. And concerning themselves to inquire about it, in order to be certain of the truth, two physicians and a surgeon were ordered to go to the house and make inspection. This they did; and finding evident tokens of the sickness upon both the bodies that were dead, they gave their opinions publicly, that they died of the plague. The people shewed a great concern at this, and began to be alarmed all over the town, and the more, because in the last week in December, 1664, another man died in the same house, and of the same distemper."

Long Acre leads us into Queen Street, which

* "Richardsoniana."   Johnson's "Life of Prior."   Spence's "Anecdotes of Men and Manners."

was built in the reign of Charles the First, and
derives its name from his consort, Henrietta Maria.
Like Drury Lane, it was once one of the most fashionable streets in London. In the reign of Charles
the First here stood Paulet House, the residence of
the Marquis of Winchester, and Conway and Rivers
House, the residences of the Earls of Conway and
Rivers. Here, too, stood the house,—in which he
died in 1776, — of the once celebrated George
Digby, Earl of Bristol, with whose inconsistencies
of character Walpole has amused himself in his
"Royal and Noble Authors." "His life," says
Walpole, "was one of contradiction. He wrote
against Popery and embraced it; he was a zealous
opposer of the court, and a sacrifice for it; was con-
scientiously converted in the midst of his prosecution
of Lord Strafford, and was most unconscientiously
a prosecutor of Lord Clarendon. With great
parts, he always hurt himself and his friends; with
romantic bravery, he was always an unsuccessful
commander; he spoke for the Test Act, though
a Roman Catholic; and addicted himself to astro-
logy, on the birth-day of true philosophy."

But Lord Bristol is now, perhaps, principally remembered from his connection with the " Mémoires
du Comte de Grammont." It was in his house in
Queen Street, apparently, that he gave his luxu-
rious parties to Charles the Second, and, with the
addition of the seductive charms of his two beautiful relations, the Miss Brooks, one of them afterwards the celebrated Lady Denham, sought to wean

the merry monarch from the alluring influence of
Lady Castlemaine, and the grave counsels of Lord
Clarendon. "The Earl of Bristol," says Count
Hamilton, " ever restless and ambitious, had put in
practice every art to possess himself of the King's
favour. He knew that love and pleasure had entire
possession of a master, whom he himself governed
in defiance of the Chancellor; thus he was continually giving entertainments at his house, and
luxury and elegance seemed to rival each other in
those nocturnal feasts, which always led to other
enjoyments. The two Miss Brooks, his relations,
were always of those parties; they were both formed
by nature to excite love in others, as well as to be
susceptible of it themselves; they were just what
the King wanted. The Earl, from this commencement, was beginning to entertain a good opinion of
his project; but Lady Castlemaine, who had recently gained entire possession of the King's heart,
was not in a humour, at that time, to share it with
another, as she did very indiscreetly afterwards, with
Miss Stewart. As soon, therefore, as she received
intimation of these secret practices, under pretence
of attending the King in his parties, she entirely
disconcerted them, so that the Earl was obliged to
lay aside his projects, and Miss Brook to discon-
tinue her advances." From Evelyn we learn that
Lord Bristol's house in Queen Street consisted of
seven rooms on a floor, with a long gallery and
gardens, and that it was furnished with "rich hangings of the King's."

But a far more remarkable nobleman, whose residence in Queen Street has thrown a deep interest over the spot, was the chivalrous and eccentric Edward Lord Herbert of Cherbury. It was in this house, probably, that " one fair day in the summer, his casement being open towards the south, the sun shining clear, and no wind stirring," he took his famous philosophical work, *De Veritate*, in his hand, and, kneeling down, prayed solemnly to the Supreme Being to grant him some sign from heaven, which was to justify him either in the publication or suppression of the work. Although his book was professedly written against revealed religion, and the existence of miracles, such is human vanity, that Lord Herbert imagined that the Divine will had been communicated in a miraculous manner to himself.

" He no sooner," he says, " had offered up his prayer, than, 'in the serenest sky that ever he saw,' a gentle noise came from the heavens, which so comforted and cheered him, that he regarded it as the sign he had prayed for, and resolved to print his work. And this, he adds, 'strange however it may seem, I profess before the eternal God is true.' "

Lord Herbert, though a disbeliever in Christianity, was at least a conscientious Deist. Aubrey tells us that he had prayers twice a day in his house, and that on Sundays his chaplain preached a sermon. His house in Queen Street witnessed the dying scene of the gallant courtier and unbelieving

philosopher. In his last illness, when he was aware
that his end was fast approaching, he expressed a
wish that Archbishop Usher might be sent for to
attend him. When it was proposed to him to receive the Sacrament, he said, indifferently, that if
there was good in anything it was in that, and
at all events it could do him no harm. Under these
circumstances the Primate refused to administer it,
for which he was afterwards much blamed. Lord
Herbert died serenely. Shortly before he breathed
his last, he inquired the hour, and on receiving a
reply, " An hour hence," he said, " I shall depart."
He then turned his face to the opposite side, and
shortly afterwards expired.

There are some other remarkable names which
throw an interest over Queen Street. Here, at one
period, lived Sir Godfrey Kneller; here resided
John Hoole, the translator of Tasso; and lastly, at
Coachmaker's Hall in this street met the Protestant
Association, which led to the famous riots fomented
by Lord George Gordon in 1780.

On entering Lincoln's Inn Fields from Queen
Street, the corner house, built by the Marquis of
Powis in 1686, is interesting as having been the
residence of the well-known minister, the Duke of
Newcastle. Lincoln's Inn derives its name from
having been the site of the palace or *Inne*, as it was
styled in the olden time, of Henry de Lacy, third
and last Earl of Lincoln, the powerful and accomplished soldier and statesman in the reign of Edward the First. His house and gardens stood on

the site of the present law-buildings, the ground of which,— recently deserted by the Dominicans, or Black Friars,—had been conferred on him by his royal master. It was here that the great Earl breathed his last, in 1312, "at his mansion-house, called Lincoln's Inn, in the suburbs of London, which he himself had erected in that place, where the Blackfriars' habitation anciently stood." His eloquent dying admonition to his son-in-law, the Earl of Lancaster, whom he summoned to his bed-side, is well-known. "Seest thou," he said, "the church of England, heretofore honourable and free, enslaved by Romish and the King's unjust oppression? Seest thou the common people impoverished by tributes and taxes, and from the condition of freemen reduced to servitude? Seest thou the nobility, formerly venerable through Christendom, vilified by aliens, in their own native country? I therefore charge thee, in the name of Christ, to stand up like a man, for the honour of God, and his church, and the redemption of thy country, associating thyself to that valiant, noble, and prudent person, [Guy] Earl of Warwick, who is so judicious in counsel, and mature in judgment. Fear not thy opposers, who shall contest against thee in the truth; and if thou pursuest this my advice, thou shalt gain eternal heaven."

After the death of the Earl of Lincoln, his palace, together with some adjoining land which had belonged to the bishops of Chester, passed into the hands of a society of lawyers; who, retaining the

name of Lincoln Inne, founded here the present
famous Inn of Court. The site of the ancient
palace of the Bishops of Chichester was, within the
last few years, pointed out by some houses known
as Chichester Rents. In point of architecture, the
present buildings possess but little merit. The
chapel, which was built by Inigo Jones, is altogether
unworthy of that great architect, and shews how
little capable he was of appreciating, or excelling in,
the Gothic style. The most interesting object is
the fine old gateway which faces Chancery Lane,
which was built about the year 1517, almost
entirely at the expense of Sir Thomas Lovell,
formerly a member of the society of Lincoln's Inn,
and afterwards a Knight of the Garter, and
Treasurer of the Household to Henry the Seventh.
The arms of the De Lacys and the Lovells still
adorn the ancient gateway.

But if Lincoln's Inn is wanting in architectural
beauty, the spot is at least deeply interesting as
associated with the history of some of our greatest
statesmen and lawyers. As we stroll along, how
many illustrious persons occur to us, who have
crossed and recrossed its time-honoured courts,—
the witty, and ill-fated Sir Thomas More, the great
Bacon, from whose title Verulam Buildings derive
their name—Coke, Hale, and Thurlow—the courtly
Mansfield,—

> Equal the injured to defend,
> To charm the mistress or to fix the friend,
> He with a hundred arts refined ;—
>
> POPE.

and lastly Camden, Erskine, Canning, Reginald Heber, and many other persons, whose names have been rendered celebrated in our own time.

We would willingly give an account of the famous masques, revels, and christenings, of which Lincoln's Inn was constantly the scene from the reign of Elizabeth to that of Charles the Second, — the days of the Yule wood, of boars' heads, and barons of beef, when the Lord of Misrule and the King of the Cockneys performed their fantastic fooleries; and when, in the words of Justice Shallow,—

> 'Twas merry in hall,
> When beards wag all, &c.

Such descriptions, however, appertain rather to a history of ancient manners and customs, than to such a work as the present. As late as 1661, we find King Charles the Second accompanied by the Duke of Ormond, Lord Clarendon, and other celebrated men, attending the Christmas revels in Lincoln's Inn.

One of the most interesting names connected with the old court of law, is that of Ben Jonson. "His mother," says Aubrey, "after his father's death, married a bricklayer, and 'tis generally said, that he wrought some time with his father-in-law, and particularly on the garden wall of Lincoln's Inn, next to Chancery Lane, and that a bencher walking through, and hearing him repeat some Greek verses out of Homer, discoursed with him, and finding him to have a wit extraordinary, gave him some exhibition to maintain him at Trinity College, in Cambridge."*

The learned and celebrated Puritan, William Prynne, was a member of, and apparently a resident in Lincoln's Inn at the time when he published his well-known Histrio-Mastix, which sent him twice to the pillory, with the additional infliction of losing an ear on each occasion. When he was subsequently branded on each cheek with the letters *S. L.*, (seditious libeller) for his virulent production, "News from Ipswich," he must indeed have presented a very uncouth appearance. When Charles the First was compelled to succumb to his parliament, Prynne was released from his imprisonment in the Island of Jersey, and was readmitted a member of Lincoln's Inn, from which society he had been expelled for writing the Histrio-Mastix. He died at his chambers here, on the 24th of October, 1669, and lies buried in the chapel of the society.†

In his chambers in Lincoln's Inn died a no less remarkable man, John Thurloe, Secretary to Oliver Cromwell, Secretary of State during the Protectorate, and the trusted friend of the Protector. His chambers were in the great court leading out of Chancery Lane, formerly called the Gatehouse Court, but now Old Buildings. His rooms are known to have been those numbered 24, in the south angle of the court, and are the chambers on the left hand, on the ground floor. These

* " Letters of Eminent Men."
† " Athenæ Oxon." Biog. Brit.

rooms were the scene of a singular passage in the secret history of Oliver Cromwell. One night, the Protector came privately to Thurloe's chambers, and had proceeded to some lengths in disclosing an affair of the utmost secrecy and importance, when, for the first time, he perceived a clerk asleep at his desk. This person was Mr. Morland, (afterwards Sir Samuel Morland) the famous mechanist, not unknown as a statesman, and at whose house in Lambeth, Charles the Second passed the first night of his Restoration with Mrs. Palmer, afterwards the celebrated Duchess of Cleveland. Cromwell, apprehensive that his conversation had been overheard, drew his dagger, and would have despatched the slumberer on the spot, had not Thurloe, with some difficulty, prevented him, assuring him that his intended victim was unquestionably asleep, since to his own knowledge, he had been sitting up two nights together. The nature of the secret interview between Cromwell and Thurloe subsequently transpired, and was no less than a design to inveigle Charles the Second, then an exile at Bruges, and his young brothers, the Dukes of York and Gloucester, into the Protector's power. It had been treacherously intimated to them, through the agency of Sir Richard Willis, that if, on a stated day, they would land on the coast of Sussex, they would be received by a body of five hundred men, which would be augmented the following morning by two thousand horse. Had they fallen into the snare, it seems that all three would have been shot immediately on reaching the shore. Morland, however, had not been asleep, as was supposed by Thurloe and Cromwell, and through his means the King and his brothers were made acquainted with the design against their lives.[*]

Lincoln's Inn Fields were laid out in the early part of the reign of Charles the First, by Inigo Jones, and are said to cover nearly the same number of square feet as the great pyramid of Egypt.[†] On the south side of the square, formerly called Portugal Row, died, in 1666, Sir John Glynne, the celebrated Chief Justice in the reign of Charles the First. Here also stood Lindsey House,—the seat of the Earls of Lindsey, and afterwards of their descendants the Dukes of Ancaster,—built after a design of the great architect; and on this side also were the residences of the celebrated Chancellor, Lord Erskine, and the still more celebrated Lord Mansfield. Lastly, in 1670, Nell Gwynne was residing in Lincoln's Inn Fields, and here, on the 8th of May, she was delivered of her eldest son, Charles Beauclerk, first Duke of St. Albans.

But unquestionably the most interesting event connected with Lincoln's Inn, is the death of the high-minded Lord Russell, who was executed in the centre of the square, on the 1st of July, 1683. We will reserve the particulars of his memorable

[*] This story is corroborated by an anecdote related by Thurloe himself. See also Welwood, and Burnet's " History of his Own Time."

[†] " Pennant's London."

fate, to our notices of the Tower of London. Here also, under circumstances of peculiar cruelty, were executed Chidiock Titchbourne, and others of that devoted and romantic band of conspirators, who perished for their attachment to the cause of the unfortunate Mary Queen of Scots, and the Roman Catholic religion. The story of their melancholy fate will also be found in our notices of the Tower.

Portugal Street, which runs parallel with the south side of Lincoln's Inn Fields, derives its name from the Queen of Charles the Second, and is the site of the theatre, styled the "Duke's Theatre," in compliment to the Duke of York, and also to distinguish it from the King's company, whom we have mentioned as performing at the Cock-pit, or Phœnix, in Drury Lane. This theatre was built after a design by Sir Christopher Wren, and was opened under a patent granted to Sir William Davenant, with the play of the "Siege of Rhodes," in the spring of 1662; Sir William transferring his company here from the theatre in Rutland Court, near the Charter House. On the night of its opening, it was honoured by the presence of Charles the Second and his gay court, being the first occasion on which the King had visited a theatre since his Restoration. The Duke's Theatre is conspicuous as having been the first playhouse where *scenes* were introduced and regularly used; and, if I remember right, where women first appeared on the boards; female characters, previous

to the Restoration, having been invariably performed by youths in female attire. The only exception
appears to have been in the theatrical representations at Court, in which we find Henrietta Maria,
and other ladies of high rank, performing in the
exquisite Masques of Ben Jonson. It was, indeed,
for his allusion, in the "Histrio-Mastix," to the im-
propriety of the Queen exhibiting herself in theatrical representations, that Prynne was exposed on
the pillory, and lost his ears.

Charles the Second, who delighted in theatrical
exhibitions, was a constant visitor at the Duke's
Theatre, and when Davenant's play of "Love
and Honour" was first acted here, he presented
Betterton with his splendid coronation suit, in which
the actor performed the character of Alonzo. The
Duke of York followed the King's example, by
giving the suit, which he had worn on the same
occasion, to Haines, who acted the part of Prince
Prospero; while the Earl of Oxford gave his to
Joseph Price, who supported the character of
Lionel, son to the Duke of Parma.

Kynaston, who performed for some time at the
Duke's Theatre, was one of the handsomest men of
his day, and, before it was the custom to admit the
presence of women on the stage, was generally
selected, from the exceeding delicacy of his features, for the personification of female characters.
In connection with this circumstance, an amusing
anecdote is related. Charles the Second, happening
one evening to enter the theatre rather earlier

than usual, found the actors unprepared to commence the performances. A messenger was dispatched to inquire the reason of the delay, on which the manager presented himself before the royal box. Believing, from his knowledge of the King's character, that the best excuse would be the true one, he plainly told his majesty, that the Queen (Kynaston) was not yet *shaved*. Charles, with his usual good humour, was amused at the excuse, which entertained him till the performances commenced. Later in life, we are surprised to read of the "lion-like majesty" of Kynaston in Don Sebastian, and of his representation of a tyrant being "truly terrible."

Charles appears to have visited Killegrew's Theatre, in Drury Lane, quite as frequently as he attended the performances at the Duke's Theatre. The principal performers at the former were Mohun, Hart, Lacy, and Nell Gwynne. Of Mohun and Hart he said, on seeing them act together in the same part, that "Mohun, (or Moon, as it was pronounced,) was like the sun, and Hart like the moon." But Lacy was the especial favourite of the merry monarch. So delighted was he with his acting, that he caused his picture to be taken in three different characters,— Teague, in "The Committee," Scruple, in "The Cheats," and Galliard, in "The Variety."

Twelve years after the erection of the Duke's theatre, it being found inconveniently small the company removed to the well-known playhouse in Dorset Gardens. Though deserted for

a time, the theatre in Portugal Street was subsequently more than once thrown open to the
public with considerable success. The celebrated Betterton formed a company here from 1695 to 1704,
when he transferred his patent to Sir John Vanbrugh,
who, a few years afterwards, removed to a more
spacious theatre which he erected in the Haymarket. In 1714, it was again opened by Rich,
—a name familiar to those who delight in the
annals of the stage,—who continued here till 1733,
when he removed his company to the theatre which
he founded in Covent Garden, under the patent
which had been granted by Charles the Second to
Sir William Davenant. Thus was this little playhouse the parent tree of the celebrated theatres
which branched off and took root in Covent Garden
and the Haymarket. In 1735, it was for the last
time opened by Gifford, the proprietor of the
theatre in Goodman's Fields, who acted here with
indifferent success till 1737, when the house was
for ever closed as a theatre. After a dreadful
fire which took place, on the 17th of September,
1809, in Bear Yard,—or, as it was formerly styled
Little Lincoln's Inn Fields,—some interesting remains of the old theatre were discovered. The front
appears to have faced Clare Market. The site is
now occupied by a pottery and china warehouse.

We must not forget to mention that the celebrated Sir William Davenant had apartments in the
theatre in Portugal Street,* in which he breathed

* Aubrey, "Athenæ Oxon."

his last on the 17th of April, 1668. It was in this street, also, that Macklin, the actor, killed a brother performer, Hallam, in May 1735,—an event which he survived sixty-two years. The dispute arose on the subject of a wig, which Hallam had worn in Fabian's play of "Trick for Trick," and which Macklin claimed as his property. High words arose between them, and, in a moment of passion, the latter struck his brother-actor a blow in the eye, the effects of which sent him to his grave. Macklin was brought to trial for the offence, but there being no evidence that the injury was premeditated, he was acquitted.

Close to Portugal Street is Clare Market, which takes its name from having been in the immediate neighbourhood of the residence of John Earl of Clare, whom we find residing here " in the most princely manner," in 1657. The site was originally called Clement's Inn Fields, and was first built upon in 1640, by one Thomas York, who obtained a licence for the purpose from Charles the First.* Clare Market, obscure and filthy as the locality now is, was in former days a fashionable locality. The Bull Head Tavern we find especially mentioned as an aristocratic house of entertainment. When the failure of a speculation in which he had embarked involved the eccentric physician, Dr. Radcliffe, in a heavy pecuniary loss, it was while "drinking" at the Bull Head Tavern, "with several persons of the first rank," that he received the disagreeable tidings.†

* Malcolm's " London."
† Biog. " Brit. Art." Radcliffe.

It was in Clare Market, that Orator Henley, whose buffooneries we have already referred to, was at one period in the habit of delivering his lectures.

The last street which we shall mention in connection with Lincoln's Inn is Duke Street, which derives its name apparently from James Duke of York. To those who take an interest in the infirmities and calamities of genius, this spot will always be remarkable, as having witnessed the dying scene of the friendless and ill-fated dramatic poet Nathaniel Lee. Oldys tells us, in his MS. notes to Langbaine, " Lee was returning one night from the Bear and Harrow in Butcher Row [near Temple Bar] through Clare Market, to his lodgings in Duke Street, over-laden with wine, when he fell down on the ground, as some say : according to others, on a bulk, and was killed or stifled in the snow." He died young, about the year 1691 or 1692.

Opposite to the Roman Catholic chapel, which narrowly escaped the fury of the mob during the Protestant riots of 1780, were the lodgings, in early life, of the celebrated Benjamin Franklin. The great philosopher and statesman worked close by, as a journeyman printer, in Great Wyld Street. He himself tells us, " I worked at first as a press-man, conceiving that I had need of bodily exercise, to which I had been accustomed in America, where the printers work alternately as compositors and at the press. I drank nothing but water; the other workmen, to the number of fifty, were great drinkers of beer. I carried, occasionally, a large form of

H 2

letters in each hand, up and down stairs, while the
rest employed both hands to carry one.   They
were surprised to see by this, and many other exam-
ples, that the ' American aquatic,' as they used to
call me, was stronger than those that drank porter.
The beer-boy had sufficient employment during the
day in serving that house alone.   My example,"
adds this great man, " prevailed with several of
them to renounce their abominable practice of bread
and cheese, with beer, and they procured, like me,
from a neighbouring house, a good basin of warm
gruel, in which was a small slice of butter, with
toasted bread and nutmeg.   This was a much better
breakfast, which did not cost more than a pint of
beer, namely, three half-pence, and at the same time
preserved the head clearer.   Those who continued
to gorge themselves with beer, often lost their credit
with the publican, from neglecting to pay their
score."

In 1766, when the great philosopher again visited
London to plead the cause of his countrymen at
the bar of the House of Commons, he paid a visit
to the printing establishment in Great Wyld Street,
in which, forty years before, he had laboured as a
humble journeyman.   Walking up to the press
which had been his accustomed station, he entered
familiarly into conversation with two workmen who
were employed at it, and sending for some liquor to
regale them with, related to them the particulars of
his early career.   The press, some years since, was
purchased of Messrs. Cox, the printers, and sent by

some Americans across the Atlantic, to be preserved in Franklin's native city, as a relic of the
illustrious philosopher.

From Lincoln's Inn, a short walk leads us to the
populous district of St. Giles's, once the retired village of St. Giles's-in-the-Fields. The ground on
which the church now stands, was formerly the site
of a hospital for lepers, founded, about the year
1117, by Matilda, wife of Henry the First. To
this hospital a small chapel was attached, which was
resorted to by the inhabitants of the scattered cot-
tages in the neighbourhood. It was in front of this
hospital, that the unfortunate and high-minded martyr, Sir John Oldcastle, Lord Cobham, was so cruelly
put to death, in the reign of Henry the Fifth, for
professing the tenets of Wyckliffe. Having been
suspended from a gibbet, by a chain fastened round
his body, a fire was lighted beneath him, and he
was slowly burnt to death.

It is necessary to observe that, at this period, the
spot we have mentioned was the common place of
execution. About the year 1413, it being thought
expedient to remove the gallows from so crowded a
district as Smithfield, they were re-erected at the
north end of the garden-wall of St. Giles, near the
junction of High Street and Crown Street. This
was certainly a place for executing criminals as late
as the reign of Queen Elizabeth, when Ballard, Babington, and some others of the gallant youths, who
conspired to place Mary Queen of Scots on the
throne, and to restore the Roman Catholic religion,

suffered death at this spot. When the gallows were
afterwards moved further to the westward, it became
a melancholy custom for malefactors, on their way
to execution, to be allowed to stop a few minutes
opposite St. Giles's church, when a large goblet of
ale,—the famous *St. Giles's Bowl*,—was offered to
them as the last refreshment they were to receive in
this life. The gallows at Tyburn, it is almost needless to remark, stood nearly at the end of Park
Lane, which appears to have been used as a place of
execution as early as the middle of the twelfth
century. When we read, however, of a criminal
being executed at *Tyburn*, we are not as a matter of
course to presume that it was at this particular spot.
The gallows were unquestionably shifted at different
periods to different places, and the name of Tyburn
appears to have been given for the time being to
each distinct spot.

The present St. Giles's church was rebuilt by
Flitcroft in 1735, and does great credit to the taste
of that architect. The exterior, which is of Port-
land stone, is plain and striking; the steeple is
peculiarly light and graceful; and the interior is a
happy combination of elegance and simplicity. The
great fault of the artist is in the small size of the
doors, which gives a certain poverty of appearance
to the rest of the building.

But the principal interest which attaches to St.
Giles's church, is the number of celebrated persons
whose remains are interred here. In the church-
yard, near the south side of the church,—as Anthony

PLAN OF
St GILES'S
in the
FIELDS.

From an original Sketch made in the Reign of
QUEEN ELIZABETH.

1 *The first St Giles's Church.* 2 *Remains of the Walls anciently enclosing the Hospital precincts.* 3 *Site of
the gallows and afterwards of the pound.* 4 *Way to Uxbridge now Oxford St* 5 *Elde Street since called
Hog Lane.* 6 *The Lane now Monmouth St.* 7 *Site of the 7 Dials formerly called Cock and Pye Fields.*
8 *Elm close since called Long Acre.* 9 *Drury Lane.*

London Richard Bentley 1851

Wood informs us in his Athenæ Oxonienses,—rests
the honoured dust of George Chapman, the poet;
the friend and companion of Shakspeare, Spenser,
Daniel, and Marlowe, but principally remembered
by his translation of Homer, which is still read
and appreciated, notwithstanding the more modern
versions of Pope and Cowper. He lived to the advanced age of seventy-seven, and, according to
Wood, was a person of reverend aspect, religious
and temperate. He was the intimate and beloved
friend of the great architect, Inigo Jones, who
erected a monument over his grave.

Chapman died in the neighbourhood of St.
Giles's church, as did also the celebrated dramatic
poet, James Shirley. The end of the latter was a
painful one. He had previously resided in Fleet
Street, when the great fire of 1666 burnt his house
to the ground, and compelled him to seek refuge in
some lodgings in St. Giles-in-the-Fields. Deeply
affected, either by the loss of his property, or by the
sublime and terrible sight which he had just witnessed, he survived his change of residence scarcely
twenty-four hours. Overcome by the same melancholy events, and by the loss of a beloved husband, his wife expired the same day, and both were
buried in the same grave in St. Giles's church-
yard.*

It is remarkable how many of the devoted adherents of the unfortunate house of Stuart rest in the
church or church-yard of St. Giles. Shirley him-

* " Athenæ Oxonienses."

self, in the civil wars, had followed his patron, the
Duke of Newcastle, to the field; but, on the de-
cline of the royal cause, had returned to London,
where, in order to obtain a livelihood, he set up a
school in Whitefriars. Here, too, sleeps another
author, the celebrated controversialist, Sir Roger
L'Estrange, who defended the cause of Charles the
First, with equal zeal, both with his sword and
his pen.   In the middle pillar, on the north
side of the church, may be seen the following
brief inscription :—

> Sir Roger L'Estrange, Knt.
> Born 17th of December, 1616,
> Dyed 11th of December, 1704,
> Anno Ætatis suæ, 87.

Alluding to his well-known failings, the Queen of
William the Third is said to have composed the
following anagram, if so it may be called, on his
name.*

> Roger L' Estrange,
> Lying Strange Roger.

In the church of St. Giles lies the body of the
gallant Philip Stanhope, first Earl of Chesterfield,
who took up arms for Charles the First, and suffered
imprisonment for his loyalty.† His monument in
the old church, we are told, was ornamented by
" *enrichments of seraphims, coronets, cartouches, &c.*"
In the old church was also a monument to another
gallant cavalier who lies buried here, on which was
the following inscription, " This monument was
erected, Anno 1670, in memory of the Honourable

* " Biog. Brit." Art. L' Estrange.
† Collins' " Peerage," Art. Chesterfield.

John Lord Bellasyse, Baron Worlaby, second son of Thomas Lord Viscount Fauconberg; who for his loyalty, prudence, and courage, was promoted to several commands of great trust by their Majesties King Charles the First and Second, viz., Having raised six regiments of horse and foot in the late civil wars, he commanded a tertia in his Majesty's Armies at the battles of Edgehill, Newbury, and Naseby, and the sieges of Reading and Bristol. Afterward being made Governor of York, and Commander in Chief of all his Majesty's Forces in Yorkshire, he fought the battle of Selby with the Lord Fairfax, and, being Governor of Newark, valiantly defended that Garrison against the English and Scotch Armies, till his Majesty came in person to the Scotch quarters, and commanded the surrender of it; at which time he also had the honour of being General of the King's Horse-guards." The inscription then proceeds to inscribe the names of his three wives and their respective progeny, in whose history the reader perhaps would take but little interest. One of the benefactors to the poor of the parish, as appeared by an inscription on a marble tablet in the old church, was the Honourable Robert Bertie,—son of Robert Bertie, Earl of Lindsey, Lord High Chamberlain and Lord High Admiral of England,—who was appointed General of the King's Forces at the breaking out of the civil war, and who fell at the battle of Edgehill in 1642.

But we have not yet concluded our notices of the

loyalists, whose remains rest in St. Giles's church,
or in its precincts. In the church-yard, near the
south-east corner of the church, may be seen an
interesting monument to the trusty and noble-
minded Richard Pendrell, who was so instrumental
in effecting the escape of Charles the Second after
the battle of Worcester. Richard was the wood-
man of Hobbal Grange, near Boscobel, whose
"noggon coarse shirt," and green suit and leathern
doublet, Charles put on at White-Ladies, for the
purpose of effecting his romantic escape;—who
when Lord Wilmot cropped the King's hair with
a common *knife*, refused to burn it, and kept it
as a memorial of his sovereign;—who conducted
Charles on his stealthy and dangerous expedition by
night from White Ladies to Madely,—and who
subsequently, with his noble-minded brothers, led
the King in safety to Lord Wilmot at Moseley.
Richard Pendrell was not forgotten at the Restoration. A pension was settled on him, as well as on
his brothers, and it is remarkable that though more
than one of their descendants are residing as subjects under the republican government of America,
they still continue to enjoy the advantages of their
ancestral loyalty. Richard Pendrell,—"trusty Dick,"
as he was styled,—died on the 8th of February,
1671, and was buried, as we have already mentioned,
in St. Giles's church-yard. The inscription on his
tomb is as follows:—" Here lyeth Richard Pendrell,
preserver and conductor of his Sacred Majesty King
Charles the Second, of Great Britain, after his

escape from Worcester Fight, in the year 1651, who
died February 8, 1671.

> Here, passenger, here's shrouded in his hearse,
> Unparalleled Pendrell through the universe,
> Like when the eastern star from heaven gave light,
> To three tost kings ; so he in such dark night
> To Britain's monarch, tossed by adverse war,
> On earth appeared a second eastern star.
> A pole astern in her rebellious main,
> A pilot to her royal sovereign.
> Now to triumph in Heaven's eternal sphere,
> He's hence advanced for his just steerage here ;
> Whilst Albion's chronicles, with matchless fame,
> Embalm the story of great Pendrell's name."

The present monument to the memory of Richard
Pendrell, in St. Giles's churchyard, is said to have
been erected at the expense of Charles the Second,
and George the Second has had the credit of having restored it.   The latter fact, however, from
the absence of all romance in his character, and
that indifference to all matters of taste and feeling
which has, generally speaking, been the characteristic of his family, may be perhaps doubted.   The
author was assured, on a recent visit to the spot,
that the descendants of the Pendrells still continue
to select St. Giles's churchyard for their burial-
place.

Among other devoted adherents of the house of
Stuart, I was not a little surprised and pleased to
find, that the staunch loyalist, Mrs. Cotton, the
mistress of Boscobel *(Domina de Boscobel,* as she is
styled in the inscription on her tomb), was buried
in St. Giles's Church.   As the inscription is interesting we will give it at length : — *Huic juxta
dormit prænobilis Heroina Fr. Cotton, Vid., Domina*

de Boscobel (loco ob Regem conservatum celebri),
serenissimæ Reginæ à privatioribus cubiculis Fœmina,
vitæ innocentiâ, morum suavitate, pietate in Deum,
charitate in proximum planè admirabilis.   Animam
placide efflavit die sept. Novemb. Anno Dom., 1677,
Ætat. suæ, 63.   Presuming *à privatioribus cubiculis*
fœmina to mean a lady of the privy chamber, the
following is a translation of the inscription :—" Near
to this spot sleeps the right noble lady of honour,
Frances Cotton, widow, Lady of Boscobel (a place
celebrated on account of the King having been preserved there), a Lady of the Privy Chamber to the
most serene Queen, eminent for the innocency of
her life, the sweetness of her manners, and her piety
towards God.   She calmly breathed forth her soul
on the 7th of November, 1677, at the age of 63."

In St. Giles's Church lies buried the ill-fated
Charles Radcliffe, by legitimate descent Earl of
Derwentwater, who was executed in 1746, for his
share in the rebellions of 1715 and 1745.   Here, too,
previous to their removal to the burial-place of his
ancestors at Dilstone, in Northumberland, rested the
remains of his elder brother, the young Earl of Derwentwater, who was beheaded for his loyalty to the
Stuarts, in 1716.   From this church his body was
carried by stealth to Dilstone, where it was interred
in the chapel by the side of his father.   According
to Hogg, the Ettrick Shepherd, " A little porch
before the farm-house of Whitesmocks is pointed
out as the exact spot where the Earl's remains
rested, avoiding Durham."   Every one remembers

the beautiful lines in the plaintive Jacobite lament,
" Derwentwater's Good Night :"—

> Albeit that here in London town
> It is my fate to die,
> O, carry me to Northumberland,
> In my father's grave to lie !
> There chaunt my solemn requiem
> In Hexham's holy towers ;
> And let six maids of fair Tynedale
> Scatter my grave with flowers.

The grave levels all distinctions and all ranks,
and together mingle in many memorable instances
the dust of the Royalist and the Republican, of the
just and the unjust, of the oppressor and the oppressed. Widely differing in character and principles from the Royalists, whose names we have
recorded, was the witty and celebrated poet, and
incorruptible patriot, Andrew Marvell, who lies
buried in the church of St. Giles. It was to the
credit of Charles the Second, that notwithstanding
Marvell, in his seat in Parliament, had invariably
and virulently opposed the measures of the court,
and had personally attacked the vices of the King
in his satires, Charles had generosity enough to forgive his enemy, and was alike able to appreciate
his genius and delight in his society. How much
one would like to know the site of the house in the
Strand — and perhaps the house itself may still
exist — in which Marvell spent his last days in
penury and privation, at a time when the slightest
departure from his political principles would have
crowned him with the wealth which he wanted, and
the honours which he despised. It was at the very

time when his poverty compelled him to borrow a
sovereign from a friend, in order to purchase the necessaries of life, that the poet one day went forth from
his wretched lodging in the Strand to the splendid
palace at Whitehall, for the purpose of passing the
evening with the merry monarch and his gay courtiers. Of the events and conversation of the evening we have no record : the next day, however,
while the poet was busily employed at his studies,
the door of his apartment, " up two pair of stairs,"
suddenly opened, and the Lord Treasurer, Lord
Danby, made his appearance. Marvell was much
surprised at the unexpected visit, and expressed his
opinion that the Lord Treasurer must have mistaken
his way. " No," said the other, "not now that I
have found Mr. Marvell." He then endeavoured,
by offering him a lucrative place under the government, and by every argument and persuasion, to
entice the patriot over to the court; but Marvell,
proud in his poverty and integrity, turned a deaf
ear to his solicitations. " My Lord," he said, " I
cannot in honour accept your offer; if I did I must
either be ungrateful to the King by subsequently
voting against him, or else false to my country in
succumbing to the measures of the court. The sole
favour which I have to ask of his Majesty is, that
he will believe me as dutiful a subject as any which
he has, and that I am acting far more advantage-
ously for his true interests by rejecting his offers
than I should do by accepting them." Finding
him inflexible, Lord Danby delicately alluded

to his necessities, and pressed him to receive
a thousand pounds as a free gift from his sovereign,
and as a personal compliment to his talents. This
was under the rule of the Stuarts, when our monarchs were in the habit of appreciating and associating with genius. James the First had
patronized every man of learning; Charles the
First was the friend of all the poets; and Charles
the Second, among many other acts of generosity
which proved his appreciation of genius, is known
to have presented Dryden with a sum of money,
and to have sent Wycherley five hundred pounds
to enable him to recover his health in the south of
France. There seems, therefore, the less reason to
account for Marvell rejecting the flattering gift of his
sovereign. He was firm, however, against this additional temptation; and yet it was immediately
after Lord Danby had left him that, we are told,
he sent to a friend to borrow a guinea. He died
on the 16th of August, 1678, and ten years after
his death, the town of Kingston-upon-Hull, which
he had so long and faithfully represented in Parliament, collected a sum of money to erect a monument over his grave in the church of St. Giles's-in-
the-Fields. The same prejudice which induced
Spratt, Dean of Westminster (a churchman whose
fortune had been made by being admitted to the
profligate parties of Charles the Second), to deny
Milton a burial-place in Westminster Abbey, and
which, in our own time, influenced another Dean
of Westminster to reject Thorwaldsen's fine monu-

mental effigy of Lord Byron, also induced the Rector of St. Giles's of his day to exclude both monument and inscription to the incorruptible and pure-minded Andrew Marvell!

The most conspicuous monument in St. Giles's Church is a recumbent figure of Lady Frances Kniveton, daughter of Alice, Duchess of Dudley, and granddaughter of the celebrated favourite of Queen Elizabeth, Robert, Earl of Leicester. The story of her descent is a remarkable one. After the tragical death of his beautiful wife, Amy Robsart, Leicester married Douglas, daughter of William Lord Howard, of Effingham, and widow of John, Lord Sheffield, whose life he is also said to have attempted by poison. Fearing that this second marriage might prejudice him in the eyes of his royal mistress, Queen Elizabeth, he affected to deny the legitimacy of his second marriage, and in his will styles his only offspring, his "base son."

This son, the celebrated Sir Robert Dudley, became the husband of Alice Leigh, daughter of Sir Thomas Leigh, Bart., afterwards Duchess of Dudley. His reputation has not yet faded. Eminent from his martial achievements and his discoveries in the West Indies, — distinguished by his lofty stature and graceful person, — the most adroit horseman and the most successful in the tilt-yard, — he united with these accomplishments the highest reputation as a navigator, an architect, a physician, a mathematician, and a chemist.* Dis-

* The accomplishment which, in the eyes of modern sportsmen,

gusted with his own country, from the repeated
failures which had attended his attempts to establish his legitimacy, he repaired to the court of
the Emperor Ferdinand the Second, whither the
fame of his accomplishments had preceded him,
and by that sovereign was elevated to the rank of
Duke, on which he assumed his family title of Duke
of Northumberland. " But it was the house of
Medici," says Horace Walpole "those patrons of
learning and talent, who fostered this enterprising
spirit, and who were amply rewarded for their
munificence by his projecting the free port of
Leghorn."

Like his father, the splendid favourite, Sir Robert
appears to have entertained some strange notions
respecting the marriage state, and, on his departure
to join the court of the Emperor, he repudiated his
legitimate wife, Alice Leigh, and took with him,
as the companion of his adventures, Miss Southwell, daughter of Sir Robert Southwell, of Wood
Rising in the county of Norfolk, by whom he had
several children.   To this lady, previous to his
departure, he gave his hand at the altar, affirming
that, by the canon law, his marriage with Alice
Leigh was illegal, inasmuch as she had admitted
him to her favours in the life-time of his first wife,
Miss Cavendish, daughter of the celebrated navigator Thomas Cavendish.

will render the name of Sir Robert Dudley principally deserving
of being recorded, is the fact, as old Anthony Wood informs us, that
" he was the first of all that taught a dog to sit in order to catch
partridges."

Whatever truth there may be in the stigma cast on the character of Alice Leigh in her unmarried days,—and it does not detract from the interest with which we regard her monument,—it is certain that Charles the First fully admitted the claims of her husband to be considered the legitimate son of the celebrated favourite, and also the legality of her own marriage, by creating her Duchess of Dudley. To this dignity she was advanced, by letters patent, on the 23rd of May, 1644, and doubtless the title of Northumberland would have been substituted, but for the offence which it might have given to one of the most zealous and powerful supporters of the unfortunate King, Algernon Percy, the tenth Earl who had succeeded to that ancient title. Frail as she may possibly have been in early youth, the Duchess of Dudley was afterwards distinguished for her virtues, and munificent charities. She died on the 22nd of January, 1670, at the age of ninety, and was buried at Stoneleigh, in Warwickshire, where a monument was erected to her memory. Her London residence was in the immediate neighbourhood of St. Giles's Church.

One of the most remarkable persons whose remains lie in St. Giles's church, is Lord Herbert of Cherbury, but there is no memorial of his resting-place, neither can I find that a monument was ever erected to his memory. He was buried in the chancel of the church on the 5th of August, 1648. Lastly, in this interesting church lies buried the great sculptor, John Flaxman, whose remains were carried to the grave on the 15th of December, 1826, attended by the President and Council of the Royal Academy. Allan Cunningham relates an interesting circumstance connected with the death of this celebrated artist. "The winter," he says, "had set in, and, as he was never a very early mover, a stranger found him rising one morning, when he called about nine o'clock. ' Sir,' said the visitant, presenting a book as he spoke, ' this work was sent to me by the author, an Italian artist, to present to you, and at the same time to apologize for its extraordinary dedication. In truth, sir, it was so generally believed throughout Italy that you were dead, that my friend determined to shew the world how much he esteemed your genius, and having this book ready for publication, he has inscribed it " *Al Ombra di Flaxman*." No sooner was the book published than the story of your death was contradicted, and the author, affected by his mistake, which, nevertheless he rejoices at, begs you will receive his work and his apology.' Flaxman smiled, and accepted the volume with unaffected modesty, and mentioned the circumstance as curious to his own family, and some of his friends." * This circumstance took place on the 2nd of December, when the great artist was apparently in excellent health and spirits. The next day he was suddenly taken ill with a cold, and, five days after the visit of the stranger, he was

* " Lives of the British Sculptors."

no more. His epitaph tells us, that, "his mortal
life having been a constant preparation for a blessed
immortality, his angelic spirit returned to the
Divine Giver on the 7th of December, 1826, in the
seventy-second year of his age."

CHARING CROSS AND WHITEHALL.

STATUE OF CHARLES THE FIRST.—EXECUTION OF GENERAL HARRISON
AND HUGH PETERS. — ANECDOTES OF LORD ROCHESTER AND
RICHARD SAVAGE.—OLD ROYAL MEWS.—COCKSPUR AND WARWICK
STREETS. — SCOTLAND YARD. — ATTEMPT TO ASSASSINATE LORD
HERBERT.—SIR JOHN DENHAM.—WALLINGFORD HOUSE.—DUKES
OF BUCKINGHAM.—ADMIRALTY.

At Charing Cross, observed Dr. Johnson, flows
the full tide of human existence. At this distance
of time, the imagination does not easily reconcile
itself to contemplate the period, when the site of
the present populous and animated spot was occupied by a shady and retired grove, in the midst of
which stood a hermitage and a fair chapel dedicated
to St. Catherine. And yet, in 1261, we find William de Radnor, Bishop of Llandaff, requesting
permission of his sovereign, Henry the Third, to
take up his abode in the cloister of his hermitage
at Charing during his occasional visits to London.*
Whether, at this period, the ground on which
Charing Cross now stands belonged to the King, or
to the See of Llandaff, there is some doubt.

Here, as late as the days of Charles the First,
stood one of those beautiful architectural memorials
raised by Edward the First, in 1296, to the memory

* Willis's "History of the See of Llandaff," p. 51.

of his beloved consort, Eleanor of Castile. This, as well as the others, were built after designs by Cavalini, and were erected, as is well known, on each spot where her remains rested in their passage from Horneby, in Lincolnshire, where she died, to their last home in Westminster Abbey. Anciently the small village of Charing stood in the open country between the cities of London and Westminster, and it has been conjectured, with much ingenuity, that it derived its name from the cross dedicated to *la chère reine*. Unfortunately, however, we find from the petition of William de Radnor, as above quoted, that the name of Charing existed thirty-five years before the death of the devoted princess to whose memory the cross was erected. During the civil troubles in the reign of Charles the First, this interesting memorial of a past age was unfortunately regarded by the fanatics as a relic of Popish superstition, and in a moment of religious frenzy, was razed to the ground by an illiterate rabble.

Nearly on the site where the cross anciently stood, is the equestrian statue of King Charles the First, which was cast in 1633, by Le Sœur, for the Earl of Arundel. A curious anecdote is related connected with this beautiful work of art. Previous to the period fixed upon for its erection, it was seized by the Parliament, who ordered it to be sold and broken into pieces. According to M. d'Archenoltz, it was purchased by one John River, a brazier, who carefully concealed the statue in hopes of better times, and who subsequently realized a considerable sum of money by selling a variety of small household articles in bronze, which he professed to have manufactured out of the mutilated man and horse. By the royalists they are said to have been eagerly bought out of affection to their martyred sovereign, and by the rebels as a memorial of their triumph. After the Restoration, River is said to have exhumed the statue, and to have returned it uninjured to the Government; and, in 1678, it was erected at Charing Cross, on its present pedestal, the work of Grinlin Gibbons. It appears by the parish books, that, during the Interregnum, the statue was preserved in the vaults of St. Paul's church, Covent Garden.

Charing Cross is replete with historical and literary associations. It was here that the fight took place, in the days of Queen Mary, between Sir Thomas Wyatt and the Earl of Pembroke,—a conflict on which the Marquis of Northampton, Sir Nicholas Penn, and other courtiers, are described as quietly gazing from the leads of St. James's Palace; while so loud were the screams of women and children that they were heard at the top of the White Tower, and "the great shot was well discerned there out of St. James's Fields."*

It was in "Hartshorn Lane, near Charing Cross,"— situated on the south side of the Strand, to the east of Northumberland House,—that the father and mother of Ben Jonson lived, when, as we have already mentioned, the future dramatist was sent to take his daily lessons in St. Martin's church; and it

* Stow.

was at Charing Cross that a still greater man than Ben Jonson once resided,—the immortal John Milton. He lived, we are told, for some weeks, in some lodgings "at one Thomson's, next door to the Bull Head Tavern, Charing Cross, opening into Spring Gardens."*

Milton had ceased to live in this neighbourhood, and had himself become blind and a fugitive, when those turbulent men with whom he had been associated in the days of their prosperity,—the surviving regicides who had brought Charles the First to the block,—were dragged on hurdles to expiate their daring crime at Charing Cross. The scene of their execution appears to have been nearly on the spot where the statue of their murdered sovereign now stands, and consequently in sight of the Banqueting-house at Whitehall, from the windows of which Charles had walked forth to the scaffold. Of those who suffered on this occasion, the two principal malefactors were the celebrated General Harrison and the fanatic preacher Hugh Peters, who met their fate, attended by all those frightful circumstances of terror and barbarity, which the law anciently denounced on those who were condemned for the crime of high treason.

Actuated by a sincere, though blind and intolerant bigotry, they died true to the principles which

* It was during his residence at Charing Cross that Milton wrote his, "Johannis Philippi Angli Responsio ad Apologiam anonymi cujusdam Tenebrionis pro Rege et Populo Anglicano infantissimam." "Biog. Brit." v. 5, p. 3114, note.

they had so daringly advocated. Harrison met his
fate with the confidence of a Christian, and with the
stoicism of an ancient Roman. As he was passing
on his sledge to the scene of execution he appeared extremely cheerful, and called out several
times on the way, "I go to suffer for the most
glorious cause that ever was in the world." Some
one in the crowd asking him, in derision, "Where
is your good old cause now?" he smiled, and,
placing his hand upon his heart, observed, "Here
it is, and I am going to seal it with my blood."
When he came in sight of the gallows, he is described as transported with joy, and when his
servant asked him how he felt, "Never," he said,
"better in my life." When he was taken off the
sledge, the hangman asked him to forgive him:
"I do forgive thee," he said, "with all my heart;"
"alas! poor man, thou dost it ignorantly; the Lord
grant that this sin may not be laid to thy charge."
He then gave the executioner what money he had,
and, having affectionately embraced his faithful
servant, mounted the ladder with a serene countenance. During a speech which he addressed to the
assembled multitude, he happened to overhear some
remarks made by the crowd that his hands and legs
trembled. "Gentlemen," he said, "by reason of
some scoffing that I do hear, I judge that some do
think I am afraid to die, by the shaking I have in
my hands and knees: I tell you, No; but it is by
reason of much blood I have lost in the wars, and
many wounds I have received in my body, which

causes this shaking and weakness in my nerves; I
have had it these twelve years: I speak this to the
praise and glory of God: he hath carried me above
the fear of death; and I value not my life, because
I go to my Father, and am sure I shall take it up
again." He was then hanged; and, being cut down
from the gallows while yet alive, his bowels were
torn out and thrown into the fire, and his body
quartered.*

Pepys was present at the execution. In his
diary of the 13th of October, 1660, he observes,
" I went out to Charing Cross to see Major General
Harrison hanged, drawn, and quartered, which was
done there; he looked as cheerful as any man could
be in that condition. He was presently cut down,
and his head and heart shewn to the people, at
which there were great shouts of joy. It is said,
that he said he was sure to come shortly, at the
right hand of Christ, to judge them that now
judged him, and that his wife do expect his coming
again. Thus it was my chance to see the King
beheaded at Whitehall, and to see the first blood
shed in revenge for the King at Charing Cross."

Three days after the execution of the military enthusiast, Harrison, Hugh Peters followed him to the
scaffold at Charing Cross, and met his death, accompanied by the same terrible paraphernalia. According
to Bishop Burnet, he had been "a very vicious man,"
and a sermon which he preached in Newgate, the
day after his trial, shews, that at this period he was

* "Trial of Charles I., and of some of the Regicides."

afflicted by the reproaches of conscience and great
despondency of mind.   " He was the man of all of
them," says Burnet, " that was the most sunk in his
spirit, and could not in any sort bear his punishment: he had neither the honesty to repent,
nor the strength of mind to suffer for it as
the rest did : he was observed all the while to
be drinking some cordial liquors to keep him
from fainting."   He suffered on the same scaffold
with Cook, the lawyer who had conducted the
prosecution against Charles the First.   On Cook's
hurdle was actually placed the severed head of
Harrison, with the livid countenance turned
towards him ; but the circumstances attending the
execution of Peters were even more harrowing.
He was placed within the rails of the scaffold,
where he was compelled to witness the dying
agonies and the disembowelling of his friend.   It
was during this awful scene, that,—as if by some
peculiar dispensation of Providence,—courage and
constancy were restored to him, and he met his
fate with a decency, a meekness, and a courage,
which would have done credit to a martyr.   To
one, who loaded him with opprobrious epithets, as
a rebel and a regicide, " Friend," he said, " you do
not well to trample upon a dying man ; you are
greatly mistaken ; I had nothing to do in the death
of the King."   One other anecdote connected with
his dying scene is interesting and even touching.
On his way to the gallows, recognising a friend in
whose kind offices he could confide, he beckoned

him towards his hurdle. Drawing forth a piece
of gold, he bent it, and desired him to carry it to
his daughter, at the same time naming the place
where she lodged. "Take it to her," he said, "as a
token from me, and let her know that my heart is
as full of comfort as it can be ; and that before this
piece shall come to her hands, I shall be with God
in glory." When he was upon the ladder, he observed to the Sheriff, "Sir, you have butchered one
of the servants of God before my eyes, and have
forced me to see it, in order to terrify and discour-
age me, but God has permitted it for my support
and encouragement."* The last expression which
was observed on his countenance was a smile. Like
Harrison, he addressed a speech to the surrounding
multitude, but from the weakness of his voice and
the execrations of the crowd, much that he said was
inaudible.†

From such inflammable enthusiasts as General
Harrison and Hugh Peters, we turn with pleasure
to brighter names and better men, or, at all events,
to safer members of society. Near Charing Cross
died, in 1677, Dr. Isaac Barrow, the eminent
mathematician and divine. There is something
very pleasing in the admiration expressed by
Dr. Pope for the memory of departed worth
and genius, and in the gratification which he
feels at having formed the acquaintance of so celebrated a man, even though at the close of his

* Ludlow's "Memoirs."
† "Trials of Charles I., and of some of the Regicides."

valuable career. "The last time he was in London,"
says Dr. Pope, "he went to Knightsbridge to give
the Bishop of Salisbury a visit. I cannot express
the rapture of joy I was in, having, as I thought,
so near a prospect of his charming and instructive
conversation; I fancied it would be a heaven upon
earth, for he was immensely rich in learning, and
very liberal and communicative of it, delighting in
nothing more than to impart to others, if they
desired it, whatever he had attained by much time
and study. Some few days after, he came to
Knightsbridge, and sat down to dinner, but I observed he did not eat. Whereupon I asked him
how it was with him; he answered, that he had a
slight indisposition hanging upon him, with which
he had struggled two or three days, and that he
hoped by fasting and opium to get it off, as he had
removed another and more dangerous sickness, at
Constantinople, some years before. But these
remedies availed him not; his malady proved an
inward, malignant, and insuperable fever, of which
he died, May 24, 1677, in the 47th year of his age,
in mean lodgings, at a sadler's near Charing Cross;
an old, low, ill-built house, which he had used for
several years; for though his condition was much
better by his obtaining the mastership of Trinity
College, yet that had no bad influence on his
morals; he still continued the same humble person, and could not be prevailed upon to take more
reputable lodgings."* In 1685-6, we find Wil-

* Dr. Pope's "Life of Dr. Seth Ward, Bishop of Salisbury."

liam Penn, the great legislator of Pennsylvania,
dating his letters from "Charing Cross."[*]

There are few persons, who are curious in literary biography, who are not aware of the circumstances under which Sir William Davenant lost his
nose in Axe Yard. Some years after his loss, we are
told, he was passing "along the Mews, at Charing
Cross, when he was followed by a beggar-woman,
who prayed God to preserve his eye-sight. Davenant, who had nothing the matter with his eyes,
inquired, with some curiosity, what on earth could
induce her to pray for his eye-sight, for, he said, ' I
am not purblind as yet.' ' No, your honour,' she
said, ' but if ever you should, I was thinking you
would have no place to hang your spectacles on.'"[†]

Charing Cross was still an ill-lighted and half-
populated spot, when, in the days of Charles the
Second, it was the scene of the forcible abduction
of Elizabeth Mallet,— celebrated as *la triste héritière* of De Grammont, — by the famous and profligate Earl of Rochester. She was the daughter
of John Mallet Esq., of Enmere, in Somerset-
shire, and was possessed of a fortune of 2500*l.*
a-year, a large portion in the days of Charles
the Second. One evening, she had been supping at
Whitehall with the beautiful Miss Stewart, afterwards Duchess of Richmond, and was returning
home with her grandfather, Lord Haly, when their
coach was suddenly arrested at Charing Cross. In

[*] " Biog. Brit." v. 5, p. 3321, note.
[†] " Biog. Dram." Art. Davenant.

a moment they were surrounded by a number of
men, on foot and horseback, who forcibly carried
the lady to another coach, in which she found herself hurried along by six horses, with the companion-
ship of two strange females.   A pursuit was immediately instituted, and, not far from Uxbridge,
Rochester was discovered skulking by himself, and
having been conducted to London, was committed
to the Tower.   Charles, subsequently, interested
himself on behalf of his witty favourite, and the lady
having been induced to forgive the outrage, after a
short delay they were married, and she became the
mother of his children.

The mention of Lord Rochester recalls the name
of a kindred genius and profligate, the unfortunate
poet, Richard Savage, whose well-known adventure at Charing Cross nearly cost him his life on
the scaffold.   "Mr. Savage," says Dr. Johnson,
"accidentally meeting two gentlemen, his acquaint-
ances, whose names were Merchant and Gregory,
he went with them to a neighbouring coffee-house,
and sat drinking till it was late, it being in no time
of Mr. Savage's life any part of his character to be
the first of the company that desired to separate.
He would willingly have gone to bed in the same
house, but there was not room for the whole company, and therefore they agreed to ramble about
the streets and divert themselves with such amusements as should offer themselves till morning.   In
this walk they happened unluckily to discover a
light in Johnson's coffee-house, near Charing Cross,

and therefore went in. Merchant with some rudeness demanded a room, and was told that there was
a good fire in the next parlour, which the company
were about to leave, being then paying their reckon-
ing. Merchant, not satisfied with this answer,
rushed into the room, and was followed by his companions. He then petulantly placed himself between
the company and the fire, and soon after kicked
down the table. This produced a quarrel; swords
were drawn on both sides, and one Mr. James Sinclair was killed. Savage, having likewise wounded
a maid that held him, forced his way with Merchant
out of the house; but being intimidated and confused, without resolution either to fly or stay, they
were taken in a back court by one of the company,
and some soldiers whom he had called to his assistance. Being secured and guarded that night, they
were in the morning carried before three Justices,
who committed them to the Gatehouse, from whence,
upon the death of Mr. Sinclair, which happened the
same day, they were removed in the night to Newgate, where they were, however, treated with some
distinction, exempted from the ignominy of chains,
and confined, not among the common criminals, but
in the press-yard." * Several witnesses swore positively that it was at the hands of Savage that Sinclair received his death-wound, and consequently at
his trial the jury brought him in guilty of murder.
As is well known, every attempt was made by his
unnatural mother, the Countess of Macclesfield, to

---

* Johnson's " Lives of the Poets."

prevent the royal mercy being extended towards him, but fortunately the kind and strenuous exertions of Lady Hertford, Lord Tyrconnel, and his charming friend, Mrs. Oldfield, the actress, counteracted her designs, and on the 9th of March, 1728, the unfortunate poet received the King's pardon.

On the site of the present National Gallery, on the north side of Charing Cross, stood, within the last few years, the Royal Mews. Here, as early as the reign of Richard the Second, were kept the King's hawks, at which period we find the accomplished Sir Simon Burley, Knight of the Garter, holding the appointment of Keeper of the Royal Falcons at the Meuse, near Charing Cross. At length, in 1537, the King's stables at Bloomsbury, then called Lomesbury, having been destroyed by fire, Henry the Eighth directed the falcons to be removed from Charing Cross; and from this reign to that of George the Fourth, it continued to be the site of the royal stables. In the reign of Richard the Second, we find the great poet, Geoffrey Chaucer, holding the appointment of Clerk of the Works at the King's Mews at Charing Cross, and here it was that Cornet Joyce, who seized the person of Charles the First at Holmby, was impri·soned, some years afterwards, by order of Oliver Cromwell.

Till within the last few years, Charing Cross was one of the usual places for exposing offenders on the pillory. Here Titus Oates underwent this punishment for his infamous perjuries, as did also, at a later period, Parsons, the author of the well-known imposition, "The Cock Lane Ghost."

On the south-east side of Charing Cross is Cockspur Street. Here still remains the British Coffee House, which appears to have been the favourite resort of many of the unfortunate Jacobite gentlemen who suffered for their share in the romantic enterprise of 1745; and here Boswell mentions his dining with Dr. Johnson in 1772. "We spent a very agreeable day," he says, "though I recollect but little of what passed."* There may be some persons to whom it may possibly be interesting to be informed that O'Brien, the "Irish giant," breathed his last in Cockspur Street.

Out of this street runs Warwick Street, at the western extremity of which formerly stood Warwick House, where the lamented Princess Charlotte resided with a small household, close to the residence of her father, the Prince of Wales, at Carlton House. It was at the further end of Warwick Street that this interesting heroine of imaginary grievances entered the hackney-coach, in which she eloped from the protection of her father, and proceeded to the residence of her mother, the Princess of Wales, in Connaught Place. The event is now nearly forgotten, but those who remember its occurrence, will not easily forget the extraordinary sensation which it created.

If we are to place any credit in tradition, Oliver Cromwell resided nearly on the spot where Drum-

* Boswell's "Life of Johnson."

mond's Bank now stands.   Milton, too, must have
resided close by, for we are expressly told that his
house in Charing Cross overlooked the Spring Gardens.

As we descend towards Whitehall, a small court
may be discovered on the east side of the street,
between Nos. 13 and 15, in which formerly stood
the celebrated " Rummers' Tavern," the resort of
the wits and the courtiers of the days of Charles
the Second.   Not many years since, the " Rummers' " was converted into a house of very indifferent repute, and is now used as a printing establishment.   This spot will always be considered
interesting as connected with the fortunes of Matthew Prior, the poet.   " Prior," says Bishop Burnet,
" had been taken a boy out of a tavern, by the
Earl of Dorset, who accidentally found him reading
Horace ; and he, being very generous, gave him an
education in literature."*   This is an illiberal statement of the Bishop's, coloured by party prejudice,
and Burnet probably knew as much when he penned it.   The fact is, that Prior's father, a respect-
able citizen, happening to die when his son was
extremely young, committed the boy to the care
of his uncle, who was then the landlord of the
" Rummers'" tavern.   That the uncle was true to
his trust is proved by his having sent the future
poet to Westminster School, under the care of the
learned Dr. Busby.   It was at this period that the
famous Earl of Dorset,—

* Burnet's " History of his Own Times."

K 2

The best good man, with the worst-natured muse,

happened to dine at the "Rummers'" with a select
party of men of rank and talent, when a dispute
arose respecting the meaning of a passage in one of
the odes of Horace. In the heat of the discussion,
one of the party exclaimed,—" I am much mistaken
if there is not a young lad in the house who will set
us all right." Prior was immediately sent for, and
gave his interpretation of the disputed passage with
so much modesty and good sense, that Lord Dorset
removed him from the tavern, and subsequently
caused him to be entered at St. John's College,
Cambridge, where he defrayed a portion of the
expenses of his education.[*]

Prior, in his "Epistle to Fleetwood Shepherd,"
one of the boon companions of Charles the Second,
writes,—

"My uncle, rest his soul! while living,
Might have contrived me ways of thriving;
Taught me with cider to replenish
My vats, or ebbing tide of Rhenish;
So, when for hock, I draw pricked white-wine,
Swear 't had the flavour, and was right wine."

As late as the 14th of October, 1685, we find the
annual feast of the nobility and gentry, residing in
the parish of St. Martin's-in-the-Fields, held at the
tavern kept by Samuel Prior, the uncle of the
poet.

The house No. 30, Whitehall, now a military
and naval bookseller's, may be noticed as having
been inhabited by Thomson, the author of the
"Seasons." His apartments were on the first floor,

* Humphrey's "Life of Prior," attached to his works.

and in these rooms he is said to have composed his
" Summer."

Some doors lower down the street, and on the
same side, is a large arch-way leading into Scotland
Yard, the latter a spot of much historical interest.
It derives its name from a palace which was built
here by King Edgar for the reception of Kenneth
the Third, King of Scotland, when the latter paid
his annual visits to London to swear fealty for
his kingdom. By degrees, according to Stow, it
grew into a magnificent palace, and was set apart
as the regular residence of the Scottish monarchs,
on the occasion of their humiliating journeys to the
southern metropolis to do homage for the fiefs
which they held under the English crown. The
last notice which we have of this palace, is in the
reign of Henry the Eighth, when his sister, Margaret, widow of James the Fifth of Scotland, made
it her residence after the death of her husband.
It was shortly afterwards demolished.

When Milton, in 1650, was appointed Latin
Secretary under the Commonwealth, we find him, in
order to be nearer the scene of his official duties,
residing in "an apartment which had been prepared for him" in Scotland Yard. The great poet,
who appears to have been fond of change of scene,
had recently removed from High Holborn to his
temporary lodgings opening into Spring Gardens,
and from thence to Scotland Yard.* Here, in 1712,
died the well-known Beau Fielding, the "Orlando

* " Life of Milton," by Philips.

the Fair" of " The Tatler," whose curious career has
already been noticed in our Memoir of Pall Mall;
and, lastly, " at his house in Scotland Yard," died,
in 1726, Sir John Vanbrugh, the architect and dramatic writer.[*]

It was at the entrance into Scotland Yard that
Sir John Ayres lay in wait with his retainers, in
the reign of James the First, to assassinate Lord
Herbert of Cherbury; and it was in the open
street, opposite, that the bloody encounter took
place between them, of which Lord Herbert has
given us so graphic an account in his " Life of
Himself." Infuriated by the conviction that Lord
Herbert had won his wife's affections and corrupted
her virtue,—which, however, the latter solemnly
asserts was not the fact,—Sir John Ayres determined at all hazards to take away the life of the
destroyer of his peace. The account which Lord
Herbert gives of this extraordinary affair, throws a
curious light on the manners of the period :—
" Coming one day into her chamber," he says, " I
saw her through the curtains lying upon her bed
with a wax candle in one hand, and a picture in the
other. I coming thereupon somewhat boldly to her,
she blew out the candle, and hid the picture from
me; myself thereupon being curious to know what
that was she held in her hand, got the candle to be
lighted again, by means whereof I found it to be my
picture she looked upon with more earnestness and

---

[*] " Memoir of Vanbrugh," by Leigh Hunt, attached to his
works.

passion than I could have easily believed, especially since myself was not engaged in any affection towards her. I would willingly have omitted this passage, but that it was the beginning of a bloody history which followed ; howsoever I must before the eternal God declare her honour. Sir John Ayres, finding he could take no advantage against me, in a treacherous way resolved to assassinate me in this manner. Hearing I was to come to Whitehall on horseback with two lackeys only, he attended my coming back in a place called Scotland Yard, at the hither end of Whitehall, as you come to it from the Strand, hiding himself here with four men armed on purpose to kill me. I took horse at Whitehall Gate, and passing by that place, he being armed with a sword and dagger, without giving me so much as the least warning, ran at me furiously, but, instead of me, wounded my horse in the brisket, as far as his sword could enter for the bone. My horse hereupon starting aside, he ran him again in the shoulder, which, though it made the horse more timorous, yet gave me time to draw my sword: his men thereupon encompassed me, and wounded my horse in three places more. This made my horse kick and fling in that manner, as his men durst not come near me, which advantage I took to strike at Sir John Ayres with all my force, but he warded the blow both with his sword and dagger: instead of doing him harm, I broke my sword with a foot of the hilt ; hereupon some passenger that knew me, and observing my horse bleeding in so many places, and so many men assaulting me, and my sword broken, called out to me several times, ' Ride away, ride away;' but I, scorning a base flight upon what term soever, instead thereof alighted as well as I could from my horse.

"I had no sooner put my foot upon the ground, but Sir John Ayres, pursuing me, made at my horse again, which the horse perceiving, pressed me on the side I alighted, in that manner that he threw me down, so that I remained flat upon the ground, only one foot hanging in the stirrup, with that piece of a sword in my right hand. Sir John Ayres hereupon ran about the horse, and was thrusting his sword into me, when I, finding myself in this danger, did, with both my arms reaching at his legs, pull them towards me, till he fell backwards on his head. One of my footmen, hereupon, who was a little Shropshire boy, freed my foot out of the stirrup; the other, which was a great fellow, having run away as soon as he saw the first assault. This gave me time to get upon my legs, and to put myself in the best posture I could with that poor remnant of a weapon. Sir John Ayres by this time likewise was got up, standing betwixt me and some part of Whitehall, with two men on each side of him, and his brother behind him, with at least twenty or thirty persons of his friends, or attendants of the Earl of Suffolk. Observing thus a body of men standing in opposition against me, though to speak truly I saw no swords drawn but by Sir John Ayres and his men, I ran violently

against Sir John Ayres; but he, knowing my sword
had no point, held his sword and dagger over his
head, as believing I could strike rather than thrust;
which I no sooner perceived but I put a home
thrust to the middle of his breast, that I threw him
down with so much force that his head fell first to
the ground, and his heels upwards.

"His men hereupon assaulted me, when one Mr.
Mausel, a Glamorganshire gentleman, finding so
many set against me alone, closed with one of them;
a Scotch gentleman, also closing with another, took
him off also. All I could well do to those who
remained was to ward their thrusts, which I did
with that resolution that I got ground upon them.
Sir John Ayres was now got up a third time, when
I, making towards him with intention to close,
thinking that there was otherwise no safety for me,
put by a thrust of his with my left hand, and so
coming within him, received a stab with his dagger
on my right side, which ran down my ribs as far as
my hip; which I feeling, did with my right elbow
force his hand, together with the hilt of the dagger,
so near the upper part of my right side, that I made
him leave hold. The dagger now sticking in me,
Sir Henry Cary, afterwards Earl of Falkland and
Lord Deputy of Ireland, finding the dagger thus in
my body, snatched it out. This while I being
closed with Sir John Ayres, hurt him on the head,
and threw him down a third time; when, kneeling
on the ground and bestriding him, I struck at him
as hard as I could with my piece of a sword, and

wounded him in four several places, and did
almost cut off his left hand. His two men this
while struck at me, but it pleased God even miracu-
lously to defend me; for, when I lifted up my sword
to strike at Sir John Ayres, I bore off their blows
half a dozen times. His friends now finding him in
this danger, took him by the head and shoulders and
drew him from betwixt my legs, and carried him
along with them through Whitehall, at the stairs
whereof he took boat. Sir Herbert Croft (as he
told me afterwards) met him upon the water, vomiting all the way, which I believe was caused by the
violence of the first thrust I gave him. His servants, brother, and friends, being now retired also, I
remained master of the place and his weapons;
having first wrested his dagger from him, and afterwards struck his sword out of his hand. This being
done, I retired to a friend's house in the Strand,
where I sent for a surgeon, who, searching my
wound on the right side, and finding it not mortal,
cured me in the space of some ten days, during
which time I received many noble visits and messages from some of the best in the kingdom."*

It appears by an old plan of the Palace of Whitehall, printed in the days of Charles the Second, that
the house adjoining the entrance to Scotland Yard
(now occupied by a chemist and the offices of a
Railway company) was formerly the residence of Sir
John Denham, the poet, who held the appointment
of Surveyor of the Works in the reign of the

* Lord Herbert of Cherbury's " Life of Himself."

"merry monarch."* This house was the scene of
one of the most curious passages in the romance
of real life. Sir John Denham,—then considerably
advanced in years, and, as he is described in De
Grammont's Memoirs, an "old and limping man,"
—had united himself to Miss Brooke, a lively and
beautiful girl, and niece of George Digby, second
Earl of Bristol. On her first appearance at the
Court of Charles the Second, — an unmarried
maiden of eighteen,—she captivated the affections,
such as they were, of the Duke of York, afterwards
James the Second ; who, on her marriage with the
aged and sarcastic poet, redoubled his attentions to
the flattered beauty. It was in an age when every
body made love. Pepys informs us that the Duke
used to follow the young bride up and down the
presence-chamber at Whitehall "like a dog ; " and
he adds, " The Duke of York is wholly given up to
his new mistress, my Lady Denham ; going at noon-
day with all his gentlemen to visit her in Scotland
Yard ; she declaring she will not be his mistress, as
Mrs. Price, to go up and down the Privy Stairs:
Mr. Brouncker, it seems, was the pimp to bring
it about." According to Count Hamilton, in his
" Mémoires de Comte Grammont," the Duke was
not left long to complain of the obduracy of his
beautiful mistress. " She suffered him," he says,
" to entertain hopes which a thousand considerations

* The front of this house, facing Whitehall, has been modernized ;
but a glance at the back part of it, which looks into Scotland Yard,
will sufficiently prove its antiquity.

had prevented her holding out to him before her
marriage;" and he adds, " It was soon brought to a
conclusion, for where both parties are sincere in a
negotiation, no time is lost in cavilling." The ter-
mination of this profligate intrigue was indeed a
tragical one. Sir John Denham (who had long
been distinguished for his biting sarcasms against
the marriage state, but who had been vain enough
to exempt himself from the general doom, when he
united himself to a young and giddy wife) was so
afflicted by the intelligence of her frailty that it
produced a temporary aberration of intellect. In a
paroxysm of jealousy he is said to have administered
poison to the partner of his bed, but with what
truth it is now impossible to ascertain. It is certain,
however, that three contemporary writers, Aubrey,
Count Hamilton, and Pepys, affirm that her death
was produced by unfair means. The latter inserts
in his "Diary" of the 10th of November, 1666,
" I hear that my Lady Denham is exceedingly sick,
even to death, and that she says, and every body else
discourses, that she is poisoned." Count Hamilton,
moreover, unhesitatingly lays her untimely death at
the door of her implacable husband; "As no person," he says, " entertained any doubt of his having
poisoned her, the populace of his neighbourhood
threatened to tear him in pieces as soon as he
should come abroad; but he shut himself up to
bewail her death, until their fury was appeased by a
magnificent funeral, at which he distributed four
times as much burnt wine as had ever been drunk

at any funeral in England." Twenty-one years
afterwards, in March, 1688, Sir John Denham himself breathed his last at " his office near Whitehall,"
the scene of his wife's frailty, and untimely end.*

In Whitehall, as is proved by an ancient print,
Oliver Cromwell had a house previous to his ag-
grandisement; and here also lived Gay, the poet,†
before he was received into the family of the Duke
and Duchess of Queensberry.

Opposite to the house which we have mentioned
as the residence of Sir John Denham, is the Admiralty. It stands nearly on the site of Wallingford
House, which was built in the reign of James the
First, by William Knollys, Viscount Wallingford,
created, on the 18th of August, 1626, Earl of Bun-
bury. Wallingford House is connected with many
historical associations. Here, in 1632, " of a disease
as strange and horrible as her depravity," and of
which Arthur Wilson has left us such disgusting
particulars,‡ is said to have died Frances Howard,
the beautiful and depraved Countess of Essex. It
was at this period in the possession of her brother-
in-law, Lord Wallingford. From Lord Wallingford
it passed to the magnificent favourite, George Vil-

* "Athenæ Oxonienses."
† Swift's " Correspondence."
‡ We mention the fact of the Countess of Essex having died
at Wallingford House entirely on the authority of Mr. Croker, who
quotes as his authority, Wilson (p. 83.) On turning, however, to
Wilson, we merely find the loathsome details of her last moments
referred to in the text. By an order of the Privy Council, dated
Whitehall, 18th January, 1622, it is ordered as " His Majesty's
gracious pleasure and command, that the Earl of Somerset and his
lady do repair either to Grays or Cowsham (Caversham,)

liers, Duke of Buckingham. Here, on two different occasions, we find Bassompierre paying him a visit, and here was born, in January, 1627, his son, George Villiers, the second and witty Duke.

It was at Wallingford House that the Lord Keeper Williams found the great favourite lying on a couch overwhelmed with grief, at that crisis of his fortunes when the Spanish ambassador, Iniosa, had half persuaded the imbecile James that his beloved " Steenie " was engaged in a plot against his life. When Buckingham had last met his sovereign James had turned to him reproachfully and said, " Ah, Steenie, Steenie, wilt thou kill me !" Shortly afterwards, the old King took coach for Windsor, and Buckingham, as usual, was proceeding to accompany him, and, indeed, had set his foot on the step of the coach, when James invented some excuse for leaving him behind. According to Bishop Hacket, the favourite burst into tears. It was immediately afterwards that the Lord Keeper visited him at Wallingford House, and found him in the state of distress we have mentioned. By the Lord Keeper's advice, Buckingham immediately repaired to Windsor, and by his respectful and affectionate demeanour and his extraordinary personal influence

---

the Lord Wallingford's houses in the county of Oxon, and remain confined to one or either of the said houses, and within three miles compass of the same, until further order be given by his Majesty." Hearne's preface to Robert of Gloucester's Chronicle. Mr. Croker probably may have read that Lady Essex was confined for life to one of Lord Wallingford's houses, and may thus have been led to infer that she died at the London residence of that nobleman, Wallingford House.

over the King, he eventually contrived to make
his peace.*

As Wallingford House was the scene of Buckingham's triumphs, so was it the scene of his
funeral obsequies. From hence, in darkness and
in stealth, his body was conveyed to Westminster
Abbey. According to Stow, the murdered remains
of the Duke, after his assassination by Felton, were
brought to Wallingford House, while, on the other
hand, Frankland asserts that they were conveyed
to York House in the Strand. Stow, however, as
usual, is in the right, for we find the point set
at rest by a contemporary writer, Mr. Meade, in a
letter to Sir Martin Stuteville :—" Notwithstanding," he says, " that Saturday was se'nnight, all the
heralds were consulting with my Lord Treasurer
to project as great a funeral for the Duke as ever
any subject of England had: nevertheless, last
night, at twelve of the clock, his funeral was solemnized in as poor and confused a manner as hath
been seen, marching from Wallingford House over
against Whitehall to Westminster Abbey; there
not being above one hundred mourners, who attended
upon an empty coffin borne upon six men's shoulders,
the Duke's corpse itself being interred yesterday, as
if it had been doubted the people in their madness
might have surprised it. But to prevent all disor-
der, the trainbands kept a guard on both sides of
the way all along, from Wallingford House to West-

* Wilson, p. 271, Weldon, p. 142, " Lives of the Chancellors,"
i. p. 112.

minster Church, beating up their drums loud, and
carrying their pikes and muskets upon their shoulders as in a march, not trailing them at their heels,
as is usual at a mourning. As soon as the coffin was
entered the church, they came all away, without
giving any volley of shot at all. And this was the
obscure catastrophe of that great man." *

After the decapitation of Charles the First, Wallingford House appears to have fallen, with other
appanages of the crown, and of the aristocracy, into
the hands of the Commonwealth. From the roof
of this house Archbishop Usher, then residing with
the Countess of Peterborough, was prevailed upon
to take a last look at his beloved master, Charles the
First, when he was led forth to the scaffold in front
of the Banqueting Hall at Whitehall. He sunk
back, we are told, in horror at the sight, and was
carried in a swoon to his apartments.† Subsequently we find Wallingford House the residence of
the celebrated General Fleetwood, and it was in his
apartments, in 1659, that the council of general

* Ellis's "Original Letters," iii. p. 265. After this corrobora-
tive evidence, it is curious to find Mr. Croker conjecturing to which
of the Duke's London residences, (Wallingford House or York
House,) the remains of the powerful favourite were conveyed after
his assassination. Mr. Croker seems to imply a doubt, on the
authority of Howell, whether Wallingford House was ever the
settled residence of the Duke of Buckingham. We have seen
Bassompierre, however, visiting him there in 1626 ; we have seen
that his son and successor was born there the following year ; we
have seen the Lord Keeper Williams visiting him there about the
same period, and the next year we find it the depository of his
remains, previous to their interment in Westminster Abbey.
These facts seem sufficiently to prove that Wallingford House was
the " settled residence " of Buckingham.
† Pennant, p. 104.

officers,—styled the Cabal of Wallingford House,—
voted their adhesion to the " good old cause," and
the necessity of intrusting the whole military power
of the kingdom to a single individual. Their ma_
chinations, as is well known, led to the dissolution
of the Parliament, and consequently to the deposition of Richard Cromwell.*

On the Restoration, Wallingford House returned
into the possession of the Villiers' family, and was
the occasional residence of George Villiers, the
second and witty Duke of Buckingham. It was
here, at the wish of the Duke, that the body of
Cowley, the poet, lay in state on the way from
Chertsey to Westminster,† and from its portals
flowed the long funeral procession of peers and
poets who followed the remains of the illustrious
poet to his last home.‡ It was a singular compliment to the memory of Cowley, that Charles the
Second should have observed of him, on hearing
of his death, that "he had left no better man behind him in England," and that a still more profligate man, the Duke of Buckingham, should have
followed him to the grave, and subsequently have
raised a monument over his remains. Buckingham
Court, a narrow passage which runs by the side of
the present Admiralty, is all that remains to point

* Hume's "Hist. of Eng." Noorthouck's "Hist. of London,"
p. 203.
† Heath's "Chronicle," continuation.
‡ "Honorificâ pompâ elatus ex ædibus Buckinghamianis, viris
illustribus omnium ordinum exequias celebrantibus, sepultus est die
M. Augusti, Anno Domini, 1667." *Dr. Sprat's Inscription on
Cowley's Monument, in Westminster Abbey.*

out the site of what was once the princely residence
of the ducal house of Villiers.

In the present Admiralty there is little that is
interesting in its local associations, and nothing that
is pleasing in its architecture. The office was
originally situated in Duke Street, Westminster, as
we find from "Pepys' Memoirs," but in the reign
of William the Third, was removed to Whitehall.
The present ponderous pile was built by Ripley,
in the reign of George the Second, and some years
afterwards, the screen which partially veils it from
the street, and which has sometimes had its admirers, was raised by one of two brothers of the
name of Adams, whose names are now principally
remembered from their having been the architects
of the Adelphi. There are those, however, to whom
the Admiralty will always be an object of interest,
from the reflection that under the portal which
leads to its gloomy and cob-webbed hall, have passed,
without an exception, the many celebrated naval
heroes, who within the last century have thrown an
unfading lustre on the annals of their country. It
was from hence that Lord Anson departed on his
voyage to circumnavigate the world,—that famous
voyage varied by hurricanes, pestilence, and splendid
conquests,—when half his followers were carried off
by the scurvy at one time, and the capture of Manilla
galleons, and the plunder of Mexican cities enriched
them at another. Here Cook took leave of his employers, to discover new regions, and, as it proved,
to lose his valuable life on the savage shore of

Owhyhee. Here Lord Rodney received the latest orders which enabled him to sweep away the French fleet, in the Carribean seas,—and from hence Lord Nelson departed to reap immortal laurels, which were too dearly earned when he fell in the hour of victory, at Trafalgar. The Board-room, too, of the Admiralty is interesting, both from the beautiful carvings of Grinlin Gibbons, which decorate its walls, as well as from its having listened to the eloquence of the many celebrated men who have sat at its Board, from the strong sense of Earl St. Vincent, to the sparkling wit of Charles Fox. At his apartments here, when first Lord of the Admiralty, died, in 1733, the celebrated Admiral Byng, the first Lord Torrington, and in the Board-room of the Admiralty was signed, twenty-four years afterwards, the death-warrant of his gallant and ill-fated son, Admiral John Byng, who was shot at Portsmouth, in 1757. Lastly, it may be mentioned, that in the room to the left, as we enter from the hall, the body of Lord Nelson lay in state previous to its interment in St. Paul's.

THE OLD PALACE OF WHITEHALL.

ALTHOUGH the ancient palace of Whitehall has
been almost entirely swept away, there still remain
sufficient traces of the old building to enable us to
link the present with the past; nor is it easy to pass
unmoved over ground which is associated with so
many historical events and romantic incidents.

> How cold and dull the wanderer's footsteps fall,
> Where stood thy glittering chambers, proud Whitehall!
> Where is the pile the haughty churchmen reared?
> Where are the classic halls by time endeared?
> Mark, where the dark meandering waters lave
> These time-worn steps, descending to the grave.
> Here kings embarked with all their rich array,
> Girt with the young, the beautiful, the gay;
> And pleasure bade the gilded vessel glide,
> And music float upon the laughing tide.
> Now, while I stand upon the cold damp stone,
> The river's mournful ripple sounds alone;
> No more I see the gorgeous train pass by;
> No more, proud pile! thy splendours meet my eye;
> No more thy gardens, sloping to the Thames,
> Are filled with high-born men and courtly dames;
> Changed is the spot where beauty twined her bowers,
> Where fountains sparkled midst a waste of flowers;
> Where, rapt in thought, great Cromwell loved to rove,
> And Henry walked with Boleyn in the grove.—J. H. J.

The Cockpit partially exists in the present Treasury; and the beautiful Banqueting House still remains, from the windows of which Charles the First passed to the scaffold. The Tilt Yard recalls the time when the open space, which still retains its ancient name, was alive with armed warriors, and streaming pennons, and glittering heralds; and when waving plumes and brilliant eyes looked down from galleries covered with cloth of gold on the stirring scene below. Lastly, the Privy Gardens still point out the site of verdant lawns and shady labyrinths, where Wolsey discussed affairs of state with Cromwell; where Henry toyed with the delicate hand of Anne Boleyn; and where Charles the Second gazed on the dazzling beauty of the Duchess of Cleveland, or laid his head in soft dalliance on the lap of *la belle Stuart*.

Among the few on whom the mantle of taste has descended in this methodical and unromantic age, there is one I would recall who has often wandered with me through these deserted scenes of departed splendour; when, with the plan of the ancient palace in our mind's eye, we have fancied back the days when the song and the dance were heard in its lighted chambers, tracing the individual scenes of its ancient splendour and hospitality, from its gay saloons and gorgeous galleries, to its crowded butteries and spacious wine-cellars,—those days when silken pages sauntered in its courts, and stately warders lounged at its royal thresholds. Such scenes have long since passed away, and with them nearly all of the ancient spirit of chivalry, hospitality, and romance.

Whitehall Palace was originally built by Hubert de Burgh, Earl of Kent, that proud and powerful noble, who, in the days of King John, stood by the side of his royal master on the famous field of Runnymede, and who, in the following reign, was dragged an ignominious traitor to the Tower. He bequeathed it to the Convent of the Black Friars in Holborn, in whose church his body was honourably interred. By this religious order, it was transferred, in 1248, to Walter de Grey, Archbishop of York, and from this period till the fall of Cardinal Wolsey, it continued to be the London residence of the prelates of that see, and from thence derived the name of York House.

York House appears to have been almost entirely rebuilt by Wolsey. Here the Cardinal Archbishop resided during many years, in a style of regal splendour, which has seldom been surpassed even by the most magnificent of our monarchs. According to Storer, in his "Metrical Life of Wolsey,"

> Where fruitful Thames salutes the learned shores
> Was this grave prelate and the muses placed,
> And by those waves he builded had before
> A royal house with learned muses graced,
> But by his death imperfect and defaced.

Here Wolsey entertained the learned, the witty, the beautiful, and the gay, and here he accumulated his vast libraries and exquisite picture-galleries. The walls of his apartments were covered with hangings of cloth of gold and tissue, and his tables with velvets, satins, and damasks of various hues. The great gallery is described as a scene of unparalleled magnificence; and in two other apartments, known as the Gilt and Council Chamber, two large tables were covered with articles of plate of solid gold, many of them studded with pearls and precious stones.

The household of this haughty churchman consisted of eight hundred persons, many of whom were knights and noblemen. Among them we find the Earl of Derby and the young Lord Percy, the heir of the great Northumberland family, who was subsequently compelled to quit the family of the Lord Cardinal for winning the affections of Anne Boleyn. It would fill pages to transcribe the description which Cavendish, Fiddes, and others give of the splendid hospitality of Wolsey, and the multitude of dependents whom he maintained at Whitehall. The numbers who were employed in his kitchens, and who were feasted at his board,— his heralds, physicians, secretaries, and cofferers; his marshals, purveyors, gentlemen ushers, and " counsellors learned in the law ; " his clerks of the check, of the hanaper, and of the wax ; the chaplains who attended him at his meals, and the deans and choristers who ministered in his chapel,—comprise such a list of attendants and retainers as no modern court in Europe could surpass. " Of gentlemen ushers," says Stowe, " he had twelve daily waiters, besides one in the privy chamber, and of gentlemen waiters in his privy chamber he had six ;

of lords, nine or ten, who had each of them two
men allowed to attend upon them, except the Earl
of Derby, who always was allowed five men. Then
had he of gentlemen cup-bearers, carvers, servers,
both of the privy chamber and of the great chamber,
with gentlemen and daily waiters, forty persons;
of yeomen ushers, six; of grooms in his chamber,
eight; of yeomen in his chamber, forty-five daily.
He had also almsmen, sometimes more in number
than at other times."

These numerous retainers were clad in the most
magnificent liveries, and even the master-cook of
the Cardinal was dressed in velvet and satin, and
wore a chain of gold round his neck. Wolsey
himself, whenever he was seen in public, appeared
with extraordinary splendour. His cardinal's robe
was of the finest satin, and of the richest scarlet die,
and over his shoulders he wore a tippet of costly
sable. He was the first clergyman in England who
wore silk and gold, and this, not only on his person, but on his saddles and the trappings of his
horses. His Cardinal's hat was borne before him by
a person of rank; and even in the King's chapel it
was always placed upon the altar. Wolsey, as
a priest, rode on a mule, the trappings of which
were of crimson velvet, and the stirrups of silver
gilt; while his attendants, consisting of gentlemen
and pursuivants-at-arms, were mounted on horses
admirably trained and gorgeously caparisoned. Two
priests, " the tallest and most comely he could find,"
immediately preceded him, carrying ponderous silver

crosses ; the one, the symbol of his being a cardinal, and the other appertaining to his dignity as Archbishop of York.

> Alas ! how silent and how sad the spot,
> Each glory vanished, and each pomp forgot !
> Yet still imagination loves to trace
> Where Wolsey triumphed in his pride of place,
> Recalls the churchman and his liveried train,
> The great, the wise, the haughty, and the vain !
> The silken thousands feasted at his board,
> The ermined prelate, and the gartered lord ;
> The glittering banquet, and the regal state,
> The great within, the suppliants at his gate ;
> When Wolsey shared a more than monarch's power,
> And reigned the mighty despot of an hour.
> Calmly he sleeps in Leicester's cloistered aisle,
> Above a people's hate, a tyrant's smile ;
> Proclaiming from the tomb the ill that springs,
> For those who build upon the faith of kings.—J. H. J.

Cavendish, in his life of Wolsey, has given us an account of an entertainment given by the great Cardinal at Whitehall, which is not only curious as throwing a light on the pastimes and manners of the sixteenth century, but is doubly interesting from its being the occasion on which Shakspeare introduces the first love scene between Henry the Eighth and Anne Boleyn. "The banquets," says Cavendish, "were set forth with masks and mummeries, in so gorgeous a sort and costly manner that it was heaven to behold. There wanted no dames or damsels meet or apt to dance with the maskers, or to garnish the place for the time, with other goodly desports. Then was there all kind of music and harmony set forth, with excellent voices both of men and children. I have seen the King suddenly come in thither in a mask, with a dozen of other maskers, all in garments

like shepherds, made of fine cloth of gold, and fine
crimson satin paned, and caps of the same ; their
hair and beards either of fine gold wire, or else
of silver, and some being of black silk ; having
sixteen torch-bearers besides their drums, and other
persons attending upon them with vizors, and clothed
all in satin of the same colours. And at his coming,
and before he came into the hall, ye shall understand that he came by water to the water-gate,
without any noise : where, against his coming, were
laid charged many cannon, and at his landing they
were all shot off, which made such a rumble in the
air that it was like thunder. It made all the noblemen, ladies, and gentlemen to muse what it should
mean coming so suddenly, they sitting quietly at
a solemn banquet.

" First, ye shall perceive that the tables were set
in the chamber of presence, banquet-wise covered,
my Lord Cardinal sitting under the cloth of estate,
and there having his service all alone ; and then was
there set a lady and a nobleman, or a gentleman and
gentlewoman, throughout all the tables in the
chambers on the one side, which were made and
joined as it were but one table. All which order
and device was done and devised by the Lord Sands,
Lord Chamberlain to the King; and also by Sir
Henry Guilford, Comptroller to the King. Then
immediately after this great shot of guns, the
Cardinal desired the Lord Chamberlain and Comptroller to look what this sudden shot should mean,
as though he knew nothing of the matter. They,

thereupon looking out of the windows into the Thames, returned again, and shewed him that it seemed to them there should be some noblemen and strangers arrived at his bridge, as ambassadors from some foreign prince. 'With that,' quoth the Cardinal, 'I shall desire you, because ye can speak French, to take the pains to go down into the hall to encounter and to receive them according to their estates, and to conduct them into this chamber, where they shall see us, and all these noble personages, sitting merrily at our banquet, desiring them to sit down with us, and to take part of our fare and pastime.' Then they went incontinent down into the hall, where they received them with twenty new torches, and conveyed them into the chamber, with such a number of drums and fifes, as I have seldom seen together at one time in any masque. At their arrival into the chamber, two and two together, they went directly before the Cardinal where he sat, saluting him very reverently; to whom the Lord Chamberlain for them said, 'Sir, forasmuch as they are strangers, and can speak no English, they have desired to declare unto your Grace thus:—They, having understanding of this your triumphant banquet, where was assembled such a number of excellent fair dames, could do no less, under the supportation of your good grace, but to repair hither to view as well their incomparable beauty, as for to accompany them at mumchance, and then after to dance with them, and to have of them acquaintance. And, Sir, they furthermore require of your grace licence to accomplish the cause of their repair.' To whom the Cardinal answered, ' that he was very well contented they should do so.'

"Then the maskers went first and saluted all the dames as they sat, and then returned to the most worthiest, and there opened a cup full of gold, with crowns and other pieces of coin, to whom they set diverse pieces to cast at. Thus, in this manner perusing all the ladies and gentlewomen, and to some they lost, and of some they won. And this done, they returned unto the Cardinal with great reverence, pouring down all the crowns in the cup, which was about two hundred crowns. ' At all ?' quoth the Cardinal, and so cast the dice, and won them all at a cast, whereat was great joy made. Then quoth the Cardinal to my Lord Chamberlain, ' I pray you,' quoth he, ' shew them that it seemeth me that there should be among them some noble man, whom I suppose to be much more worthy to sit and occupy this place and room than I, to whom I would most gladly, if I knew him, surrender my place according to my duty.' Then spake my Lord Chamberlain unto them in French, declaring my Lord Cardinal's mind, and they rounding him again in the ear, my Lord Chamberlain said to my Lord Cardinal, ' Sir, they confess,' quoth he, ' that among them there is such a noble personage, whom, if your Grace can appoint him from the others, he is contented to disclose himself, and to accept your place most worthily.' With that the Cardinal, taking a good advisement among them, at the last quoth he, ' Me seemeth the gentleman with the black beard should be even he.' And with that he arose out his chair, and offered the same to the gentleman in the black beard, with his cap in his hand.

"The person to whom he offered then his chair, was Sir Edward Neville, a comely knight, of a goodly personage, that much more resembled the King's person in that mask than any other. The King, hearing and perceiving the Cardinal so deceived in his estimation and choice, could not forbear laughing, but plucked down his visor, and Master Neville's also, and dashed out with such a pleasant countenance and cheer, that all noble estates there assembled, seeing the King to be there amongst them, rejoiced very much. The Cardinal eftsoons desired his Highness to take the place of estate; to whom the King answered that he would go first and shift his apparel; and so departed, and went straight into my lord's bed-chamber, where was a great fire, made and prepared for him, and there new-apparelled him with rich and princely garments. And in the time of the King's absence, the dishes of the banquet were clean taken up, and the tables spread again with new and sweet perfumed cloths; every man sitting still until the King and his maskers came in among them again, every man being newly apparelled. Then the King took his seat under the cloth of estate, commanding no man to remove, but sit still, as they did before. Then in came a new banquet before the King's Majesty, and to all the rest through the tables, wherein, I suppose, were served two hundred dishes, or above, of wondrous costly meats and devices subtlely devised. Thus passed they forth the whole night with banqueting, dancing, and other triumphant devices, to the great comfort of the King, and pleasant regard of the nobility there assembled."

If Whitehall possessed no other feature of historical interest, the site of the ancient palace would be sufficiently endeared to us from the single circumstance of Shakspeare, having fixed there the principal scenes of his magnificent play of "Henry the Eighth." It is, indeed, not a little interesting to find how closely one of the finest scenes in the play, as pourtrayed by the immortal dramatist, coincides with the account of Cavendish, even in its minutest details; and yet "Henry the Eighth," was acted as early as 1603, and Cavendish's "Life of Wolsey," was not published till 1641. It is impossible to resist transcribing an extract from the parallel scene in Shakspeare.

SCENE 4.—*The Presence Chamber in* YORK PLACE.

A small table under a state canopy for the CARDINAL, *a longer table for the guests. Enter at one door* ANNE BOLEYN, *and divers* LORDS, LADIES, *and* GENTLEWOMEN, *as guests ; at another door enter* SIR HENRY GUILDFORD.

Guild. Ladies, a general welcome from his grace
  Salutes ye all : This night he dedicates
  To fair content, and you : none here, he hopes,
  In all this noble bevy, has brought with her
  One care abroad : he would have all as merry
  As first-good company, good wine, good welcome,
  Can make good people.—O, my lord, you are tardy.

Enter Lord Chamberlain, LORD SANDS, *and* SIR THOMAS LOVELL.

  The very thought of this fair company
  Clapped wings to me.
Chamb. You are young, Sir Harry Guildford.
Sands.   By my life,
  They are a sweet society of fair ones.
Chamb. Sweet ladies, will it please you sit ? Sir Harry,
  Place you that side, I'll take the charge of this :
  His grace is entering. —Nay, you must not freeze ;
  Two women placed together makes cold weather :
  My Lord Sands, you are one will keep them waking ;
  Pray sit between these ladies.
Sands.   By my faith,
  And thank your lordship. By your leave, sweet ladies.

   Seats himself between ANNE BOLEYN *and another lady.*

  If I chance to talk a little wild, forgive me ;
  I had it from my father.
Anne.   Was he mad, sir ?
Sands. O, very mad, exceeding mad, in love too ;
  But he would bite none : just as I do now,
  He would kiss you twenty with a breath.   [*kisses her.*]
Chamb.   Well said, my Lord.
  So, now you are fairly seated : —Gentlemen,
  The penance lies on you, if these fair ladies
  Pass away frowning.

   Enter CARDINAL WOLSEY, *attended ; and takes his state.*

Wol. You are welcome, my fair guests, ; that noble lady,
  Or gentleman, that is not freely merry,
  Is not my friend : This, to confirm my welcome ;
  And to you all good health.

   [*Drum and trumpets within : Chambers discharged.*]

         What warlike voice,
  And to what end is this? nay, ladies, fear not ;
  By all the laws of war you are privileged.
Serv.   A noble troop of strangers ;
  For so they seem ; have left their barge and landed ;
  And hither make, as great ambassadors
  From foreign princes.
Wol.   Good Lord Chamberlain,
  Go, give them welcome, you can speak the French tongue ;
  And, pray, receive them nobly, and conduct them
  Into our presence, where this heaven of beauty
  Shall shine at full upon them :—Some attend him.

Enter the KING, *and twelve others, as maskers, habited like shepherds,*
 with sixteen torch-bearers ; ushered by the LORD CHAMBERLAIN.

They pass directly before the CARDINAL, *and gracefully salute him.*

Wol. A noble company! what are their pleasures?

Chamb. Because they speak no English, thus they prayed
    To tell your grace ;—that having heard by fame
    Of this so noble and so fair assembly
    This night to meet here, they could do no less,
    Out of the great respect they bear to beauty,
    But leave their flocks; and under your fair conduct,
    Crave leave to view the ladies, and entreat
    An hour of revels with them.

Wol.   Say, Lord Chamberlain,
    They have done my poor house grace; for which I pray them
    A thousand thanks, and pray them take their pleasures.

[*Ladies chosen for the dance.* The KING *chooses* ANNE BOLEYN.]

K. Hen. The fairest hand I ever touched! O beauty,
    Till now I never knew thee.

Wol. My Lord,——

Chamb.   Your Grace?

Wol. Pray tell them thus much for me:
    There should be one amongst them, by his person,
    More worthy this place than myself; to whom
    If I but knew him, with my love and duty
    I would surrender it.

Chamb.   I will, my lord.

[CHAMB. *goes to the company, and returns.*]

Wol. What say they?

Chamb.   Such a one, they all confess,
    There is, indeed; which they would have your grace
    Find out, and he will take it.

Wol.   Let me see then, [*Comes from his state.*]
    By all your good leaves, gentlemen ;—Here I'll make
    My royal choice.

K. Hen.   You have found him, Cardinal; [*Unmasking.*]
    You hold a fair assembly; you do well, lord:
    You are a churchman, or I'll tell you, cardinal,
    I should judge now unhappily.

Wol.   I am glad
    Your Grace is grown so pleasant.

K. Hen.   My Lord Chamberlain,
    Pr'ythee, come hither: What fair lady's that?

Chamb. An't please your Grace, Sir Thomas Boleyn's daughter,
    The Viscount Rochford, one of her highness' women.

K. Hen. By Heaven she is a dainty one.—Sweetheart,
    I were unmannerly, to take you out,
    And not to kiss you. A health, gentlemen,
    Let it go round.

Wol. Sir Thomas Lovel, is the banquet ready
      I' the privy chamber?
Lov.   Yes, my lord.
Wol.   Your Grace,
      I fear, with dancing is a little heated.
K. Hen. I fear too much.
Wol.   There 's fresher air, my lord,
      In the next chamber.
K. Hen. Lead in your ladies, every one.   Sweet partner,
      I must not yet forsake you :—Let 's be merry ;
      Good my lord Cardinal, I have half a dozen healths
      To drink to these fair ladies, and a measure
      To lead them once again ; and then let 's dream
      Who 's best in favour.—Let the music knock it.
                              [*Exeunt with trumpets.*]

After the star of Wolsey's grandeur had set, it
was in his gorgeous apartments at York House,
that the Duke of Suffolk waited on him to require
his resignation of the Great Seal ; and here it was
that the great Cardinal bade farewell, —" a long
farewell,"—to all his greatness. Having directed
that a careful inventory should be taken of his
valuable plate and costly stores, — the whole of
which he ordered to be delivered over to the King,
—" he took barge at his privy stairs, and so went
by water to Putney," on his way to Esher. In
December, 1529, he surrendered his palace into the
hands of his royal master, shortly after which the
name of York House was prohibited, and that of
Whitehall substituted in its stead. In the play of
" Henry the Eighth," where the coronation of Anne
Boleyn is described, we find,—

                    So she parted,
      And with the same full state paced back again
      To York-place, where the feast is held.
1st. Gent.   Sir,
      You must no more call it York-place—that is past :

For, since the Cardinal fell, that title's lost ;
'Tis now the King's, and called Whitehall.
3rd. Gent.   I know it ;
But 'tis so lately altered, that the old name
Is fresh about me.   *Act iv. Scene* 1.

After the disgrace of Wolsey, Henry seems to
have lost no time in occupying the palace of his
discarded favourite, for, in November, the same
year, we find him giving audience at Whitehall to
a deputation from the House of Commons, and
here, on the 6th of December following, he conferred Earldoms on the Viscounts Rochford and
Fitzwalter, and Lord Hastings.

Change we the scene ! a brighter throng is there ;
See Henry's throne usurps his favourite's chair ;
No more the pomp of Papal Rome we trace ;
The jewelled courtier fills the churchman's place ;
And beauty's peerless form and glorious eye,
Shine in the gilded hall and gallery high ;
And music pours her soft delicious strains,
And love looks blest, and age forgets its pains ;
And youth and beauty mingle in the dance,
Exchange the mutual vow, and melting glance.
But see, with flashing eyes and angry mien,
In lonely state sits Henry's injured queen !
See youthful Mary, destined bride of France,
Half pleased, half angry, blush at Brandon's glance ;
See Cromwell muse on Wolsey's closing hour,
Nor deems how near his own descent from power ;
While Surrey breathes his own impassioned line,
In gentle dalliance to his Geraldine.
But mark, in yonder rich recess apart,
Where Henry woos the lady of his heart !
Deaf to his consort's claims,—all sacred ties,—
He looks for love in Boleyn's azure eyes ;
Toys with her small white hand, allays her fears,
And pleads his suit to no unwilling ears ;
While she, the envy of that glittering ring,
Blushes to hear the praises of her King.
Ill-fated Boleyn ! when thy childhood strayed
Through Hever's primrose walks and hawthorn glade ;
When swelled thy rich notes in thine own loved bowers,
With one solicitude, thy birds and flowers ;

Or, when young Percy, seated by thy side,
Took thy soft hand, and claimed thee as his bride ;
Snatched his first kiss, and breathed th' enamoured vow,
Or circled flowery chaplets for thy brow ;
Were not thy thoughts more calm, thy heart more blest,
Than when a monarch clasped thee to his breast ?
Fair transient plaything for a tyrant's lust,
How soon shall foes and rivals breed mistrust !
Possession cloys, satiety begins,
And venial faults are blackened into sins.
See ! darkly lower the gathering clouds of fate,
Gleams the sharp axe, and yawns the Traitor's Gate ;
And Boleyn's latest look and dying moan,
Reproach the charms that raised her to a throne.—J. H. J.

At Whitehall, on the 25th of January, 1533,
Henry was married to the ill-fated Anne Boleyn.
On that day, according to Stow, "King Henry
privately married the Lady Anne Boleyn, in his
closet, at Whitehall, being St. Paul's day." Early
in the morning, it seems, Dr. Lee, one of the royal
Chaplains, and afterwards Bishop of Lichfield and
Coventry, was sent for to perform mass in the
King's closet, where he found, with the King, Anne
Boleyn and her train-bearer, Mrs. Savage, afterwards Lady Berkeley, and two of the grooms of the
bed-chamber. According to Lord Herbert of Cherbury, Archbishop Cranmer assisted at the ceremony.

Henry made great additions to Whitehall. Having purchased and enclosed the ground, now known
as St. James's Park, he raised a tennis court, cock-
pit, and bowling-green, on the site of the present
Treasury and the public offices adjoining. He
built also a splendid gallery overlooking the tilt-
yard, on the site of a part of the present Horse
Guards and Dover House. These buildings Henry

connected with the old palace, by a magnificent
gateway and arch,—from the designs of Holbein,
—which spanned the street immediately below the
present Banqueting House.* From the gallery
above mentioned, both Henry and his daughter,
Elizabeth, were accustomed to view the jousts and
tournaments in the tilt-yard below; and from its
windows, in May, 1539, when the invasion was
threatened by the Catholic potentates of Europe,
Henry reviewed the 15,000 armed citizens, consisting of gunners, pikemen, archers and billmen, whose
appearance Holinshed describes as presenting so
splendid a sight. Holbein's beautiful gate was removed in 1750, for the purpose of widening the
street. It was the intention of William, Duke of
Cumberland, the son of George the Second, to re-
build it at the top of the Long Walk, at Windsor,
but for some reason the design was never put into
execution.

Whatever may have been the vices or the crimes
of Henry the Eighth, he has at least the merit of

* " To Holbein," says Pennant, " was owing the most beautiful
gate at Whitehall, built with bricks of two colours, glazed, and
disposed in a tesselated fashion. The top, as well as that of an
elegant tower on each side, were embattled. On each front were
four busts, in baked clay, in proper colours, which resisted to the
last every attack of the weather: possibly the artificial stone revived in this century. These, I have been lately informed, are
preserved in a private hand. This charming structure fell a sacrifice to conveniency within my memory; as did another in 1723,
built at the same time, but of far inferior beauty. The last
blocked up the road to King Street, and was called King's Gate.
Henry built it as a passage to the Park, Tennis Court, Bowling
Green, the Cock Pit, and Tilting Yard; for he was extremely
fond of athletic exercises; they suited his strength and his temper."
" History of London," p. 93.

having been a munificent patron of the arts. He
himself united the qualities of a scholar, a musician,
an architect, and a poet. His collection of pictures,
at Whitehall, was the foundation of the famous
gallery formed by Prince Henry, and his brother,
Charles the First; both Raffaelle and Titian were
invited by him to England, and Holbein had apartments at Whitehall, and was engaged, by an annual
salary of two hundred florins, to decorate the interior of the palace. At Whitehall, Henry closed
his selfish career of profligacy, rapine, and crime.
Here he signed his will on the 30th of December,
1547, and here, on the 28th of January following,
he died. He had become more fretful and impatient as his disease increased, and as many persons had suffered as traitors during his reign, for
foretelling the King's death, it was long before any
one could be found who would inform him of his
condition. At length Sir Anthony Denny was bold
enough to undertake the task, and exhorted him to
prepare for the fate which awaited him. Henry
expressed his resignation, and desired that Cranmer
might be sent for, but before the arrival of the
Archbishop he was speechless. He still, however,
retained his senses, for when Cranmer desired him
to give some sign of his dying in the faith of Christ,
he pressed the Prelate's hand, almost immediately
after which he expired.

During the brief reign of the studious and accomplished Edward the Sixth, Whitehall presented
a very different aspect to what it had worn in the

days of his father. In the Privy Gardens, — so recently filled with the beauty and chivalry of the land,—Bishop Latimer was to be seen preaching, in a raised pulpit, to the young King and a devout audience; while the silent hours of the night, which Henry had devoted to revelry and the dance, were passed by his successor in study, meditation, and prayer.

It is the hush of night ! the moon-beams fall
On flower and fount, on turret and on hall;
And all is still and silent ; save at times
Toll the far midnight melancholy chimes.
While slowly pacing o'er the echoing ground,
The sentry takes his solitary round.
A single lamp in yonder turret gleams,
Far o'er the Thames its trembling halo streams.
There sits the sceptred boy, the student King !
For him no joys the dance or banquet bring.
Though youth, wealth, honour, lineage, are his own,
And more than earthly beauty, and a throne ;
For him in vain the flatterer spreads his net,
Or beauty lures with eyes of luscious jet.
His mind is fixed on nobler thoughts than these,
On loftier studies which instruct and please.
Immersed in holy or in classic lore,
His ermine lies neglected on the floor;
Above the joys that fade, the tastes that cloy,
For genius' fatal gift is thine, fair boy ;
And fell disease on that pale brow I trace,
And burns consumption's hectic on thy face.
But hovering angels smile on virtue's friend,
And smooth thy path, young Edward, to thine end ;
Well pleased the blameless sufferer lays him down,
And yields an earthly for a heavenly crown.—J. H. J.

During the reign of Queen Mary, we discover little or no interest connected with Whitehall. We find her residing here, however, shortly after her accession, and from hence her coronation procession passed by water to Westminster, her sister Elizabeth bearing the crown before her.

In the reign of Queen Elizabeth, Whitehall resumed its ancient glory. Immediately after the
death of her sister, we find her taking up her residence here; and here she kept the first Christmas
after her accession. The last time, apparently, that
she had passed a night within its walls, was when
she had been led here a prisoner for her presumed
share in Sir Thomas Wyatt's conspiracy.   Here it
was that she received the startling tidings that she
was to be incarcerated in the Tower, and from hence
she was led, on Palm Sunday, 1554, to the private
water-entrance of the palace, where a boat was in
waiting to convey her to the fatal fortress, within
the walls of which the axe had fallen on the neck
of her unfortunate mother, Anne Boleyn.

After the accession of Elizabeth, Whitehall became the scene of her pastimes and diversions, and
here she surrounded herself with those eminent
statesmen, scholars, and poets, whose names have
thrown so much lustre on her reign.

Lo! where Eliza holds her stately court,
Genius, the muses, and the loves resort.
Queen of the lion mien! I see thee stand,
Girt with the high-born magnates of the land!
Warriors and bards, the statesman and the sage,
The master-spirits of a giant-age.
There leans the bard who sang by Avon's tide;
There frown the chiefs who quenched the Armada's pride;
There glitters courtly Walsingham; and there
Young Essex sits in dalliance with the fair.
See great Eliza, throned in purple state,
With reverend Burleigh hold the close debate;
Or now with Bacon speak of Nature's stores,
With Raleigh rove on India's palmy shores;
Now glide with Hatton through the stately dance,
Now throw on Leicester's form a tenderer glance;

Leicester whose words, in Windsor's shady grove,
Had dared to breathe the honeyed tale of love.
But time and grief have wrought their change : proud Queen,
I mark thy drooping eye, thine altered mien ;
Long years have ploughed their furrows on thy face,
And dimmed thine awful charms and boasted grace ;
Where are thy days of mirth, thy nights of ease ?
Lo ! flattery cloys, and pleasures cease to please ;
Stretched on her splendid solitary bed,
The fretful monarch clasps her throbbing head ;
Peevish she turns from Burleigh's soothing tone,
Loathing herself, she dreads to be alone ;
While conscience, piercing with its scorpion fang,
Provokes the dreary thought, the cankering pang.
Through each long day, with anxious gaze is scanned
A small bright ring that glitters on her hand ;
Dear sad memorial of a tenderer hour,
When love and Essex proved their dangerous power.
Essex, thine own loved Essex,—where is he ?
Nay frown not, lady, 'twas thine own decree.
Nor start thus wildly from thy feverish bed ;
'Twas only fancy drew that severed head !
Less peace for her who lives than him who dies :
Calm in his crimsoned shroud the loved-one lies ;
What if his fiery soul, his rival's hate,
And woman's treacherous friendship, sealed his fate,
'Twas thine, the great prerogative to save,
And yet thou doom'dst him to an early grave ;
Doom'dst him to curse thee with his latest breath ;
The cold stern author of his bloody death.—J. H. J.

It was in the great gallery, built by her father, that Elizabeth received the deputation from Parliament, when they presented themselves humbly and respectfully " to move her grace to marriage ;" and from hence she proceeded in procession, in 1559-60, to meet her first Parliament. " On Wednesday, Jan. 25," says Holinshed, " the Parliament began, the Queen's Majesty riding in her parliament robes, from her Palace of Whitehall to the Abbey Church of Westminster, with the Lords Spiritual and Temporal attending her, likewise in their parliament robes."

Elizabeth, like her father, took an especial delight
in the Tilt Yard. Here, in 1581, when the Commissioners arrived in England to treat concerning the
projected marriage between the Queen and the Duc
d'Anjou, Elizabeth entertained her illustrious guests
with the most magnificent tournament which had
perhaps ever been held in England. She herself
was seated in the gallery overlooking the Tilt Yard,
which, says Holinshed, "was called, and not without reason, the castle or fortress of perfect Beauty."
Among the defenders of the castle of Beauty we
find the Queen's devoted champion, Sir Henry Lee,
the gallant Knight of the Garter, who had made a
vow to present himself armed at the Tilt Yard at
Whitehall on the 27th of November annually, till
he should be disabled by age.

The challengers, who personated the four foster-
children of Desire, were the Earl of Arundel, the
Lord Windsor, Sir P. Sidney, and Sir Fulke Greville.

This "amorous foolery," as it is styled by Pennant, commenced with the challengers summoning
the fortress to surrender in a "delectable song,"
commencing with the following verses :—

> Yield, yield, O yield, you that this fort do hold,
>   Which seated is in spotless Honour's field ;
> Desire's great force, no forces can withhold,
>   Then to Desire's desire, O yield, O yield !
> Yield, yield, O yield ;—trust not to beauty's pride ;
>   Fairness, though fair, is but a feeble shield ;
> When strong Desire, which Virtue's love doth guide,
>   Claims but to gain his due ;—yield, yield, O yield !

The fortress still refusing to surrender, "two
cannon were fired off, one with sweet powder, and

the other with sweet water; and after there were
store of pretty scaling ladders, and then the footmen
threw flowers and such fancies against the walls, with
all such devices as might seem shot from Desire."
Suddenly, while this pleasant siege was being carried on, the defenders of Beauty, clad in sumptuous
apparel, entered the lists, and attacking the challengers and their partisans, a regular "tourneie" took
place, in which Sir Henry Lee "brake his six
staves," and many others "jousted right valiantly,"
till twilight separated the combatants. "These
courtly triumphs," as they are described by Holinshed, —" set forth with the most costlie braverie
and gallantness," — were continued the following
day, and concluded with a fantastic pageant, in
which the challengers made their submission to the
Queen, and expressed their sense of their own "de-
generacy and unworthyness in making Violence accompany Desire."

> Here, where I stand, when chivalry was young,
> The courser neighed, the clattering armour rung ;
> Here stood the lists ; the crimson pennon streamed,
> And bright the helm and flashing falchion gleamed.
> Here stood the herald in his glittering garb,
> Here pawed the earth the warrior's foaming barb ;
> With vizors closed, their lances in the rest,
> Their white plumes waving from each iron crest,
> See, with fierce speed, the rival knights advance,
> Deal the rude blow, or break the pointed lance ;
> While, from the silken galleries above,
> Fair ladies flung their anxious looks of love.—J. H. J.

Elizabeth retained her taste for these buffooneries
to the close of her long life. When she was in her
sixty-seventh year, and when her heart was pro-

fessedly in the bloody tomb of her beloved Essex, we find her attending a masque given by Lord Cobham at Blackfriars, on the occasion of Lord Herbert's marriage with a daughter of the Earl of Shrewsbury.   Lord Herbert was one of her handsome favourites of the Tilt Yard.

> The Herberts, every Cockpit-day,
> Do carry away,
> The gold and glory of the day.*

In the course of the evening, she was "wooed to dance" by a masque who personated Affection. "Affection!" she exclaimed bitterly.   "Affection is false!"   And yet we find the royal harridan,—whom Hentzner describes at this period as having a wrinkled face, little eyes, hooked nose, and black teeth,— actually rising up and dancing.†   In another letter, written about the same time, we find, "Her Majesty is very well: this day she appoints to see a Frenchman do feats in the Conduit Court.   To-morrow she hath commanded the bears, the bull, and the ape to be baited in the Tilt Yard; upon Wednesday she will have solemn dancing." ‡   Such was the extraordinary old woman, who could admirably direct the affairs of a great monarchy at one moment, and attend a bull-bait or dance a minuet the next; she who could sign the death of a sister-queen, or of a beloved favourite, with the same pen with which she had previously translated a play of Euripides, or an oration of Isocrates.

Hentzner, the German traveller, who visited Eng-

---

* Lodge's "Illustrations."   † "Sydney Papers."   ‡ Ibid.

land at the close of the reign of Elizabeth, has left
us an account of Whitehall, which he styles a palace
" truly royal." The royal library, he says, was well
stored with Greek, Latin, Italian and French books,
and among the rest was a little French work, upon
parchment, written in Elizabeth's own hand, and
addressed to her father.* Hentzner's further description of Whitehall is chiefly confined to a catalogue of curiosities to be seen in the various apartments. They consist principally of embroidered
quilts, silver cabinets containing writing materials,
the passion of our Saviour, in painted glass, a chest
containing the Queen's jewellery, a piece of clock-
work, surmounted by an Ethiopian riding on a
rhinoceros, and other fantastic articles, the names
of which are not worth transcribing.

It was from the *orchard* at Whitehall, where
they had assembled after the breath quitted the
body of Elizabeth, that the Lords of the Council
despatched a messenger to James the First, to ac-
quaint him of his accession to the English throne.
At the same time he was proclaimed by Sir
Robert Cecil in front of the palace. He arrived
at Whitehall on the 7th of May, 1603, and, on
the 22nd, we find him conferring the honour of
knighthood in the garden of the palace on the principal law officers, his gentlemen-ushers, and others.
Among the former was the too-celebrated Lord Bacon.

---

* "To the most high, puissant, and redoubted Prince, Henry VIII.
of the name, King of England, France, and Ireland, Defender of
the Faith; Elizabeth, his most humble daughter, health and obedience. Hentzner's " Journey to England," p. 29.

The tastes and amusements which were introduced at Whitehall by the Scottish monarch differed widely from the chivalrous pastimes and
amusements which had distinguished the court of
his predecessor. "The King," says Sir Anthony
Weldon, "would come forth after supper to see
pastimes and fooleries, in which Sir Edward Zouch,
Sir George Goring, and Sir John Finett, were the
chief and master-fools: and surely this fooling got
them more than any other's wisdom, far above them
in desert. Zouch's part was to sing bawdy songs
and tell bawdy tales, Finett to compose these
songs. Then were a set of fiddlers brought up on
purpose for this fooling; and Goring was master of
the game for fooleries, sometimes presenting David
Droman and Archie Armstrong on the back of the
other fools, to tilt one at the other, till they fell
together by the ears: sometimes the property was
presented by them in antic dances.   But Sir J.
Millisent, who was never known before, was commended for notable fooling, and so was, indeed, the
best extemporary fool of them all."   These buffooneries, however, were in a great degree redeemed
by the taste of the King's consort, Anne of Denmark, under whose patronage were introduced and
represented those magnificent masques, many of
them the productions of Ben Jonson, which, we are
told, made "the nights more costly than the days."
We may, hereafter, have to allude to these gorgeous
entertainments.

During the reign of James the First, there occurred more than one incident which throws an additional interest over the ancient palace of White-hall. Here, in January, 1604-5, when only four years of age, the unfortunate Charles the First was created Duke of York, and made a Knight of the Bath, with great solemnity. A sword was girded on the side of the royal infant, a coronet of gold was placed on his head, and a golden verge in his hand. "There was a public dinner," writes Sir Dudley Carleton, "in the great chamber, where there was one table for the Duke and his Earls assistants, another for his fellow Knights of the Bath. At night we had the Queen's mask in the Banquetting House, or rather her pageant. There was a great engine at the lower end of the room which had motion, and in it were the images of sea-horses, with other terrible fishes, which were ridden by Moors. The indecorum was, that there was all fish and no water. At the further end was a great shell, in the form of a shallop, wherein were four seats. In the lowest sat the Queen, with my Lady Bedford; in the rest were placed my Ladies Suffolk, Derby, Rich, Effingham, Ann Herbert, Susan Herbert, Elizabeth Howard, Walsingham, and Bevil. Their appearance was rich, but too light and courtezan-like for such great ones."* The pageant was succeeded by a ball, at which the Queen was "taken out" by the Spanish Ambassador, and concluded with a magnificent banquet.

* Letter from Sir Dudley Carleton to Mr. Winwood, dated Jan. 1604. Winwood's "Memorials."

It may be mentioned that Ben Jonson's "Masque of Blackness" was performed on this occasion, the Queen and her ladies having their faces and hands painted to represent Ethiopians: the expense of the entertainment amounted to three thousand pounds.

The marriage which took place at Whitehall, in October, in 1604, between Philip Herbert, Earl of Montgomery,—the "memorable simpleton" of Horace Walpole,—and Lady Susan Vere, daughter of Edward, 17th Earl of Oxford, presents a still more curious picture of the manners of a past age. The bride was led to church by Henry, Prince of Wales, and the Duke of Holstein, and the King himself gave her away to his unworthy favourite. So lovely, we are told, did she look in her tresses and jewels, and bridal array, that the King observed, "were he unmarried, he would keep her himself," a great compliment from James, who was, generally speaking, no very ardent admirer of female beauty. The marriage ceremony was followed by a splendid banquet, and terminated by as magnificent a masque. "There was no small loss that night," says Sir Dudley Carleton, "of chains and jewels, and many great ladies were made shorter by the skirts. The presents of plate and other things, given by the noblemen, were valued at 2,500*l.*; but that which made it a good marriage, was a gift of the King's, of 500*l.* land, for the bride's jointure. They were lodged in the Council-chamber, where the King, *in his shirt and night-gown,* gave them a *reveille-matin* before they

were up, *and spent a good time in or upon the bed.*
No ceremony was omitted of bride-cakes, points,
garters, and gloves, which have been ever since the
livery of the court; and at night there was sewing
into the sheet, casting off the bride's left hose, and
many other pretty sorceries."*

It was to the King's bed-chamber at Whitehall,
that Guy Fawkes was dragged, bound hand and
foot, after his apprehension by Sir Thomas Knevett,
at the door of the cellar beneath the House of
Lords.   Here he was examined by the timid James
and his astonished councillors, and notwithstanding
the frightful nature of his projected crime, retained
the bearing of a gentleman and a soldier, even with
the rack and the gibbet staring him in the face.
He met the taunts of the Lords of the Council
with scorn, and retorted their inquisitive glances
with looks of defiance.   When asked by one of
the numerous Scottish favourites of James, what
he had intended to have done with so many bar-
rels of gunpowder, "One of my objects," he replied contemptuously, "was to blow Scotchmen
back into Scotland."   He unhesitatingly admitted
his crime, and added, that, had he been within the
doors of the cellar at the time, he would have blown
himself up and those who arrested him, without the
least scruple.   From Whitehall he was conveyed to
the Tower, and on the 31st of January, 1606, was
executed, with three of his associates, in Old Palace
Yard, Westminster.

* Winwood's " Memorials."

Six months afterwards, on the occasion of the arrival in England of the Queen's brother, Christian King of Denmark, we find the Gunpowder Plot apparently forgotten, and Whitehall again the scene of the most magnificent pageants and banquets. " I will now in good sooth," writes Sir John Harrington, "declare unto you, who will not blab, that the gunpowder fright has gone out of all our heads, and we are going on hereabouts, as if the devil was contriving every man to blow up himself by wild riot, excess, and devastation of time and temperance." In the " Nugæ Antiquæ,"* will be found a very entertaining and graphic description of one of the entertainments given to the Danish monarch.

On the 12th of June, 1610, the lamented Prince Henry was created Prince of Wales at Whitehall. The ceremony occasioned a succession of balls, banquets, and pageants, which lasted three days. On the first day was a most magnificent banquet ; on the second there was exhibited " a most glorious maske," which continued till "within half an hour of the sun's rising ; " and on the third day was a grand " tilting-match, a gallant sea-fight, and many rare and excellent fire-works, which were seen by almost a million of people."

But Whitehall is endeared to us by a still more interesting personage, the amiable Elizabeth, Queen of Bohemia, daughter of James the First. Here she passed her happy childhood, and here, " in

* Vol. i. 348.

flower of youth and beauty's pride," she was affianced to her future husband, Frederick the Fifth,
Count Palatine of the Rhine, "cupbearer" of the
empire, and afterwards King of Bohemia. The
ceremony, both of her *fiançailles* and of her espousals, was solemnized with a greater outlay of wealth,
than have perhaps been ever squandered on any
similar ceremonials either before or since. The expense of the dresses and jewels, lavished on the
ladies who attended her, amounted to 3,914*l*.; the
fitting up of her bridal chamber cost 3,023*l*.; and
the expenses of the fireworks, exhibited in the
gardens of Whitehall and on the banks of the
Thames, amounted to 7,600*l*. I have now the
items of the total expenditure before me, and they
amount to as much as 93,278*l*.

Elizabeth was affianced to the Elector Palatine,
on the 27th of December, 1612, in the Banqueting
House of Whitehall. The Palsgrave, as he was
then styled, was led in first, attended by Prince
Charles and several of the nobility, and clad in
a black velvet cloak, adorned with gold lace. Then
followed the Princess, in a black velvet gown,
" semé of crosslets, or quaterfoils, silver; and a
small feather on her head, attended with ladies."
Shortly afterwards entered the King, who, having
seated himself under the canopy of state, the Palsgrave and the Princess stepped forward, and stood
together on a rich Turkey carpet. Sir Thomas
Lake then formally read in French, from the book
of Common Prayer, " I, Frederick, take thee, Eliza-

beth, to my wedded wife," which was repeated by
the Palsgrave *verbatim*. The same words having
been repeated by the Princess, the Archbishop of
Canterbury pronounced the benediction. It may
be remarked, that the marriage was asked by the
publication of common banns in the Chapel Royal.
It is also curious to find the royal bride and bridegroom habited on this joyous occasion in black.
The fact, however, is, that Henry Prince of Wales,
—lamented by every one except his own father,—
had died scarcely more than seven weeks previously; and James, partly perhaps jealous of the
popularity of his deceased son, and partly from
motives of convenience, had thus indecently hurried on the espousals of his daughter.

The marriage ceremony was finally performed
at Whitehall on the 14th of February, 1614.
We have an account of this gorgeous ceremony,
from the pen of Sir John Finett, the Master of
the Ceremonies, who minutely describes the splendid dresses, and the "draughts of Ippocras" out
of golden bowls. "The bravery," he says, "and
riches of that day were incomparable; gold and
silver, laid upon lords', ladies', and gentlewomen's
backs, was the poorest burthen : pearls and costly
embroideries being the commonest wear." The
jewels worn by the royal family are said to have
been worth nearly a million of money; according
to common report, the dress worn by the Lady
Wotton "cost fifty pound the yard the embroi-
dering;" and Lord Montague presented his two

daughters with fifteen hundred pounds to provide themselves with suitable apparel. With the exception of the three Lord Chief Justices, no person was admitted to view the ceremony under the rank of a Baron.*

At Whitehall was solemnized on the 26th of December, 1613, with scarcely less magnificence, the marriage of Robert Carr, Earl of Somerset, the unworthy favourite of James the First, with Frances Howard, the beautiful murderess and adulteress.† Notwithstanding her previous marriage with the young Earl of Essex, afterwards the celebrated Parliamentary General, she had the effrontery to appear at the altar with the white dress and flowing tresses of a virgin. The marriage ceremony was performed by the Bishop of Bath and Wells, in the presence of the King and Queen, and the principal

---

* For an account of the espousals of the Queen of Bohemia, see Winwood's "Memorials," vol. iii. p. 421 ; Coke, vol. i. p. 64 ; Ellis's "Orig. Letters," vol. iii. p. 110 ; and "Finetti Philoxenis," p. 11.

† It was at a splendid tournament in the Tilt Yard at Whitehall, that Robert Carr first attracted the notice of James the First. On this occasion Carr had been selected by Lord Hay to present the shield and device of the latter to the King. As he rode up the lists, his horse became unmanageable, and threw him before the King's face. James, struck with the beauty of his person, and concerned at the severity of his accident,—for his leg had been broken by the fall,—gave directions that he should be conveyed to the palace, and carefully attended by the royal surgeons. As soon as the tilting was over, the King paid him a visit. He returned the next day, and, indeed, as long as the confinement lasted, was daily in the habit of passing an hour or two in the chamber of the fortunate invalid. On his recovery, for which James was exceedingly impatient, he was knighted and made a gentleman of the bedchamber. On the subsequent rapid progress which he made in the royal favour there is no reason to expatiate. See Wilson, p. 55 ; Weldon, p. 58.

nobility. " Whitehall," says Coke, " was too narrow to contain the triumphs of this marriage, and
they must be extended into the city." Notwithstanding the shameful notoriety which attached to
the amours of this profligate couple, the City of
London were subservient enough to pander to the
wishes of the court, by celebrating the nuptials with
almost a greater parade than had previously been
exhibited in the presence of peers and bishops at
Whitehall. On the 4th of January, nine days after
the marriage, we find the bride and bridegroom,
attended by the Duke of Lennox, the Lord Chamberlain, and a numerous train of the nobility, proceeding in great state to the city. A magnificent
entertainment awaited them in Merchant Taylors'
Hall; the music struck up joyously as they entered;
speeches of congratulation were offered to them,
and the Lord Mayor and Aldermen came forward
in their scarlet gowns to do honour to the King's
favourite and his bride. In the pride of regal
favour, they were conducted to a sumptuous banquet, where they were waited upon by deputations
from the twelve companies. After supper, there
were plays, masques, and dancing, and, late at night,
the rejoicings were concluded with a second banquet.
At three o'clock in the morning, the favourite and
his beautiful bride returned to their nuptial chamber at Whitehall. How widely different was the
closing scene of this favoured pair! Within a little
more than two years, these two envied and glittering beings were the inmates of a prison! Deprived

of fortune, flattery, and the pomp of circumstance, they were dragged as murderers to the bar of a criminal tribunal, and narrowly escaped suffering by the hands of the common executioner.

The present Banqueting House was built in this reign. It is but a small part of a glorious edifice, projected by Inigo Jones; but still it is sufficient to explain to us how magnificent would have been the entire building, of which this admired relic was intended to be but an insignificant portion. The designs for this beautiful pile are well known. It was intended to have extended to no less than 1150 feet on the banks of the Thames, and to the same distance in front of the present street of Whitehall. Its completion, however, was prevented, partly by the extravagance of James the First, but principally by the misfortunes which befell his ill-fated son. The Banqueting House was commenced in 1619, and was finished, in about two years, at the expense of 17,000*l*. But for the interruption of the civil wars, it is said to have been the intention of Charles the First to have engaged Vandyke to decorate its walls with scenes connected with the history of the Order of the Garter. The expense was computed at 80,000*l*.* Such a building, decorated by such an artist, would indeed have been the glory of Europe.† This splendid room, the scene of

* Fenton's " Waller," notes, p. 37; Walpole's " Works," vol. i. p. 235.

† It is curious to find how small were the wages of the great artist, Inigo Jones, during the period he was employed in the renovation of Whitehall. His allowance was only 8*s*. 4*d*. a day as

the drivelling amusements of James the First, and
of the magnificent masques of Ben Jonson,—where
Charles the First so often dined in state with Henrietta Maria,—where Cromwell entertained a puritanical parliament,—and where Charles the Second so
often led out a fair lady to dance the gay "Coranto,"
—is now converted into a *chapel*. The dais, on which
the second Charles so often debauched, is converted
into an *altar*, and a *pulpit* hides the spot from which
his unfortunate father passed to the scaffold! The
ceiling of the Banqueting House was painted by Rubens at the cost of 3,000*l.*, and represents, in nine
compartments, the apotheosis of James the First.
In the centre is conspicuous the besotted face of
the English Solomon, surrounded by various Pagan
deities and other allegorical figures, consisting of
Mars, Commerce, and the Fine Arts.

On the accession of Charles the First, the Court
of Whitehall presented an union of magnificence
and decorum, and such a treasury of all that is
exquisite in sculpture and painting, as has never
been surpassed by any Court in Europe. Walpole
observes, " During the prosperous state of the
King's affairs, the pleasures of the Court were carried on with much taste and magnificence. Poetry,
painting, music, and architecture were all called in

surveyor, with 46*l.* a year for house-rent, the maintenance of a
clerk, and other occasional expenses. The masonry of the Banqueting House was executed by Nicholas Stone, a famous statuary
in the reign of James the First, who died on the 24th of August,
1647. There is a print of him in the "Anecdotes of Painting."
Granger, vol. ii. p. 163. His allowance, when employed at Whitehall, was "4*s*. 10*d.* the day."

to make them rational amusements; and I have no
doubt but the celebrated festivals of Louis the Fourteenth were copied from the shows exhibited at
Whitehall, in its time the most polite court in Europe.   Ben Jonson was the laureat, Inigo Jones
the inventor of the decorations; Laniere and Fera-
bosco composed the symphonies; the King, the
Queen, and the young nobility danced in the inter-
ludes."   To the names mentioned by Walpole, we
may add those of Milton, Fletcher, Carew, and Selden.   The "Masque of Comus," written by the
former, and the beautiful scenic decorations and
contrivances of the latter, may afford some con-
ception of the rational amusements of the court
of Charles.   Even Marshal Bassompierre, perhaps
the most refined and fastidious man in Europe, has
done full justice to the elegant and dignified character of the Court of Whitehall at this period. Speaking of his state introduction to Charles and Henrietta
Maria, he says, "I found the King raised on a stage
two steps, the Queen and he on two chairs, who rose
the first bow I made them on coming in.   The company was magnificent, and the order exquisite."*

The magnificent masques which were represented
at Whitehall, under the auspices of Charles, will
be remembered as long as Milton, Ben Jonson,
Fletcher, and Inigo Jones, shall continue to be
classic names.   Mr. D'Israeli informs us, — " The
fullest account I have found of one of these entertainments, which at once shew the curiosity of the

* "Embassy to England" in 1626.

scenical machinery, and the fancy of the poet, the richness of the crimson habits of the gentlemen, and the white dresses, the white herons' plumes and jewelled head-dresses and ropes of pearl, of the ladies, was in a manuscript letter of the time, with which I supplied the editor of 'Jonson,' who has preserved the narrative in his 'Memoirs' of that poet." * "Such were the magnificent entertainments," says Mr. Gifford, in his introduction to Massinger's Works, "which, though modern refinement may affect to despise them, modern splendour never reached even in thought."

During the earlier period of the reign of Charles, these splendid entertainments took place in the present Banqueting House, but the King, dreading that the numerous lights might injure the many choice pictures which decorated the walls,† caused a building, of light construction, to be erected purposely for the representation of his favourite masques. In a letter of the period, we find,— " The Masking House is nearly ready, and 1400l. is appointed for the charge of a Masque at Twelfth Night." ‡ This building was the "Boarded Masque House," which the Parliament ordered to be pulled down, in 1645.

The following passage, written in the succeeding reign, enables us to form a tolerable notion of the splendid hospitality exercised by Charles, at Whitehall. "There were daily in his court, eighty-six

* "Curiosities of Literature." † "Strafford Letters."
‡ Collins's "Memorials."

tables, well furnished each meal; whereof the King's
table had twenty-eight dishes; the Queen's twenty-
four; four other tables, sixteen dishes each; three
other, ten dishes; twelve other, seven dishes; seventeen other, five dishes; three other, four; thirty-two
had three; and thirteen had each two; in all about
five hundred dishes each meal, with bread, beer,
wine, and all other things necessary. There was
spent yearly in the King's house, of gross meat, fifteen hundred oxen; seven thousand sheep; twelve
hundred calves; three hundred porkers; four hundred young beefs; six thousand eight hundred
lambs; three hundred flitches of bacon, and twenty-
six boars. Also one hundred and forty dozen of
geese; two hundred and fifty dozen of capons; four
hundred and seventy dozen of hens; seven hundred
and fifty dozen of pullets; fourteen hundred and
seventy dozen of chickens; for bread, three hundred
and sixty-four thousand bushels of wheat; and for
drink, six hundred tons of wine and seventeen
hundred tons of beer; together with fish and fowl,
fruit and spice, proportionably. This prodigious
plenty in the King's court caused foreigners to put
a higher value upon the King, and was much for
the honour of the kingdom. The King's servants,
being men of quality, by his Majesty's special order,
went to Westminster Hall, in term-time, to invite
gentlemen to eat of the King's viands, and, in
Parliament-time, to invite the Parliament men
thereto."*

* " Present State of London," 1681.

Charles the First is one of the very few of our monarchs to whom the arts may be considered as under an obligation. The price of pictures, we are told, rose to double their value, in consequence of the competition between Charles and Philip the Fourth of Spain, another royal collector. Through the agency of Rubens, the celebrated cartoons of Raffaelle were transferred from Flanders to England; and, at the cost of 18,000*l*., Charles purchased the entire cabinet of the Duke of Mantua, considered the finest in Europe. In the collection at Whitehall alone, (and it must not be forgotten that the King had *eighteen* other palaces *) were twenty-eight pictures by Titian, eleven by Correggio, sixteen by Julio Romano, nine by Raffaelle, four by Guido, and seven by Parregiano, besides many exquisite works by Rubens and Vandyke. To the blind zeal and besotted ignorance of a puritanical Parliament we owe the dispersion of this glorious collection. Such pictures and statues as they chose to style *super-stitious* were ordered to be destroyed, and the rest to be sold. The inventory, which was entrusted to the most ignorant appraisers, took a year in drawing up, and the collection three years in selling. Thus, to the disgrace of civilization, were dispersed, mutilated, or destroyed, the splendid effects, the gems and antiquities, the costly statue-galleries, the unique cabinet of Charles the First,

* Granger incidentally mentions the number of the King's palaces as twenty-four. Including the old Scottish palaces they probably may have amounted to even more than this number.

the delight of his leisure hours, and the envy of Europe!

It was to Whitehall that Charles conducted his young and beautiful bride after the consummation of their nuptials, at Canterbury, on the 16th of June, 1625. But as Whitehall was the scene of his bridal pleasures, so did it witness the last agony of the unfortunate monarch. It was here that he was insulted by the brutal soldiery; here he spent so many melancholy hours in the course of his tedious trial; and here it was that he passed from the walls of his own Banqueting House to a bloody death.

Silent and sad, the sacred spot we tread,
Where fell, unhappy Charles! thy severed head:
By all the graces, all the arts bemoaned,
With thee triumphant, and with thee dethroned;
Here flew thy moments of domestic bliss,
Here soared thy thoughts to higher worlds than this;
Here, while thine infants prattled in thine arms,
Strayed thy fond glance to Henrietta's charms;
Here, too, when faction reared her rampant band,
And foul rebellion revelled through the land;
Here, in the ancient palace of thy race,
Triumphant treason fixed thy dungeon-place;
Here, where each spot recalled thy days of power,
Thy bridal rapture, and thy social hour;
Here broke the rabble soldier on thy rest,
With paltry insults and the ribald jest;
Here, o'er the infant offspring of thy care,
Fell thy last tear, and rose thy dying prayer;
How fondly gazing, as the closing door
Hid the young forms thou must behold no more;
Then did thy last, thy tenderest feeling stray,
To her, thy queen, thy loved-one, far away.
But lo! they come, in melancholy state,
Ill-fated King! to bear thee to thy fate;
Frown the mailed sentries at thy palace doors,
And line its courts and gilded corridors;
The crowd is gathered, and the axe prepared,
Fixed is the block, the headsman's arm is bared.

Yet, 'midst the horrors of that awful scene,
No terror shook thy calm majestic mien :
Though gazing thousands wept thine hour of woe,
And shrunk appalled, or cursed the hovering blow ;
Thine was that inward peace which can illume,
The last dark pangs which marshal to the tomb ;
Thine was the heaven-lit smile, the wish resigned,
The even pulse, th' unconquerable mind ;
The blissful visions of a soul forgiven,
That tastes the joys before it mounts to Heaven !—J. H. J.

" Every night," says Hume, " the King slept
sound as usual, though the noise of workmen employed in framing the scaffold, and other preparations for his execution, continually resounded in his
ears." This description is graphic, but it is not
true; inasmuch as it is well-known that the King
passed the night previous to his execution at St.
James's Palace. From thence, on the fatal morning, he passed on foot through the Park, between
an avenue of soldiers, to Whitehall; and being
conducted along the gallery,—which at that time
ran across the street, and connected the royal buildings in the Park, with the opposite part of the
palace,—he was led to the bed-chamber which he
had occupied in the days of his prosperity. This
apartment appears to have overlooked the river,
and consequently was at a considerable distance
from the scene of his execution. It adjoined the
private stairs leading to the river, and was subsequently occupied by the Queen of Charles the
Second.

The scaffolding having only been commenced the
preceding evening, and not having been completed, the unfortunate monarch was allowed a

considerable time for prayer. While he was still
engaged at his devotions, some pushing members
of the puritan clergy knocked at the door of his
apartment, and offered to assist him in preparing
for his fate. He told them calmly, that they had
so often prayed against him, they should never
pray with him in his agony; but, he added, he
should be grateful if they would remember him
in their prayers. As soon as he had finished his
devotions,—"Now," he says, "let the *rogues* come;
I have forgiven them, and am prepared for all
I am to undergo. When Colonel Hacker gave the
last signal at the door of his apartment, Bishop
Juxon, his spiritual adviser, and his faithful attendant, Herbert, fell on their knees before him and
wept: the King gave them his hand to kiss, and
Juxon being an old man, he kindly assisted him to
rise. To Colonel Tomlinson, a republican officer,
who had shewn him every attention consistent with
his duty to his employers, he presented his gold
tooth-pick case, and requested him to attend him to
the last. Then, desiring that the door might be
opened, and telling Hacker he was prepared to
follow him, he passed, with a cheerful countenance,
through an avenue of guards which lined the once
splendid galleries, to the scaffold.

Much doubt has existed in regard to the exact
spot at Whitehall on which Charles was beheaded.
"The King," says Pennant, "was conducted from
his bedchamber along the galleries and the banqueting-house, through the wall, in which a passage was

broken, to his last earthly stage. This passage still remains, at the north *end* of the room, and is at present the door to a small additional building of late date." Mr. Croker* falls into the same error as Pennant. " It is generally supposed," he says, " that Charles was beheaded on a scaffold erected in the front of the Banqueting House. This is, I believe, a mistake. *The street in the front of the Banqueting House did not then exist.*" The fact, however, is that not only was there a street in front of Whitehall, running under Holbein's famous gateway, but it was then, as it is now, the only thoroughfare between the cities of London and Westminster. Moreover, not only does every ancient print of the King's execution represent him as having been beheaded in *front* of the Banqueting House, and not at the *end*, but the warrant for the execution expressly lays down that the execution shall take place " *in the open street before Whitehall.*" The fact is, that Charles, agreeably with the terms of the warrant, was executed immediately in front of the Banqueting House, passing through a passage broken in the wall, which passage was exactly in the centre of the building, between the upper and lower window. Herbert, who attended his unfortunate master in his last moments, informs us, " The King was led along all the galleries and Banqueting House, and there was a passage broken through the wall, by which the King passed unto the scaffold." The reason for breaking through the

* Notes to Bassompiere's " Embassy," p. 61.

wall is obvious. Had Charles passed through one of the *lower* windows, the scaffold must necessarily have been so low that it would have been on a level with the heads of the people, a circumstance, for many evident reasons, to be carefully avoided; while, on the other hand, had he passed through one of the *upper* windows, the height would have been so great that no one could have witnessed the scene except those who were immediately on the scaffold. Without, however, continuing the digression, it is perhaps sufficient to observe, that at the renovation of the Banqueting House a few years since, a fact was made apparent, which I imagine will be considered as setting the question at rest. Having curiosity enough to visit the interior of the building, — the walls of which were then laid bare,—a space was pointed out to me, between the upper and lower centre windows, of about seven feet in height and four in breadth, the bricks of which presented a broken and jagged appearance, and the brickwork introduced was evidently of a different date from that of the rest of the building. There can be little doubt that it was through this passage that Charles walked to the fatal stage. Indeed, when we consider how conclusive is the evidence that the execution took place in *front* of the Banqueting House, and how improbable it is that such solid and beautiful masonry should have been disturbed and broken through for any other purpose, we shall perhaps be pardoned for looking upon it as setting the question for ever at rest.

The King passed to the fatal scaffold with
a cheerful countenance and with a firm undaunted step. In the words of one* who differed
widely from him in all religious and political
opinions,—

> While round the armed bands
> Did clasp their bloody hands,
> He nothing common did or mean,
> After that memorable scene ;
> But with his keener eye
> The axe's edge did try ;
> Nor called the gods, with vulgar spite,
> To vindicate his helpless right ;
> But bowed his comely head
> Down, as upon a bed.

Charles was attended to the scaffold by Bishop
Juxon, and by two of the gentlemen of his bed-
chamber, Harrington and Herbert. The stage was
covered with black cloth ; in the centre of it lay
the block, with the axe resting on it ; and close by,
the King's coffin lined with black velvet. The
scaffold was surrounded by a large body of soldiers,
both foot and horse, and beyond them were a vast
multitude of human beings, who came to witness the
memorable scene. To the last Charles appeared
cheerful, resigned, and even happy. Having put on
a satin cap, he inquired of one of the two executioners, both of whom were in masques, if his hair
were in the way. The men requested him to push
it under his cap. As he was doing so, with the
assistance of the Bishop and of the executioner, he
turned to the former and said, "I have a good
cause, and a gracious God on my side." "There is

* Andrew Marvell.

but one stage more," replied the Bishop, " It will
carry you from earth to heaven ; and there you will
find a great deal of cordial joy and comfort." To
which the King responded, " I go from a corruptible
to an incorruptible crown, where no disturbance can
be, no disturbance in the world." Then again
inquiring of the executioner, " Is my hair well ? "
he took off his cloak and *George*, and, delivering the
latter to the Bishop, exclaimed with a marked
emphasis " *Remember !* " To the executioner he
said, " I shall say but short prayers, and when I
thrust out my hands——." Looking at the block,
he said, " you must set it fast." The executioner
replied that it was fast. The King remarked that
it might have been higher. Being told that it
could not have been higher, he said, " when I put
out my hands this way——." In the mean time,
having divested himself of his doublet, he again put
on his cloak. Then lifting up his hands and eyes to
heaven, and repeating a few words which were inaudible to the bystanders, he knelt down and laid his
head upon the block. The executioner stooping to
put his hair under his cap, the King, thinking he
was about to strike, bid him *wait for the sign*. After
a short pause he stretched out his hand, and the
executioner at one blow severed his head from his
body. The head was immediately lifted up by
the other headsman and exhibited to the people.
" Behold," he exclaimed, " the head of a traitor."
The dismal and almost universal groan which burst
forth at that moment from the dense population

around, was never forgotten by those who heard it.
The multitude, however, were allowed but a short
interval for reflecting on the scene they had witnessed, for almost immediately a party of cavalry
rode rapidly from Charing Cross to King Street,
and another from King Street to Charing Cross, for
the purpose of dispersing the people ; and within a
few minutes, with the exception of the scaffold and
its bloody paraphernalia, Whitehall presented but
the ordinary appearance of every day.

> But thou, dark man! by whose relentless doom
> The martyred monarch found a bloody tomb;
> What dost thou here within these regal walls,
> Where every glance thy daring crime recalls ?
> Here, where thy victim's latest tear was shed ?
> Here, in the silent chamber of the dead,
> Why sit'st thou, brooding, mournful, and alone,
> Thou dark usurper of the Tudor's throne ?
> Why does thy heart no proud content avow ?
> There sits no triumph on thy lordly brow ;
> Whence was the pang that iron frame that shook ?
> Whence was that sudden start, the haggard look ?
> Can airy trifles shake that giant mind?
> The rustling tapestry, the moaning wind ?
> Yes ! round thy feverish couch and tortured brain,
> Avenging conscience groups her shadowy train ;
> Brings the pale phantoms of the good and brave,
> By thee condemned to many a headless grave ;
> The waking agony, the nightly fear,
> Thy daughter's curses ringing in thine ear ;
> The dread of death that seeks for lengthened days,
> By craven arts which ill the end repays ;
> The secret armour, and the trebled guard,
> Each foe suspected, from each friend debarred ;
> The mean intelligence, the watchful eye,
> The ready poniard, and the hireling spy ;
> Thy soul a torment, and thy life a lie.—J. H. J.

On the 16th of December, 1653, Oliver Cromwell was solemnly installed Lord Protector of the
Commonwealth of England, Scotland, and Ireland.

He occupied at this period apartments in the Cock-pit, on the site of the present Treasury, from whence, after a " seeking of the Lord," he proceeded,—surrounded by his body guard, and preceded by the Barons of the Exchequer, the Judges in their robes, and the Lord Mayor, Aldermen, and Recorder, in their scarlet gowns,—to Westminster Hall, where the ceremony of Installation was performed with great magnificence. On the return of the procession, Cromwell was immediately preceded by the Lord Mayor, bearing the sword of maintenance. They again assembled in the Banqueting House, from whence, after an exhortation by Nicholas Lockyer,—Cromwell's puritan chaplain, and afterwards Provost of Eton, — they dispersed to their respective homes.

From this period we find the Protector receiving the House of Commons, and the congratulations of Foreign Ambassadors, in the Banqueting House at Whitehall, and on the 14th of April, 1654, he formally took up his abode in the regal palace of the Stuarts, and apparently in the same apartments which had been occupied by the ill-fated Charles. In the public journals of the day there is more than one notice of the removal of the Protector and his family to the stately apartments of Whitehall. "April 14, 1653. His Highness, the Lord Protector, with his lady and family, this day dined at Whitehall, whither his Highness and family are removed, and did this night lie there, and do there continue." And again in the " Weekly Intelligencer," "The Privy Lodgings for his Highness, the Lord Protector, in Whitehall, are now in readiness, as also the lodgings for his Lady Protectress; and likewise the Privy-kitchen, and other kitchens, butteries, and offices; and it is conceived the whole family will be settled there before Easter. The tables for diet prepared are these : —

A table for his Highness.	A table for the gentlemen.
A table for the Protectress.	A table for coachmen, grooms, and other domestic servants.
A table for chaplains and strangers.	
A table for the steward and gentlemen.	·A table for inferiors, or sub-servants." *

A few days afterwards we find the Protector giving a sumptuous entertainment at his new abode. "April 27, 1654: The Lords Ambassadors of the United Provinces this day dined with his Highness, the Lord Protector, at Whitehall, and the Lords of the Council, with some Colonels and other gentlemen, at two tables in the same room; and the Lords Ambassadors, the Lord President, and the Lord Lisle, at the same table with his Highness; and twenty gentlemen were taken into his Highness's life-guard of foot, who carried up the meat, and many gentlemen attended; and after dinner there was a banquet. The coats of the guards are grey cloth, with black velvet collars, and silver trace and trimming."†

Notwithstanding his professed godliness, Cromwell shewed but little disinclination to surround

---

* "Weekly Intelligencer," March 14th, to 21st, 1654.
† "Select Proceedings in State Affairs," April 27th, to May 4th, 1654.

himself with the trappings of monarchy and the paraphernalia of a court. Sir Gilbert Pickering was appointed his Lord Chamberlain, and his son-in-law, Claypole, Master of the Horse. His processions were attended by heralds and pursuivants-at-arms, and at his second installation in Westminster Hall, we find his former simple dress of black velvet exchanged for robes of purple lined with ermine. Evelyn, who visited Whitehall in 1656, observes, " I ventured to go to Whitehall, where of many years I had not been, and found it very glorious and well furnished."

If the entertainments given by Cromwell, at Whitehall, were wanting in taste and refinement, they were at least characterized by a profuse and generous hospitality. Every Monday he kept an open table for all the officers of his army who had attained the rank of captain, besides a smaller table, every day of the week, for such officers as came accidentally to court. " With these," says Heath, " he seemed to disport himself, taking off his drink freely, and opening himself every way to the most free familiarity." More than once in the Banqueting House at Whitehall,—beneath that famous roof which had witnessed alike the refined amusements of Charles and his latest agony,—we find him entertaining, in a body, the Commons of England, many of whom, like himself, had set their signatures to the death-warrant of their royal master. Heath mentions the Parliament being " gaudily entertained " by him in the Banqueting House, in 1656, having previously attended a sermon in St. Margaret's Church, Westminster;* and Burton more than once records these liberal entertainments. In February, 1657, he writes, " Mr. Speaker acquainted the House, that his Highness hath invited all the members of the House to dine with his Highness on Friday next, (being the day of public thanksgiving), in the Banqueting House at Whitehall."† It would save much trouble if invitations in our time could be delivered in a similar summary manner.

We must not conclude our notices of the court of Cromwell, at Whitehall, without giving a brief account of a remarkable entertainment which took place in the present Banqueting House,—a building endeared to us by so many historical associations. The buffooneries of the great Protector, —his thorough enjoyment of a practical joke, his delight in flinging napkins at the ladies, and cushions at his dragoons,—are well known. At the entertainment to which we allude, while the sweetmeats were being served, a lady who was *enceinte*, and who happened to be a spectator, requested Colonel Pride, who was seated at the same table with Cromwell, to give her some candied apricots, for which she had conceived a longing. The gallant Colonel, we are told, "instantly threw into her apron a conserve of wet sweetmeat with both his hands, and stained it all over; when, as if it had been the sign, Oliver catches up his napkin

* Heath's " Chronicle."
† " Parliamentary Diary," 18th February, 1657.

and throws it at Pride; he at him again, while all the table were engaged at the scuffle: the noise whereof made the members rise before the sweet-meats were set down, and believing dinner was done, go to this pastime of gambols, and be spectators of his Highness's frolics. Were it worth a description, I would give the reader a just and particular account of that Arab festival, as it was solemnized in the Banqueting House at Whitehall."* Similar frolics are recorded as having taken place at the nuptial banquets of the Protector's daughters, Mrs. Claypole and Mrs. Rich.

At Whitehall, on the 6th of April, 1657, Cromwell refused the crown of Great Britain, which was formally tendered to him by the assembled Commons of the realm. Here also, on the 3rd of September, the following year,—on the anniversary of his great victories of Worcester and Dunbar, and on the day which he had always regarded as the luckiest of his life,—the mighty usurper breathed his last. The fearful tempest, which howled around his death-bed, was listened to with superstitious awe by those who were aware of the great extremity of this extraordinary man. Ships were dashed against the shore; houses were swept from their foundations; trees were uprooted in vast numbers, and especially those in St. James's Park, almost under the windows where the Protector lay expiring.

That Cromwell died imbued with the religious enthusiasm which he had professed in his life time

* "Court and Kitchen of Mrs. Elizabeth Cromwell," Lond. 1664.

there can be no doubt. He was constantly seen absorbed in his devotions, and such was his fanaticism, and so confident was he of being received among the saints in Heaven, that, to use the words of Hume, "he assumed more the character of a mediator, interceding for his people, than that of a criminal, whose atrocious violation of social duty had, from every tribunal, human and divine, merited the severest vengeance." If, at times, any doubt was entertained by him as to the real state of his soul, and the efficacy of those illusions of eternal happiness with which he so fondly flattered himself, it seems to have been dispersed by the assurances of the fanatical preachers who attended him. Of Godwin, a popular divine, he inquired earnestly whether a person, who had once been in a state of grace, could again fall from it and suffer the reprobation awarded to the damned. On being assured that such was impossible, "Then am I safe," he exclaimed, "for I am sure that once I was in a state of grace." In his last extremity, when paroxysm was succeeding paroxysm, and when it was too evident that the hours of the Protector were numbered, a deputation from the Council of State waited at his bed-side to know his will with regard to his successor. His senses, however, were nearly gone, nor had he strength enough to express his wishes. Some one, however, named his son Richard, at which he is said to have shewn sufficient signs of approbation to justify the subsequent measures taken by the Council.

Richard Cromwell was immediately installed as Lord Protector in the room of his father, and took up his abode in the palace of Whitehall. His rule, it is needless to remark, was of short duration ; nor is it necessary to enter into the circumstances which led to the downfall of this singular personage. For some time before he quitted Whitehall, his creditors had become pressing and even insolent. According to Heath, within a day or two after he had resigned the Protectorship, instead of his guards, Whitehall was besieged by half the bailiffs of Westminster, who were actually armed with writs against the unfortunate Richard.

At the Restoration of Charles the Second, Whitehall presented a very different appearance to what it had worn under what Voltaire styles *la sombre administration de Cromwell*. Never, perhaps, in the social history of any country, has there been effected so sudden a revolution in *fashion*,—for such in fact it was,—from the black doublets and the long sallow faces of the Puritans, to the dainty coxcombry and the open and unblushing profligacy which were the immediate characteristics of the Restoration of Charles the Second. In the same apartments—in which a few months before were held solemn " exhortations" and "seekings of the Lord,"—we turn, as it were, by the shifting of a magic lantern, to such scenes as Buckingham building houses of cards to amuse *la belle Stuart*, or Rochester slipping indecent lampoons into the pockets of his good-humoured sovereign. Let us turn only, and it is a

task equally amusing and instructive, from the "Parliamentary Diary" of Burton and the public journals under the rule of Cromwell, to the gossiping
pages of Pepys and Count Hamilton, and we shall
be readily struck with the extraordinary change.

With Cromwell died,—not, indeed, the spirit of
puritanism, for it still continues to throw a blight
on our religious institutions, to deprive the hard-
worked labourer of his day of rest, and to drive him,
from manly and harmless amusements on the
Sabbath day, to the debaucheries of an alehouse,—
but with Cromwell died the fashionable assumption
of sanctity and sour faces, the straining after theatrical effect, and the affectation of conventional costume.   Whether, indeed, for better or for worse,
Whitehall, at the Restoration, wore a very different
appearance to what it had presented in the days of
the Protectorate.   In lieu of puritan chaplains with
hypocritical faces and Geneva frills; in lieu of sanc-
tified members of Parliament with long cloaks and
steeple-crowned hats, we find yeomen of the guard
in bright costumes, and pages in silken attire, again
sauntering through its ancients courts; once more
were seen gallant cavaliers, and fair ladies with
flowing tresses and scarlet plumes, riding laughingly
forth from under its heavy portals; again the love-
song was heard by moonlight in the shady labyrinths of Privy Gardens; music and the dance once
more resounded in the lighted galleries; and here
the merry monarch sauntered among his witty
courtiers, and toyed with his languishing and beau-

tiful mistresses, as gay, as thoughtless, and as
unconcerned, as if the blood of his father had never
dimmed the axe of the common executioner within
a few feet of him, or as if he himself had never
been driven forth by a mighty revolution to be
a wanderer on the face of the earth.

> Awake the dance, the revel, and the song,
> Light the gay hall for pleasure's laughing throng!
> Young, gifted Charles! when bounteous Heaven restored
> Thy father's sceptre to its graceless lord ;
> Could not thy heart be tempted to retrace
> Th' ancestral sorrows of thy fated race ;
> These stones ensanguined with a father's gore,
> Thy friends who died on many a foreign shore ?
> Could not their fate one serious thought impress ?
> Could not thine own long exile and distress
> One tear of pious gratitude impart,
> Or wring reflection from that rebel heart ?
> No ! fill the bowl to beauty's sparkling eyes ;
> " Live while we live," the frolic monarch cries ;
> Away with thought in joy's delicious hours,
> Of love and mirth, of melody and flowers !
> Lo ! on the ear voluptuous music falls,
> The lamps are flashing on the mirrored walls ;
> How rich the odours, and how gay the rooms
> With sparkling jewels and with waving plumes !
> Bright names that live in history's page we trace,
> Hyde's mournful look, and Monmouth's angel face ;
> Portsmouth's dark eye, and Cleveland's haughty charms
> That chained a monarch to her snowy arms ;
> There royal Catherine checks the jealous tear,
> While pleads her lord in beauty's flattered ear;
> There gleams the star on graceful Villiers' breast,
> Here the grouped courtiers laugh at Wilmot's jest :
> There glittering heaps of tempting gold entice
> The wealthy fool to chance the dangerous dice ; .
> Here floats young beauty through the graceful dance,
> Feigns the fond sigh, or throws the wanton glance ;
> There the soft love-song, to yon group apart,
> Steals with delicious sweetness o'er the heart ;
> The easy monarch glides from fair to fair,
> Hints the warm wish, or breathes the amorous prayer ;
> Such the gay scene the joyous night displays,
> But mark the change to-morrow's sun surveys !

The song is hushed, the revellers are fled,
The monarch sleeps upon his funeral bed ;
Coldly it yawns, yon vault's sepulchral gloom ;
There are no lords-in-waiting in the tomb !
No sorrowing friend, no weeping child is there,
No loved-one sobbing with dishevelled hair :
All, whom his bounty fed, his grandeur won,
Have flown to worship at the rising sun.
Of all who courted, pandered, cringed, or sued,
Pleasure's gay swarm, or Flattery's hollow brood ;
One heart alone, within her widowed bower,
Mourns with convulsive sobs their parting hour ;
The only friend who watched his closing scene,
His injured spouse, his own neglected Queen !—J. H. J.

Charles the Second returned to Whitehall on his
birth-day, the 29th of May, 1660.   In St. George's
Fields, Southwark, he was met by the Lord Mayor
and aldermen in their scarlet gowns, and, being conducted by them under a rich canopy, was regaled
with a magnificent banquet.   From Southwark to
Whitehall, the streets through which he passed were
hung on each side with tapestry; bands of music
were stationed at appointed places ; the train-bands
of the city, in rich dresses, lined the way, and
the conduits flowed with excellent wine.   Charles
entered the palace of his ancestors amidst the roar
of cannon and the acclamations of thousands.   At
night the sky was illumined with bonfires and fire-
works, and the people were regaled with a profusion
of wine and food.   Late at night, Charles went in
stealth from Whitehall to the house of Sir Samuel
Morland, at Lambeth, where he passed the first night
of his almost miraculous restoration with Mrs. Palmer, afterwards the celebrated Duchess of Cleveland.

In the pages of Pepys and De Grammont will be

found many amusing particulars connected with the history of Whitehall in the days of the "merry monarch." Pepys, in particular, has bequeathed us a very graphic account of a Court entertainment which he witnessed in the old palace. "The room," he says, "where the ball was to be, was crammed with fine ladies, the greatest of the Court. By-and-by comes the King and Queen, the Duke and Duchess, (of York,) and all the great ones; and, after seating themselves, the King takes out the Duchess of York, and the Duke the Duchess of Buckingham; the Duke of Monmouth my Lady Castlemaine, and so other lords, other ladies, and they danced the brantle. After that, the King led a lady a single coranto; and then the rest of the lords, one after another, other ladies; very noble it was, and great pleasure to see. Then to country dances; the King leading the first, which he called for; which was, says he, 'Cuckolds all awry,' the old dance of England. Of the ladies that danced, the Duke of Monmouth's mistress, and my Lady Castlemaine, and a daughter of Sir Harry de Vic's were the best. The manner was, when the King dances, all the ladies in the room, and the Queen herself, stand: and indeed he dances rarely, and much better than the Duke of York."

From the pen of the same amusing writer we have a charming description of the return of a Court party from a ride, at which Charles and his Queen were present, and at which *la belle Stuart,* afterwards Duchess of Richmond, presents the most

prominent figure. "I followed them," says Pepys,
"into Whitehall, and into the Queen's presence,
where all the ladies walked, talking and fiddling
with their hats and feathers, and changing and trying
one another's by one another's heads, and laughing.
But it was the finest sight to me, considering their
great beauty and dress, that ever I did see in all my
life. But, above all, Miss Stuart, in this dress,
with her hat cocked and red plume, with her
sweet eye, little Roman nose, and excellent *taille*,
is now the greatest beauty I ever saw, I think, in
my life." On horseback, Miss Stuart is said to
have looked exquisitely beautiful. It was this
charm which captivated George Hamilton, when he
presented her with his heart and one of " the pret-
tiest horses in England."

Such charms as those of *la belle Stuart* could not
fail to captivate the amorous monarch. " The
King," writes Pepys, in 1663, "is now besotted
with Miss Stuart, getting her into corners ; and
will be with her half an hour together, kissing
her, to the observation of all the world ; and she
now stays by herself, and expects it, as my Lady
Castlemaine did use to do." The feeling of Charles
for Miss Stuart seems to have approached nearer
to what may be termed love than any other of his
libertine attachments. It seems that the young
maid of honour was constantly detained by the
Duchess of Cleveland to pass the night in her apartment, and as it was the daily practice of Charles to
visit his mistress before she rose, he constantly

found them in bed together. Miss Stuart, however, had sense enough to prefer a substantial match
to a splendid intrigue, and therefore readily listened to an offer of marriage, which she received
from Charles Stuart, fourth Duke of Richmond.
The remaining scenes of the drama are laid at
Whitehall. The Duchess of Cleveland, it seems,
furious at seeing her influence over her royal lover
eclipsed by a younger rival, determined to en-
lighten Charles as to the inconstancy of his new
mistress. Accordingly, one night, in the course of
a stormy interview, the Duchess bitterly taunted
him with being the dupe of his rival, and the laugh-
ing-stock of the Court, — " Miss Stuart," she said
jeeringly, " had doubtless dismissed him from her
apartment, on the ground of affected indisposition, or
some pretended scruples of delicacy; but, she added,
he had only to return to her chamber, and he would
find his happy rival, the Duke of Richmond, occupying his place." While Charles was hesitating
how to act, the Duchess took him by the hand, and
led him towards the spot. " Chiffinch," says De
Grammont, " being in her interest, Miss Stuart
could have no warning of the visit : Miss Stuart's
chamber was in the middle of a little gallery,
which led, through a private door, from the King's
apartments to those of his mistresses. The Duchess
of Cleveland wished him good night as he entered
her rival's chamber, and retired in order to wait the
issue of the adventure." It was near midnight.
The King, in his way, was met by Miss Stuart's

waiting-maid, who attempted to oppose his entrance, telling him her mistress had been ill and had only just fallen asleep, but Charles insisted on forcing his way into the apartment. " He found Miss Stuart in bed," says De Grammont, " but far from be-ing asleep: the Duke of Richmond was seated at her pillow, and in all probability was less inclined to sleep than herself. The confusion of the one party, and the rage of the other, were such as may be easily imagined on such an occasion. The King, who of all men was the most mild and gentle, ex-pressed his resentment to the Duke of Richmond, in such terms as he had never before made use of. The Duke was speechless and almost petrified: he saw his master and his King justly irritated. The first transports which rage inspires on such occasions are dangerous; Miss Stuart's window was very convenient for a sudden revenge, the Thames flow-ing close beneath it: he cast his eyes upon it, and seeing those of the King more inflamed with indig-nation than he thought his nature capable of, he made a profound bow, and retired without replying a single word to the torrent of reproaches and menaces that was poured upon him." The Duke retired from Court, but shortly afterwards returned privately, and carried off his beautiful prize. On a stormy night, in March, 1667, Miss Stuart eloped from her apartments at Whitehall, and joined the Duke at a small inn in Westminster. They then fled on horseback into Surrey, where they were married the following morning by the Duke's chaplain. According to Bishop Burnet, nothing could exceed the violence of the King's rage on hearing of his mistress's flight. Within twelvemonths, however, the good-humoured monarch was reconciled to her as well as her husband; and it is said, that, from this period, not only had Charles no reason to complain of her want of complaisance, but that he was once so intoxicated at a party at Lord Townshend's, as to boast to the Duke of Richmond of the favours which the Duchess had conferred on him.

It was through the " little gallery" (which we have mentioned as leading by a " private door" from the King's apartments to those of the ladies of the palace,) that Charles was one day passing, when he heard the voice of Miss Howard singing a popular satirical song, in which his familiar *soubriquet* of " Old Rowley" was not very reverentially introduced. After satisfying his curiosity for a few moments, he mischievously tapped at the door of her apartment. Miss Howard inquired who was there ?—" Only old Rowley," was his good-humoured reply.

According to Evelyn, the apartments of the Duchess of Portsmouth,—another mistress of Charles, —at Whitehall, had ten times the " richness and glory" of the Queen's. An account of a morning visit which the philosopher paid to them in 1683, in company with the King, is amusingly detailed in his "Diary." "Following his Majesty," he says, " through the *gallery* I went with the few who attended him into the Duchess of Portsmouth's dressing-room within her bedchamber, where she was in her morning loose garment, her maids combing her, newly out of bed, his Majesty and the gallants standing about her: but that which engaged my curiosity, was the rich and splendid furniture of this woman's apartments, now twice or thrice pulled down and rebuilt to satisfy her prodigal and expensive pleasures, while her Majesty's does not exceed some gentlemen's wives in furniture and accommodation. Here I saw the new fabric of French tapestry, for design, tenderness of work, and incomparable imitation of the best paintings, beyond anything I had ever beheld. Then, for Japan cabinets, screens, pendule clocks, great vases of wrought plate, tables, stands, chimney furniture, sconces, branches, braseras, &c., all of massive silver, and out of number, besides some of his Majesty's best paintings."

According to Pennant, the celebrated Nell Gwynne, " not having the honour to be on the Queen's establishment," had no apartments at Whitehall. This, however, I presume to be a double error. That Nell Gwynne, strange as it may appear, was one of the ladies of the Privy Chamber to Catherine of Braganza is proved beyond a doubt by the books in the Lord Chamberlain's office ;* and that she had apartments at Whitehall in her official capacity appears to be no less certain. Anthony Wood, speaking of the King's

* She was sworn into the post in 1675. See "Pegge's Curialia," p. 58.

convivial parties, says, "They met either in the
lodgings of Louisa, Duchess of Portsmouth, or in
those of Chiffinch, near the back-stairs, or in the
apartment of Eleanor Gwynne, or that of Baptist
May; but he losing his credit, Chiffinch had the
greatest trust amongst them." Occasionally these
agreeable supper-parties took place in the apartment of Miss Kirk, one of the maids of honour to
the Queen. The company seems to have generally
consisted of the Duke of Richmond, Lord Taaffe,—
the admirer and apparently the seducer of Miss
Kirk,—Miss Stuart, the Count de Grammont, and,
for the sake of appearances, the governess of the
maids of honour.

In the days of Charles the Second, the old palace
of Whitehall was of vast size and magnificence.
"It extended," says Pennant, "along the river, and
in front along the present Parliament and Whitehall Street, as far as Scotland Yard, and on the
other side of those streets to the turning into Spring
Gardens beyond the Admiralty, looking into St.
James's Park. The merry King, his Queen, his
royal brother, Prince Rupert, the Duke of Monmouth, and all the great officers, and all the courtly
train, had their lodgings within these walls; and all
the royal family had their different offices, such as
kitchens, cellars, pantries, spiceries, cyder-house,
bake-house, wash-yards, coal-yards, and slaughter-
houses." The source from which Pennant drew this
sketch of the old palace is from the interesting plan
taken by John Fisher in 1680, and engraved by

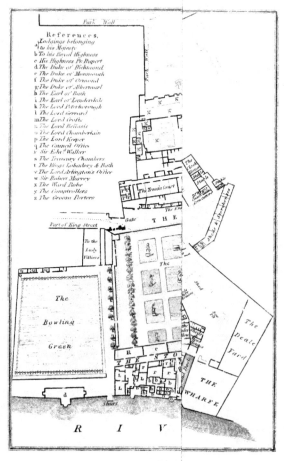

PALACE

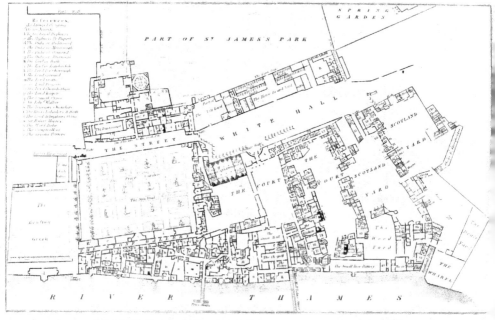

PALACE OF WHITEHALL, IN CHARLES THE SECONDS REIGN ANNO 1680.

Virtue in 1757. This plan is now before me, and
it is not a little interesting to be able to fix the
identical spot inhabited by the Chiffinches and the
Killegrews, by the wrong-headed Prince Rupert,
and by the right-minded Duke of Ormond. Here,
on the site of the present Treasury, overlooking the
Park, lived the celebrated George Monk, Duke of
Albemarle; and here, overlooking the street, on
the site of the Board of Trade, lived the unfortunate
Duke of Monmouth.

The public stairs, or water-entrance to the Palace,
still remain on the spot where they existed in the
days of Wolsey. The private stairs, however, which
were used by royalty alone, no longer exist, though
the arch of the portal still remains in the wall
adjoining Fife House. With how many interesting events and recollections is this spot identified!
Through this arch Wolsey passed when he took
his long farewell of human greatness, when, em-
barking on board his barge for Esher, he fixed his
mournful glance for the last time on the princely
palace which was to be his no more. Here Henry
the Eighth so often embarked amidst fair dames
and gallant men, on his magnificent water progresses to Greenwich and Richmond; — down its
steps his daughter Mary descended on her way to
her coronation in Westminster Abbey;—here Elizabeth was handed into her barge by the courtly
Leicester or the ill-fated Essex;—under its portal
Charles the First passed with his beautiful bride
to their nuptial apartments;—and here, in after-

years, he descended between an avenue of soldiers on his way to his trial in Westminster Hall.
Here Charles the Second must have often departed
on his midnight frolics, and here his brother descended in darkness and in stealth, on the night
that he fled an exile to a foreign shore.

Immediately to the east of the private water
entrance to the palace were the apartments of
Catherine of Braganza, which had been previously
occupied by Charles the First and Cromwell; and
immediately to the west were those of Charles the
Second, both looking on the Thames. By the plan
of the Palace we have just referred to, we find that
the King's apartments joined those of the maids of
honour, as described by De Grammont; and the
"little gallery" into which they opened is plainly
perceptible. Adjoining the water-entrance and
the back-stairs, we trace the apartment of William
Chiffinch,—the indefatigable panderer to the pleasures, and the depositary of the secrets of the
voluptuous Charles,—whose name has been immortalized by Sir Walter Scott.

In a scarce and curious little work published in
the reign of Charles the Second, the author observes,
"To describe all particularities relating to this royal
seat would be too tedious. There is a most magnificent and stately banqueting house, built by King
James, and the delicate Privy Garden was lately
enlarged towards the south, with a pond of an oval
form, supplied with water from Hyde Park, where
you may see the water shoot, or forced up to a great

height from the surface of the pond, and, by its winding fall, delights the eye and the ear with its pretty murmur." *

Charles the Second breathed his last at White-hall on the 6th of February, 1685, after a short illness, and not without suspicion of having been poisoned. Evelyn, in a passage written on the night of the King's death, has left us a very striking description of Whitehall, as he beheld it only on the *Sunday* preceding. " I can never forget," he says, " the inexpressible luxury and profaneness, gaming, dissoluteness, and, as it were, total forgetfulness of God (it being Sunday evening), which this day se'night I was witness of; the King sitting and toying with his concubines, Portsmouth, Cleveland, and Mazarine, &c., a French boy singing love songs in that glorious gallery, whilst about twenty of the great courtiers and other dissolute persons were at basset round a large table, a bank of at least 2000*l.* in gold before them, upon which two gentlemen who were with me made reflections with astonish-ment. Six days after was all in the dust !" A short time before his death Charles gave his keys to his brother James, who is described as kneeling by his bed-side and in tears. He recommended to his care and protection all his natural children, except the Duke of Monmouth, who had deeply offended him. He begged him also to be kind to the Duchess of Cleveland, and especially to the Duchess of Portsmouth ; and he added, " Do not let Nelly

* " The Present State of London," 1681."

starve." In his last moments he received the
sacrament of extreme unction from a Roman Catholic priest, Father Huddleston, who had assisted him
in his flight after the battle of Worcester, and who
was brought privately into the King's bedchamber
by the back-stairs.

The priest was introduced into the sick chamber
by James the Second, who is described as kneeling, deeply affected, by the bed-side of his dying
brother. Notwithstanding their dissimilarity of
character, the scene which parted the two brothers
for the last time appears to have been deeply affecting. From the pen of the Reverend Francis
Roper, Chaplain to the Bishop of Ely, who was
admitted to the sick chamber of the "merry
monarch," we have an interesting account of what
passed on the occasion. " He often in extremity of
pain," says Roper, "would say he suffered, but
thanked God he did so; and that he suffered
patiently. He every now and then would seem
to wish for death, and beg the pardon of the standers-
by, and those that were employed about him, that
he gave so much trouble; that he hoped the work
was almost over; he was weary of this world; he
had enough of it, and was going to a better. There
was so much affection and tenderness expressed
between the two royal brothers, the one upon the
bed, *the other almost drowned in tears upon his knees,
and kissing of his dying brother's hand*, as could not
but extremely move the standers by."* Such was

* Ellis's "Orig. Letters," vol. iii. p. 335.

the scene which passed in the death chamber of
Charles the Second at Whitehall! On the following day James received the congratulations of
his council, and was formally proclaimed at the
gates of the palace, and in other places. According to the prejudiced account of Burnet, the pro-
clamation was read in solemn silence. " There were
no tears," he says, "for the last King, and no shouts
for the present one." Welwood and Dr. Calamy,
however, have left us a very different account of the
manner in which James's accession was hailed by
the people.

On the eve of that memorable Revolution, when
the bigotry and misconduct of the misguided James
was gradually bringing about the change which deprived him of the sovereignty of three kingdoms,
it was at Whitehall that he first received the
tidings of the projected invasion of his dominions
by the Prince of Orange, and that he silently and
sullenly awaited his fate. Here, too, it was that
the last of the male line of the Stuarts, who
reigned over these realms, took his farewell of
human greatness.

It was not unnatural perhaps, that it should be
long before James could believe that the vast naval
armament, which was preparing by his own cousin
and son-in-law in the ports of Holland, was intended
to wage war against himself. When the nature
of the Prince of Orange's intentions became at
length but too evident, he is said to have turned
deadly pale, and the despatch which brought the

tidings fell unconsciously to the ground. Among
other evidences of the disquietude displayed by the
unfortunate monarch, previous to the landing of
his Dutch son-in-law, was the fact of his causing
a weather-cock, of no ordinary dimensions, to be
erected immediately opposite his private apartments, on the roof of the Banqueting House at
Whitehall. It was intended to give him momentary notice of the state of the wind, whether
favourable or not to the approach of the Dutch
fleet to the English ports. The weather-cock may
still be seen at the north end of the Banqueting House, and is rendered the more remarkable from its being transversely ornamented with
a cross, the symbol of that religion, his devotion
to which proved so fatal to his posterity as well as
to himself. The anxiety which prevailed as to the
shifting of the wind was not confined to the King
himself, but, according as it happened to blow from
the east or from the west, was styled the Popish
or the Protestant wind. This circumstance is alluded to in the well known poetical ballad of
Lillibulero,—

> Oh, but why does he stay behind?
> By my soul 'tis a Protestant wind!

At length it became positively known that the
Prince of Orange had landed on the shores of England, and was advancing towards the metropolis.
It was then,—betrayed by the friends who ought to
have been most devoted to him, deserted by his army,
shunned by the summer crew of parasites and

flatterers who had buzzed about him in his prosperity, abandoned at his utmost need by his own
connections, and even by his favourite daughter,
the Princess Anne of Denmark,—that the broken-
hearted monarch came to the resolution of effecting his escape to the Continent. His first thought,
however, was for his young wife, Mary of Modena, and for his infant heir, afterwards invidiously
known as the "Pretender;" and their flight is not
the least romantic incident in the history of Whitehall.

The particulars are as follow.—On the evening of
the 6th December, 1688, the King, without previously communicating his intentions to the Queen,
sent for the Count de Lauzun, the well known
favourite of Louis the Fourteenth, and desired him
to make instant preparations for her departure: he
then retired harassed and miserable to bed. Everything having been duly prepared, at the appointed
hour the Count de Lauzun, accompanied by Mon-
sieur de St. Victor, proceeded to the King's apartment, and informed him of the steps they had
taken. James instantly rose from his bed, and
proceeded to awake the Queen, who, being unexpectedly made aware of the plan which was laid
for her sudden departure, threw herself at her husband's feet, and, in a passion of grief, implored him
to allow her to remain and share the dangers which
surrounded him. James, however, was inflexible,
and gave orders that the two nurses of the Prince
should be awakened. When the infant was brought

into the room, the feelings of the father overcame
his usual coldness, and tenderly embracing his child,
he gave the most particular injunctions to the
Count de Lauzun to watch carefully over his
charge.

It was now between three and four o'clock in the
morning, in the most inclement season of the year,
when the Queen, carrying her infant in her arms,
stole in disguise down the back stairs at Whitehall,
to the private water entrance leading to the Thames.
The fugitives seem to have been in great dread
that the cries of the royal infant would attract the
attention of the guards; fortunately, however, it
slept, equally unconscious of the inclemency of the
elements, and of the change which was taking place
in its own fortunes. At the foot of the stairs an
open boat was in readiness, in which, in almost total
darkness, with the discomforts of a high wind, a
heavy rain, and the Thames being unusually tempestuous and swollen, the unfortunate Queen and
her attendants crossed the river to Lambeth. A
coach had been hired, but by some accident it
was delayed. "During the time that she was
kept waiting," says Dalrymple, "she took shelter
under the walls of an old church at Lambeth,
turning her eyes streaming with tears, sometimes
upon the Prince, unconscious of the miseries which
attend upon royalty, and who upon that account
raised the greater compassion in her breast, and
sometimes at the innumerable lights of the city,
amidst the glimmerings of which she in vain ex-

plored the palace in which her husband was left, and
started at every sound she heard from thence."
While in this disagreeable situation, the fugitives
had a narrow escape from discovery. "The Queen,"
says Father Orleans, "waiting in the rain under
the church-wall for a coach, the curiosity of a man,
who happened to come out of a neighbouring inn
with a light, gave considerable cause of alarm.
He was making towards the spot where she was
standing, when Riva, one of her attendants, suddenly rushed forward and jostled him, so that they
both fell into the mire. It was a happy diver-
sion, as the stranger believing it to be the result
of accident, they both apologized, and so the matter
ended." From Lambeth, the Queen proceeded by
land to Gravesend, where a vessel was waiting for
her, in which, after a safe and expeditious voyage,
she arrived at Calais about four o'clock on the
following afternoon.

It was not long after the flight of the Queen,
that the ground opposite Whitehall very nearly
became the scene of a sanguinary encounter. The
general commanding the royal guards was the celebrated Lord Craven, who had figured as the gay and
accomplished courtier in the reign of James the
First; who, in the field of battle, had frequently
dared death in the cause of his sovereign, and who,
amidst the horrors of the Great Plague, had braved
it with equal cheerfulness in the cause of humanity.
Though now approaching his eightieth year, he
still retained the command of the royal guards,

in which capacity he continued to perform his military duties with the same zeal and alacrity, as when, in the vigour of his youth, and under the influence of an honourable ambition, he had fought under the illustrious banner of the great Gustavus Adolphus.

One more duty was still left for the gallant old soldier to perform. Ascertaining that the Dutch troops had entered London, he assembled his men before the palace of Whitehall, and placing himself at their head, prepared to die in defence of his legitimate sovereign. The minds of men were eagerly alive to the result, when, about eleven o'clock at night, the sound of the approaching Dutch was plainly perceptible. Learning that Lord Craven was prepared to receive them, they marched through St. James's Park in order of battle; their matches lighted, and their drums beating. In the midst, however, of the general suspense and trepidation, Lord Craven received positive orders from James to retire from his post; a sentence which seems to have been as reluctantly obeyed by his humblest follower, as by the veteran hero himself. It must, indeed, have been a bitter blow to the old soldier; nor would it be easy to analyze the feelings of that good and gallant man, when drawing off the noble troops, whose fine discipline and gallant appearance constituted the pride and pleasure of his existence, he left the threshold of his sovereign, and the palace of the ancient monarchs of his native country, to be insulted by the sight of a Dutch burgher-guard standing as sentries at its gates.

The moment had now arrived when the unfortunate James found it imperative to consult his own safety. Accordingly, on the night previous to his flight, he communicated his determination to the Duke of Northumberland, the lord in waiting, desiring him on his allegiance to keep it a profound secret, till the necessity for concealment should no longer exist. On the following morning, the 11th of December, about three o'clock, the King withdrew from Whitehall by the private water-entrance to the palace, and entered a boat, which was in waiting for him.

The next morning the King's ante-chamber at Whitehall was thronged as usual by the officers of state, the gentlemen of his household, and others who were in the habit of attending his levee, and their surprise was excessive, when, on the door of the bed-chamber being thrown open, instead of the King, the Duke of Northumberland made his appearance, and informed them of His Majesty's flight. Having performed this last act of kindness for his sovereign, the Duke, who was a natural son of Charles the Second, immediately placed himself at the head of his regiment of Guards, and declared for the Prince of Orange.

James, in the meantime, had proceeded as far as Feversham, where he was boarded by a boat, containing thirty-six armed men, who, ignorant of his rank and mistaking him for a fugitive Roman Ca-

tholic priest, detained and ill-treated him in the
most shameful manner. During the progress of
these events, the Prince of Orange had advanced
as far as Windsor, and as it was unquestionably his
interest that James should quit the kingdom, he
was naturally annoyed and disconcerted at the
King's progress having been arrested. The Prince
immediately despatched a messenger to his persecuted father-in-law, desiring him on no account to
proceed nearer to London than Rochester. The
despatch, however, arrived too late, for James was
already far advanced on his way to London, and
at night his return to the metropolis was hailed by
the ringing of bells, the blazing of bonfires, and
every manifestation of popular delight. Reresby, a
contemporary writer, mentions the "loud huzzas"
which were heard as the King passed through the
city, and Father Orleans also observes, "This was
a day of triumph: no man ever remembered to
have seen the like; ringing of bells, bonfires, and
all the solemnities that are usually exhibited to
testify joy, were practised on this occasion."

But when James for the last time re-entered the
ancient palace of Whitehall, he found its gorgeous
chambers almost deserted. Gratifying as must have
been the evidences of reviving royalty which were
even now ringing in his ear, they proved of no substantial advantage to the fallen monarch. The herd
of sycophants and time-servers had already gone to
worship the rising sun. He was approached but by
few persons of distinction, and had the mortification

of seeing Dutch sentries doing duty beneath his
windows.

James was in bed at Whitehall, and was probably
but little inclined to sleep, when, about midnight,
his privacy was broken in upon by Lords Halifax,
Shrewsbury, and Delamere, who informed him that
he must quit London the next morning. For the
purpose of being near the sea-coast, he requested
that he might be allowed to make Rochester his
residence, and, as it suited the views of his adversaries, his request was readily granted. He was
conveyed down the river, attended by a Dutch
guard, on a very tempestuous night, not without
danger from the elements as well as from man.
He remained at Rochester till the 23rd of December, when, on another dark and stormy night,
he proceeded with his natural son, the Duke of
Berwick, and two other faithful followers, in a
small boat down the river Medway, and about midnight reached a sailing vessel, which was expecting
him near the fort at Sheerness. After encounter-
ing much adverse and boisterous weather, the fugitives, on Christmas day, 1688, arrived safely at
Ambleteuse, in Picardy.

It was not many days after the expulsion of
James, that his daughter, Queen Mary, installed
herself, with the most indecent feelings of exultation and joy, in the very apartments which had so
recently witnessed the sorrows and the flight of her
ill-fated father. The scene is described by the
Duchess of Marlborough, in her " Account of Her

Own Conduct." Speaking of the Queen's want of
feeling, she says, " Of this she seemed to me to give
an unquestionable proof the first day she came to
Whitehall. She ran about it, looking into every
closet and conveniency, and turning up the quilts
upon the bed, as people do when they come to an
inn, and with no sort of concern in her appearance ;
behaviour which, though at that time I was extremely caressed by her, I thought very strange and
unbecoming ; for whatever necessity there was of
deposing King James, he was still her father, who
had so lately been driven from that chamber and
that bed ; and if she felt no tenderness, I thought
she should still have looked grave, or even pensively
sad, at so melancholy a reverse of his fortune."

Had the truth of this picture rested entirely on
the prejudiced authority of so virulent a partizan as
the Duchess of Marlborough, we might be inclined
to regard it as exaggerated and malicious. But the
description which Evelyn gives of Mary's behaviour, on her first arrival, sufficiently establishes
the veracity of the Duchess. " She came," he
says, " into Whitehall, laughing and jolly, as to
a wedding, so as to seem quite transported. She
rose early the next morning, and, in her undress,
as it was reported, before her women were up,
went about from room to room to see the convenience of Whitehall ; lay in the same bed and apartments where the late Queen lay, and within a night
or two sat down to play at basset, as the Queen, her
predecessor, used to do." Even her panegyrist,

Bishop Burnet, admits that he could not witness the Queen's unseemly levity without censure.

Whitehall, convenient and even picturesque as was its situation, magnificent as were its princely chambers, and suited to all the purposes of a court, was never the fixed residence of the phlegmatic usurper, King William. I cannot discover, indeed, that he ever passed a night within its walls. Probably its apartments, — and they had witnessed his courtship in the gay time of the "merry monarch," — were too intimately associated with the dark and melancholy annals of a past dynasty, and with the misfortunes of a race whom he had been so instrumental in driving into misery and exile. He took up his abode in the distant and Dutch-looking palace of Kensington, where he lived to bemoan the desolation of his domestic hearth, and to curse the ingratitude of the people whom he had saved from bigotry and slavery; where he drank brandy in secret, and where he died. Whitehall may be said to have ceased to exist with the House of Stuart. In 1697, nearly the whole of this magnificent structure, which contained upwards of a thousand apartments, was consumed by fire.

In wandering over the site of Whitehall,—once the scene of so much splendour, and of so many interesting historical events,—the antiquarian and the lover of the past will find but little that escaped the great fire of 1697. The Banqueting House,—the rooms occupied by Oliver Cromwell, forming part of the present Exchequer Office,—the old water entrance,—and probably some of the apartments of the Treasury, are all, we believe, that remain of the ancient palace.

On the site of the present Treasury and part of the Board of Trade, stood, as has already been mentioned, the famous Cock-pit,—the spot where our sovereigns gazed complacently on the cruel sports which were the delight of a past age,—where afterwards arose the celebrated structure, where the ministers of Queen Anne transacted the affairs of the realm,—and which, though considerably changed and altered, has continued, from that day to the present, to be the Treasury of Great Britain. Several of the old offices were taken down in 1733, in order to erect the present building which faces the parade in the Park; the expense of which was estimated at 9000*l.*

The Cock-pit, once a portion of the ancient palace, is associated with many illustrious names. Here were the apartments of George Monk, Duke of Albemarle; and here that celebrated man breathed his last. After his death, they were conferred by Charles the Second on his own niece, the Princess Anne of Denmark, afterwards Queen Anne. From hence it was, on the approach of the Prince of Orange to London, in 1688, that she fled at midnight down the back-stairs in "her night-gown and slippers," with only the Duchess of Marlborough for her companion, to join the deadly enemies of her unfortunate father. A few years afterwards, the harsh conduct of King William, and of her sister, Queen Mary, compelled her to quit the Cock-pit under very different circumstances. Lord Dartmouth, speaking of the compulsory removal of the Princess from Whitehall, observes, " She was carried in a sedan to Sion, being then with child, without any guard or decent attendance ; where she mis-carried, and all people forbid waiting ; which was complied with by everybody but the Duke of Somerset, whose house she was in, and Lord Rochester, who was her uncle." The Princess subsequently removed to Berkeley House, Piccadilly, where she remained till the death of her sister, when she became reconciled to King William, and probably returned to her old apartments at the Cock-pit.

In 1708, we find the Treasury spoken of as being " kept at the Cock-pit near Whitehall." Here, during the reign of Queen Anne, was the office of the celebrated Godolphin, and of the no less celebrated Harley, Earl of Oxford. Here, in full council, Guiscard made his attempt on the life of Harley ; here the assassin himself fell pierced with many wounds, of which he afterwards died in Newgate ; and, lastly, here it was that Bishop Atterbury underwent his memorable examination before the Privy Council, previous to his committal to the Tower. From Dodsley we learn, that as late as 1761, the Treasury retained its ancient name of the Cock-pit.

THE THAMES AT LONDON.

THE THAMES IN ANCIENT TIMES. — THAMES BY MOONLIGHT. — OLD
PALACE OF WHITEHALL. — NORTHUMBERLAND, YORK, DURHAM,
SALISBURY, WORCESTER, AND SOMERSET HOUSES.—TEMPLE GARDEN.
ALSATIA.— BRIDEWELL. — BAYNARD'S CASTLE. — QUEENHITHE. —
BANKSIDE.—WATER PROCESSIONS.

LET us take boat at Whitehall Stairs and pass
down the river to the Tower, noting, as we glide
along, a few of the more remarkable places associated with the history of the past.   Let us recall
to mind the time when the Thames was the great
thoroughfare, the "silent highway," as it has been
styled, between London and Westminster; when
its banks were adorned with a succession of stately
palaces and fair gardens; when it was crowded
with gilded barges covered with silken awnings,
and with a thousand wherries freighted with hooded
churchmen, and grave merchants, and laughing
beauty, in all the glittering or fantastic costume
of a past age.

Heave and how, rumbelow,

was the ancient chorus of the London watermen in
the days of the Plantagenets, and, as late as the
reign of Charles the First, we find this peculiar
race still famous for keeping time to their oars with
some characteristic song.

Row the boat, Norman, row to thy leaman,

was the first line of a song composed by the Lon-
donwatermen in honour of John Norman, Lord
Mayor of London in the reign of Henry the Sixth,
who, in 1454, first introduced the custom of the
Lord Mayor proceeding on state occasions, by water
from London to Westminster instead of on horseback.

To the philosopher, the Thames, as it presents
itself in our own time,—with its immense commerce, its crowded navigation, its magnificent
bridges, its busy wharfs and its forest of masts at
London Bridge,— presents matter of reflection of
deep and varied interest. Such reflections may be
indulged even when we are jostled along the
crowded bridges; and even the smoke from ten
thousand furnaces and manufactories, which usually
obscures the mid-day in London, may furnish additional food for meditation, as evincing the wealth
of the mighty city. But to the poet, the painter,
and the lover of past history, it is not at such a
time that the Thames wears its most inviting aspect. Those only, indeed, have witnessed it in its
full perfection, who have stood, on a summer morning, on one of its glorious bridges, when the inhabitants of the vast human hive are asleep, and
when every object is rendered distinct, and picturesque, and beautiful, from the meanest wharf
to the magnificent dome of St. Paul's, with its
golden cross glittering in the early sunrise.

But I confess that to me it is on a moonlight

night that the Thames at London wears its fairest
aspect.   If the reader has any taste for what is
beautiful in nature or in art; if, like the author, he
is sometimes willing to forget the turmoil of the
present to live in the silent world of the past, let
him, on a fair night, pass from the noisy streets of
Westminster into Dean's Yard, and thence into the
still and solemn cloisters of the old Abbey.   There,
standing on the tombs of mitred abbots and name-
less monks,—with the massive walls and buttresses
of the venerable cathedral steeped in the moonlight,
and with all its innumerable associations crowding
on his mind,—he will witness a scene of almost
unequalled interest and beauty.   Let him then
take boat at Westminster Bridge.   He will hear no
sound but the splash of his own oars; he will see
the light reflected in long lines of radiance from the
different bridges; he will call to mind the many
gorgeous processions, or the many illustrious prisoners who were led along the same "silent highway"
to their dungeons in the Tower, and their pillow on
the block; he will rest on his oars at each remembered spot of interest or beauty, and at midnight he
will hear the iron tongues of a thousand clocks
answering each other over the sleeping city, and,
far louder than the rest, the solemn and deep-toned
knell of St. Paul's.   The days have gone by when
the oar of the London waterman was entangled in
the stems of the water-lily; when, as described by
Paulus Jovius in 1552, the river "abounded in
swans, swimming in flocks;" or when, as men-

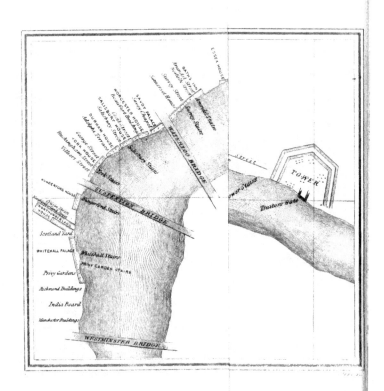

PLAN OF THE RIVER THAMES BUILDINGS.

tioned in the Spectator, " ten sail of apricock boats"
were seen landing their cargoes at Strand Bridge,
having previously taken in melons at Nine Elms.
But though the Thames at London may have lost
much as regards the picturesque, there still remains
much to charm and interest us, and the lapse of
time has at least had the effect of adding to its
thousand historical associations.

In proceeding by water from Westminster to the
Tower, the first spot of interest which we pass is
the site of the old palace of Whitehall, with its
traces of the ancient water-entrance, where our
monarchs were accustomed to embark in all their
splendour and triumph, from the days of Henry
the Eighth to those of the last of the Stuarts.
Further on are the gardens of Northumberland
House, which formerly extended to the water; and
adjoining them, Hungerford Market points out
the site of the London residence of the powerful
family of the Hungerfords of Fairleigh, in Wiltshire, whose mansion was pulled down by Sir Edward
Hungerford, in the reign of Charles the Second.   A
little beyond Hungerford Market stood York House,
formerly the inn, or residence, of the Bishops of
Norwich, and afterwards of the Archbishops of York.
Here lived the celebrated Lord Chancellor Egerton,
and here the great Bacon was born: here, also, in the
days of his magnificence, lived the great favourite,
George Villiers, Duke of Buckingham, and from
its beautiful gateway—the work of Inigo Jones—
which is still an ornament to the river, he must

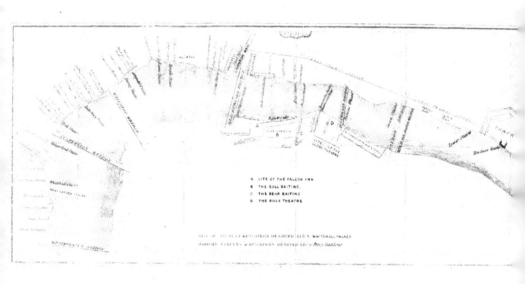

A   SITE OF THE FALCON INN
B   THE BULL BAITING.
C   THE BEAR BAITING
D   THE ROSE THEATRE

SITE OF ANCIENT BUILDINGS OF KOTHERHITH'S WHITEHALL PALACE
MODERN STREETS & BUILDINGS DENOTED THUS *this Curtons*

OF THE RIVER THAMES, SHOWING THE CORRESPONDING SITES OF ANCIENT & MODERN BUILDING

tioned in the Spectator, " ten sail of apricock boats"
were seen landing their cargoes at Strand Bridge,
having previously taken in melons at Nine Elms.
But though the Thames at London may have lost
much as regards the picturesque, there still remains
much to charm and interest us, and the lapse of
time has at least had the effect of adding to its
thousand historical associations.

In proceeding by water from Westminster to the
Tower, the first spot of interest which we pass is
the site of the old palace of Whitehall, with its
traces of the ancient water-entrance, where our
monarchs were accustomed to embark in all their
splendour and triumph, from the days of Henry
the Eighth to those of the last of the Stuarts.
Further on are the gardens of Northumberland
House, which formerly extended to the water; and
adjoining them, Hungerford Market points out
the site of the London residence of the powerful
family of the Hungerfords of Fairleigh, in Wiltshire, whose mansion was pulled down by Sir Edward
Hungerford, in the reign of Charles the Second. A
little beyond Hungerford Market stood York House,
formerly the inn, or residence, of the Bishops of
Norwich, and afterwards of the Archbishops of York.
Here lived the celebrated Lord Chancellor Egerton,
and here the great Bacon was born: here, also, in the
days of his magnificence, lived the great favourite,
George Villiers, Duke of Buckingham, and from
its beautiful gateway—the work of Inigo Jones—
which is still an ornament to the river, he must

often have passed to his sumptuous barge, in all the pomp and pride of human greatness.

Close to York House stood Durham House, the residence of the Bishops of Durham, now occupied by Durham Yard and the Adelphi. In July, 1258, at a time when the treachery and insincerity of Henry the Third, the exactions with which he oppressed his unfortunate subjects, and his contempt of all solemn obligations, threatened to draw down on him the judgments of Heaven and the anathemas of the church, we find the misguided monarch entering his barge at Westminster Stairs, and passing down the river towards the Tower. He had proceeded only a short distance, when the sky became obscured, and so violent a storm of thunder and lightning followed, that Henry, who was at all times terrified by any conflict of the elements, ordered the rowers to put him on shore. The barge was nearly opposite Durham House, which was then occupied by Simon de Montfort, Earl of Leicester, who had married the King's sister, and who was at the head of the associated barons, with whom Henry was then on the worst terms. The Earl, perceiving the approach of the royal barge, hastened to receive the King on his landing, and after respectfully saluting him, endeavoured to dispel his fears. "Your majesty," he said, "should not be afraid since the tempest is over." At these words, the King's countenance put on a severe expression, and he exclaimed passionately, "Above measure I dread thunder and lightning; but, by the head of God,

I am in more terror of thee, than of all the thunder and lightning in the world."*

Next to Durham House stood Salisbury House, built by Robert Cecil, Earl of Salisbury, in the reign of James the First; and adjoining it stood Worcester House, the site of which is now covered with Beaufort Buildings. Farther on, extending as far as Waterloo Bridge, stood the magnificent palace of the Savoy, — the residence of the great Plantagenets, Dukes of Lancaster,—the place of captivity of John, King of France, who was taken prisoner at the battle of Poictiers,—and which was devoted by Wat Tyler to the flames, in 1381, from the hatred which he bore to its owner the celebrated John of Gaunt, Duke of Lancaster.

Somerset House, which stands on the site of the famous palace erected by the Protector, Duke of Somerset, recalls a host of interesting associations. Beyond it stood Bath's Inn, the residence of the Bishops of Bath and Wells, till the reign of Edward the Sixth. It afterwards became the property of the celebrated high-admiral, Lord Thomas Seymour, and was one of the scenes of his "indecent dalliance" with the Princess Elizabeth, during the life-time of her sister, Queen Mary. Subsequently it became the residence of the Howards, Earls of Arundel and Dukes of Norfolk, whose titles are still preserved in Arundel Stairs and Surrey Stairs.

Between the site of Arundel House and the Temple, " Essex Stairs " points out the spot where

* Matthew Paris.

stood the garden or water entrance to Essex House,
once the residence of the ill-fated favourite of Queen
Elizabeth, and the scene of his conspiracy against
his royal mistress.   The Temple Garden,—whether
we people it in imagination with the Knight Templars of the olden time, or with the many learned
and peaceful men who have since sauntered beneath its green avenues,—is a spot especially interesting.   Here it is, in his play of Henry the
Sixth, that Shakspeare places the scene between
Richard Plantagenet and the Earl of Somerset,
when, in hot blood, they quitted the Temple Hall
for the secluded garden, and where the contention
took place, which, in the subsequent bloody quarrel
between the rival houses of York and Lancaster,
gave rise to the party distinctions of the White
and Red Rose.

> Within the Temple Hall we were too loud!
> The garden here is more convenient.
> *Plan.* Let him that is a true-born gentleman,
> And stands upon the honour of his birth,
> If he suppose that I have pleaded truth,
> From off this brier pluck a white rose with me.
> *Som.* Let him that is no coward nor no flatterer,
> But dare maintain the party of the truth,
> Pluck a red rose from off this thorn with me.
> *Warwick.* I love no colours; and, without all colour
> Of base insinuating flattery,
> I pluck this white rose with Plantagenet.
> *Suffolk.* I pluck this red rose, with young Somerset;
> And say withal, I think he held the right.

It indeed led to a contest, which

> —— dyed the white rose in a bloody red.

Adjoining the Temple, was Alsatia, the place of
refuge for the outcasts of society in the reigns of Eli-

zabeth and James the First, now perhaps, principally
familiar to the reader from Scott's admirable romance,
the "Fortunes of Nigel." Immediately to the east
stood the church and convent of the Carmelites, or
White Friars,—a name preserved, within the last
century, in "Whitefriars Stairs,"—and close to it
is the site of Dorset House, formerly the residence
of the Bishops of Salisbury, and afterwards inhabited by the celebrated Thomas Sackville, Earl of
Dorset. Here he composed his tragedy of "Porrex
and Ferrex," which was performed before Queen
Elizabeth at Whitehall, and here more than one
of his successors, a race of warriors and poets,
breathed their last.

We next pass by the site of Bridewell, a formidable castle in the days of William the Conquerer,
and the favourite palace of our early Norman sovereigns. Its walls were formerly washed by the clear
waters of the Fleet River,—a name afterwards degraded into the Fleet Ditch,—which Pope has immortalized in his "Dunciad," and which, from its
having been converted into an underground sewer,
is now only to be seen where it pours its black
waters into the Thames, near the foot of Blackfriars
Bridge. Pope says, alluding to the "Dunces:"—

> By Bridewell all descend,
> (As morning prayer and flagellation end,)
> To where Fleet-ditch, with disemboguing streams,
> Rolls the large tribute of dead dogs to Thames,
> The king of dykes! than whom no sluice of mud
> With deeper sable blots the silver flood.

When London was anciently a fortified city, the
great wall ran along the Fleet Ditch, extending to

the river nearly where Blackfriars Bridge now
stands. *Within* the walls stood the great house
of the Dominicans, or Black Friars, a spot famous
in the history of our country; and immediately to
the east of the bridge is the site of Baynard's
Castle, which takes its name from Baynard, a follower of William the Conqueror, who died in the
reign of William Rufus. This spot is also endeared
to us from being associated with the pages of Shakspeare, and with some of the most interesting passages in the history of our country. But, as regards
these, and other sites of past splendour to which we
have alluded in our progress down the river,—as we
may have to dwell more fully on their local histories
in our future rambles through the streets of London,
—we must not too much anticipate the interest
which remains to be dwelt upon elsewhere.

Proceeding in our progress down the river, we
pass under the shadow of the great cathedral of St.
Paul's. At its foot is Queenhithe, or Queen's Harbour, — anciently called Edred's-hithe, — the spot
where vessels discharged their cargoes as early as
the days of the Saxons. We find it royal property
in the time of King Stephen, who bestowed it on
William de Ypres, who, in his turn, conferred it on
the convent of the Holy Trinity, " within Aldgate."
In the reign of Henry the Third it again came into
the possession of the crown: the vessels which
brought corn from the Cinque Ports were compelled to land their cargoes here; and apparently,
from the harbour dues being conferred on the Queen,

it obtained its name of *Ripa Reginæ*, or Queen's Wharf.

On the opposite, or southern bank,—between Blackfriars Bridge and Southwark Bridge, — is Bankside. Here was the Globe Theatre immortalized as the spot where Shakspeare trod the stage; here was the celebrated " Paris Garden ; " here stood the circuses for " bowll-bayting " and " beare-baytynge," where Queen Elizabeth entertained the French ambassadors, with the baiting of wild beasts ; here stood the Falcon Tavern, the daily resort of Shakspeare and his dramatic companions,—the " Folken Ine " as it is styled in the ancient plans of Bankside,—and here also, between Southwark Bridge and London Bridge, were the "pike ponds" which supplied our monarchs with fresh-water fish, and adjoining them the park and palace of the Bishops of Winchester.

The history of old London Bridge we shall reserve for our notices of Southwark and its interesting locality. But, before landing at the Tower, let us pause to mention one or two incidents which throw a charm over the old river.

In the reign of Edward the Third, when that warlike monarch was holding his court at Westminster, and when his captive, King John, of France, was residing in the Palace of the Savoy, we frequently find the latter proceeding by water to pay private visits to the English monarch. " He went," says Froissart, " as often as he pleased, *privately by water*, to visit King Edward at his palace of Westminster."

In the succeeding reign, it was on the occasion of one of the royal processions of Richard the Second on the Thames, that the monarch espied Gower the poet passing by in his wherry, and summoning him on board the royal barge entered familiarly into conversation with him, and commanded him to

> Make a book after his hest.

The result was the production of the "Confessio Amantis," in which the poet, in a simple but graphic manner, thus describes his interview with his sovereign :—

> As it befel upon a tide,
> As thing which should then betide;
> In Thames, when it was flowing,
> As I by boat came rowing,
> So as fortune her time set,
> My liege lord perchance I met,
> And so befel, as I came nigh,
> Out of my boat, when he me sygh;
> He bade me come into his barge;
> And when I was with him at large,
> Among other things he said
> He hath this charge upon me laid,
> And made me do my business,
> That to his high worthiness
> Some new thingé I should book,
> That he himself might look,
> After the form of my writing.
> And thus upon his commanding,
> My heart is well the more glad
> To write so as he me bade.

A few years afterwards, in the reign of Henry the Sixth, we find the Thames connected with the troubles of the unfortunate Eleanor Cobham, wife of Humphrey Plantagenet, Duke of Gloucester She was accused (with one Bullinbrooke, "a priest very expert in the art of necromancy," and Margery

Goudmain, commonly called the Witch of Eye,) of conspiring against the King's life, with the object of elevating the Duke of Gloucester to the throne. The accusation set forth, that she, "Eleanor Lady Cobham, Duchess of Gloucester, to bring her husband to the crown, had procured and contrived with the said persons to make an image of wax like unto the King; which image they dealt so with by their devilish incantations and sorceries, that as the image consumed by little and little, the King's person should so daily decay, till he was brought to his end."*

That the Duchess tampered with the necromancers there can be no doubt. One of the charges brought against her, was administering love potions to her husband " to make him love her ;" the truth of which she admitted, though she positively denied having conspired against the life of the King. Bullinbrooke was hung, drawn, and quartered, and the Witch of Eye was burnt. The Duchess escaped with performing penance, and suffering imprisonment for life. On three different occasions, she was compelled to walk through Fleet Street, and other places, with her head uncovered, and with a taper of two pounds weight in her hand, which she offered at the high altar of St. Paul's Cathedral. On each of these occasions the unfortunate lady was brought from Westminster to the city by water. On the 13th of November, 1440, she was landed at the Temple Stairs; on the 15th at the Old Swan Stairs,

* Kennett's " Complete History."

close to London Bridge, and on the 17th at Queenhithe. It is remarkable that, notwithstanding the
lapse of more than four hundred years, the three
"stairs" we have just mentioned should be still in
existence, with the same names by which they were
distinguished in the reign of Henry the Sixth.

When Henry the Seventh consented to the coronation of his young wife,—the Princess Elizabeth,
daughter of Edward the Fourth, that "gentle,
beautiful, and fruitful lady," as she is styled by
Lord Bacon,*—she was conducted by water from the
palace at Greenwich to Westminster with extraordinary magnificence, being attended by "barges
freshly furnished with banners and streamers of
silk." The fair young queen was crowned in Westminster Abbey, in the presence of her cold-blooded
husband, by Morton, Archbishop of Canterbury,
on Sunday, the 25th of November, 1487. Ive, in
his account of the "Coronacion of Queene Elizabeth," describes her passage by water from Greenwich; thus affording us a very curious picture of a
royal procession in the fifteenth century. "She was
royally apparelled," he says, "and accompanied
with my lady, the King's mother, and by many
other great estates, both lords and ladies, richly
besene, came forward to the coronation; and at
their coming forth from Greenwich by water there
was attending upon her there the mayor, sheriffs,
and aldermen of the city, and diverse and many
worshipful commoners, chosen out of every craft,

* " Life of Henry the Seventh."

in their liveries, in barges freshly furnished with banners and streamers of silk, richly beaten with the arms and badges of their crafts; and especially a barge, called the bachelor's barge, wherein were many gentlemanly pageants, well and curiously devised to do her highness sport and pleasure with."

It was while passing down the river in his sumptuous barge, in 1521, that the powerful subject, Edward Bohun, Duke of Buckingham, the lineal descendant of Edward the Third, and the victim of his arch enemy Cardinal Wolsey, was arrested on the Thames by the Captain of the King's guard, Sir Henry Marney, and carried through the Traitor's Gate to the Tower. From hence, on the day of his trial, he was conveyed by water to Westminster Hall, with all the ceremony due to his high position as a prince of the Blood Royal, and the most powerful nobleman in the realm. Before night the scene had changed, and when he re-entered his barge at Westminster Stairs it was as a condemned criminal. The vessel was furnished with a carpet and cushions befitting his high rank, but he declined taking the seat which he had previously occupied. To Sir Thomas Lovell, Constable of the Tower, he said, " When I came to Westminster, I was Lord High Constable and Duke of Buckingham, but now—poor Edward Bohun!" He was landed at the Temple Stairs, where, with the fatal axe carried before him, he was conducted through the city to the Tower on foot, as a "cast man." A few days afterwards, amidst the tears and lamentations of a vast concourse

of people, he perished by the hands of the heads-
man on Tower Hill.

It was not long before Cardinal Wolsey shared
the fallen fortunes of his victim, the Duke of Buckingham. In the pages of the chroniclers of the
period, we find more than one graphic picture of the
great churchman, as he occasionally appeared in his
gorgeous progresses on the Thames; more especially
when the famous conclave was sitting in the great
hall at Blackfriars to decide on the divorce between
Henry the Eighth, and his injured and high-minded
queen, Catherine of Arragon.   At this eventful
crisis in the life of the voluptuous tyrant, we find
the great Cardinal constantly passing to and fro in
his barge, from the court at Blackfriars to the palace of Bridewell, in order to communicate, from
time to time, to the irritated monarch,—love-sick
with the charms of Anne Boleyn,—the result of the
day's proceedings. On one occasion, we find the
Cardinal closeted for several hours with his royal
master, whom he seems to have quitted in the worst
of humours.   On re-entering his barge, the companion of the Cardinal was the Bishop of Carlisle,
who, wiping, as we are told by Cavendish, the per-
spiration from his face, hazarded the trite observation that it was a " very hot day."—" Yes," said the
Cardinal pithily, " and if you had been as well chafed
as I have been within this hour, you *would* say it
was very hot."

On the occasion of the nuptials of Henry the
Eighth and Anne of Cleves, in 1540, the King and

his bride proceeded by water from Greenwich to Westminster, in great state. "On the fourth of February," says Holinshed, "the King and Queen removed to Westminster by water, on whom the Lord Mayor and his brethren, with twelve of the chief companies of the city, all in barges gorgeously garnished with banners, pennons, and targets, richly covered, and furnished with instruments sweetly sounding, gave their attendance; and, by the way, all the ships shot off, and likewise, from the Tower, a great peal of ordnance went off hastily."

A few years afterwards, when Henry the Eighth declared his marriage with Anne Boleyn, the young Queen was conducted "by all the crafts of London," from Greenwich to the Tower. The scene is described by the old chroniclers with great spirit. There were "trumpets," we are told, "shawms, and other divers instruments, all the way playing and making great melody." "The Lord Mayor's state barge," says Mr. Tytler, "led the way, adorned by flags and pennons hung with rich tapestries, and ornamented on the outside with scutcheons of metal, suspended on cloth of gold and silver. It was preceded by a wafter, or flat vessel, full of ordnance, on the deck of which a dragon pranced about furiously, twisting his tail and belching out wildfire. The Mayor's was followed by fifty other barges belonging to the trades and merchant-companies, all sumptuously decked with silk and arras, and having bands of music on board. On his lordship's left hand was seen a raft with an artificial mountain, having on its summit a wheel of gold, whereon was perched a white falcon crowned and surrounded by garlands of white and red roses. This was the Queen's device, and on the mountain sat virgins who sang and played sweetly. This civic cavalcade rowed down to Greenwich, where Anne appeared habited in cloth of gold, and, entering her barge, accompanied by her suite of ladies and gentlewomen, set forward to the Tower. Around her were many noblemen,—the Duke of Suffolk, the Marquis of Dorset, her father, the Earl of Wiltshire, with the Earls of Arundel, Derby, Rutland, Worcester, and others, all in their private barges. She thus rowed to the Tower, amidst the shouts of the people, and peals of ordnance from the ships which were anchored close in shore. On arriving at the fortress she was received by the Lord Chamberlain, and brought to the King, who met her at the postern, and kissed her. She then turned to the Mayor, and having gracefully thanked him and the citizens for the honour they had done her, entered the Tower." Less than three years afterwards the young and beautiful Queen was re-conducted over the same "silent highway," and landed a miserable prisoner at the Traitor's Gate of the Tower!

In the reign of Queen Elizabeth the Thames again became the scene of many a royal procession, when the regal barge was followed by attendant vessels, freighted with the household guards and bands of musicians. It was on the occasion of one

of her progresses on the Thames, that Sir Walter
Raleigh, from his prison-window in the Tower,
caught a glimpse of his royal mistress as she was
landing at Blackfriars. Arthur Gorges writes to
Cecil, in 1592,—" Upon a report of her Majesty's
being at Sir George Carew's, Sir Walter Raleigh,
having gazed and sighed a long time at his study-
window, from whence he might discern the barges
and boats about the Blackfriars' Stairs, suddenly
broke out into a great distemper, and swore that
his enemies had on purpose brought her Majesty
thither to break his gall in sunder with Tantalus'
torment, that when she went away he might see
death before his eyes, and many such like conceits.
And, as a man transported with passion, he swore to
Sir George Carew that he would disguise himself,
and get into a pair of oars, to ease his mind but
with a sight of the Queen."

In the following reign, on the occasion of the
marriage of the interesting Elizabeth, daughter
of James the First, with the Elector Palatine,
the Thames at Whitehall was the scene of extraordinary splendour and rejoicings. Winwood
tells us, in his " Memorials," that the fireworks
alone, which were exhibited in the gardens of
Whitehall on the banks of the Thames, cost nearly
eight thousand pounds. Among those who took
a share in the pageant, and who subsequently presented a masque at Court, were the members of
the Inner Temple and of Gray's Inn. " These
maskers," we are told, " with their whole train

in all triumphant manner and good order, took barge at Winchester Stairs, about seven of the clock that night, and rowed to Whitehall against the tide. The chief maskers went in the King's barge royally adorned, and plenteously furnished with a great number of great wax lights, that they alone made a glorious show: other gentlemen went in the Prince's barge, and certain other went in other fair barges, and were led by two admirals. Besides all these, they had four lusty warlike galleys to convoy and attend them; each barge and galley being replenished with store of torch-lights, made so rare and brave a show upon the water, as the like was never seen upon the Thames."

On the occasion of the marriage of Charles the First and Henrietta Maria, the Thames at London once more presented a stirring and splendid scene. The King had met his young bride at Dover: the marriage was consummated the same night at Canterbury, and on the 16th of June, 1625, Charles arrived with his bride in the capital. They had embarked on board the royal barge at Gravesend, from whence, attended by several of the magnificent vessels of the nobility, they proceeded up the river in regal state. From London Bridge to Whitehall the procession resembled a triumph. Thousands of vessels crowded the Thames; every lighter and barge was filled with spectators, and the banks appeared a moving mass of population. The guns roared from the Tower, as well as from the various ships in the neighbourhood; while the populace,

notwithstanding the plague raged around them, and
the rain fell in torrents, vied with each other in the
clamour of their gratulations. The King and Queen
were each dressed in green. The windows of the
barge, notwithstanding the pelting rain, were kept
open, Henrietta frequently acknowledging the shouts
of the populace by gracefully waving her hand. It
was observed that her head already reached the
King's shoulder, and that she was young enough to
grow taller.*

In the " Strafford Letters " will be found more
than one interesting notice of the unfortunate Archbishop Laud passing between his episcopal palace at
Lambeth and the palace of Whitehall. In one of
his letters to the Earl of Strafford, speaking of the
state of his health, he regrets that, in consequence
of his elevation to the See of Canterbury, he has
only to glide across the river in his barge, when
summoned either to the Court or the Star-chamber;
whereas, when Bishop of London, there were five
miles of rough road between the palace of Fulham
and Whitehall, the jolting over which in his coach
he describes as having been extremely beneficial to
his health.

In our notices of Whitehall we have mentioned
the particulars of the flight of the ill-fated James
the Second by night, when he was compelled to leave

* See Ellis's " Orig. Letters;" " The Life and Death of that
Matchless Mirror of Magnanimity, Henrietta Maria de Bourbon;"
and " A true Discourse of all the Royal Passages, Triumphs, and
Ceremonies, observed at the Contract and Marriage of the High
and Mighty Charles, King of Great Britain."   London, 1625.

his kingdom and his palace to the tender mercies of his Dutch son-in-law. The boat which lay in wait for him at the private water-entrance to the palace was rowed by only two watermen, and the only companions of his flight were Sir Edward Hales and two trustworthy servants. The misguided King had contrived to obtain possession of the Great Seal, and, as he passed down the river, he let it fall into the water. The circumstance possibly occasioned some temporary inconvenience, but the instrument was shortly afterwards recovered by a fisherman, and restored to the government.

We have mentioned also the stormy passage across the water to Lambeth, of the young and interesting Mary of Modena; when, with her infant slumbering in her arms, she passed silently and stealthily down the private stair-case at Whitehall, and blessing the howling of the wind and the raging of the waters, because they drowned the cries of her infant, stepped into the boat which was to convey her on her first stage from the inhospitable country of which she had seen but little, and which she had so little reason to leave with regret. With these notices we will quit our memoir of the Thames. Under the rule of our Dutch and German monarchs, we find it connected with scarcely an incident of the slightest interest; indeed its romance appears to have expired with the flight and fallen dynasty of the ill-fated Stuarts.

THE TOWER.

DESCRIPTION OF THE FORTRESS.—ITS PRINCIPAL BULWARKS.—TOWER
CHAPEL.—TRAITOR'S GATE.—KINGS WHO BUILT, ENLARGED, AND
LIVED IN IT.—DISTINGUISHED PRISONERS WHOSE MISFORTUNES
OR CRIMES HAVE THROWN A DEEP INTEREST OVER ITS DUNGEONS.

ASSOCIATED with almost every great and every
tragic event in the history of our country, there
is no building in Europe, which, to an English-
man, is replete with feelings and recollections of
such deep and varied interest as the Tower of London. Who is there, indeed, whose philosophy is so
rigid, or whose heart is so dead to every sentiment
of poetry and romance, as to be able to pass without
deep emotion through its dreary courts, every stone
of which, could they speak, would chronicle some
fearful crime, or some melancholy tale of suffering
and distress! Whether, indeed, we recall the time
when the Roman sentinel looked down from its
ramparts on the quiet waters below;—whether
we identify ourselves with the period when it was
the proud palace of our Norman sovereigns, di-
versified with terraced walks and verdant labyrinths;—whether we conjure up the shadows of
the headless and illustrious dead who have ex-

piated here their patriotism or their crimes; —
whether we recall the foul murders which have
been perpetrated in its fearful dungeons, — the
screams of tortured guilt, or the silent sufferings of
innocence and beauty,—this memorable pile cannot
fail to awaken a train of thought and reflection to
which no pen could do justice. But, before we
proceed to touch on the many heart-stirring events
with which the Tower is associated, it is necessary to
give a brief description of the ancient fortress itself.

The fact of a Roman fortress having existed on
the site of the present Tower of London has occasionally been called in question, but we believe
without reason ; nor would we willingly deprive it
of one of its most interesting associations. That
the White Tower, or, as it was formerly styled,
Cæsar's Tower,* was originally founded by Julius
Cæsar is unquestionably a fiction, the Roman emperor never having advanced so far as London in
either of his expeditions. On the other hand, that
the Romans had a fortification here, and indeed a
Mint, at a later period, there can be little doubt.

That the Keep or White Tower is the most

---

* Shakspeare more than once designates it as Cæsar's Tower.
In " Richard the Second," Act v. Sc. 1, we find,

This is the way

To Julius Cæsar's ill-erected Tower.

And, again, in " Richard the Third," Act iii. Sc. 1.

Prince.	Did Julius Cæsar build that place, my Lord ?
Gloster.	He did, my gracious Prince, begin that place ;
	Which, since, succeeding ages have re-edified.
Prince.	Is it upon record ? Or else reported
	Successively from age to age, he built it ?
Buckingham.	Upon record, my gracious Lord.

ancient part of the present fortress there can also
be no question. It was erected, about the year
1078, by William the Conqueror; the architect
being the celebrated Gundulph, Bishop of Rochester, who also built Rochester Castle. In the following reign, William Rufus surrounded the Tower
with a stone wall, and his successor, Henry the
First, made several important additions. Fitzste-
phen, who wrote about the year 1180, informs
us, "London hath on the east part a Tower Palatine, very large and very strong, whose court and
walls rise up from a deep foundation: *the mortar
is tempered with the blood of beasts.*"* When Fitz-
stephen penned these lines, little did he imagine
how symbolical were the materials, which ce-
mented the walls of the Conqueror, of the bloody
scenes which were destined hereafter to be enacted
in its secret dungeons.

> Ye Towers of Julius, London's lasting shame,
> By many a foul and midnight murder fed!

The principal entrance to the Tower is by three
gates to the west, one within the other. The first
of these opens into a small court, on the right of
which is the Lions' Tower, where the royal mena-
gerie was formerly kept; the second opens to a stone
bridge built over the moat; and at the further end is
the third gate, which is defended by a portcullis,
and is otherwise much stronger than the others, and
where, for centuries, the principal guard of the

* " Arcem palatinam maximam et fortissimam, cujus areæ muri
à fundamento profundissimo exsurgunt, cemento cum sanguine ani-
malium temperato."

Tower, consisting of soldiers and warders, has always
been stationed.

There still exists a curious and ancient ceremony, connected with the opening and closing of
the Tower gates. In the morning, the yeoman-
porter, attended by a sergeant's guard, proceeds to
the Governor's house, where the keys of the fortress are delivered to him. From hence he proceeds to open the three gates, and, as the keys pass
and repass, the soldiers on duty lower their arms.
The yeoman-porter then returns to the innermost
gate, and calls on the warders in waiting to take in
Queen Victoria's keys, on which the gate is opened,
and the keys are lodged in the warder's hall till
night-time. At the closing of the gates, the same
formalities are used as in the morning. As soon
as the gates are shut, the yeoman-porter, followed
by a sergeant's guard, proceeds to the main guard,
who are all under arms, with the officer upon duty
at their head. The usual challenge from the main
guard is, "Who comes here?" To which the yeoman-porter answers, "The Keys." The challenger
returns, "Pass, Keys." As they pass, the main
guard lower their arms, on which the yeoman-porter exclaims, "God save Queen Victoria," and the
guards answer, with loud voices, "Amen." The
yeoman-porter then proceeds with his guard to the
Governor's house, where the keys are lodged for
the night.

The principal bulwarks in the Tower of London
are the White or Cæsar's Tower; the Bell Tower;

the Beauchamp or Cobham Tower; the Devereux Tower; the Bowyer's Tower; the Jewel Tower; the Broad Arrow Tower; the Salt Tower; the Record or Wakefield Tower; and the Bloody Tower. Some other towers might be mentioned of ancient date, many of which may have been the dark scenes of torture and death, but it is not known that any particular interest is attached to them. The site of those we have mentioned, and of which we are about to give a brief account, may be traced by the annexed curious plan of the Tower, taken from a survey made in the reign of Queen Elizabeth. By a document, drawn up in 1641, shewing the manner in which the different buildings are appropriated, it appears that as many as eleven towers were used as "*prison lodgings.*"

We have already mentioned that the WHITE TOWER, or Keep, is the most ancient part of the fortress. This fine building is of a quadrangular form. The walls are of vast thickness: and at each of its four angles is a lofty turret, one of which was formerly used by the learned Flamstead as an observatory. Besides its antiquity, the White Tower is especially an object of interest, as having been formerly an integral part of the ancient palace of the Kings of England. Its chapel, its hall, and its council-chamber still remain. In addition to some capacious vaults beneath its foundations, the White Tower consists of three stories, each of which has its particular interest. The ground, or basement story, consists of three apartments; two of which are of considerable size, while the third is not a little remarkable from the peculiarity of its vaulted roof, and the appearance which it presents of great antiquity. That these gloomy chambers were for centuries used as prisons there can be little doubt. Here, in the reign of Queen Mary, were imprisoned several unfortunate persons who were implicated in Sir Thomas Wyatt's rebellion, and here, if we are to place any credit in tradition, Sir Walter Raleigh composed his "History of the World." These interesting rooms,—on the walls of which the inscriptions left by more than one unhappy criminal may still be traced,—are now, to the disgrace of the Government, used as store-rooms for arms, and a magazine for gunpowder.

The second story in the White Tower, besides two other apartments, consists of the beautiful chapel dedicated to St. John the Evangelist, which rises to the roof of the Tower. It was here that our sovereigns and their households for centuries offered up their devotions. Formerly, through many a reign, it was redecorated and rebeautified with religious care and at regal expense; but it has been left to the present tasteless age to convert it into an emporium for dirty records and musty parchments! Such is the fate, in the nineteenth century, of the most interesting and perfect specimen of the Norman style of architecture in England!

In the uppermost story of the White Tower, the apartments are far loftier and more imposing, and

also have all the appearance of being of an ancient
date. The largest of them—the roof of which consists of vast beams of timber supported by massive
pillars of wood — is deeply interesting, as being,
according to tradition, the famous council-chamber
where our sovereigns sat at debate when they
held their Court in the regal fortress. Here it was
that Richard the Second, clad in all the appurtenances of royalty, and surrounded by " Dukes,
prelates, Earls, and Barons," took his crown from
his devoted head and delivered it to the usurper
Bolingbroke! Here occurred that striking scene at
the council-table, when the Protector Gloucester
bared his shrivelled arm, and when, striking his
hand upon the table, the guard rushed in, and hurried the unfortunate Hastings to the block; and
lastly, here it was that Anne Boleyn stood, serene
and beautiful, before her judges, on that memorable occasion when every cheek was blanched and
every eye was wet but her own! And yet,—shame
on the age,— this apartment also has been converted into a Record Office!

The private apartments of the palace, where for
nearly five hundred years the sovereigns of England
experienced their joys, their sorrows, or their bridal
pleasures, were situated at the south-east angle of
the fortress, having an immediate communication
with the chapel and the state rooms in the White
Tower. The bedchamber and the private closet of
the sovereign were in the Lanthorn Tower, of which
no vestige now remains, but which formerly ad-

joined the great gallery, and overlooked the private garden of the palace. The position of these buildings may be easily understood by a reference to the annexed plan, and it may be interesting to bear the locality in the mind's eye, as hereafter we shall find them the scene of more than one historical, or romantic incident, in the annals of the Tower.

Immediately on the left hand, after entering the fortress, is the BELL TOWER, which derives its name from containing the alarm bell of the garrison. Here was confined the pious and venerable John Fisher, Bishop of Rochester, for refusing to take the oath of supremacy to Henry the Eighth, and from hence he was led forth to the scaffold on Tower Hill. The apartment in which he was imprisoned was probably the gloomy and vaulted room on the basement floor. His dungeon is described as miserable in the extreme; and here he was allowed to remain, though in his eightieth year, with no covering but rags, and these scarcely sufficient to hide his nakedness. Over a chimney-piece in an apartment adjoining the Bell Tower, has recently been discovered the following interesting inscription :—" *Upon the twenty daye of June, in the yere of our Lord a thousande five hundred three score and five, was the Right honorable countes of Lennox Grace commettede prysoner to thys lodgynge for the marreage of her sonne, My Lord Henry Darnle and the Quene of Scotland. Here is their names that do wayte upon her noble Grace in thys place. M. Elizh. Hussey, M. Jane Baily, M. Elizh. Chamberlain, M.*

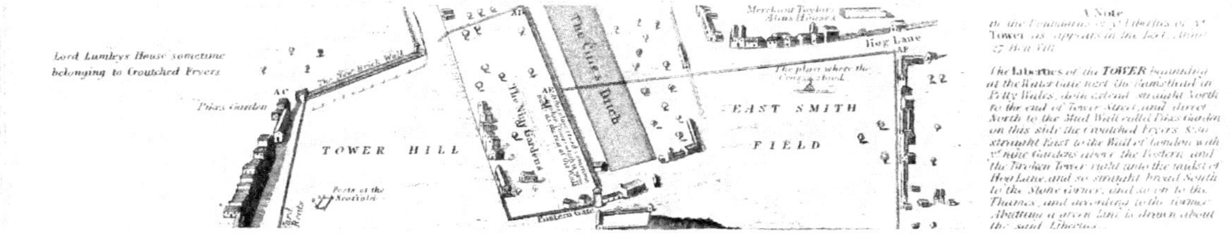
Lord Lumleys House sometime
belonging to Croutched Fryers
The New Brick Wall
TOWER HILL
Posts at the Scaffold
The Cities Ditch
Postern Gate
EAST SMITH FIELD
Merchant Taylors Alms Houses
Hog Lane
A Note

joined the great gallery, and overlooked the private garden of the palace. The position of these buildings may be easily understood by a reference to the annexed plan, and it may be interesting to bear the locality in the mind's eye, as hereafter we shall find them the scene of more than one historical, or romantic incident, in the annals of the Tower.

Immediately on the left hand, after entering the fortress, is the BELL TOWER, which derives its name from containing the alarm bell of the garrison. Here was confined the pious and venerable John Fisher, Bishop of Rochester, for refusing to take the oath of supremacy to Henry the Eighth, and from hence he was led forth to the scaffold on Tower Hill. The apartment in which he was imprisoned was probably the gloomy and vaulted room on the basement floor. His dungeon is described as miserable in the extreme; and here he was allowed to remain, though in his eightieth year, with no covering but rags, and these scarcely sufficient to hide his nakedness. Over a chimney-piece in an apartment adjoining the Bell Tower, has recently been discovered the following interesting inscription :—" *Upon the twenty daye of June, in the yere of our Lord a thousande five hundred three score and five, was the Right honorable countes of Lennox Grace commettede prysoner to thys lodgynge for the marreage of her sonne, My Lord Henry Darnle and the Quene of Scotland. Here is their names that do wayte upon her noble Grace in thys place. M. Elizh. Hussey, M. Jane Baily, M. Elizh. Chamberlain, M.*

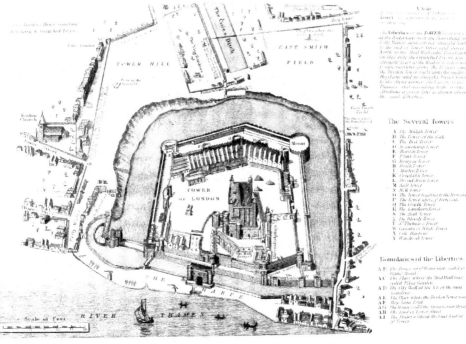

A Note

The Liberties of the TOWER beginning at the Bulve Gate near the Bramditch to Little Tower ditch and so straight North to the end of Tower Street and down North to the Mud Wall called East Smithfield and so unto the Crooked Tree it was straight East to the End of London wall & so northward across the Ditch and the Brazen Tower right unto the end of Hog Lane and so straight West Church to the Stone cross and down to the Thames and ascending to the same. Position in green line is shown about the said Liberties.

The Several Towers

A The Midak Tower
B The Tower of the Hall
C The Bell Tower
D Bauchamp Tower
E Develin Tower
F Flint Tower
G Bowyer Tower
H Brick Tower
I Martin Tower
K Constable Tower
L Broad Arrow Tower
M Salt Tower
N Well Tower
O The Tower leading to the Iron Gate
P The Tower above y.e Iron Gate
Q The Cradle Tower
R The Lanthorn Tower
S The Bell Tower
T The Bloody Tower
V S.t Thomas's Tower
W Graces or Wake Tower
X Cole Harbour
Y Win Arrak Tower

Boundaries of the Liberties

A B The House or Water side called y.e Bulve Hotel
A C The Place where the Mud Wall was called Flagg Garden
A D The City Wall at the N.t of the was Liberties
A E The Place where the Brazen Tower was
A F Hog Lane End
A G The House called the Stone cross Rose
A H The End of Tower Street
A I The Stairs without the East End of y.e Tower

THE TOWER AND ITS LIBERTIES.

Robert Partington, Edward Cuffin, anno Domini,
1566."

According to tradition, it was in the Bell Tower
that Queen Elizabeth was lodged when she was
committed to the Tower by her sister, Queen
Mary. This, however, could not have been the
case, as we are expressly told that her prison adjoined the Queen's garden, where, when her health
began to suffer from close confinement, she was
occasionally allowed to take the air. The Bell
Tower has long formed a part of the lodgings of
the Lieutenant of the Tower, now the residence
of the Lieutenant-Governor. This latter building
was erected in the reign of Henry the Eighth,
and contains little that is interesting, with the exception of an apartment on the second floor, in
which Guy Fawkes, and the other conspirators
concerned in the Gunpowder Plot, underwent their
examination. A bust of James the First, as well
as a marble monument in the wall, — giving an
account of the conspiracy, in Latin, and the names
of the conspirators and the examining commissioners,—are still preserved in the apartment.

The BEAUCHAMP or COBHAM TOWER appears to
have been erected about the reign of King John,
and is highly interesting, as having been apparently the principal state prison in the fortress, and
the spot where the most illustrious criminals were
probably immured. In the reign of Henry the
Eighth it was known as the Beauchamp Tower;
but in consequence of some of the Cobhams having

been confined there for their share in Sir Thomas
Wyatt's rebellion, it afterwards became more familiarly known as the Cobham Tower. The principal
apartment, which is of large size, is on the first
floor, with two small cells adjoining it, in which,
probably, the prisoners were secured for the night.
It is difficult to enter this interesting apartment
without feelings of deep emotion. The walls are
literally covered with inscriptions, engraved by the
hands of a succession of unhappy prisoners,—some
of them bearing names familiar to us by their misfortunes and violent deaths,—others breathing the
purest piety,—others bewailing in some touching
sentence their miserable lot. For instance, let us
take the following inscription by Charles Bailly, a
young man who involved himself in the ruined fortunes of Mary Queen of Scots;—

"*Principium sapientiæ timor Dei, I.H.S. X.P.S.
Be friend to one. Be enemye to none. Anno D.,
1571, 10 Sept. The most unhappy man in the world
is he that is not pacient in adversities ; for men are
not killed with the adversities they have ; but with the
impatience which they suffer.*

"*Tout vient apoient, quy peult attendre. Gli sos-
piri ne son testimoni veri dell' angoscia mia. Æt. 29.
Charles Bailly.*"

Again, how touching is the following inscription,
the original of which is in Italian! "*Since fortune
hath chosen that my hope should go to the wind to complain, I wish the time were destroyed, my planet being
ever sad and unpropitious. William Tyrrel, 1541.*"

Over the fire-place is an inscription, in his own hand, by the unfortunate Philip, Earl of Arundel, who languished here for many years, till he was released by death on the 19th of November, 1595. The inscription is as follows :—

Quanto plus afflictionis pro Christo in hoc sæculo, tanto plus gloriæ cum Christo in futuro. *Arundell. June* 22, 1587.

Gloria et honore eum coronasti, Domine,
In Memoria eterna erit justus.
At . . .

Lastly, on the site of the fire-place, is a well-executed piece of sculpture, by John Dudley, Earl of Warwick, (eldest son of John, Duke of Northumberland,) who was imprisoned for his share in the rash attempt to place the crown on the head of his sister-in-law, Lady Jane Grey. His name, in the spelling of the age, is encircled by a border of oak-sprigs, roses, and other flowers, and above it is his family badge, of the lion, and bear and ragged staff. There is also an inscription of four lines in verse, part of which is obliterated. The Earl was afterwards arraigned for high treason in Westminster Hall, and, together with his father and the Marquis of Northampton, was condemned to death, but died shortly afterwards in the Tower.

The word JANE, on the walls of the principal apartment in the Beauchamp Tower, has occasionally excited great attention, as being supposed to be the autograph of the beautiful and accomplished Lady Jane Grey. From her sex, however, her high rank, and her near relationship to the Queen, it is far more likely that she was imprisoned either in the royal apartments, or in the private residence of the Lieutenant of the Tower; though, on the other hand, the name may not impossibly have been engraved either by her husband, Lord Guildford Dudley, a fellow prisoner in the Tower with his brother, the Earl of Warwick, or by some other affectionate relative or adherent. The following couplet is known to have been written by Lady Jane Grey, on the wall of the apartment in which she was confined, but unfortunately no trace of it can now be discovered :—

> Non aliena putes homini quæ obtingere possunt,
> Sors hodierna mihi, cras erit illa tibi.

The Beauchamp Tower, like every other interesting part of the ancient fortress, has been converted to a strange purpose. That famous apartment, the walls of which formerly listened to the dying prayers and groans of many an illustrious criminal, is now condemned to the unseemly uses, and resounds to the boisterous joviality, of a mess-room. There seems but little prospect of better times; let us, however, hope and pray that a government may yet spring up with sufficient taste and liberality to erect a proper repository for our public records; to clear the fine old towers of the present lumber; to restore them, internally as well as externally, to their ancient architecture; and to gratify, not only our own countrymen, but men of taste and feeling of all countries, by admission to those time-honoured apartments, which, in point of historical and romantic interest, are not to be surpassed by any building in Europe.

The DEVEREUX, or, as it was anciently called, the DEVELIN TOWER, is situated at the north-west angle of the fortress, and seems for centuries to have been set apart as a state-prison; the appearance of which, with its massive walls, its gloomy cells, and iron-gratings, it still partially retains. It bears its present name from having been the prison of Robert Devereux, Earl of Essex, the ill-fated favourite of Queen Elizabeth. It has every appearance of being of a much earlier date than the Beauchamp Tower.

The BOWYER'S TOWER derives its name from having been formerly the residence of the master and provider of the King's bows. Of this Tower, the only remains are the basement story, which consists of a vaulted and gloomy apartment, the walls of which also are of great thickness. According to tradition, it was in this dismal chamber, that George, Duke of Clarence, was drowned in a butt of Malmsey.

The JEWEL TOWER, or, as it was styled in the days of Queen Elizabeth, the MARTIN TOWER, flanks the north-east angle of the Tower. It derives its name from having been long the repository of the Regalia, which were formerly kept in a small building on the south-side of the White Tower. It was here that Blood made his famous attempt to steal the crown. Of this ancient tower also, little is left but the basement floor, the roof of which is vaulted and groined in the elegant style of architecture that prevailed in the reign of Henry the Third. It was formerly one of the principal prison-lodgings in the Tower, and, till modern alterations barbarously swept them away, some interesting inscriptions, left by unfortunate prisoners, were to be traced on its walls.

The BROAD ARROW TOWER, which consists of two stories, appears to be of the same date as the Beauchamp Tower, and also formed one of the ancient prisons of the fortress. The most interesting part is the basement floor, which consists of a dismal chamber, and a still more dismal cell, about six feet long and about four feet wide. On the walls are still to be traced some interesting inscriptions, engraved by the guilty, the penitent, or the oppressed.

The SALT TOWER, a small circular tower, formerly adjoined the east end of what was called the King's gallery, and probably formed an integral part of the ancient palace. The ground floor consists of a vaulted dungeon, connected by a small spiral staircase of stone with the upper chamber. On the walls of the former there still exist many melancholy memorials of those who languished within this gloomy prison house.

The RECORD TOWER, formerly known as the HALL TOWER, and sometimes as the WAKEFIELD TOWER, is a large circular building, the lower part of which is apparently of the reign of William Rufus, and, with the exception of the White Tower, is unquestionably the most ancient part of the fortress. In this Tower, from the reign of Henry the

Eighth, and probably from a still earlier period, the ancient records of the kingdom have been preserved. If we are to place any faith in tradition, it was in the fine and lofty chamber on the second story, that the "meek usurper," Henry the Sixth, met with his untimely end.

We might mention several other towers which anciently formed a part of the bulwarks of the royal fortress, but either all remains of them have passed away, or they possess no particular interest. We will content ourselves, therefore, with noticing not the least remarkable one,—the Bloody Tower.

The BLOODY TOWER, formerly called the GARDEN TOWER, is situated close to the Record Tower, and from the style of architecture, appears to have been built about the reign of Edward the Third. This tower derives its chief interest from the popular belief that exists, that in one of its gloomy chambers Edward the Fifth, and his infant brother Richard, Duke of York, were smothered by order of their inhuman uncle Richard, Duke of Gloucester; and from this circumstance it has been said to derive its name of the Bloody Tower. In the reign of Charles the Second, some workmen who were employed in the Tower, discovered the bones of two youths, corresponding in size with the two children of Edward the Fourth, and it has generally been supposed that the spot where they were found was beneath the basement story of the Bloody Tower. This, however, is not the case: the real spot where they were discovered being at the foot of an ancient staircase on the south side of the White Tower. There are many circumstances, indeed, which lead us to question whether the popular story of the murder of the young princes is not altogether an idle fiction ; but even admitting the fact that they met with an untimely end, there is no reason to imagine that the Bloody Tower was the scene of the tragedy. There is every reason, indeed, to be-lieve that the supposition is the mere invention of more recent times. It was not till the latter end of the reign of Queen Elizabeth, that the Bloody Tower received its present name, and as Mr. Bailey conjectures, in his history of the Tower of London, it is far more likely to have been so called from having been the scene of one of the many " foul and midnight murders " which disgraced the sixteenth century, and not improbably from the tragical end of Henry, Earl of Northumberland, who destroyed himself in the Tower, in 1585, but whose death was popularly attributed to the hand of the midnight assassin.

Perhaps the most interesting spot in the ancient fortress is the " Tower Chapel," erected in the reign of Edward the First, and not inappropriately dedi-cated to St. Peter ad Vincula. Who is there that has ever entered that narrow portal, through which so many of the headless dead have been carried in their bloody shrouds to their last home, without feelings of the deepest emotion? How many high hopes ! what turbulent passions ! what fair forms ! rest calmly beneath our feet !

After life's fitful fever they sleep well!

Here for a time rested the headless trunk of Sir
Thomas More, and here lie the remains of the
amiable and undaunted martyr, John Fisher, Bishop
of Rochester. In front of the altar sleep the two
ill-fated wives of Henry the Eighth, the gentle and
beautiful Anne Boleyn, and the no less beautiful
adulteress, Catherine Howard; and between them,
—in the same grave with his turbulent and ambitious brother, Lord Seymour, of Sudley, and side
by side with his powerful rival, John Dudley, Duke
of Northumberland, — sleeps the great Protector
Duke of Somerset.

Not far off rest the headless remains of George,
Lord Rochford, who was involved in the fate of his
innocent sister, Anne Boleyn; and here also lies,
the wise and powerful minister of Henry the Eighth,
Thomas Cromwell, Earl of Essex. It is singular
that in no history have I been able to trace the burial-place of the gifted and ill-fated Lady Jane
Grey, or of her ambitious father, Henry Grey, Duke
of Suffolk, who was executed a few days after his
accomplished daughter. As it is certain, however,
that her young husband, Lord Guildford Dudley,
who was beheaded on the same day with her, was
interred in the Tower Chapel, it is not improbable
that Lady Jane, and her turbulent father, were laid
in the same grave.

In the afternoon of the day on which death terminated his dreadful sufferings, was committed, almost stealthily, to the earth, in the Tower Chapel

the remains of the accomplished courtier and poet,
Sir Thomas Overbury, the victim of the subtle
poisons administered to him in his dungeon in the
Tower by the agents of Frances Countess of Essex.
Here lies the mutilated corpse of Robert Devereux,
Earl of Essex, the ill-fated favourite of Queen Elizabeth; and, under the communion-table, reposes
one no less gifted and ambitious, the unfortunate
James Duke of Monmouth. Lastly, here lie buried
more than one of the gallant and devoted men, who
lost their lives in the cause of the ill-fated Stuarts.
Here repose, in one grave, the intrepid Lord Balmerino, the gay and handsome Lord Kilmarnock,
and the arch-traitor, Simon, Lord Lovat.

Pitied by gentle minds Kilmarnock died,
The brave, Balmerino, were on thy side.

Some years since, on removing the pavement of
the chapel, their coffin-plates were discovered, and
are now preserved in the building. They bear the
following inscriptions:—

Arthurus
Dominus de Balmerino
Decollatus 18° die Augusti 1746.
Ætatis suæ 58°.

Willielmus
Comes de Kilmarnock
Decollatus 18° die Augusti 1746.
Ætatis suæ 42°.

Simon Dominus
Frazer de Lovat
Decollat. Apr. 9. 1747.
Ætat. suæ 80.

In the days when our sovereigns and their house-

holds performed their orisons in the Tower Chapel,
we find it constantly re-beautified and re-decorated
by successive monarchs. It then contained rich
stalls for the King and Queen; and there were two
chancels, one dedicated to the Holy Virgin, and the
other to St. Peter. It was adorned with a fine cross
and with pictures and statues of saints; its two
altars were profusely ornamented, and the windows
filled with beautiful stained glass. Its appearance,
alas! has been sadly changed for the worse. It is
now deformed by modern pews, and in vain do we
search for any trace of the magnificence of the past.
But that which principally disappoints us on entering the Tower Chapel, is the absence of all memorials to the illustrious dead who sleep beneath our
feet, and whose misfortunes have been familiar to
us from our childhood. Not a single one is to be
found! We still hope, however, that the time may
come when this interesting spot will be thrown open
to the public, and that some memorial will be
raised, however simple, to point out the names of
those who rest below, and the spot where they
severally lie.

But though the resting-places of the headless
dead remain unrecorded, there is more than one
interesting memorial to persons more fortunate or
less ambitious, who died peaceably in their quiet
homes. There is a fine monument to Sir Richard
Blount, and his son, Sir Michael, and another to
Sir Richard Cholmondely, who fought under the
Earl of Surrey at Flodden Field. All three, in

their respective lifetimes, held the appointment of
Lieutenant of the Tower. But the monument to
which we turn with the greatest interest, is a small
tablet of stone in the floor, at the upper end of
the nave, to the memory of Talbot Edwards, the old
man who was gagged and stabbed by the ruffian
Blood, when the latter made his famous attempt to
seize the crown jewels. "*Here lieth ye body of
Talbot Edwards, gent., late keeper of His Ma^{ty's} Regalia, who dyed ye 30th of September, 1674, aged 80
yeares and 9 moneths.*" The old man lived to
see himself neglected, and his assailant pensioned!

The open space in front of the Chapel is scarcely
less interesting than the chapel itself. When the
rage of the Protector, Richard Duke of Gloucester,
sent the unfortunate Lord Hastings from the Council-table to the block, "without time for confession
or repentance," it was here that he was hurried by
the guard, and beheaded on a "log of timber,"
which his executioners found conveniently at hand.
Here the lovely Anne Boleyn submitted her slender
neck to the stroke of the executioner; here the
no less beautiful Queen Catherine Howard was beheaded, together with the unprincipled Lady Rochford, the confidante of her amours; and here perished the pious and gentle Lady Jane Grey.
Lastly, it was here that the Earl of Essex, the
ill-fated favourite of Queen Elizabeth, submitted
serenely and piously to his fate. In the "yard belonging to the chapel" also lie buried Sir Francis
Weston, Henry Norris, and William Brereton, the

three reputed lovers of Anne Boleyn, who were involved in her ruin, and who were beheaded a few days before her, on Tower Hill.

Before we proceed to notice some of the more distinguished prisoners, whose misfortunes or whose crimes have thrown so dark and deep an interest over the dungeons of the Tower, let us pause for a moment at the famous Traitor's Gate. As we look down upon that gloomy water-entrance, what a crowd of melancholy recollections rushes to our minds! How many illustrious persons, who wantoned so lately in the full pride of pomp and power, have been hurried through this dark passage, never more to return! How often, when its dripping walls have received the armed barge, and have echoed back the last melancholy splash of the advancing oars, has the increasing darkness sent the colour from the cheek of the prisoner, and struck terror into his heart. Within the last year or two, the ancient wooden gates, blackened by age and the action of the water, have been removed from the Traitor's Gate. Whether they have been converted into fire-wood, or turned to some baser purpose, we know not; but we do know, that, in any other country but England, they would have been religiously preserved as a priceless and most interesting relic of the past.

The first person who is recorded to have been committed a prisoner to the Tower was the famous soldier-prelate, Ralph Flambard, Bishop of Durham, whose extortions and oppressions rendered him so

unpopular as minister and first favourite of William
Rufus. Uniting in his own person the appointments
of High Treasurer, Justiciary, and Bishop of Durham,
he fell at once, on the accession of Henry the First,
from the highest position which could be held by a
subject to be an inmate of a prison.   Here he continued to lead that life of revelry and intemperance
which had distinguished him in the days of his
greatness.   At length, we are told, his friends
having contrived to convey a rope to him in a
flagon of wine, he let himself down from the tower
in which he was imprisoned, and, with the exception of a few bruises, reached the ground uninjured.
He subsequently managed to reach the court of
Robert of Normandy, whom he afterwards assisted
in his fruitless endeavours to obtain possession of
the English throne.

It is not till the succeeding reign of King
Stephen, that we have any positive evidence of the
Tower having been a royal residence.   It is certain,
however, that this monarch was residing here in
1140, when, according to William of Malmesbury,
he kept his court in the Tower, during Whitsuntide,
with great magnificence.   In this reign we find the
custody of the Tower conferred on Geffrey de Mandeville, Earl of Essex, grandson of the powerful
Geffrey de Mandeville, who had accompanied the
Conqueror to England.   De Mandeville proved a
traitor to his master, and retained the fortress for
the Empress Maude; nor was it till he was arrested
and made prisoner at St. Alban's, in 1143, that the

Tower again came into the possession of King Stephen.

During the reign of Henry the Second we find but little interest connected with the Tower, nor is it ascertained that he ever kept his court here. It may be mentioned, however, that in the early period of this reign it was in the custody of the celebrated Thomas à Becket.

When Richard the First departed for the Holy Land, in 1189, he conferred the important post of custodian of the Tower on his Chancellor, Longchamp, Bishop of Ely. Foreseeing, perhaps, the opposition which he was likely to encounter in his career of haughtiness and oppression, the Bishop raised round the fortress an "embattled wall of stone," far stronger than that of William Rufus, and surrounded the whole with a "broade and deepe ditch." At length his repeated acts of violence and extortion having completely incensed the nation, a convocation of barons and prelates was summoned, by the King's brother, Prince John, to meet at Reading, with the view of concerting measures for opposing the Regent in his tyrannical career. The result was, that he was formally cited to appear before them, on the Monday following, at Loddon Bridge. Instead of obeying the summons, he hastened to the Tower, where he shut himself up with his retainers, and prepared to stand the siege with which he was threatened. However, finding himself environed by a powerful army, and forseeing that resistance was of little avail, he ap-

peared at night on the walls of the eastern part of
the fortress, and held a parley with the principal
nobles who headed the conspiracy. His safety
having been guaranteed to him, with permission to
retire to the Continent, he consented to surrender
the Tower, which was immediately entered by
Prince John and his followers. The charge of the
fortress was forthwith conferred on the Archbishop
of Rouen, in whose custody it remained till the
return of King Richard from the East.

King John appears to have frequently held his
court at the Tower, and, following the example of
his predecessors, that unhappy monarch added considerably to the strength of the fortress. It underwent a siege by the Barons in 1215, and when the
Magna Charta was signed at Runnimede, in that
year, we find it still in the possession of the King.
One of the stipulations of the Charter, was the surrender of the Tower of London to the Barons, till
the King should have fulfilled the articles of agree-
ment which he had signed with his people, and accordingly it was delivered in trust to the Archbishop
of Canterbury.

Henry the Third not only added considerably to
the strength of the Tower, but it was also to his
taste for the fine arts that his successors were indebted for that internal comfort and magnificence
which continued to render this palatial fortress a
suitable residence for the sovereigns of England,
even as late as the reign of James the First. As a
specimen of the architectural taste of Henry the

Third, we may mention the beautiful chapel erected under his auspices in the White Tower. In the records of the period are numerous entries of the sums spent by Henry in beautifying and strengthening the Tower; comprising the cost of statues and paintings, of which unfortunately no relic remains to us. It is especially directed that the King's chamber of state shall be decorated with paintings from the story of Antiochus.

As the Tower was the spot where Henry passed the happy days of his minority, so also was it the scene of more than one of his fierce struggles with his imperious barons, and of more than one eventful incident in his chequered career. Here it was that his sister Isabel was kept in restraint till her marriage with the Emperor Frederick, in 1235; here the unfortunate King sought for safety during his contest with his powerful nobles; here, at one period, we find him retreating in the dead of night, and at another presiding over festivals of gorgeous magnificence; and, lastly, here it was that he signed those humiliating conditions, which delivered over, not only the Tower of London, but every other fortress in the kingdom, to the custody of the Barons. From this period the Tower remained in the possession of that domineering faction, till, at the battle of Evesham, the success of the King's gallant son, afterwards Edward the First, restored the royal authority.

During this reign we find more than one person of distinction a prisoner in the Tower. Here, in

1232,—to the very fortress of which he had recently been the dreaded governor,—was committed
that powerful Baron and distinguished soldier and
statesman, Hubert de Burgh, Earl of Kent. The
valuable services which he had rendered to King
Richard and King John, and even to Henry himself,
deserved a very different requital. In 1209 we find
him sent abroad to negotiate a treaty of marriage
between King John and a Princess of Portugal, and
two years afterwards he was made Chamberlain of
the King's household, Warden of the Marches of
Wales, Sheriff of Cornwall, and Governor of the
Castles of Launceston and Dover. The following
year he was sent on an embassy to France to de-
mand restitution of the Duchy of Normandy, and
in 1215 he was one of the Commissioners who
treated with the Barons, at Runnimede, on the
occasion of the signing of the Magna Charta. As
a soldier, his services were no less eminent than
as a statesman. In 1216, when Lewis, the French
Dauphin, invaded England at the invitation of the
rebels, we find him successfully defending the Castle
of Dover against a powerful force, although the
garrison consisted only of his own servants and a
hundred and forty soldiers. Again, a short time
afterwards, when a large fleet, under the conduct of
the celebrated Eustace the Monk, was approaching
the shores of Kent, with supplies from France, the
Earl set sail from Dover, and, though having only
eight ships under his command, dispersed the
enemy, and took captive and beheaded their leader.

At the death of King John, De Burgh hastened to
serve his young sovereign, Henry the Third, with
the same zeal and alacrity with which he had served
his late master; nor at first had he any reason to
complain that his services were rewarded with a
niggard hand. The accession of honours, indeed,
which yearly flowed in to him; the variety of appointments which he held under the crown; and
his numerous castles and vast wealth, almost exceed
belief. In 1219, on the death of William Marshall,
Earl of Pembroke, he was appointed Guardian of
the King and Kingdom; the following year he married Margaret, sister of the King of Scotland; and,
in 1228, was created Earl of Kent, and appointed
Chief Justiciary of England for life: lastly, in 1231,
he was made Chief Justiciary of Ireland, and Constable of the Castles of Odiham and Windsor, and
of the Tower of London. Such an accumulation of
dignities and honours could not fail to raise him
many enemies. By degrees they contrived to under-
mine him in the favour of his sovereign, and, in
1232, he was deprived of all his honours, appointments, and estates, and compelled to seek refuge in
the sanctuary of Merton Priory, in Surrey. From
hence his enemies followed him to a residence of
the Bishop of London, in Essex, where, under a
promise of protection, he had taken up his residence. Hearing that an armed force was approaching to seize his person, he repaired to an adjoining
chapel, and when his enemies entered, he was found
standing before the altar with the cross and host in

his hands. These were immediately wrested from him; he was dragged from the sanctuary, and with every circumstance of ignominy, was carried, with his legs tied, on a wretched jade to the Tower. It would occupy many pages to follow the subsequent miserable fortunes of this once powerful minister. The treatment which he experienced in the Tower, where he was loaded with chains, and exposed to every indignity which the malice of his enemies could devise ; — his restoration to the sanctuary in Essex, occasioned by the Bishop of London threatening excommunication to all those who had dared to violate the sacred privileges of the church ;—the solitary nights which he spent at the altar, deprived of food and of all intercourse with his kind ;—the starvation which eventually compelled him to deliver himself up to his enemies ;—his re-imprisonment in the Tower ;— the cruelties to which he was subsequently exposed in the dungeons of Devizes Castle ;—his romantic escape ;—the attempts which were again made to starve him to death when he sought refuge before the high altar of the church of St. John, at Devizes ;—and lastly, his being carried in safety to the borders of Wales by a band of devoted friends ; —all these incidents partake rather of the character of romance than of a matter-of-fact history of real life. De Burgh subsequently leagued himself with those nobles who took up arms to redress the wrongs of their country, and, being included in the general amnesty at Gloucester, was restored to a great portion of his estates. He died in 1243, and was buried in the church of the Friars Preachers, in London.

Another unfortunate prisoner in the Tower about this period, was Griffin, eldest son of Llewellin, Prince of Wales. Deprived of his birth-right, and delivered up to the King of England by the treachery of his younger brother, he passed four miserable years a prisoner in the fortress of his hereditary foe. At length, having found means to elude the vigilance of his keepers, the unfortunate Prince contrived to form a rope of the clothes and furniture of his bed, which he made fast to the battlements of the turret in which he was confined. In the dead of night he made the perilous trial. In his descent, however, the rope broke, and the next morning he was discovered a lifeless corpse, with his head and neck crushed beneath his shoulders.

The last prisoner of any celebrity who was confined to the Tower in the reign of Henry the Third, was William Marish, or de Marescis, who, though descended from a long line of ancestors, was content to establish himself as the chief of a band of daring freebooters in the Isle of Lundy, where he continued to be long an object of terror to the inhabitants of the western coast of England. At length, notwithstanding the strength of his island stronghold, having been overpowered and taken, he was confined with four or five of his most formidable associates in the Tower, where he was loaded with irons and committed to the securest dungeon. His fate was such as he must have anticipated. Having been hanged, and his body disembowelled, his quarters were sent to be exposed in the four principal cities of the kingdom.

It was in accordance with the martial tastes of Edward the First to add considerably to the strength of the Tower. He greatly enlarged the moat, and threw up fresh outworks, especially towards the western entrance; and, indeed, since his time, but little has been added to the military defences of the celebrated fortress. One would wish to be able to identify the Tower with the personal history of the "mighty victor," but it would seem that he seldom held his court within its walls. Nevertheless, the history of the Tower in this reign is not devoid of interest. Here it was, when the unfortunate Jews were accused of adulterating the coin of the realm, that six hundred were huddled together at one time, of whom two hundred and eighty were hung in London alone. Here, too, the conquest of Wales, and the subjection of Scotland, conducted many a noble and knightly prisoner; here the timid Baliol wept over his fallen greatness, and here languished the flower of Scottish chivalry, comprising the Earls of Athol, Ross, and Monteith, Comyn of Badenoch, Richard Syward, John Fitz-Geffrey, Andrew de Moravia, John de Inch Martin, David Fitz-Patric de Graham, Alexander de Meners, and Nicholas Randolf, all of whom had been eminently distinguished for the valour with which they had fought the battles of their country.

Lastly, here it was that the glorious patriot, William Wallace, was led a prisoner in 1305. In the dungeons of the Tower he breathed his last prayer for the land which had given him birth ; and under its portals he was led forth, tied to a horse's tail, to expiate on the common gallows his only offence, namely, a generous ardour to revenge the wrongs of his country. This illustrious man was executed with all the accompaniments of horror which were peculiar to a semi-barbarous age, and which have only been omitted within the last century. His body was removed from the gallows before life was extinct ; his bowels were taken out and burnt; his head was set on London Bridge, and his quarters sent to Scotland to arouse the tears and curses of his affectionate countrymen. His gallant companion in arms, the dauntless Sir Simon Frazer, suffered the same fate, and had his head affixed next to that of Wallace, on London Bridge.   Many other brave men were led forth from the Tower to suffer for the same cause, and among them the Earl of Athol, whose royal descent proved of no avail, and who underwent his doom under circumstances of peculiar cruelty.

In tracing the history of the Tower at this period, we find other very curious evidence of Edward's arbitrary power. While the victorious monarch was absent in Scotland, in 1303, his treasury in West-minster Abbey was broken into, and robbed of the large sum, it is said, of one hundred thousand pounds. Edward immediately committed the whole of the sacred establishment,—consisting of the abbot, the monks, and their servants,—to the Tower of London. They were subsequently tried and acquitted, nor does it appear that the real perpetrators of the robbery were ever discovered. To the Tower also, in this reign,—when their vice and enormities led to the breaking up of their establishments in 1307, —were committed the Grand Master of the Knight Templars, and all the members of their powerful Order south of the Tweed.

The ill-fated Edward the Second appears to have occasionally kept his court in the Tower. Here his Queen gave birth to her eldest daughter, from this circumstance styled Joan of the Tower, and here we find him more than once taking refuge when threatened by the fury of his exasperated subjects. After the murder of the King, his young son, Edward the Third, was kept closely watched here by his mother, Queen Isabel, and her paramour, Lord Mortimer. It was soon evident, however, that the fiery spirit of Edward the First had descended unabated to his young grandson. By his orders, Mortimer was suddenly arrested in Nottingham Castle, and, with his two sons, was loaded with chains and thrust into the darkest dungeons of the Tower. Here the unworthy favourite lingered for some time, till he was led forth to the gallows on Tower Hill.

With Edward the Third the Tower appears to have been a favourite residence, and during his reign it is connected with some of the proudest

events in our history. Here, after his great and
brilliant victories in France and Scotland, were
conducted as prisoners the chivalry of both those
countries, including the French and Scottish monarchs, who both of them suffered captivity in the
Tower. The first prisoner of importance in this
reign appears to have been the gallant John, Earl of
Murray, one of the most devoted supporters of the
Scottish throne, who was taken prisoner in 1336,
In those days the liberation of a prisoner of high
rank was procurable only by the payment of a large
ransom, and accordingly when the Earl was delivered
by Edward to the possession of the Earl of Salisbury,
the latter received written permission to "do with
him as most for his advantage." Being unable to
pay the large ransom required for his freedom,
Murray remained in the Tower for as long as four
years, when, singularly enough, on Salisbury's being
made prisoner in France, he was exchanged, on the
intercession of the King of Scotland, for his former
keeper.

The year 1346 witnessed the surrender to the
victorious arms of Edward of the important town of
Caen in Normandy, "a goodly town," we are told,
"full of drapery and other merchandise, and rich
burgesses, and noble ladies and damsels, and fair
churches, and one of the fairest castles in all
Normandy." Here were captured the Count d' Eu,
constable of France, and the Count de Tankerville,
who, with many of the most influential citizens
were brought to England ; and, having been con-

ducted in triumph through London, were lodged in the Tower.

The same year the eyes of the citizens of London were regaled with the sight of a far more splendid triumph, and the royal fortress became the prison of still more illustrious captives. At the battle of Neville's Cross, near Durham, there fell into the hands of the English the Scottish sovereign, David Bruce, as well as the Earls of Fife, Monteith, Wigton, and Carrick, the Lord Douglas, and fifty other powerful chieftains, all of whom were ordered to be sent as prisoners to the Tower. They were conducted thither by an escort of twenty thousand men. The Scottish monarch, mounted on a lofty black charger, was a conspicuous object in the procession. On his entrance into the city, he was met by the different companies clad in their respective liveries, and with every show and circumstance of honour, was conducted through the crowded streets to the gates of the Tower, where he was formally and respectfully delivered over to the custody of Sir John Darcy, the constable of the fortress. The unfortunate monarch remained a prisoner in England for as many as eleven years, when he was ransomed for the vast sum of one hundred thousand marks. Many of his gallant companions in arms also suffered long confinements, and the Earls of Fife and Monteith, in consequence of their having previously performed fealty to Edward, were sentenced to death. The former owed his escape to his affinity to the royal blood, but Monteith was hung and quartered agreeably to his sentence, and his head was exposed on Tower Hill.

Other and more brilliant successes followed the victory of Neville's Cross. In 1347,—after a siege of nearly eleven months, during which they had suffered every possible kind of misery and privation,— the city of Calais surrendered to the victorious arms of Edward. Finding it impossible to hold out any longer, its brave defenders,—followed by the principal burgesses,—proceeded one by one, and bareheaded, to the camp of the English monarch ; the former with their swords transversed, and the latter with a rope in each hand, to denote that their lives were at the disposal of the victor, either to hang or spare them. Edward, moved with compassion at their melancholy condition, not only saved their lives, but immediately ordered food to be sent into the town to relieve the hunger of their suffering fellow-citizens. These brave men must have presented an interesting spectacle, as—headed by their valiant leader John de Vienne, a knight of Burgundy,—they were led through the streets of London on their way to the Tower. The same year was conducted to the Tower the celebrated Charles de Blois, who so long and valiantly asserted, on the field of battle, his claims to the dukedom of Brittany. He continued a prisoner for nine years, when he obtained his release on the payment of a large ransom. He fell at the battle of Auray, in 1364, while still maintaining his pretensions to the ducal throne.

The splendid victory of Poictiers, in 1357, filled the Tower with still more illustrious captives. The triumphant entry of Edward the Black Prince into London, in that year, must have presented a scene of striking magnificence to which no description could do justice. The principal captives who graced his triumph consisted of John, King of France, his son Philip, four other Princes, eight Earls, and many others of the chief nobility of France. Conspicuous in the cavalcade was the French King, clad in royal robes, and mounted on a beautiful milk-white charger, while by his side, in plain attire, rode the Black Prince on a small black palfrey. The French King, on his first arrival, was confined in the Savoy, where, we are told, he " kept his house a long season, and was frequently visited by the King and Queen, who made him great feast and cheer." During the subsequent absence, however, of Edward in France, in 1359, it was thought necessary to remove the French King to a place of greater security, and he was accordingly conducted to the Tower, where he had at least the advantage of having his captivity lightened by the society of many of the most illustrious and high-born of his own countrymen. " To be more sure of them," says Froissart, " the French King was set in the Tower of London, and his young son with him, and much of his pleasure and sport restrained, for he was then straitlier kept than he was before." The French King remained a prisoner till the following year, when the treaty of

Bretigny restored him to his country and his throne.

It remains to notice only two other prisoners of distinction who were committed to the Tower in the reign of Edward the Third. These were William de Thorp, Chief Justice of the Common Pleas, who had been condemned to death for bribery and corruption, and the young, graceful, and gallant Valeran, Earl of St.-Paul, who had been taken prisoner in a skirmish near Lyques, in 1375. The former narrowly escaped an ignominious death on the scaffold. St.-Paul was more fortunate After a long confinement in the Tower, he was removed to the " fayre castell of Wynsore," where the Princess of Wales, and her daughter, the Lady Maude, " the fayrest ladye in all Englande," were then residing. St.-Paul and the Lady Maude sometimes met at " daunsynge and carollyng," and the consequence was, that an attachment sprung up between them, which subsequently ended in their union.

The history of the Tower, during the reign of Richard the Second, presents matter of interest widely different from that which had characterized it during the reign of his warlike predecessor. Here, at one time, we find the unfortunate monarch residing in great magnificence, and at another flying here for refuge from his turbulent nobles. From under its portals he sallied forth, clad in white robes and in regal state, to the ceremony of his coronation ; here he formally resigned his kingdom to the usurper Bolingbroke ; and lastly, here it was that his murdered corpse was brought, previous to its exposure and burial.

The coronation of the young and ill-fated King was solemnized with great magnificence. A few days before the ceremony took place, Richard proceeded from the palace of Richmond to the Tower, where he remained till the appointed day, the 15th of July, 1377. He then issued forth from the Tower, "clad in white garments," and accompanied by the principal nobles; Sir Simon Burleigh holding the sword of state before him, and Sir Nicholas Bond, on foot, leading the King's horse by the bridle, for he was then only in his eleventh year. In the open space before the Tower, he was greeted by an immense assemblage of nobles and knights, together with the Lord Mayor, sheriffs, and Aldermen of London, in their scarlet robes, who formed themselves into procession, and thus accompanied the young King to Westminster. "The noise of trumpets and other instruments," says Holinshed, "was marvellous. The city was adorned in all sorts most rich. The water conduits ran with wine for the space of three hours together. In the upper end of Cheape was a certain castle made with four towers, out of the which castle, on two sides of it, there ran forth wine abundantly. In the towers were placed four beautiful virgins, of stature and age like to the King, apparelled in white vestures, in every tower one, who blew in the King's face, at his approaching near to them, leaves of gold; and as he approached also, they threw on him and his horse florins of gold counterfeit. When he was come before the castle, they took cups of gold, and filling them with wine at the spouts of the castle, presented the same to the King and to his nobles. On the top of the castle, betwixt the four towers, stood a golden angel, holding a crown in his hands, which was so contrived, that when the King came, he bowed down and offered to him the crown. But to speak of all the pageants and shows which the citizens had caused to be made and set forth in honour of their new King, it were superfluous; every one in their quarters striving to surmount the other, and so with great triumphing of citizens, and joy of the lords and noblemen, he was conveyed unto his palace at Westminster, where he rested for the night."

Among the prisoners of the Tower, during this reign, we discover many illustrious names. In 1386, when the powerful confederacy under the King's uncles, the Dukes of York and Gloucester, had reduced the unfortunate monarch to the last extremity, we find many of his personal friends and advisers committed to the dungeons of that very fortress, in the saloons of which they had so recently been welcomed as the cherished guests of their sovereign. Among these was the gallant and accomplished Sir Simon Burley, who had been selected by the Black Prince to be the companion and adviser of his son, while Richard was still a boy. In vain did the Queen fall on her knees before the inexorable Gloucester, and with floods

of tears implore him to save the life of one so
honoured and beloved. He was sentenced to be
drawn, hung, and quartered, but in consideration of
his being a knight of the Garter, the sentence was
afterwards changed to beheading, which was accordingly carried into effect on Tower Hill. "To write
of his shameful death," says Froissart, "right sore
displeaseth me; for when I was young I found him
a noble knight, sage and wise; yet no excuse could
be heard, and he was brought out to the Tower,
and beheaded like a traitor: God have mercy on
his soul!"

The unfortunate Richard was subsequently enabled to avenge the death of his faithful adviser.
On the breaking up of the confederacy, its leaders
fell into the hands of the King. The Duke of
Gloucester perished in a mysterious manner in the
castle at Calais; and the Earls of Arundel and
Warwick, Lord Cobham, and Sir John Cheyney,
were committed prisoners to the Tower. The life
of Warwick was spared, and his sentence commuted
to banishment in the Isle of Man. Arundel was
less fortunate. That turbulent and once powerful
nobleman was condemned to be drawn, hung and
quartered; but in consideration of his high rank the
King commuted his sentence to the axe and the
block. On the very day of his condemnation he
was led from Westminster to Tower Hill, with his
hands tied ignominiously behind him, and there,
without being allowed a moment for prayer, was
hurried into eternity. Among the spectators the

unfortunate Earl happened to observe his own son-
in-law, the Earl of Nottingham, and his nephew,
the Earl of Kent.   Turning reproachfully to them,
he said, " It would have more beseemed you, my
lords, to have been absent on this occasion ; but the
time will come when as many will marvel at your
misfortunes as do at mine at this time."

During the memorable rebellion of Wat Tyler,
we find King Richard taking refuge in the Tower
with about six hundred of the principal nobles and
churchmen in the realm.   The fortress was invested
by an infuriated rabble, who are described by Froissart as yelling and shouting " as though all the de-
vylles of hell had been amonge them."   The Savoy,
—the magnificent palace of the Duke of Lancaster,
—was pillaged, and the Temple, and several houses
of the wealthy merchants and others, shared the same
fate. At length, all supplies being cut off, the King
consented to grant the rebels a conference at Mile
End.   Accordingly, at the appointed time, Richard,
having previously heard mass in the Tower, was
proceeding to quit the fortress, when a body of
the rebels forced their way in, and committed
the most atrocious barbarities.   Simon Sudbury,
Archbishop of Canterbury,—the Chancellor Sir Robert Hales,—the Treasurer,—the King's confessor,
—and others, were dragged from the chapel, where
they had taken refuge, and put to the sword.   Stow,
speaking of the murder of the Archbishop, observes,
—" There lay his body unburied (on Tower Hill,)
all that Friday, and the morrow, till the afternoon,

none daring to deliver his body to sepulture : his
head these wicked took, and nailing thereon his
hood, they fixed it on a pole, and set it on London
Bridge, in place where before stood the head of
Sir John Minstarworth." Other atrocities were committed by the exasperated mob. They not only
burst open and pillaged the royal apartments, but
entering the chamber of the Queen's mother, treated her with the most wanton cruelty. The sequel
of the story is well known. The King met the
rebels at Smithfield, when the gallant Lord Mayor
of London, Sir William Walworth, struck their
daring leader, Wat Tyler, to the ground, and thus
sent dismay into the hearts of his followers. Wat
Tyler was shortly afterwards executed, and the head
of the Archbishop having been taken down from
London Bridge, that of the rebel chief was set up
in its place.

In 1389, we find King Richard holding a most
magnificent tournament in the Tower, at which
many of the most celebrated knights of France and
Germany presented themselves. On the first day,
called the feast of challenge, " there issued," says
Froissart, " out of the Tower of London, first, threescore coursers apparelled for the jousts, and on
every one an esquire of honour riding a soft pace ;
and then issued out threescore ladies of honour
mounted on fair palfreys, riding on the one side,
richly apparelled ; and every lady led a knight
with a cheque of silver, which knights were appa-
ralled to joust ; and thus they came riding along

the streets of London with great number of trumpets and other minstrelsy, and so came to Smithfield, where the King and Queen and many ladies
and demoiselles were ready in chambers richly
adorned to see the jousts." At night, we are told,
" there was goodly dancing in the Queen's lodging, in the presence of the King and his uncles,
and other Barons of England, and ladies and demoiselles, continuing till it was day, which was time
for every person to draw to their lodgings." In
1396, King Richard was united to his second wife,
Isabel, daughter of Charles the Sixth of France.
On her arrival in England she was conducted to
the Tower, and from thence proceeded in great
state to her coronation at Westminster.

It was to the apartments in the Tower which had
witnessed his bridal pleasures, that the ill-fated
Richard was brought a prisoner at the close of his
reign, and here he formally abdicated his throne in
favour of Henry, Duke of Lancaster. The scene
as described by Froissart, is striking in the extreme.
On the appointed day, he says, " The Duke of Lancaster, accompanied with lords, dukes, prelates,
earls, barons, and knights, and with the notablest
men in London, and of other good towns, rode to
the Tower, and there alighted. Then King Richard
was brought into the hall, apparelled like a king
in his robes of estate, his sceptre in his hand, and
his crown on his head. Then he stood up alone,
not holden nor stayed by any man, and said aloud,—
' I have been king of England, Duke of Aquitaine,

and lord of Ireland above twenty-two years, which signory, royalty, sceptre, crown, and heritage, I clearly resign here to my cousin, Henry of Lancaster ; and I desire him here in this open presence, in entering on the same possession, to take this sceptre ;' and so delivered it to the Duke, who took it. Then King Richard took his crown from his head with both his hands, and set it before him, and said, ' Fair cousin, Henry Duke of Lancaster, I give and deliver you this crown, wherewith I was crowned King of England, and therewith all the right thereto depending.' " The unfortunate monarch was shortly afterwards removed to the castle of Leeds in Kent, and thence to Pomfret Castle, where he met with his mysterious and untimely end. His body was conveyed to London, and lay one night in the Tower previous to its interment in Westminster Abbey.

The only other prisoner of importance who appears to have been confined in the Tower during the reign of Richard the Second, was the great poet, Chaucer. Here it was that he composed his prose-work "The Testament of Love ;" following the example of Boethius, who, under similar circumstances, wrote his famous work, the "Consolations of Philosophy." Chaucer appears to have been liberated about the year 1389.

The history of the Tower during the reign of Henry the Fourth presents but few incidents of particular interest. The usurper, however, unquestionably resided here in the early period of his reign, and from hence issued forth in magnificent state to his coronation in Westminster Abbey. He was attended on this occasion by his eldest son, Prince Henry, six dukes, six earls, eighteen barons, and nine hundred knights and esquires. The King himself, who was clad in a short tunic of cloth of gold, with the garter on his left leg, rode on a white courser with his head uncovered; all the streets through which he passed being hung with tapestry and arras, and the conduits flowing with wine. The number of horsemen who formed the cavalcade is said to have amounted to no less six thousand.

The discovery of the conspiracy, which was formed at Oxford for taking away the King's life, led to the arrest and execution of some of the first nobles in the kingdom. The Earls of Kent and Salisbury were put to death at Cirencester; the Earl of Gloucester and Lord Lumley shared the same fate at Bristol, and Sir Thomas Blount and nine-and-twenty other knights and esquires at Oxford. Many others were committed to the Tower, among whom were the Earl of Huntingdon, Thomas Merks, Bishop of Carlisle, Sir John Shelley, and Magdalen, King Richard's chaplain. The Earl of Huntingdon, who was King Henry's brother-in-law, was captured near his own castle at Pleshey, and, having been condemned, was executed after an imprisonment of only five days, and his head fixed on London bridge. The sacred office held by the Bishop of Carlisle probably saved his life. This was the gallant and noble-minded churchman, who, almost alone, had stood

forward as the champion of his friendless and unfortunate sovereign, King Richard, and with the most
undaunted courage had opposed those infamous proceedings which led to the deposition of Richard,
and subsequently deluged the country with so much
of its noblest blood. From the Tower the Bishop
was discharged to the custody of the Abbot of
Westminster, where he shortly afterwards died.
Magdalen, the King's chaplain, was not so fortunate.
Having been conveyed to the Tower, he was sentenced to death without a trial, and having been
hanged, drawn, and quartered, his head was placed
among the many ghastly visages, with which London
Bridge was at this period disfigured.

Two other prisoners in the Tower, in this reign,
were Griffin, son of the celebrated Owen Glendower;
and the young and accomplished James the First of
Scotland. The latter, in the life-time of his father,
King Robert the First, was on his way to be educated in France, when he was captured at sea, and
committed by order of King Henry to the Tower.
After suffering an imprisonment of nearly eighteen
years, he contracted his romantic marriage with
Lady Jane Beaufort, daughter of the Earl of Somerset, and cousin of Henry the Sixth. The young
King shortly afterwards obtained his release, and
returned to Scotland, where his subsequent eventful
history is well known.

During the glorious reign of Henry the Fifth, the
Tower appears to have been but rarely used as a
regal residence; and yet, though there is little to

identify it with the personal history of the victor of
Agincourt, there is much that is interesting connected with it at this period. Here, at the first dawn
of the Reformation, on account of his religious principles, was imprisoned the brave and virtuous Lord
Cobham. Having been found guilty at his trial, he
was sentenced to be hanged and burnt as an obsti-
nate heretic and traitor. In the meantime, however,
he found means to escape from the Tower, and, notwithstanding the great exertions which were made,
and the vast rewards which were offered, for his apprehension, he continued for nearly four years to
elude the vigilance of his enemies. At last, in December, 1417, this excellent man was taken prisoner
by Lord Powis on the borders of Wales, and was
conducted to his former dungeon in the Tower. A
short time afterwards, having resisted every endeavour which was made to induce him to recant his
errors, his original sentence was carried relentlessly
into execution. Having been drawn from the
Tower to St. Giles's-in-the-Fields, he was hanged
by the middle with a chain, and a fire being lighted
under him, he was slowly burnt to death.

The victory gained by Henry the Fifth at Agincourt, in 1415, and his other glorious successes
in France, were the means of filling the Tower
with many prisoners of high rank. Here were
imprisoned the Duke of Orleans, father of Louis the
Twelfth of France, the Duke de Bourbon, Louis
Earl de Vendôme, Marshal Boucicaut, and the
Count d'Eu, all of whom had been taken prisoners

on the field of Agincourt. They each remained in
captivity for many years; Henry thinking it so es-
sential to the interests of his country that they
should be kept in safe custody, that, with his
latest breath, he enjoined his brother, the Duke
of Bedford, to turn a deaf ear to any overtures
which might be made for their release, till his young
son should at least have obtained his majority. The
Duke de Bourbon and Marshal Boucicaut died in
captivity;—the Earl de Vendôme obtained his release from the Tower, in 1423, and was placed
under the custody of Sir John Cornwall;—and, in
1435, the Count d'Eu was also released, and given
in charge to the Earl of Morton. The Duke of
Orleans remained a prisoner in England till 1440,
when he was released on the payment of a ransom
amounting to 50,000*l.* During his captivity in this
country, he solaced himself with writing his volume
of poems entitled " Poieses de Charles Duc d'Orleans," more than one of which he is said to have
composed in the Tower of London.

Many of the Scottish nobility,—including the Earl
of Crawford, Alexander Lord Gordon, William
Lord Ruthven, William Lord Aberdalgy, James
Lord Calder, Walter Lord Dirleton, and William
Lord Abernethy,—were also confined in the Tower,
in this reign. These persons had been given up as
hostages for the payment of 40,000*l.*, which sum
was demanded for the expenses of King James's
entertainment and maintenance while a prisoner in
England. Some of the Scotch noblemen were

afterwards exchanged for others of their countrymen, who were sent to fill their places, while others
were less fortunate, and continued in captivity for
many years.

During the sanguinary struggle between the
Houses of York and Lancaster, we find the Tower
associated with many events of stirring interest.
With the fortunes of the ill-fated Henry the Sixth,
its history is particularly connected; that monarch
having been frequently its inmate, sometimes as a
monarch, and sometimes as a miserable captive.

On the breaking out of Cade's rebellion, in 1450,
and the defeat of Sir Humphry Stafford by the
rebels, near Seven Oaks, a strong garrison was
placed in the Tower, under the command of Lord
Scales, and, in order to appease the popular fury,
Lord Say was committed a prisoner within its
walls. That unfortunate nobleman, being sometime
afterwards imprudently taken before the judges at
Guildhall, was seized by an infuriated mob, and
having been dragged to Cheapside, was inhumanly
butchered by the people. Elated by success, Cade
and his followers proceeded to lay siege to the
Tower, where the Archbishop of Canterbury, the
Chancellor, and several other persons of high rank
had taken refuge. For some time the city continued to be a frightful scene of plunder, cruelty,
and rapine; nor was it till, at the suggestion of
the Bishop of Winchester, a general pardon under
the great seal was promised to all offenders, that
tranquillity was restored to the affrighted metro-

polis. Cade, however, was excepted from the general amnesty, and shortly afterwards suffered the penalty of his cruelty and his crimes.

In 1460, we find Lord Scales besieged in the Tower by the Earl of Salisbury, Lord Cobham, and Sir John Wenlock. The fortress continued to hold out till King Henry was made prisoner, the following year, when Lord Scales, in endeavouring to effect his escape by water, was taken prisoner and slain. The various successes and reverses which attended the arms of the opposing factions of York and Lancaster, and the circumstances which raised Edward the Fourth to the throne, are well known. Having escaped from the fatal conflict of Hexham, the unfortunate Henry wandered for some time in disguise on the borders of Scotland, till, being delivered over to his enemies, he was ignominiously conducted to one of the prisons of that fortress, in the regal halls of which he had formerly reigned, the envied and all-powerful Lord. Here the weak monarch remained till 1471, when the revolution, effected by the Earl of Warwick, forced King Edward into a temporary exile, and for a brief period restored Henry to his rights. He was immediately removed from the solitary rooms in which he was confined, to the royal apartments, where he was shortly afterwards waited upon in great state by the Duke of Clarence, the Earls of Warwick and Shrewsbury, Lord Stanley, and other noblemen of high rank. Thence, clad in a long robe of blue velvet, and with the crown on his head, he proceeded in solemn state to St. Paul's, where, amidst the hollow shouts of the fickle populace, he returned thanks for his extraordinary deliverance from the power of his enemies.

But a fresh storm was brooding over the head of the ill-fated monarch. Edward shortly afterwards returned from his brief exile, and after a series of events as extraordinary as they were rapid, succeeded in regaining a throne which previously he had almost as rapidly lost. Henry once more fell into the hands of his enemies, and had the misery inflicted on him of being a compulsory witness of the fatal battle of Barnet, and of the slaughter of his faithful followers and friends. After the battle, which was fought on Easter Sunday, 1471, King Henry was brought back to his old prison, in the Tower, where he was committed to the charge of Anthony Wydvile, Earl Rivers. In the mean time, the usurper marched his forces to give battle to the devoted and dauntless Queen Margaret, who with her young son, Edward, had recently landed at Weymouth, from France. The opposing armies encountered each other on the field of Tewkesbury, and the result is well known. Young Edward was taken prisoner and inhumanly put to death, and on the 21st of May, 1471, King Edward returned to the capital in triumph. A few days afterwards, the unfortunate Henry was found dead in the Tower.

Shortly after the battle of Tewkesbury, the noble-minded, Margaret,—whom the tragic events of a

few days had rendered childless and husbandless,—
was discovered in a small convent in Worcester-
shire, and from thence was conducted to a miserable prison in the Tower. In the mind of this extraordinary woman, with what painful recollections
must the gloomy fortress have been associated! She
remained here a prisoner till 1475, when, in accordance with the treaty of Picquigni, she obtained her
release on the payment of 50,000*l.*

Among the remarkable persons confined in the
Tower, in the reign of King Henry, is said to have
been Owen Tudor, grandfather to King Henry the
Seventh. Here also was imprisoned, William de la
Pole, Earl of Suffolk, the prime minister and declared favourite of Margaret of Anjou. His name
is now principally remembered from its connection
with the loss of many of the splendid territorial ac-
quisitions which England had won from her hereditary foe, and especially from the discomfiture which
he received from Joan d'Arc, beneath the walls of
Orleans. On the eleventh day of the siege, the
maid,—arrayed in her military costume, and dis-
playing her consecrated banner,—descended into the
fosse, at the head of the assailing force. In the
heat of the fray she received a blow on the head
from a stone, which struck her to the ground, and
for a moment deprived her of her senses. She
soon, however, recovered herself, and was again foremost in the assault. Fortune decided against the
English, and Suffolk fell into the hands of the
enemy. The person who took him prisoner was one

Renaud, a Frenchman, of whom he inquired, before
he surrendered himself, whether he was a gentleman? The reply being satisfactory, he again demanded whether he was a knight? Renaud replying that he had not yet attained that honour,—
"Then," replied Suffolk "I will make you one," and
dubbing him a knight with his sword, immediately
surrendered himself as his prisoner. It was more
than twenty years afterwards that the Duke of Suffolk fell a victim to the popular clamour, which
attributed to his tyranny and injustice every misfortune which had befallen England during the unfortunate reign of the imbecile Henry. He was
doubtless a bad man and a bad minister, but he
was devoid neither of moral nor personal courage.
Sensible of the odium which he had incurred, and
aware that articles of impeachment were preparing
against him in the House of Commons, Suffolk
acted the part of a bold man, and rising in his
seat in the House of Lords, endeavoured to over-
awe his enemies by the undaunted manner in which
he asserted his own innocence, and insisted on
the claims which his services, and those of his family, had entailed on the gratitude of the public.
The Commons of England, however, were not to
be diverted from their purpose, and, on the 28th
of January, 1451, the powerful minister was committed to the Tower. On the 9th of March following, he was brought from thence to the bar of the
House of Lords. He denied the being guilty of
the crimes of which he was charged, but submitted

to the King's mercy. It was expected that his condemnation would immediately have followed, but,
to the surprise of all men, the King, doubtless
at the instigation of Queen Margaret, took the
law into his own hands, and, dispensing with the
formalities of a trial, banished him the kingdom for
five years. The hatred of the people, however,
was not so easily to be pacified. On his passage
from Dover to Calais, he was seized by a vessel
belonging to the Duke of Exeter, and being carried
back to Dover, was beheaded with a rusty sword,
on the side of a long-boat, and his body, having
been stripped of his "gown of russet, and his
doublet of velvet mailed," was thrown on the sands
of Dover.

The only other prisoners of importance, in this
reign, were Edmund, Duke of Somerset, who succeeded to the power and unpopularity of the Duke
of Suffolk, and who was killed in the first battle of
St. Albans;—Lord Dudley, who had been wounded
and taken prisoner at the battle of Bloreheath,—
John De Vere, twelfth Earl of Oxford, and his
eldest son, Lord Aubrey De Vere,—and George
Nevil, Archbishop of York, Chancellor of the kingdom, and brother of the Earl of Warwick, the king-
maker. The Earl of Oxford and his heir expiated
their attachment to the House of Lancaster on the
scaffold, but the others had the good fortune to
escape with their lives.

The handsome and amorous usurper, Edward the
Fourth, frequently kept his gay court at the Tower.

It was from hence, on the 29th of June, 1461, that he rode forth in great magnificence to his coronation in Westminster Abbey ; the Knights of the Bath preceding him, arrayed, we are told, "in blue gowns, with hoods and tokens of white silk upon their shoulders." It was here also, in 1465, that Edward conducted his fair and interesting Queen, Elizabeth Wydvile, after their romantic union had been announced to the world. This lady was the daughter of a private gentleman, Sir Richard Wydvile, whom Jaqueline of Luxembourg, Duchess of Bedford,—sacrificing her pride to her affections,—had allowed to claim her hand at the altar. Their daughter,—the destined successor of the haughty Margaret of Anjou on the throne of the Plantagenets,—had married Sir John Gray of Groby, who died gallantly fighting for Henry the Sixth at the second battle of St. Albans, and whose estates had consequently been confiscated by the usurper. Left a young, beautiful, but impoverished widow, the lady Elizabeth Gray was residing, in comparative seclusion, with her mother, the Duchess of Bedford, when King Edward, being on a hunting expedition in the neighbourhood, happened to pay an accidental visit to the house. "As the occasion," says Hume, "seemed favourable for obtaining some grace from the gallant monarch, the young widow flung herself at his feet, and with many tears entreated him to take pity on her impoverished and distressed children. The sight of so much beauty in affliction strongly affected the amorous Edward; love stole insensibly into his heart under the guise of compassion; and her sorrow, so becoming a virtuous maiden, made his esteem and regard quickly correspond to his affection. He raised her from the ground with assurances of favour; he found his passion increase every moment by the conversation of the amiable object; and he was soon reduced, in his turn, to the posture and style of a supplicant at the feet of Elizabeth."

The idol of the young and gay of both sexes,— a young king, withal, eminently handsome in his person and insinuating in his address,—it might have been supposed, with these advantages, that Edward would have found little difficulty in obtaining access to the bedchamber of the beautiful widow, without previously passing through the church. But whether conscious of her power over the amorous monarch, or whether actuated by a virtuous indignation, the object of his passion turned a deaf ear to every importunity which flowed from dishonourable love. "She obstinately refused to gratify his passion," says Hume, "and all the endearments, caresses, and importunities of the young and amiable Edward proved fruitless against her rigid and inflexible virtue. His passion, irritated by opposition, and increased by his veneration for such honourable sentiments, carried him at last beyond all bounds of reason; and he offered to share his throne, as well as his heart, with the woman, whose beauty of person and dignity of

character, seemed so well to entitle her to
both."

The marriage of Edward and Elizabeth Wydvile
was privately celebrated at Grafton, and shortly
afterwards Edward carried his bride in triumph to
the Tower, from whence, on Whitsun-eve, 1465,
she was conducted in state to Westminster Abbey,
where she was crowned by the Archbishop of Canterbury.

Before quitting the history of the Tower in the
reign of Edward the Fourth, we must recall one
of the most remarkable tragedies which has ever afforded the ground-work for romance,—the execution
of the ill-fated George, Duke of Clarence, the son-
in-law of the king-maker Warwick, and the brother
of the reigning monarch. Who is there, who has
ever visited the Tower of London, whose imagination
has not identified its gloomy walls with the glorious
imageries of Shakspeare! Who is there who has
not longed to be able to point out the dungeon,
where " false, fleeting, perjured Clarence" dreamed
his last frightful dream, when he awoke from his
troubled and fitful slumbers to start at the pale
faces of the remorseless murderers, who were waiting to bear him to his doom. The night-scene in
the dungeon, between the unfortunate Clarence, and
Sir Robert Brakenbury, the lieutenant of the
Tower, is one of those magnificent passages in poetry,
which make the earliest and deepest impressions on
our imaginations, and continue to be remembered
and quoted to the last.

Brak. What was your dream, my Lord, I pray you, tell me?
Clar. Methought that I had broken from the Tower,
And was embarked to cross to Burgundy:
And in my company, my brother Gloster,
Who from my cabin tempted me to walk
Upon the hatches; thence we looked toward England,
And cited up a thousand heavy times,
During the wars of York and Lancaster,
That had befallen us. As we paced along
Upon the giddy footing of the hatches,
Methought that Gloster stumbled; and, in falling,
Struck me, that thought to stay him, overboard,
Into the tumbling billows of the main.
O Lord! methought, what pain it was to drown!
What dreadful noise of water in mine ears!
What sights of ugly death within mine eyes!
Methought I saw a thousand fearful wrecks;
A thousand men, that fishes gnawed upon;
Wedges of gold, great anchors, heaps of pearl;
Inestimable stones, unvalued jewels,
All scattered in the bottom of the sea.
Some lay in dead men's skulls; and, in those holes
Where eyes did once inhabit, there were crept,
As 'twere in scorn of eyes, reflecting gems,
That wooed the slimy bottom of the deep,
And mocked the dead bones that lay scattered by.
Brak. Had you such leisure in the time of death,
To gaze upon the secrets of the deep?
Clar. Methought I had; and often did I strive
To yield the ghost: but still the envious flood
Kept in my soul, and would not let it forth
To seek the empty, vast, and wandering air:
But smothered it within my panting bulk,
Which almost burst to belch it in the sea.
Brak. Awaked you not with this sore agony?
Clar. O, no, my dream was lengthened after life;
O, then began the tempest of my soul!
I passed, methought, the melancholy flood,
With that grim ferryman which poets write of,
Unto the kingdom of perpetual night.
The first that there did greet my stranger soul
Was my great father-in-law, renowned Warwick,
Who cried aloud,—*What scourge for perjury*
Can this dark monarchy afford false Clarence?
And so he vanished. Then came wandering by
A shadow like an angel, with bright hair
Dabbled in blood; and he shrieked out aloud,
Clarence is come,—false, fleeting, perjured Clarence,—

That stabbed me in the field by Tewkesbury ;
Seize on him, furies, take him to your torments !
With that, methought, a legion of foul fiends
Environed me, and howled in mine ears
Such hideous cries, that, with the very noise,
I trembling waked, and, for a season after,
Could not believe but that I was in hell ;
Such terrible impression made my dream.

Brak. No marvel, lord, that it affrighted you !
I am afraid, methinks, to hear you tell it.

Clar. O, Brakenbury, I have done those things,—
That now give evidence against my soul,—
For Edward's sake ;—and, see, how he requites me !
O God ! if my deep prayers cannot appease thee,
But Thou wilt be avenged on my misdeeds,
Yet execute thy wrath on me alone ;
O, spare my guiltless wife, and my poor children !

The motives which induced King Edward to sign
the death-warrant of his own brother will probably
ever continue to be a mystery. Clarence, fickle in
character, and imprudent in speech, had formerly
joined his father-in-law, the Earl of Warwick,
in his confederacy against the King: but they had
long since been reconciled ; all unkindness seemed
to have been forgotten ; the royal brothers had
fought side by side at the battles of Barnet and
Tewkesbury, and their interests were to all appearance the same. But whatever may have been the
follies or the crimes of the misguided Clarence, his
enemies, headed by the King himself,—who was probably urged on by his younger brother, the Duke of
Gloucester,—were evidently determined on his death.
On the 16th of January, 1478, he was committed
to the Tower, and in the course of the same month
was brought to trial, on charges of high treason,
at the bar of the House of Lords. With suborned

witnesses, and a parliament, in those days, slavishly
devoted to the wishes of the reigning sovereign,
it may readily be imagined that the doom of Clarence was fixed. Edward himself pleaded in person against his unfortunate brother; he was found
guilty by the peers, and both Houses petitioned
the King to consent to his execution. The only favour which Edward shewed his brother was giving
him the choice of the manner of his death. Clarence accordingly expressed the whimsical wish of
being drowned in a butt of malmsey, which was
privately carried into effect in the Tower on the
18th of February. The fate of Clarence has been
connected with a prophecy, which was current at
the period, that the King's son would be murdered by a person, the initial of whose name was
G., and as the Christian name of the Duke was
George, and as his violent and unsteady character
was but too well known, public opinion, it is said,
fixed upon him as the future murderer of his
nephew. Even, however, in the ignorant and superstitious days of Edward the Fourth, it is difficult
to believe that so idle a tale could have sealed the
fate of a prince of the blood. Hume, however, has
condescended to give it a place in his " History of
England," and Shakspeare has immortalized it in
his play of " Richard the Third." He makes Richard
say in his opening soliloquy :—

> Plots have I laid, inductions dangerous,
> By drunken prophecies, libels, and dreams,
> To set my brother Clarence, and the king,
> In deadly hate the one against the other :

And if King Edward be as true and just,
As I am subtle, false, and treacherous,
This day should Clarence safely be mewed up ;
About a prophecy, which says—that G
Of Edward's heirs the murderer should be.
Dive, thoughts, down to my soul ! here Clarence comes.

It seems far more probable, however, that the prophecy is the invention of a later period, founded on the reputed murder of King Edward's children by the Duke of Gloucester.

King Edward died on the 9th of April, 1483, and the same day his young son, Edward the Fifth, then in his thirteenth year, was proclaimed his successor. He was then residing in the Castle of Ludlow, on the borders of Wales, under the guardianship of his maternal uncle, Anthony Wydvile, Earl Rivers, a nobleman equally distinguished for his literary accomplishments and his chivalrous gallantry on the field of battle. The breath had no sooner quitted the body of the late King, than the Duke of Gloucester commenced playing that subtle part, for which his talents and unprincipled character alike fitted him, and which has been rendered famous both in the pages of history and romance. He was then absent in the north of England, but no sooner did he receive intelligence of his brother's death, than he addressed letters, teeming with expressions of unalterable allegiance and affection, to his young nephew. Moreover he was one of the first to swear fealty to him, and, placing his large retinue in mourning, he advanced to do homage to the new King at Northampton. In the evening, over the social board, the Duke of Gloucester and Earl

Rivers pledged themselves in the wine-cup; mirth
and joviality resounded in the festive chamber, and
when they parted at night, it was with every appearance of cordiality and good fellowship. But, the
next day, as Rivers was entering the town of Stony
Stratford, he was suddenly arrested by orders of the
Duke of Gloucester, and conveyed with Lord Grey,
Sir Thomas Vaughan, and Sir Richard Hawse, to
Pomfret Castle, in front of which he was shortly
afterwards beheaded, without trial, and without the
slightest means of vindicating his character. Such
was the end of that gallant and accomplished man,
—the ornament of the age in which he lived,—who
had worsted the Bastard of Burgundy in the most
famous tournament of that chivalrous period, and of
whom Walpole eloquently says, "Though Caxton
knew none like to the Erle of Worcester, and thought
that all learning in the nobility perished with Tip-
toft, yet there flourished, about the same period, a
noble person, (Anthony Earl Rivers,) by no means
inferior to him in learning and politeness; in birth
his equal, by alliance his superior, and in pilgri-
mages more abundant." The father and brother
of Earl Rivers had both previously lost their heads
during the memorable contentions between the
Houses of York and Lancaster.

There were opposed, at this period, between the
Duke of Gloucester and the sovereign power, the
numerous progeny of King Edward the Fourth,
and the two children of his elder brother, the
Duke of Clarence; but to the inordinate ambition

of this extraordinary man these were but slight
obstacles. The appointment of the Duke to the
high office of Protector, — the flight of the affrighted Queen-mother, with her younger son, the
Duke of York, to the sanctuary at Westminster,—
and the insidious means by which she was induced
to deliver up her beloved child to their future
murderer, are well known. On the 13th of April,
1483, the young King, attended by the Dukes of
Gloucester and Buckingham, made his entry into
London with great magnificence, and, after passing
a few nights in the palace of the Bishop of London,
was conducted to his last earthly resting-place in
the Tower, where he was shortly afterwards joined
by his infant brother, the Duke of York.

The 23rd of June was fixed upon as the day
of the King's coronation, and every preparation
was made for the important ceremony. But on the
13th, there took place that memorable Council at
the Tower, which the genius of Shakspeare has
rendered so familiar to every one. At the head of
the table sat the Protector, and among the principal
persons present were the Archbishop of York, the
Bishop of Ely, Lord Hastings, and Lord Stanley.
The subjects in discussion were the precedents and
formalities to be adopted at the coronation of the
young King. Richard, with that perfect and almost
demoniacal command over his feelings and countenance, which was one of his most remarkable
characteristics, was apparently in the highest spirits
and most jovial humour. Among other subjects,

he jested with the Bishop of Ely on the excellence and early growth of his strawberries, which the latter reared at his rural episcopal palace at Holborn.

> My Lord of Ely, when I was last in Holborn,
> I saw good strawberries in your garden there ;
> I do beseech you, send for some.

The Bishop immediately despatched a servant for the strawberries. The scene which followed is well known. The Duke, on pretence of business, left the council-chamber for a few minutes, and on his return appeared with a countenance, in which rage, hatred, and determined vengeance were forcibly marked. After sitting awhile in awful silence, and biting his lips with real or pretended anger, " What," he exclaimed, stamping his foot, " are they worthy of, that compassed and imagined *his* destruction, who was so nearly related to the King, and was intrusted with the administration of government ? " Hastings, — who was Chamberlain to the young King, and whose devoted and affectionate attachment to the son of his late master, had brought him under the ban of the Protector,—immediately replied, " Surely, my lord, they are worthy to be punished as traitors, whosoever they be." The rage of the Protector increased at these words. " Those traitors," he said,—openly accusing the Queen-mother,—" are the sorceress, my brother's wife, and his mistress, Jane Shore : see how by their witchcraft they have wasted my body."—" Therewith," says Sir Thomas More, " he turned up his doublet sleeve to the elbow of his left arm; where he shewed a wearish withered arm and small, as it was never other, and thereupon every man's mind misgave them, well perceiving that this matter was no quarrel ; for they wist that the Queen was too wise to go about any such folly."

Those who were seated at the council-table, knowing that the Protector's arm had been shrivelled from his infancy, looked at each other with terror and amazement.   Hastings, however, replied, " Certainly, my lord, if they have so heinously done, they be worthy of heinous punishment."—" And do you reply to me," exclaimed the Protector, " with your *ifs* and your *ands ?   You* are the chief abettor of that witch Shore; *you* are yourself a traitor : and I swear by St. Paul, that I will not dine before your head be brought me." He then struck the table with his hand ; the guard rushed in ; in the struggle Lord Stanley, either by design or accident, received a severe blow on the head with a pole-axe, and Lord Hastings was hurried a prisoner from the apartment.   Immediately afterwards, " without time for confession or repentance," he was beheaded on a log of timber on the green before the chapel.

Glouc. I pray you all, tell me what they deserve,
         That do conspire my death with devilish plots
         Of damned witchcraft ; and that have prevailed
         Upon my body with their hellish charms ?
Hast. The tender love I bear your grace, my lord,
         Makes me most forward in this noble presence
         To doom the offenders : Whosoe'er they be,
         I say, my lord, they have deserved death.
Glouc. Then be your eyes the witness of their evil,
         Look how I am bewitched ; behold mine arm
         Is, like a blasted sapling, withered up :
         And this is Edward's wife, that monstrous witch,
         Consorted with that harlot, strumpet Shore,
         That by their witchcraft thus have marked me.

Host. If they have done this deed, my noble lord,—
Glouc. If ! thou protector of this damned strumpet,
    Talk'st thou to me of *ifs ?*—Thou art a traitor :—
    Off with his head :—now, by St. Paul I swear,
    I will not dine until I see the same.—
    Lovel and Catesby, look that it be done ;
    The rest, that love me, rise, and follow me.

Immediately afterwards, Jane Shore, the beautiful mistress of the late King, was committed to
prison on charges of sorcery. This celebrated lady
had been married in early youth to a wealthy
citizen of London. Her own wishes, however, had
not been consulted in the match, and the sight
of a young, handsome, and gallant monarch languishing at her feet, proved a temptation too powerful to resist. She yielded to his importunities, and
long continued to be the beloved mistress of the
amorous Edward. All her contemporaries bear witness to her charming address, her extraordinary accomplishments, her ready wit, her goodness of heart,
and the surpassing beauty of her person. Moreover,
the influence which she exercised over her royal
paramour was employed in rewarding merit and re-
lieving the distressed. " Proper she was and fair;"
says Sir Thomas More, " nothing in her body you
would have changed, unless you would have wished
her somewhat higher. Yet delighted not men so
much in her beauty, as in her pleasant behaviour:
for a proper wit she had, and could both read well
and write ; merry in company; ready and quick of
answer; neither mute, nor full of babble ; sometimes taunting without displeasure, and not without
disport. The King would say he had three concu-

bines, who in three diverse properties diversely excelled; one the merriest, another the ugliest, and
the third the holiest in the realm. The first was
Jane Shore, in whom he therefore took especial
pleasure: for many he had, but her he loved; and
his favour, to say the truth, she never abused to
any man's hurt, but to many a man's comfort and
relief. Where the King took displeasure, she
would mitigate and appease his mind; where men
were out of favour, she would bring them to his
grace; for many that had highly offended she obtained pardon; of great forfeitures she got men
remission." Failing in his object of convicting her
of sorcery and witchcraft, the Protector delivered
her over to the tender mercies of the spiritual
court, where she was formally tried for lewdness
and adultery. Sentence was passed on her by the
Bishop of London, and this delicate, idolized, and
warm-hearted woman,—on whose bosom the head of
the all-powerful Edward had so recently reposed,
and whose favour had so lately been abjectly courted
by the most powerful nobles in the land,—was condemned to do public penance at the cathedral of
St. Paul's, walking bare-footed, in a white sheet, and
with a torch in her hand, through a line of gazing
spectators. She bore her part, however, with a
decent dignity, and a becoming grace of manner,
which, with the remembrance of her many virtues,
drew tears from the eyes of many, and won for her
the respect of all.

> Submissive, sad, and lowly was her look;
> A burning taper in her hand she bore,

And on her shoulders, carelessly confused,
In loose neglect, her lovely tresses hung;
Her streaming eyes bent ever on the earth,
Except when, in some bitter pang of sorrow,
To Heaven she seemed in fervent zeal to raise,
And beg that mercy man denied her here.

She obtained her liberty after the full performance of her painful penance, and lived to an advanced age, poor, friendless, and

Forgotten at her utmost need,
By those her former bounty fed.

"She lived," says Hume, "not only to feel the bitterness of shame imposed on her by a tyrant, but to experience, in old age and poverty, the ingratitude of those courtiers who had long solicited her friendship, and been protected by her credit. No one, among the great multitudes whom she had obliged, had the humanity to bring her consolation or relief; she languished out her life in solitude and indigence; and, amidst a court inured to the most atrocious crimes, the frailties of this woman justified all violations of friendship towards her, and all neglect of former obligations."—"She now," in the graphic language of Sir Thomas More, "beggeth of many living, who at this day would have themselves begged, if she had never been." Granger tells us that the Duchess of Montagu had a lock of Jane Shore's hair, which looked as if it had been powdered with gold dust. It is somewhat remarkable that the only three known portraits of the beautiful concubine of King Edward should have been preserved in collegiate foundations,—one at King's College, Cambridge, another at Eton College,

while the third, some years since, was in the possession of Dr. Peckard, of Magdalen College, Cambridge.

On the 25th of June, 1483, two days after the
execution of Hastings and the arrest of Jane Shore,
Richard was waited upon at Baynard's Castle, by
his creature, the Duke of Buckingham, the Lord
Mayor of London, and a body of the citizens, who,
having previously been suborned by the Protector's agents, clamorously insisted on his investing
himself with the supreme power. Being informed
that the people were assembled in the court below,
he pretended an utter ignorance of their purpose,
and it was only with great apparent reluctance
that he could be induced to admit their leaders
to an audience. Being brought into his presence,
Buckingham informed him that the people were
unanimously resolved to have him for their sovereign ; to which the Protector replied, with all
seeming humility, that no inducement could make
him swerve from his allegiance to his royal nephew,
and he strongly recommended all present to follow
his example. Being informed, however, that the
nation were resolved to withhold their fealty from
the young King; and Buckingham adding that if
he (the Protector) refused the proffered dignity,
they would be compelled to look out for a sovereign
elsewhere, he pretended to yield reluctantly to their
arguments and remonstrances. On the following
day he was proclaimed with the title of King
Richard the Third, and with the usual formalities.

Glouc.   Alas, why should you heap those cares on me ?
          I am unfit for state and majesty :—
          I do beseech you take it not amiss ;
          I cannot, nor I will not yield to you.
Buck.   If you refuse it,—as in love and zeal,
          Loath to depose the child, your brother's son ;
          As well we know your tenderness of heart,
          And gentle, kind, effeminate remorse,
          Which we have noted in you to your kindred,
          And equally, indeed, to all estates,—
          Yet know, whether you accept our suit or no,
          Your brother's son shall never reign our king ;
          But we will plant some other in your throne,
          To the disgrace and downfal of your house,
          And, in this resolution, here we leave you ;—
          Come, citizens, we will entreat no more.
                    Exeunt Buckingham and Citizens.
Cat.   Call them again, sweet prince, accept their suit ;
          If you deny them, all the land will rue it.
Glouc.   Will you enforce me to a world of cares ?
          Well, call them again ; I am not made of stone,
          But penetrable to your kind entreaties.
                              Exit Catesby.
          Albeit against my conscience and my soul.
                    Re-enter Buckingham and the rest.
          Cousin of Buckingham,—and sage grave men,—
          Since you will buckle fortune on my back,
          To bear her burden, whether I will or no,—
          I must have patience to endure the load ;
          And if black scandal or foul-faced reproach,
          Attend the sequel of your imposition,
          Your mere enforcement shall acquittance me ;
          For God he knows, and you may partly see,
          How far I am from the desire of this.
Mayor.   God bless your grace ! we see it, and will say it.
Glouc.   In saying so, you shall but say the truth.
Buck.   Then I salute you, with this royal title,—
          Long live King Richard, England's worthy King !

Such is the best authenticated account of the immediate circumstances which raised the Duke of Gloucester to the throne. When we consider, however, not only the peaceful manner in which he was allowed to take possession of it, but also that the proudest nobles of the land immediately hastened to

do homage to him,—and, moreover, that his coronation, which took place twelve days afterwards, was
graced by an unusually large attendance of the
peers of the realm,—it is difficult to believe that
the party which raised him to the sovereign power
consisted merely of a band of hungry courtiers and
paid citizens, with the addition of the capricious
mob who shouted at his heels.

On the 6th of July, the Protector passed under
the time-honoured portals of the Tower, and proceeded with great pomp through the streets of
London to Westminster Abbey to his coronation.
In the procession were as many as three dukes,
nine earls, and twenty-two barons, besides a large
assemblage of knights and esquires. Amongst the
most conspicuous in the gorgeous cavalcade was
the Protector's creature, the Duke of Buckingham. The appearance of Richard, as described by
the chronicler Hall, must have been striking in the
extreme. His robes were of blue velvet, richly
embroidered with gold, and the trappings and
caparisons of his horse were supported by footmen in rich and costly dresses, "in such solemn
fashion that all men much regarded it." Singular as it may appear, it is not a little questionable
whether the youthful and deposed monarch, Edward
the Fifth, was not compelled to play a part in the
coronation procession of his unnatural uncle.*

* That preparations were made for his attending the coronation
of the usurper, is proved beyond a doubt, by the wardrobe account for the year 1483. Among the charges is one for " the lord
Edward, son of the late King, Edward the Fourth, for his apparel

Shortly after his coronation, King Richard proceeded on a progress through the midland counties as far as York, and it was during his absence from the metropolis, that he is said to have imagined, and caused to be carried into effect, that memorable tragedy, the murder of his two nephews in the Tower. The dramatic account of Sir Thomas More, who wrote about twenty-five years after the presumed catastrophe, is that which has been followed by our principal historians. "King Richard," he says, "after his coronation, taking his way to Gloucester, devised, as he rode, to fulfil that thing which he had before intended. Whereupon he sent John Grene, whom he specially trusted, to Sir Robert Brakenbury, constable of the Tower, with a letter and credence also, that the same Sir Robert in any wise should put the two children to death. This John Grene did his errand to Brakenbury, kneeling before our Lady in the Tower, who plainly answered that he would never put them to death to die therefore.

"With that answer Grene returned, recounting the same to King Richard at Warwick, yet on his journey; wherewith he took much displeasure, and

and array, that is to say, a short gown made of two yards and three-quarters of crimson cloth of gold, lined with two yards and three-quarters of black velvet: a long gown made of six yards and a half of crimson cloth of gold, lined with six yards of green damask; a short gown made of two yards of purple velvet, lined with two yards of green damask; a doublet and stomacher, made of two yards of black satin; a bonnet of purple velvet; nine horse harness and nine saddlehousings of blue velvet, gilt spurs, with many other rich articles, and magnificent apparel for his henchmen and pages." Walpole's "Historic Doubts," pp. 65, 66.

that same night said to a page of his, 'Ah! whom shall a man trust? They that I have brought up myself; they that I thought would have mostly served me, even those fail, and at my commandment will do nothing for me.'—'Sir,' quoth the page, ' there lieth one in the pallet chamber without, that, to do your grace pleasure, the thing were right hard that he would refuse;' meaning by this Sir James Tyrrell, who was a man of goodly personage, and, for the gifts of nature, worthy to have served a better prince, if he had well served God; and by grace obtained as much truth and good-will as he had strength and wit. Whereupon the King rose and came out into the pallet chamber, where he found Sir James Tyrrell in bed with Sir Thomas Tyrrell, of person like, and brethren in blood, but nothing of him in conditions. Then said the King unto them merrily, 'What, sirs, be ye in bed so soon?' and calling Sir James Tyrrell up, brake to him secretly his mind in this mischievous matter, in which he found him to his purpose nothing strange. Wherefore on the morrow he sent him to Brakenbury with a letter, by which he was commanded to deliver to Sir James all the keys of the Tower for a night, to the end that he might there accomplish the King's pleasure in such things as he had given him in commandment."

According to the further account of Sir Thomas More, ever since the usurpation of Richard, the young King and his infant brother, the Duke of York, had been deprived of all the appurtenances of

royalty : they were kept in close confinement, their
accustomed attendants were removed from about
their persons, and their places supplied by one who
bore the *sobriquet* of Black Will, and by four other
persons, who it may be supposed were of dark and
suspicious character.   From this period the young
brothers are described as clinging to each other, as
if in the vain hope of finding succour in each other's
embraces; neglecting their dress, and anticipating
with childish horror the dark doom which awaited
them. "The Prince," says Sir Thomas More, "never
tied his points, nor anything thought of himself,
but with that young babe his brother, lingered in
thought and heaviness till the traitorous deed delivered them from their wretchedness."

The project of smothering the young princes
in their bed,—to prevent as much as possible any
ocular evidence of their having met with a violent
death,—is said to have originated with Sir James
Tyrrell, who associated with himself one Slater, and
two other ruffians of the names of Miles Forest and
John Dighton ; the latter a " big, broad, square, and
strong knave." The hour fixed upon for the perpetration of the crime was midnight, when the inmates
of the Tower were wrapped in sleep. "Then," says
Sir Thomas More, "this Miles Forest and John
Dighton, came into the chamber, and suddenly
wrapped them up amongst the clothes, keeping
down by force the feather bed and pillows hard
upon their mouths, that within awhile they smothered
and stifled them, and their breaths failing, they gave

up to God their innocent souls into the joys of
Heaven, leaving to their tormentors their bodies
dead in bed. After which the wretches laid them
out upon the bed, and fetched Tyrrell to see them,
and when he was satisfied of their death, he caused
the murderers to bury them at the stair-foot,
deep in the ground, under a great heap of stones."
Who does not remember the soliloquy of Sir James
Tyrrell in the fourth act of "King Richard the
Third ? "

> The tyrannous and bloody act is done ;
> The most arch-deed of piteous massacre,
> That ever yet this land was guilty of.
> Dighton and Forrest, whom I did suborn
> To do this piece of ruthless butchery,
> Albeit they were fleshed villains, bloody dogs,
> Melting with tenderness and mild compassion,
> Wept like two children, in their death's sad story.
> O thus, quoth Dighton, lay the gentle babes ;—
> Thus, thus, quoth Forest, girdling one another
> Within their alabaster innocent arms ;
> Their lips were four red roses on a stalk,
> Which, in their summer beauty, kissed each other.
> A book of prayers on their pillow lay ;
> Which once, quoth Forrest, almost changed my mind ;
> But, O, the devil,—there the villain stopped ;
> When Dighton thus told on,—We smothered
> The most replenished sweet work of nature,
> That, from the prime creation, e'er she framed,—
> Hence both are gone with conscience and remorse,
> They could not speak ; and so I left them both,
> To bear this tidings to the bloody king.

After the perpetration of the crime, Sir James
Tyrrell is said to have ridden in furious haste to
King Richard, to whom he communicated "all the
manner of the murder." Richard, we are told,
thanked him for the zeal which he had displayed
in his service, and complimented him on the man-

ner in which he had accomplished his task. However, he is said to have betrayed a strange displeasure at the indecent manner in which his nephews had been committed to the earth, and to have given directions to disinter their bodies, and to remove them to consecrated ground. " Whereupon," says Sir Thomas More, "a priest of Sir Robert Brakenbury's took them up and buried them in such secrecy as, by the occasion of his death, which was shortly after, no one knew it." This is a curious passage, when we remember that, in the days of Charles the Second, when there was occasion to disturb the earth at " the stair-foot,"— the spot which is mentioned as the original site of their interment,—there were found the remains of two human beings, which are stated to have exactly corresponded with the age of the murdered princes. They were removed, by order of King Charles, to Henry the Seventh's Chapel at Westminster, where a marble monument still points out the spot where they lie.

In describing the particulars of the presumed murder of the children of Edward the Fourth in the Tower, it will be seen that we have followed, almost verbatim, the account given by an almost contemporary writer, Sir Thomas More,—a graphic picture, which, for more than three centuries, has drawn the tear from childhood, and formed the subject of many a plaintive ballad,—which Shakspeare has improved upon in his immortal drama,—which has long been borrowed by the pencil of the artist and the pen of the writer of romance,—and lastly, which, till within the last few years, has been implicitly followed by the graver historian. Whether, however, such a tragedy was ever acted in the Tower, is quite another question. That the young Princes were put to death in the manner related by Sir Thomas More, there is no little reason to disbelieve. All that is known with certainty, is the fact that they were alive, and were inmates of the Tower, at the period of Richard's accession, and that they were never afterwards satisfactorily proved to be in existence. But whether they fell by the hand of the assassin, or whether they wore out a miserable existence in the dungeons of the Tower,—whether they were removed to the continent and were transferred to the safe keeping of some foreign power,— or whether the young King was the only victim, and his brother, the Duke of York, was in reality the accomplished and unfortunate Perkin Warbeck, —will probably ever continue to be a mystery. The different arguments for and against the supposititious murder of the young Princes, would form a curious groundwork for discussion, into which, however, it is neither the province of this work, nor the inclination of the author to enter.

On the 22nd of August, 1485, King Richard expired on the famous field of Bosworth, and, the same day, the crown which he wore in the battle, having been found among the spoils, was placed by Sir William Stanley on the head of his rival, the Earl of Richmond. The ceremony of King Henry's coronation, in consequence of the sweating sickness raging violently in London, was delayed a few weeks, when he was solemnly crowned by Cardinal Bourchier, Archbishop of Canterbury, by the title of King Henry the Seventh.

During this reign we find the King, like his predecessors, occasionally maintaining his court, and holding tournaments, at the Tower. With his young Queen, also,—Elizabeth of York, sister of the unfortunate Edward the Fifth,—the Tower seems to have been a favourite residence. Hither this amiable Princess was conducted by water from Greenwich, in great state, on the eve of her coronation, and on her landing was received by the King and the principal nobility and officers of state, who conducted her to the royal apartments. The following day, the 25th of November, 1487,—" royally apparelled, and accompanied by my ladye, the King's mother, and many other great estates, both lords and ladies,"—she came forth to her coronation. The houses, in the streets through which she passed on her way to Westminster Abbey, were hung, some with arras and tapestry, and others with cloth of gold, velvet, and silk. Between the Tower and St. Paul's, were arrayed the different Companies of the city of London in their rich and showy liveries, and " in diverse places were ordained singing children, some arrayed like angels, and others like virgins, to sing sweet songs as her Grace passed by."* And through the gay and

* Ive's " Coronation of Queen Elizabeth, p. 120.

crowded streets,—the central object of attraction in a brilliant cavalcade, consisting of the noblest and fairest of the land,—passed Elizabeth of York to her coronation. Her habit of white cloth of gold rendered her especially conspicuous; her long fair hair flowed loosely down her back, and on her head was a coronet of gold glittering with precious stones. The populace, as she passed, hailed with the loudest acclamations the young and interesting Princess, whose marriage with their selfish and cold-hearted sovereign had united the two great houses of York and Lancaster, and had thus arrested that tide of misery, blood, and desolation, which had so long devastated the land.

The Tower was the scene of Elizabeth's death. On the 2nd of February, 1503, she was brought to bed here of a daughter, whose birth she survived only a few days.

There were two prisoners in the Tower in the reign of Henry the Seventh, to each of whose histories a deep interest attaches itself. These were Edward Plantagenet, Earl of Warwick, son of the ill-fated Duke of Clarence, and the accomplished and no less ill-fated Perkin Warbeck.

Jealous of any rival near his throne, one of the first acts of King Henry, on being exalted to the supreme power, had been to immure the Earl of Warwick in the Tower. Without having committed,—without even being accused of a single crime,—this unfortunate prince, the last male heir of the great race of the Plantagenets,—gifted in

all probability with the hereditary gallantry of his
family, and panting for the pleasures and enjoyments natural to his age,—was sacrificed to the
jealousy of a cold-blooded tyrant; and those years,
which are generally considered to be the most
precious, were condemned to be passed in a miserable imprisonment.   Here he remained till the
year 1499, when the gates of the Tower opened
to receive a no less remarkable prisoner, Perkin
Warbeck.   The two youths,—who were not improbably closely allied in blood, — having found
means to confer with each other in secret, contrived a plan for escaping from the gloomy fortress.   Their project, however, unfortunately transpired, and the Earl of Warwick, whose only offence was a natural longing for life and liberty,
was brought to his trial, on the 21st of November, before the Earl of Oxford, High Steward of
England.   He was condemned to death, and on
the 28th of the same month, was beheaded on
Tower Hill.   Even in that distant age,—when fearful and mysterious crimes, and the shedding of
royal and illustrious blood, were things of ordinary
occurrence, — the open crime committed by the
jealous tyrant was regarded with universal detestation.   His excuse was, that his ally, Ferdinand of
Arragon, had scrupled to give his daughter Catherine in marriage to Arthur, Prince of Wales, as
long as one of the male line of the Plantagenets
should survive to dispute the succession.   The apology was worthy of the man !

From the Earl of Warwick we turn to the still more extraordinary fortunes of Perkin Warbeck. According to the account of those who denied his claims, this person was the son of one Osbeck, or Warbeck,—a renegade Jew of Tournay, and subsequently a citizen of London,— whose wealth having introduced him to the notice of Edward the Fourth, that easy and affable monarch consented to stand god-father to his son. The account, however, given by Perkin Warbeck and his partizans was widely different. They boldly asserted that he was Richard, Duke of York, youngest son of King Edward,—that he had contrived to elude the murderous intentions of Richard the Third, as well as the watchful jealousy of Henry the Seventh,—and that he was in fact their rightful and legitimate sovereign. That the young claimant to the throne bore an extraordinary personal resemblance to Edward the Fourth,—and, moreover, that, at the time of Henry's accession, a strong rumour was prevalent that one at least of the late King's sons had escaped from the Tower, and was still living,—are facts which cannot be called in question. Whether, however, Perkin Warbeck was in reality the younger son of King Edward ;—whether, as some have conjectured, he was merely the illegitimate offspring of that monarch,—or whether, after all, he was in fact only a daring impostor,—are questions admitting of more arguments and disquisition than we have here space to enter into.

Young, handsome in his person, and eminently

graceful and courtly in his address, — the master, moreover, of several languages, and gifted with accomplishments far beyond the age in which he lived,—no one could be more admirably qualified for the conspicuous part which he was destined to play. The story of his romantic claims, his resemblance to the features of Edward the Fourth, and the fame of his many accomplishments, at length reached the ears of Margaret, Duchess of Burgundy, sister of the late King, who was induced to invite him to her court. It was not, however, till after she had caused his strange claims and previous history to be searchingly scrutinized, that the Princess was induced openly to acknowledge him as her nephew. "Diverse and sundry times," we are told, "in open audience and solemn presence, he was made to declare and shew by what means he was preserved from death and destruction; in what countries he had wandered and sought friendship; and finally, by what chance of fortune he came to her court and presence." The Duchess, having at length expressed herself perfectly satisfied of his identity, joyfully embraced him as her lost nephew, and openly declared him to be the last heir of the Plantagenets, and the legitimate sovereign of England. She usually addressed him as the "White Rose of England;" she assigned him a guard of thirty halberdiers, with liveries of "murrey and blue;" and conferred on him an income befitting his presumed rank.

The fact of the adventurer's claims having been

acknowledged by the Duchess of Burgundy,— as well as the fame which had gone abroad of his own merits and accomplishments, — could not fail to create a considerable sensation in England. Nor was it with the common people alone that his romantic tale found credence. Men of the highest rank and consequence, — including Lord Fitzwalter, Sir Simon Mountfort, Sir Thomas Thwaites, and even the Lord Chamberlain, Sir William Stanley,— entered into a secret correspondence with him. Encouraged by these circumstances, and by the increasing unpopularity of Henry the Seventh, Perkin Warbeck, assisted by pecuniary loans from his friends, enlisted a well-appointed body of men, to whom he added a number of adventurers of all nations, and with this force determined to invade England, and to dispute the possession of the throne with King Henry.   Accordingly, in the month of July, 1495, he set sail, and with little difficulty effected a landing. The gentlemen of Kent, however, were prepared to receive him, and, after a skirmish, in which he lost an hundred and fifty men, he re-embarked his force, and steered towards Scotland.

His reception by the Scottish monarch, James the Fourth, was as favourable and flattering as his fondest wishes could have anticipated; and this was afterwards improved upon by the adventurer himself, whose agreeable conversation and insinuating address entirely won for him the affections of James. The Scottish monarch publicly acknowledged him to be the legitimate sovereign of England, and, as a proof of his sincerity, conferred on him in marriage a beautiful and virtuous lady, related to the blood royal of Scotland, the lady Catherine Gordon, daughter of the Marquis of Huntley.

Assisted by James,—who parted with his plate and other valuables to afford the adventurer the means of equipping an army,— Perkin Warbeck made an irruption into England. The moment, however, soon arrived when it was no longer in the power of the Scottish monarch to assist his favourite. Without the means of carrying on a long and expensive war, and, moreover, hearing that a large army was marching northward to give him battle, James, though with great reluctance, signed a treaty of peace with the English King, leaving the unfortunate Perkin Warbeck to try his fortunes in some other quarter. He accordingly retired in the first instance to Cork, where he received an invitation from the Cornish rebels, which induced him to pass over to the coast of England. He soon found himself at the head of seven thousand men, with which force he proceeded to lay siege to Exeter. Desertion, however, and discontent soon began to take place among his ill-paid and ill-appointed followers, and at the threatened approach of the King of England with a large force, he was compelled to raise the siege, and to seek safety in flight. He found an asylum in the sanctuary of Beaulieu, in the New Forest, but some time afterwards, on receiving a promise of the King's

pardon, he surrendered himself into the hands
of his enemies, and was conducted in a kind of
mock triumph to London. The persons who had
charge of him had received the strictest orders
never to quit his person. By some means, however,
he contrived to effect his escape, and threw himself
on the protection of the prior of Sheen, in Surrey.
He again fell into the power of Henry, and was
compelled to sit in the stocks a whole day, before
the entrance to Westminster Hall. From this
period he remained a close prisoner in the Tower,
till the failure of his attempt to escape from that
fortress with the young Earl of Warwick. He was
then brought to trial on charges of high treason,
and, being found guilty, was hanged at Tyburn, on
the 23rd of November, 1499. His young and interesting widow, Lady Catherine Gordon, received
great kindness from Henry's Queen, who placed
her near her person, and conferred on her a pension which was continued to her in the following
reign.

The only other prisoner of importance who was
confined in the Tower, in this reign, was the Lord
Chamberlain, Sir William Stanley,—he who had
fought by the side of his ungrateful sovereign on the
field of Bosworth, and had placed the crown on the
head of the usurper in the hour of victory. The
only crime of which he proved to have been guilty,
was his having said in confidence to Sir Robert
Clifford, that *if he was sure that Perkin Warbeck
was the son of King Edward, he would never bear arms*

against him. Accordingly, he was formally impeached
before the merciless and cold-blooded Henry,—who
was then holding his court in the Tower,—of having
favoured the pretensions of the adventurer. On the
15th of February, 1495, he was brought to trial,
and, having been found guilty, was beheaded on
Tower Hill.

The history of the Tower, during the ensuing
reign of Henry the Eighth, is full of interest.
Here were confined, preparatory to a bloody death,
—that rich and powerful nobleman, Edward, Duke
of Buckingham ;—the wise and witty Sir Thomas
More ;—the upright minister, Cromwell, Earl of
Essex ;—the gentle and beautiful Anne Boleyn ;
—the fair and lascivious Catherine Howard ;—the
meek martyr, Anne Askew ; and the young and
gallant Earl of Surrey, the darling of beauty and
of the muses.

It was here that Henry the Eighth passed, in
comparative privacy, the days which elapsed between the death of his father and his interment
in Westminster Abbey. It was here also that he
conducted his young Queen, Catherine of Arragon,
from Greenwich, and here he passed with her a few
days previous to their gorgeous coronation at Westminster. According to the account of the old chronicler, Hall, it must have far exceeded in magnificence all former similar ceremonials. The procession, after issuing from the Tower, passed through a
long line of streets, the houses of which, as was customary on such occasions, were hung with silk, ta-

pestry, and damask. First rode, in rich dresses, two gentlemen on horseback, bearing the colours of the provinces of Guienne and Normandy. Then came two other gentlemen, carrying the King's hat and cloak; while immediately before Henry rode Sir Thomas Brandon, master of the horse, in a magnificent habit of tissue, ornamented with roses of gold. The King, who rode bare-headed, was conspicuous above the rest in a tunic of raised gold, and a robe of crimson velvet. "His placard," we are told, "was set with diamonds, rubies, emeralds, and pearls, and his bawdrick, or belt, with great rubies: the trappings of his horse were of damask and gold, with a deep border of ermine; the knights and esquires of his body were clad in crimson velvet, and all the gentlemen, and other of his chapel, and his officers and household servants, in scarlet." Immediately behind the King came the Queen, in a chariot or litter drawn by two white palfreys. She was habited in a dress of white embroidered satin, and on her head was a coronet set with precious stones, from underneath which her hair, "beautiful and goodly to behold," fell in long tresses down her back. A few years afterwards, this fair and envied princess became a divorced and degraded woman, and her rival and maid of honour, Anne Boleyn, was led forth to her coronation, from under the same portal at the Tower, with circumstances of even greater magnificence than those which had graced the triumph of her predecessor.

The first illustrious victim to the jealousy of

Henry the Eighth, was Edward Duke of Buckingham, Knight of the Garter and Lord High Chancellor of England, at whose attainder and execution sank for ever the splendour, the princely
honours, and vast wealth of the ancient and renowned family of the Staffords. The Duke was
nearly related to the blood-royal, being descended
from Anne, eldest daughter of Thomas of Wood-
stock, youngest son of King Edward the Third.
To this circumstance, and also to his having rashly
incurred the hostility of Cardinal Wolsey, may be
attributed the downfall of this wealthy and powerful nobleman. The Duke, on some occasion of
ceremony, is said to have held a basin to the King,
which his majesty had no sooner used, than Wolsey
dipped his fingers into it. This circumstance was so
offensive to the proud blood of Buckingham, that he
emptied the contents of the basin on the floor, part
of the water falling on the rich dress of the Cardinal. From this moment, Wolsey is said to have
determined on the Duke's ruin. Some time afterwards, he was arrested on charges of high treason,
and, on the 13th of May, 1521, was conveyed by
water from the Tower to Westminster Hall, where
he was solemnly tried before his peers, the Duke
of Norfolk presiding as Lord High Steward on the
occasion. Having been found guilty, and the awful
sentence awarded for the crime of high treason
having been passed upon him, he addressed the Lord
High Steward in an able and affecting speech. "My
Lord of Norfolk," he concluded, " you have said as

a traitor should be said unto ; but I was never one :
yet, my Lords, I nothing malign for what you have
now done to me, and may the eternal God forgive
you my death, as I do. I shall never sue to the
King for life ; howbeit, he is a gracious prince, and
more grace may come from him than I desire. I
beseech you, my Lords, and all my fellows, to pray
for me."

We have already mentioned, that after his condemnation, the Duke was reconducted to the barge
in which he had been conveyed to his trial, and
which was fitted up with carpets and cushions befitting the high rank of the prisoner. He refused,
however, to make use of them, and took his seat
elsewhere. To Sir Thomas Lovell he said, " When
I came to Westminster I was Lord High Constable,
and Duke of Buckingham, but now, poor Edward
Bohun."

Sir Nich. Vaux.   Prepare there
The Duke is coming ; see, the barge be ready ;
And fit it with such furniture, as suits
The greatness of his person.
Buck.   Nay, Sir Nicholas,
Let it alone ; my state now will but mock me.
When I came hither, I was Lord High Constable,
And Duke of Buckingham : now, poor Edward Bohun :
Yet I am richer than my base accusers,
That never knew what truth meant : I now seal it ;
And with that blood will one day make them groan for't.
                    King Henry VIII., Aat ii. Scene 1.

The Duke landed at the Temple Stairs, from
whence he was led to the Tower, through the city,
on foot ; the fatal axe being carried before him.
Four days afterwards, on the 17th of May, this
powerful nobleman was beheaded, in pursuance of

his sentence, on Tower Hill. He died calmly, and amidst the tears of the populace, to whom his popular manners, and princely mode of living, had greatly endeared him. When Charles the Fifth was informed of his death, he is said to have observed, in allusion to the meanness of Wolsey's origin, "that a butcher's dog had killed the finest buck in England." It is remarkable,—within the short space of one hundred and twenty years,—how many of the ancient and chivalrous family of the Staffords, perished by violent deaths! Edward Stafford, the sixth Baron, was killed at the battle of Shrewsbury; Humphrey, the seventh Baron, at the battle of Northampton; and his son, Humphrey, Earl of Stafford, at the battle of St. Albans; Henry Stafford, Duke of Buckingham, was beheaded in the market-place at Salisbury, and his son, the subject of the present notice, on Tower Hill. The office of Lord High Constable, which the Duke inherited from the Bohuns, Earls of Hereford, was forfeited by his attainder, and has never since been revived in England.

Let us now turn to the closing scene of the wise and accomplished Chancellor, Sir Thomas More, who was committed to the Tower, in 1534, for refusing to take the oath of supremacy to Henry the Eighth. His equanimity, both during his long imprisonment and on the scaffold, never forsook him. On his landing at the Traitor's Gate, the porter, according to an ancient custom, demanded his " uppermost garment " as his fee ; on which Sir

Thomas presented him with his hat, telling him *that*
was his "uppermost garment," and that he wished it
was of more value. During his imprisonment in the
Tower, he was frequently visited by the Lord Chancellor, the Dukes of Norfolk and Suffolk, and other
members of the Privy Council, who used every
argument to persuade him to take the oath of
supremacy, but no inducement could prevail upon
him to purchase existence at the expense of his
conscience. Accordingly, he was brought to his
trial at the bar of the Court of King's Bench, and
as trials for high treason in those days were little
more than formalities, he was found guilty by the
jury, and was sentenced to be hanged, drawn, and
quartered, and his head fixed on a pole on London
Bridge. This sentence, the King,—who appears
to have borne as much affection for Sir Thomas
More as it was in his nature to entertain for any
one,—afterwards changed of his own accord to beheading. On the return of Sir Thomas More to
the Tower, a severer trial than that which he had
lately undergone, awaited him. As he was being
led through the gates of the fortress, his favourite
daughter, Mrs. Roper, (a lady who is said to have
united the genius of her father with all the softer
accomplishments of her sex,) burst through the
guards, and, throwing her arms round her father's
neck, bathed him with her tears. It was not without force that the officers were able to remove her;
but, before he was out of sight, she again broke
from them, and once more throwing herself into

her father's arms, the same distressing scene was
acted over again. "Oh, my father, oh, my father!"
were the only words to which her grief enabled her
to give utterance. But, even at this painful moment, — when even the guards who surrounded
him are said to have shed tears,—Sir Thomas still
retained his wonted calmness and self-possession.
He alone, whatever were his secret feelings, appeared unmoved. In the centre of the armed circle,
he gave his daughter his solemn blessing; reminding her that if he suffered innocently, it was by
the will of God,—that it was her duty to resign
herself to His will and pleasure; and lastly, he
enjoined her to pray for mercy on his soul.

He was reconducted to his solitary dungeon,
where, even with the prospect of a painful and violent death immediately before his eyes, his cheerfulness never forsook him, and he even continued to
jest on the scaffold. Early on the morning of the
6th of July, 1535, he was unexpectedly visited by
Sir Thomas Pope, who informed him that it was the
will of the King and Council that his execution
should take place before nine o'clock on that very day.
His reply was touchingly calm and dignified. "For
your good tidings," he said, "I heartily thank you.
I have always been much bounden to the King's
kindness for the benefits and honours he hath from
time to time heaped upon me; but I am more so
for his having put me into this place, where I
have had convenient time to have remembrance
of my end; and that it pleaseth his highness so

shortly to rid me from the miseries of this wretched
world." As he was being led forth from the Tower,
a woman in the crowd reproached him with having
detained some deeds while he was in power. "Good
woman," he said, "have patience but a little while,
for the King is so gracious to me, that, within this
half hour, he will discharge me of all my business,
and help thee himself." While he was in the act
of mounting the scaffold, he said to some one near
him, "Friend, help me up, and when I come down
again, let me shift for myself." The executioner
begging his forgiveness, "I forgive thee," he said,
"but you will never get any credit for beheading
me; my neck is so short." Then laying his head
upon the block, he desired the executioner to wait
till he had put his beard aside; "for that," he said,
"never committed treason."

Thus perished on Tower Hill, in his fifty-third
year, this great ornament of his age and country.
His remains were, in the first instance, buried in
the chapel of the Tower, but were afterwards removed to the south side of the chancel of Chelsea
Church. His head was fixed on a pole on London
Bridge, where it remained for fourteen days, when
his beloved daughter contrived to obtain possession
of it. She preserved it in a leaden box till the
day of her death, when, agreeably with her own
wish, it was placed in her arms, and interred with
her in the family vault of the Ropers, in St. Dun-
stan's Church, Canterbury.

A fellow-prisoner of Sir Thomas More in the

Tower, was John Fisher, Bishop of Rochester, a
devout and learned prelate, who was also committed
for refusing to admit the King's supremacy in the
church. Notwithstanding his advanced age, for he
had attained his eightieth year, he was thrust into
a cold and gloomy dungeon, where he was allowed
no covering but rags, which were scarcely sufficient
to cover his nakedness. He was in this miserable
condition when the Pope conferred on him the
high dignity of Cardinal. Before the purple, however, could reach England, the venerable prelate
was no more. On the 17th of June, 1535, he was
tried and condemned, and on the 22nd of the
same month was led forth to his execution. On
the morning of his death he dressed himself with
unusual care, and calmly laid his head upon the
block, repeating fervently the *Te Deum*.

The same year, the unfortunate Queen, Anne
Boleyn, was committed a prisoner to the gloomy
fortress of the Tower. Less than three years before, she had issued forth to her coronation from
under the portals of that very building, amidst the
roar of cannon and the acclamations of the populace, the centre of a glittering cavalcade of gallant
men and beautiful women, the envied of thousands,
and the observed of all observers :—

> Then high-born men were proud to wait ;
> And beauty watched to imitate
>   Her gentle voice and lovely mien ;
> And gather from her air and gait
>   The graces of their queen :
> Then, had her eye in sorrow wept,
> A thousand warriors forth had leapt ;

A thousand swords had sheathless shone,
And made her quarrel all their own.
Now,—what is she? and what are they?
Can she command? or these obey?
All silent and unheeding now,
With downcast eyes, and knitting brow,
And folded arms, and freezing air,
And lips that scarce their scorn forbear,
Her knights and dames,—her court is there.

She had then been attended by mitred abbots, and by bishops, and barons, and earls, and marquises;—by Knights of the Bath in their " violet gowns with hoods purfelled with minever ;"—by judges in their scarlet robes, and peers arrayed in crimson velvet ; while she herself, young, beautiful, and joyous, followed in a fair chariot, drawn by four milk-white palfreys, her long hair flowing from under the diamond coronet which encircled her head, and her canopy of cloth of gold, supported by the choicest knights of a chivalrous age. The scene was now changed, and when, pale, friendless, and affrighted, she passed a prisoner through the Traitor's Gate,—the famous water-entrance to the Tower, —it was to quit it but once more to pass to her trial, and thence to the scaffold.

The question of the guilt or innocence of Anne Boleyn, we are not called upon to discuss. Naturally of a gay, lively, and unsuspicious disposition ; vain of her own surpassing loveliness, and naturally fond of admiration;—accustomed, moreover, by her early education in France, to the freedom and levities which were forbidden by the stricter ceremonials of the Court of England,—and prompted by a natural flow of spirits to throw off the trammels of royalty, and to associate familiarly with those who had formerly been her chosen intimates,—it was not to be wondered that she should occasionally have forgotten the exalted station she had been called upon to fill, and that, in some unguarded moments, she should have been betrayed into freedoms and familiarities, of which, however innocent in themselves, her enemies afterwards availed themselves to effect her ruin and death. That she was ever the adulteress, however, which her unfeeling husband affected to believe her, and much more that she was guilty of the incestuous crime with her own brother, Lord Rochford, with which she was so confidently charged, we believe to be entirely and utterly false.

One can almost imagine the scene of the famous tournament at Greenwich, on May-day, 1535, when the handkerchief of the lovely Queen fell from her silken balcony into the area below. Whether the circumstance was intentional, or whether it was accidental, Henry chose to interpret it as an act of gallantry to one of her presumed paramours, and, inflamed by his new passion for Jane Seymour, determined on the ruin of his beautiful Queen. He immediately quitted the gay scene, accompanied by only six attendants, and on his return to the palace at Westminster, gave orders for the arrest of the Queen's brother, Lord Rochford, Henry Norris, William Brereton, and Sir Francis Weston, three officers of his own household, and Mark Smeaton, a musician,—all of whom were accused of having shared the Queen's favours, and who were forthwith committed to the Tower.

The next day, the Queen was arrested by the Duke of Norfolk and other Lords, and on her way to the Tower by water, was informed of the charges brought against her, which she earnestly and solemnly declared to be false. Amazed by so strange and sudden a vicissitude in her fortunes, as she passed through the gloomy Traitor's Gate, she became deeply affected, and, on reaching the landing, fell down on her knees, passionately renewed her protestations of innocence, and shortly afterwards fell into violent hysterics. As she hoped God to help her, she said, she was not guilty of the crime laid to her charge.

There is extant part of a letter from Sir William Kingston, Constable of the Tower,—who was placed as a sort of spy over the words and actions of the unfortunate Queen,—which affords a very interesting picture of her miserable condition on her first admission to the Tower. To Secretary Cromwell he writes, " Upon my lord of Norfolk, and the King's council, departing from the Tower, I went before the Queen into her lodging, and she said unto me, ' Mr. Kingston, shall I go into a dungeon ?' ' No, madam, you shall go into your lodging that you lay in at your coronation.' ' It is too good for me,' she said; 'Jesus have mercy on me ;' and kneeled down, weeping apace, and in the same sorrow fell into a great laughing, which she hath done several times since. And then she desired me to move

the King's highness, that she might have the sacrament in the closet by her chamber, that she might
pray for mercy; for ' I am as clear,' she said, ' from
the company of man, as to sin, as I am clear from
you, and am the King's true wedded wife.' And
then she said, ' Mr. Kingston, do you know wherefore I am here ?' and I said, nay ; and then she
asked me, ' when saw you the King ?' and I said, ' I
saw him not since I saw him yesterday in the
tilt-yard.' And then said she, ' Mr. Kingston, I pray
you to tell me where my father is ?' and I told her I
saw him before dinner in the court. ' And where
is my sweet brother?' And I said I left him at
York Place (Whitehall), and so I did. ' I hear say,'
said she, ' that I shall be accused with three men,
and I can say no more than nay, without I should
open my body, and therewith opened her gown.'
Then she said, ' Mr. Kingston, shall I die without
justice ?' And I said, the poorest subject the King
hath, hath justice ; and therewith she laughed. All
this saying was yester-night."

There is another remarkable passage in this interesting letter, which shews that, even in her own
bedchamber, the unfortunate Queen had a secret
spy upon her actions. " I was commanded," writes
Kingston, " to charge the gentlewomen that attended
upon the Queen, that they should have no communication with her, unless my wife were present;
and so I did it, notwithstanding it cannot be so;
for my Lady Boleyn and Mistress Cofyn lie on the
Queen's pallet, and I and my wife at the door with-

out; so that they must needs talk that be within; *but I have everything told me by Mistress Cofyn* that she thinks meet for me to know."

It was at this period that Anne Boleyn addressed that touching and beautiful letter to her heartless lord, which, as a literary composition, is far superior in elegance to the style of the age in which she lived. The last paragraph, in which,—forgetting her own misfortunes, she eloquently intercedes for those innocent persons who had become involved in her ruined fortunes,—is one which never fades from the memory. "My last and only request shall be, that myself only may bear the burden of your grace's displeasure, and that it may not touch the innocent souls of those four gentlemen, who, as I understand, are likewise in strait imprisonment for my sake. If ever I have found favour in your sight; if ever the name of Anne Boleyn hath been pleasing in your ears, then let me obtain this request; and I will so leave off troubling your grace any farther, with mine earnest prayers to the Trinity to have your grace in His good keeping, and to direct you in all your actions. From my doleful prison in the Tower, this sixth of May.   Your most loyal and ever-faithful wife, ANNE BOLEYN."

On the 12th of May, Norris, Weston, Brereton, and Smeaton, underwent their trial in Westminster Hall. Norris, who was a personal favourite of the King, was offered his life, on condition that he should confess himself guilty and accuse the Queen. He was too generous, however, to save his own life at the expense of that of another, and retorted indignantly, that in his conscience he believed her to be an innocent woman, and that, for his own part, he would rather die a thousand deaths than calumniate a guiltless person. Smeaton, on the other hand, displayed a contemptible attachment to life, and though his averment obtained no credit, he confidently affirmed that he had been admitted to a criminal correspondence with the Queen. The Queen's own voluntary statement, with regard to her intercourse with this miserable musician, there is every reason to believe deserving of credit. He had never, she said, been in her chamber but twice, when he played upon the harpsichord, but she admitted that he once had the confidence to tell her that "a look sufficed him." Smeaton's meanness, however, availed him nothing, and he was executed with the rest.

Three days after the condemnation of her presumed lovers, the Queen and her brother, Lord Rochford, were brought to trial in the great hall of the Tower. The jury, which tried them, consisted of the Duke of Suffolk, the Marquis of Exeter, the Earl of Arundel, and twenty-three other peers; their uncle, the Duke of Norfolk, presiding as Lord High Steward. The defenceless Queen had by this time regained her calmness and self-possession, and when she appeared before the Court, attended by her ladies, she wore an aspect of dignified royalty and injured innocence, which the beholders were little likely to forget. There were few, who witnessed that memorable scene in the Tower, who did not depart to their own homes with a firm and full conviction of the innocence of the persecuted Queen. The frightful accusation of incest was fully entered into, but the proofs appear to have amounted to little more than that Rochford, before some company, had been seen to lean over the bed of his sister. In those days, however, the will of the sovereign readily decided the fate of his victim, and accordingly, the fair and innocent Queen was sentenced to be either burned or beheaded, according to the King's pleasure. The dreadful words were no sooner uttered, than she arose in the midst of her female attendants, and gave utterance to a most touching asseveration of her innocence. Had the verdict of her judges, she said, been given according to the expectation of the bystanders, she must inevitably have been acquitted: but there were those among them, she added,—and she seems especially to have alluded to the King's brother-in-law, the Duke of Suffolk,—who " applying themselves to the King's humour," were determined on effecting her ruin. " O Father ! O Creator !" she exclaimed fervently; "Thou who art the way, the truth, and the life ; Thou knowest that I have not deserved this death !" Till within two days of her execution, the unhappy Queen appears to have been buoyed up with expectations that her life would be spared. On the 15th of May, however, sentence of death was passed on her; on the 17th, Lord Rochford, Norris, Brereton, and Weston, were beheaded on

Tower Hill, and, on the 19th, she herself was led
forth to execution.   On the 16th, the day after
her condemnation, Kingston writes, " I desire to
know the King's pleasure touching the Queen, as
well for her confessor, as for the preparation of scaf-
folds and other necessaries ; concerning which the
King's grace shewed me that my lord of Canterbury should be her confessor, and he was here this
day with the Queen ; but not in that matter.   Sir,
the time is short, for the King supposes the gentlemen do die to-morrow.   I have told my Lord
Rochford that he must be in readiness to-morrow
to suffer execution, and so he accepts it very well,
and will do his best to be ready.   Sir, I shall desire
you, that we may here know the King's pleasure,
as shortly as may be, that we may prepare for the
same, which is necessary ; for we here have no man
to do execution.   *Yet the Queen said this day at
dinner that she should go to Hanover, and is in hope
of life;* and thus fare you well. — WILLIAM KING-
STON."

The execution of her brother, and the preparations
which were making for her own death, at length
convinced the unhappy Queen that she had no
mercy to expect from her relentless husband,
and she prepared herself to die with exemplary
piety and resignation.   Kingston, a few hours before
her execution, writes to Secretary Cromwell: The
Queen sent for me, and at my coming she said,
' Mr. Kingston, I hear say, I shall not die before noon, and I am very sorry, therefore, for I

thought to be dead now, and past my pain.'   I told her it should be no pain, it was so subtle.   Then she said, I have heard say the executioner is very good, and I have a little neck; and putting her hands about it laughed heartily.   I have seen many men, and also women executed, and that they have been in great sorrow, but, to my knowledge, this lady has much joy and pleasure in death.   Her almoner is continually with her, and has been since two of the clock after midnight."

On the night before her execution Anne, for the last time, sent a message to her husband, protesting her innocence, and acknowledging the many favours she had formerly received at his hands.   From a private gentlewoman, she said, he had raised her to be a marchioness, and from a marchioness to be a Queen; and, since he could raise her no higher, he was now sending her to be a saint in Heaven. Lastly, she solemnly recommended her infant daughter, Elizabeth, to his paternal care.

All strangers having been commanded to quit the Tower, about noon she was led forth to the scaffold, which was erected on the green in front of the chapel.   Among the persons who had been summoned to be present, were the Dukes of Suffolk and Richmond, and the Lord Mayor, sheriffs, and aldermen of London.   Her step was firm and graceful; her countenance serene and cheerful; and it was remarked that she had never looked more beautiful than she did in that awful hour.   Her beauty and gentleness nearly unmanned the executioner:

the ladies who attended her clung to her in pa-
roxysms of grief, and there was no one present who
was not deeply affected by the touching solemnity
of the scene. Anne alone appeared cheerful and
unmoved. She kindly endeavoured to soothe the
grief of her attendants, to each of whom she presented some token of her affectionate regard. Then,
after addressing a few words to the bystanders,—in
which she acknowledged the bounties she had received from the King, and desired the prayers of those
around her,—she knelt down, and, having passed a
short time in prayer, she laid her head upon the
block as resignedly as if it had been her pillow, and
submitted to the blow of the executioner. This
person had been brought from Calais; it being supposed that he was more expert than any in England. Very little regard was shewn to the Queen's
remains. They were placed in a common elm
chest, which had been used for holding arrows, and
were interred, without ceremony, among the many
headless dead in the chapel of the Tower. There
is a mound in Richmond Park,—in the garden of
the lodge occupied by Lord John Russell, — on
which, it is said, King Henry stood to watch the
bursting of the rocket, which had been agreed upon
as the signal to announce to him that his injured
Queen was no more. The next day he married her
rival, Jane Seymour.

The following year, Lord Thomas Howard, youngest son of the Duke of Norfolk, was committed to
the Tower for forming a clandestine marriage with

the King's niece, Lady Margaret Douglas. He died
of grief in the fortress, after a short imprisonment,
when his widow, who had been his fellow-prisoner,
obtained her liberty.

In 1540, the powerful and high-minded Thomas
Cromwell, Earl of Essex, was disgraced, by the
ungrateful master whom he had served so long and
faithfully, and was committed a friendless and for-
saken prisoner to the Tower. On the morning of
the 10th of June,—after passing through an antichamber lined with cringing courtiers and hungry
supplicants,—he had taken his seat at the council-
table as Keeper of the Privy Seal, Lord Chamberlain,
Master of the Wards, and a Knight of the Garter.
The same day he was suddenly arrested at that
very table by the Duke of Norfolk, and hurried to
the Tower. On the 29th he was tried and condemned, ostensibly on some ridiculous charges of
high treason; but his real crimes, as is well known,
were his having brought about the marriage with
Anne of Cleves,— whom Henry, after their first
interview, had declared to be a " great Flanders
mare,"— and afterwards his opposing the King's
marriage with his new passion, Catherine Howard.

From the Tower the fallen minister addressed
more than one pathetic letter to his royal master;
" written," to use his own language, " with the
quaking hand and most sorrowful heart of a most
sorrowful subject." One of these letters concludes,
" I, a most woeful prisoner, am ready to take the
death when it shall please God and your majesty;

and yet the frail flesh inciteth me continually to call to your Grace for mercy and grace for mine offences. And thus Christ save, preserve, and keep you. Written at the Tower, this Wednesday, the last of June, with the heavy heart, and the trembling hand of your highness's most heavy, and most miserable prisoner, and poor slave, Thomas Cromwell." And a little below he adds, " Most gracious prince, I cry for mercy, mercy, mercy!"

One of these heart-rending appeals the tyrant caused to be thrice read over to him, and was so affected at the recital as to shed tears. The arguments, however, of Cromwell's deadly enemy, the Duke of Norfolk, and the King's headstrong passion for Catherine Howard, overcame his lingering affection for his old and faithful servant, and, on the 28th of July, Cromwell was led from the Tower to the fatal scaffold on the adjoining hill, where he died pious and resigned.

On the 8th of August, 1540, eleven days after the death of Cromwell, Henry was united to Catherine Howard, niece of the Duke of Norfolk, the best beloved, and not the least beautiful of his numerous wives. Fascinated by her youth, her loveliness, her agreeable conversation, and insinuating address, the sixteen months which elapsed between the period of their marriage and the discovery of the frailty of his young wife, were perhaps the happiest of Henry's life. He made no secret of his excessive attachment, and on one occasion publicly returned thanks to Heaven in the chapel-royal, for the felicity which their union had procured for him ; the Bishop of Lincoln having composed an especial prayer for the occasion.

At length, however, rumours of the Queen's infidelity, and especially of criminal conduct before marriage, became whispered abroad, and to Archbishop Cranmer was committed the invidious and perilous task of communicating to the unsuspecting monarch the fact that he had been deceived in his beautiful Queen. Had Cranmer failed in his proofs, his head, as well as those of others, would doubtless have paid the penalty. At first, so confident was Henry of his wife's purity, that he positively refused to give the least credit to the information. But at length when undoubted proofs of her criminality were laid before him, he became so deeply affected, that he continued for a long time speechless, and at last burst into tears.

The necessary investigations having been made in different quarters, the Queen was conveyed in the first instance to Sion, where she underwent an examination before the Archbishop of Canterbury, her uncle, the Duke of Norfolk, and other lords. About the same time, Lady Rochford,—the confidante of her amours,—and three gentlemen, Mannoc, Derham, and Culpepper, on whom she was accused of having conferred her favours, were committed to prison. In the presence of the examining lords, she made a full confession of her criminality with Derham before marriage, but strenuously denied that she had since been unfaithful to the king's bed; a statement, the truth of which she subsequently insisted upon no less vehemently to Dr. White, afterwards Bishop of Winchester, when he conferred with her as her spiritual adviser immediately before her execution. We are naturally inclined to give credit to the solemnity of a dying declaration. But when we remember the fact, that Derham, who had been her paramour before marriage, was afterwards appointed to a place about her person, and, moreover, that Culpepper, during a recent progress which she had made with the King, had been admitted into her bed-chamber at eleven o'clock at night, and had remained there till four o'clock the next morning, can we wonder that her judges should have refused to give credence to her story?

From Sion the young Queen was conducted in as private a manner as possible to the Tower. Thither also were committed, as accessories of her crime, her grandmother, the old Duchess of Norfolk, her unprincipled confidante, Lady Rochford, her uncle, Lord William Howard, the Countess of Bridgewater, and some other persons of inferior rank. About the same time Derham and Culpepper were tried, and hung at Tyburn; and on the 11th of January, 1542, acts of attainders were passed against the Queen and Lady Rochford for high treason.

On the eleventh of February, the young Queen and her favourite were executed together on the green before the Tower Chapel. "Since my writing to you on Sunday last," says an eye-witness, " I

saw the queen and Lady Rochford suffer within
the Tower the day following ; whose souls, I doubt
not, be with God, for they made the most godly
and Christian end that ever was heard tell of,
I think, since the world's creation ; uttering their
lively faith in the blood of Christ only, with
wonderful patience and constancy to the death ;
and with goodly words and steadfast countenances,
they desired all Christian people to take regard
unto their worthy and just punishment with death
for their offences, and against God heinously, from
their youth upwards, in breaking all his com-
mandments.   Wherefore, they being justly condemned, as they said, by the laws of the realm
and the parliament, to die, required the people, I
say, to take example at them for amendment of
their ungodly lives, and gladly to obey the King in
all things ; for whose preservation they did heartily
pray, and willed all people so to do, commending
their souls to God, and earnestly calling for mercy
upon him."   The world looked upon the execution
of Lady Rochford as a judgment from Heaven,
for it was through her evidence that Queen Anne
Boleyn, and her own husband, Lord Rochford, had
been brought to the block.   Shortly after the
Queen's death, the Duchess of Norfolk, and most
of the others who had been condemned for mis-
prision of treason, received the King's pardon.
Lord William Howard, however, was allowed to
linger on in the Tower, where he died a few
months after the execution of his sister.

A lady of a very different character was Anne Askew, one of the early sufferers in the cause of the Reformed religion. She was the daughter of Sir William Askew, of Kelsay, in Lincolnshire, and at the time that she was committed to the Tower, and was subjected to the frightful agonies of the rack, was only in her twenty-sixth year. She had been previously condemned to death at Guildhall, and had listened undauntedly to the dreadful sentence passed upon her, that she should be burnt alive at the stake. There still, however, remained the terrors of the rack,—and as the Duchess of Suffolk, and the Countesses of Sussex and Hertford, and other ladies, were supposed to have imbibed the same religious opinions, — her persecutors determined, by agonies and terrors, to force her to a confession. She remained true, however, to her religion and to friendship, to the last. On arriving at the Tower, she was thrust into a miserable dungeon, where we have the evidence, not only of Fox, but also her own written statement, that Sir Richard Rich, a Privy Counsellor, and Sir Thomas Wriothesley, the Chancellor, actually put their hands to the rack, and assisted in the frightful work of torturing the noble-minded girl. " Rich," she says, in her unvarnished narrative, " came to me with one of the council, charging me, upon my obedience, to shew unto them if I knew any man or woman of my sect ? My answer was, that I knew none. They asked me of my lady Suffolk, my lady of Sussex, my lady of Hertford, my lady Denny, and my lady Fitzwilliams.

I said, if I should pronounce anything against them, that I were not able to prove it. Then they put me on the rack, because I confessed no ladies or gentlewomen to be of my opinion, and thereon they kept me a long time. And because I lay still and did not cry, my Lord Chancellor, and Mr. Rich took pain to rack me with their own hands, till I was well nigh dead. Then the Lieutenant [of the Tower] caused me to be loosed from the rack. Incontinently I swooned, and then they recovered me again. After that, I sat two long hours reasoning with my Lord Chancellor, upon the bare floor, whereas he, with many flattering words, persuaded me to leave my opinions. But my Lord God,—and I thank his everlasting goodness,—gave me grace to persevere, and will do, I hope, to the end."

Her prayer was not breathed in vain. When she was led to the flames, her limbs were so mangled and disjointed, that it was only with the assistance of two sergeants that she was able to stand. Yet, Strype informs us, that one who visited her in the Tower, a few hours before her execution, was so struck with the sweet serenity of her countenance, that he compared it to that of St. Stephen, " as it had been that of an angel." She was burnt to death at Smithfield, in the presence of the Duke of Norfolk, the Earl of Bedford, the Lord Chancellor, and others, on the 16th of July, 1546. At the last moment, immediately before the torch was put to the faggots, a paper was presented to her, containing the King's pardon, on condition that she would

recant her errors. She refused, however, not only
to have the document read, but even to look at it.
" Whereupon," says Ballard, " the Lord Mayor commanded it to be put in the fire, and cried with a
loud voice, *Fiat Justitia*; and, fire being put to the
faggots, she surrendered up her pious soul to God in
the midst of the flames."

The last persons who were committed to the
Tower, in this reign, on whose history and misfortunes we shall dwell at any length, were Thomas
Duke of Norfolk, and his accomplished and ill-fated
son, Henry Earl of Surrey. To the former venerable nobleman, the King, as well as his country,
lay under deep obligations for his long and valuable services. In his youth, he had signalized himself in more than one naval enterprise; he had
fought the foremost and the bravest on the famous
field of Flodden; as Lord Deputy of Ireland his
conduct had gained the approbation of all men; he
had suppressed a dangerous insurrection in the
North; on the King's advance to Boulogne, in
1544, he had commanded the vanguard of the army;
and, moreover, he had more than once vanquished
the Scots on their own territory, " with a destruction," says Buchanan, " which equally levelled the
turreted castle of the baron, and the straw-built
hut of the peasant." Allied to the blood royal by
his descent from the ancient family of the Mow-
brays; still more closely allied to it by his marriage
with a daughter of Edward the Fourth, and by
his two nieces, Catherine Howard and Anne Boleyn,

having been successively Queens of England;—
universally regarded, moreover, as the head of the
powerful Roman Catholic party in England;—we
cannot be surprised, from the knowledge which we
possess of Henry's character, that when the tyrant
had become old, peevish, and sickly, he should
have regarded the power and popularity of the
Duke of Norfolk with suspicion and dread. Accordingly, in the month of December, 1546, the
Duke was suddenly arrested and committed to
the Tower. To the ambassadors abroad it was
given out, that the Duke, and his son, Lord Surrey, had conspired to take on them the government, during the King's life, and, after his death,
to secure the person of the Prince: one of the
principal charges, however, appears to have been,
that the Duke had quartered the arms of Edward the Confessor, which his ancestors had long
borne before him, and which he himself had often
worn in the King's presence. On the 14th of
January, 1547, the House of Peers, without examining the prisoner, without trial or evidence, passed
a bill of attainder against the Duke. This infamous
bill was immediately approved by the obsequious
Commons, and, having received the royal assent by
Commissioners, the Duke's execution was ordered to
take place on the morning of the 29th of January.

The gay, the gallant, and handsome Earl of Surrey,—the soldier, the scholar, the courtier, and the
poet,—was commited to the Tower at the same
time with his venerable father. Not being a peer

of the realm, he was ordered to be tried before a common jury at the Guildhall, where he was arraigned on the 13th of January. His answers to the questions put to him were remarkable for their judgment and acuteness, and his defence was eloquent, dignified, and spirited. When one of the witnesses, who were confronted with him, repeated a conversation in which he stated that he had braved the Earl with an insolent retort, " I put it to the jury," said the noble prisoner, " whether it is probable that any man should address such a speech to the Earl of Surrey, and he not strike him ? " Notwithstanding his able defence, he was found guilty of high treason, and was carried back to the Tower, with the edge of the fatal axe turned towards him. Six days afterwards, on the 19th of January, he was beheaded on Tower Hill.

The Duke of Norfolk was more fortunate than his accomplished son. His sentence was to have been carried into effect on the 29th of January, but, on the very day previously, Henry, whose health had been long failing him, providentially breathed his last. The Duke, who survived till the reign of Queen Mary, lived to preside at the trial of his powerful rival, John Dudley, Duke of Northumberland, and, when upwards of eighty years of age, appeared in arms at the suppression of Wyatt's rebellion. It is remarkable that he should have lived in the reigns of eight sovereigns.

We have been able to dwell on the misfortunes of only a few of the numerous prisoners who were

denizens of the Tower during the reign of Henry
the Eighth.   In those days, its gloomy dungeons
appear to have been but seldom tenantless.   During the religious persecutions which prevailed in
the reign of Henry, they were crowded with hun-
dreds of human beings who were stigmatized with
the name of heretics; and, almost daily, its vaulted
chambers and passages echoed back the shrieks
extorted by the frightful tortures of the rack.

Here, in this reign, were committed prisoners,
the Earls of Casillis and Glencairn, and many of
the most powerful of the Scottish nobility, who
had been taken prisoners at the battle of Solway;
and again, in 1537, after the suppression of the
insurrections in the north, the dungeons of the
Tower were peopled with a host of prisoners, of
whom Lord Darcy was beheaded on Tower Hill,
Lord Hussey at Lincoln, and Sir Robert Constable
was hung in chains at Hull: numerous others,
— including the abbots of Fontaine, Ryval, and
Jervaux,—were taken from the Tower, to be executed at Tyburn.   Here were imprisoned the two
unworthy favourites of Henry the Seventh, Sir
Richard Epsom and Edmund Dudley, both of whom
were beheaded on Tower Hill; and here also, at
a later period, were confined the Marquis of Exeter, Henry Pole Lord Montague, Sir Edward
Neville, brother of Lord Abergavenny, and Sir
Nicholas Carew, all of whom, having been condemned to death for carrying on a treasonable correspondence with Cardinal Pole, fell by the axe

of the executioner on the adjoining hill. Lastly, the singular fate of Arthur Plantagenet, Viscount Lisle, demands a passing notice. This nobleman, an illegitimate son of King Edward the Fourth, had been committed to the fortress on suspicion of being engaged in a conspiracy to deliver over the town of Calais, of which he was the governor, to the French. His innocence, however, being afterwards clearly proved, Henry sent his secretary, Sir Thomas Wriothesley, with a present of a diamond ring to the prisoner, as a token that he was restored to favour and to life. The communication had a different effect to what was intended. So overpowered was Lord Lisle by the joyful tidings, and the suddenness of the communication, that he was seized with convulsions, of which he expired the same night.

Henry the Eighth, as we have already mentioned, died on the 28th of January, 1547, and, two days afterwards, his son and successor, Edward the Sixth, then in his tenth year, was conducted with great parade to the Tower, amidst the roar of cannon and the acclamations of the populace. The next day, the royal child was placed on a throne in the chamber of presence, where the principal nobility knelt to him and kissed his hand. Here, a few days afterwards, he was knighted by his maternal uncle, the Protector Somerset, and from hence he was conducted in great state, on the 20th of February, to his coronation in Westminster Abbey.

The first prisoner of importance who was committed to the Tower, after the accession of the young King, was his own uncle, Thomas, Lord Seymour, of Sudley, Lord High Admiral of England. This celebrated person was no less conspicuous from his high courage, his commanding figure, his graceful manners, and his success with the fair sex, than for his arrogance to his equals, his implacable animosities, and his insatiable ambition. By his insinuating address he had contrived to win the affections of Henry's widow, Catherine Parr, to whom he was married so soon after the King's death, that, had she borne a living child, it would have been difficult to identify its father. The Queen died shortly afterwards in childbed, when Lord Seymour had the boldness to fix his views on the King's sister, the young Princess Elizabeth. That he succeeded in insinuating himself into her good graces, and that some familiarities of a rather delicate nature passed between the Lord High Admiral and the young Princess, there can be no question. At one time we find him romping with her in the garden at Hanworth, and " cutting her gown into an hundred pieces;" while on another occasion we discover him entering her chamber before she had risen, when, we are told, " She ran out of her bed to her maidens, and then went behind the curtains of her bed." But with Lord Seymour love was only a secondary consideration. Aware that his brother, the Protector, would never consent to his marriage with the Princess, he en-

tered into a dark and deep-laid plot, the principal
objects of which were to supplant his brother in
the Protectorship, and to obtain possession of the
King's person and affections.

It could only have been from a stern and melancholy necessity, that a man so amiable as the
Protector could have been induced to sanction
those violent measures against his own brother,
which subsequently led that daring intriguer to
the block.   Having previously deprived him of
the office of High Admiral, the Protector, on the
19th of January, 1549, signed a warrant for com-
mitting him to the Tower.   In vain Lord Seymour
pleaded to be brought to an open trial.   On the 26th
of February, the bill for his attainder passed the
House of Lords; on the 4th of March it was rati-
fied, with only a few dissentient voices, by the House
of Commons, and, on the following day, the young
King gave his assent to the execution of his own
uncle, and the Protector signed the death-warrant
of his own brother.   Of the manner in which Lord
Seymour demeaned himself in his last moments, but
few particulars have been handed down to us.   At
his own request he was attended by the celebrated
Bishop Latimer, who informs us, in one of his ser-
mons, that the Lord Admiral died " very danger-
ously, irksomely, horribly."   He was beheaded on a
scaffold on Tower Hill, on the 20th of March, 1549.

The ruin of the Protector,—brought about by his
turbulent and ambitious rival, John Dudley, Duke
of Northumberland,—followed shortly after that of

his brother. On the 6th of October, 1551, Lord St. John, President of the Council, the Duke of Northumberland, the Earls of Southampton and Arundel, and five other members of the Privy Council, met at Ely House, Holborn, and after attributing to him every misfortune which had befallen the nation, came to the bold determination of acting independent of his authority. These astounding tidings no sooner reached the ears of the Protector, than he removed the young King from Hampton Court to Windsor, and, by arming his friends and retainers, shewed how resolved he was to defend himself to the last. Great, however, and deserved as was his popularity with the lower classes, the Protector found, to his grief and consternation, that scarcely a single person of rank was prepared to rise in his favour. It was evident therefore that his doom was fixed. On the 17th of October, he was sent to the Tower with several of his friends and adherents, and, on the 1st of December following, was brought to trial before a solemn assemblage of peers in Westminster Hall; the Marquis of Winchester sitting as Lord High Steward. The charges on which he was arraigned were high treason and felony;—the former accusing him of having projected to seize the King's person and to raise insurrections in the north, and the latter of having meditated the arrest of the Duke of Northumberland; a recent act of Parliament having declared it to be felony to conspire against a Privy Councillor.

At his trial, Somerset demeaned himself with

great dignity; and so satisfactory was his defence, that the peers acquitted him of the charge of treason, though they brought him in guilty of the felony. So beloved was he by the people, that when the verdict of acquittal was announced to the multitude who surrounded Westminster Hall, they raised so loud a shout of exultation, that it was heard at Charing Cross. Their joy, however, was suddenly damped, when they learned that he had been found guilty of the felony, and condemned to death.

From Westminster, Somerset was conducted by water to London Bridge, and from thence, escorted by a strong guard, through the streets to his former apartment in the Tower. His execution was fixed for the 22nd of January, and, accordingly, on that day, the ill-fated Protector,—lately so envied and so powerful, — was led forth to the scaffold, on Tower Hill. He ascended the fatal stage with a firm step and cheerful countenance, and kneeling down, and lifting up his hands, commended his soul to God. He then addressed himself to the multitude, and had proceeded at some length in his speech, when an incident occurred which might have put to the test the courage and composure of the bravest. Suddenly, Sir Anthony Brown was seen riding towards the scaffold, at which the people raised a loud cry of joy, and, throwing up their caps, shouted,—"A pardon, a pardon, God save the King!" The mistake, however, was soon discovered, on which the Duke, without the least discomposure, waved his hand to the people, to obtain their silence, and calmly continued his harangue.

Having concluded, he again knelt down to his devotions, and then, once more rising up, took an affectionate leave of the Sheriffs and the Lieutenant of the Tower, and presented the executioner with some money. Having untied his shirt-strings, he again knelt down in the straw, and the executioner having turned down his collar, he himself covered his face with his handkerchief. To the last, his countenance appeared unmoved by the fear of death, and it was observed that, if anything, his cheeks had more colour in them than usual. Having laid his head upon the block, he repeated three times, "Lord Jesus, save me!" and, just as he was uttering it for the third time, the axe fell and separated his head from his body. His remains were placed in a coffin, and having been carried back to the Tower, were interred between the bodies of Anne Boleyn and Catherine Howard. Thus died the great Protector, Edward, Duke of Somerset! After the axe fell, many of the crowd rushed on the scaffold, and dipping their handkerchiefs in his blood, preserved them as precious relics. Some years afterwards, when his rival, the Duke of Northumberland, was carried a prisoner through the streets to the Tower, many persons crowded round him, and shaking their bloody handkerchiefs in his face, upbraided him with his cruelty to their favourite Duke.

We have already mentioned that more than one

of the Protector's friends and partizans were committed with him to the Tower. Of these, the Earl
of Arundel, Lords Grey and Paget, and others
escaped with an imprisonment of more or less duration; but Sir Ralph Vane, a brave and veteran
soldier, Sir Michael Stanhope, a relation of Somerset, Sir Thomas Arundel, and Sir Miles Partridge,
were less fortunate. All four were executed on the
same day, the 26th of February, on Tower Hill;
Arundel and Stanhope by the axe, and Vane and
Partridge on the common gibbet. Sir Ralph Vane
died deeply lamented. He had fought gallantly on
many fields of battle, and, at his trial, had conducted his defence with great ability. When pressed
to petition for his life, he refused to make the required submission. " The wars," he said, " have
now ended, and the coward and the courageous
are alike esteemed."

Edward the Sixth expired at Greenwich, on the
6th of July, 1553, in the sixteenth year of his age.
Shortly before his decease, he was prevailed upon by
the Duke of Northumberland, to deprive his sisters,
Mary and Elizabeth, of the succession, and to be-
queath his crown to the Lady Jane Grey,—who had
married the Duke's fourth son, Lord Guildford Dudley,—and who was great-grand-daughter of Henry the
Seventh, by the marriage of Mary, daughter of that
monarch, to Charles, Duke of Suffolk. This measure,
immediately after the King's death, was confirmed
by the Privy Council and the several judges; Sir
James Hale alone refusing to give his assent.

The breath had no sooner quitted the King's body, than Northumberland,—accompanied by the Duke of Suffolk, the Earl of Pembroke, and others of the nobility,—proceeded to Sion House, where Lady Jane was then residing, and where they did homage to her as their sovereign. Immediately afterwards, she was proclaimed Queen of England with the usual solemnities; and, on the 9th of July, was conducted in state to the royal apartments in the Tower. Her reign, it is almost needless to remark, was as brief as its honours were distasteful to her.

Mary, the rightful successor, was at this period residing at Framlingham Castle, in Suffolk, where so many of the nobility and gentry flocked to her with military reinforcements, that it soon became evident, even to the aspiring Northumberland, that all hope of retaining the crown on the head of his daughter-in-law was at an end. In particular he was affected by the coldness of the people. "Many," he said to Lord Grey, "come to look at us, but I find no one cries, *God speed you!*" Deserted by his friends and followers, he was arrested by the Earl of Arundel on the 25th of July, and forthwith committed to the Tower. At the same time were seized, and sent to the same fortress, his three sons, the Earl of Warwick and Lords Ambrose and Henry Dudley; his brother, Sir Andrew Dudley, the Earl of Huntingdon, Lord Hastings, Sir Thomas Palmer, Sir Henry and Sir John Gates, and Dr. Sandys; the latter of whom

had preached a sermon at Cambridge in favour of
the Lady Jane. Two days afterwards, the Duke
of Suffolk, Lady Jane Grey, and her husband, Lord
Guildford Dudley, were committed to the Tower.

It was customary, in those times, for the kings
of England to pass the first days after their succession in the royal fortress, and accordingly, on the
3rd of August, we find Queen Mary conducted
thither with great state and magnificence. She
continued to reside there till after the funeral
of her brother, King Edward, on which occasion,
though she permitted him to be buried according to
the rites of the Protestant faith, she caused a
solemn requiem to be offered up for his soul in her
chapel in the Tower. In October following, we
find her holding her court in the royal fortress,
and it was from hence, on the 1st of that month,
that she proceeded in great state to her coronation in Westminster Abbey.

One of the first steps of Mary on entering the
Tower, had been to release the Duke of Norfolk,
who had remained a prisoner there since the death
of Henry the Eighth. She restored to liberty also
the Duchess of Somerset, widow of the Protector;
the celebrated Gardiner, Bishop of Winchester;
Tunstal, Bishop of Durham; and other prisoners of
less note. Their places, however, were merely
vacated to make room for fresh captives; indeed,
during this short reign, there seems scarcely a day
that the Tower did not open its gates to admit some
new victim, or that it did not send forth some

miserable wretch either to the axe or to the stake.

The first persons who suffered, were the turbulent and ambitious Duke of Northumberland, and his partizans, Sir Thomas Palmer and Sir John Gates. The Duke was condemned to death by his peers on the 18th of August, and on the 21st all three were executed on Tower Hill.

Notwithstanding Northumberland's established reputation for courage, the manner in which he encountered his reverse of fortunes, and looked death in the face, was widely different from the quiet fortitude, and pious resignation, which, under similar melancholy circumstances, had distinguished his rival and victim, the Duke of Somerset. When his enemy, the Earl of Arundel, arrested him at Cambridge, he fell on his knees before that nobleman, and in the most abject manner implored him to intercede for his life. Again, on the day before his execution, we find him addressing the following appeal to the Earl,— " Honourable Lord, and in this my distress my especial refuge, most woeful was the news I received this evening by Mr. Lieutenant, that I must prepare myself against to-morrow to receive my deadly stroke. Alas ! my good lord, is my crime so heinous, as no redemption but my blood can wash away the spots thereof? An old proverb there is, and it is most true, that a living dog is better than a dead lion. Oh ! that it would please her good Grace to give me life, yea, the life of a dog, if I might but live

and kiss her feet, and spend both life and all
in her honourable service, as I have done the best
part already under her worthy brother and most
glorious father. Oh! that her mercy were such
as she would consider how little profit my dead
and dismembered body can bring her; but how
great and glorious an hour it will be in all poste-
rities, when the report shall be that so gracious and
mighty a queen had granted life to so miserable
and penitent an object. Your honourable usage
and promise to me, since these my troubles, have
made me bold to challenge this kindness at your
hands. Pardon me if I have done amiss therein,
and spare not, I pray, your bended knees for me
in this distress. The God of Heaven, it may be,
will requite it one day on you or yours; and if
my life be lengthened by your mediation, and
my good Lord Chancellor's, (to whom I have also
sent my blurred letters,) I will ever owe it to be
spent at your honourable feet. Oh! my good
Lord, remember how sweet life is, and how bitter
the contrary. Spare not your speech and pains, for
God, I hope, hath not shut out all hopes of comfort
from me in that gracious, princely, and womanlike
heart; but that, as the doleful news of death
hath wounded to death both my soul and body,
so the comfortable news of life shall be as a new
resurrection to my woeful heart. But if no remedy
can be found, either by imprisonment, confiscation,
banishment, and the like, I can say no more but
God grant me patience to endure, and a heart to

forgive, the whole world. Once your fellow and loving companion, but now worthy of no name but wretchedness and misery.—"J. D."

The Duke, together with Sir Thomas Palmer and Sir John Gates, were beheaded on Tower Hill in the presence of an immense assemblage of people. At his execution, he confessed the justice of his sentence, and professing himself a firm believer in the "old religion," he told the multitude that they would have no tranquillity till they returned to the faith of their ancestors. Having concluded his speech, he "put off his gown of swan-coloured damask," and then laying his head on the block, he covered his eyes, and submitted to the stroke of the executioner. According to Fox, the martyrologist, the Duke was at heart a Protestant, but had been promised his life, even though his head should be on the block, on condition that he attended mass, and publicly avowed himself a Roman Catholic. The story, however, requires confirmation. It was certainly to the credit of Queen Mary, that, notwithstanding the numerous persons who were implicated in the late dangerous insurrection, only three persons,—Northumberland, Palmer, and Gates,—were marked out for destruction. It was not till Sir Thomas Wyatt's rebellion seemed to require increased severity, that the Queen signed the death warrants of Lady Jane Grey, Lord Guildford Dudley, and the Duke of Suffolk.

Replete as is the Tower with historical associations of deep interest, there is no story connected with it half so affecting as that of the young, the lovely, and ill-fated Lady Jane Grey; a story, which Fox tells that, when he was writing it in his " Book of Martyrs," the tears burst from his eyes. Distinguished as much by the sweetness of her disposition and her unaffected piety, as by her high birth, her deep learning, her playful wit, her surpassing loveliness, and her extraordinary female accomplishments, the Lady Jane, to the age of eighteen, had lived a life of comparative seclusion; dividing her time between the enjoyments which her passion for literature afforded her in her own closet, and the quiet pleasures and amusements of social life. We have the authority of her tutor Aylmer, and also of Queen Elizabeth's tutor, Ascham, that she was a perfect mistress of the Greek, Latin, French, and Italian languages, and was also acquainted with the Hebrew, Chaldee, and Arabic. She played on several musical instruments, which she occasionally accompanied with her voice; and she also wrote a beautiful hand, and excelled in various kinds of needlework. And all these virtues and accomplishments were " bounded within the narrow circle of eighteen!" Ascham on one occasion found her reading Plato, when all the rest of the family were hunting in the Park. " Before I went into Germany," he says, " I came to Broadgate, in Leicestershire, to take my leave of that noble lady, the Lady Jane Grey, to whom I was exceeding much beholden. Her parents, the Duke and Duchess, and all the household, gentlemen and gentlewo-

men, were hunting in the park. I found her in
her chamber reading the 'Phædon' of Plato, in
Greek, and that with as much delight as some
gentlemen would read a merry tale in Boccaccio.
After salutation and duty done, with some other
talk, I asked her why she should lose such pastime in the park ? Smiling she answered me, ' All
their sport in the park is but a shadow to that
pleasure I find in Plato.' However illustrious she
was by fortune," adds Ascham, " and by royal extraction, these bore no proportion to the accomplishments of her mind, adorned with the doctrine
of Plato, and the eloquence of Demosthenes."

To one so gentle and so retiring,—so passionately attached to literature and the arts,—the glitter
of a crown and the frivolities of a court could offer
but slight charms. Accordingly, when she was
waited upon, at Sion, by her father and father-in-
law, the Dukes of Suffolk and Northumberland,
and was hailed by them as Queen of England, she
expressed the greatest reluctance to quit a private
station, and the happy circle of which she was the
idol ; and it was only with the greatest difficulty that
she was at last induced to yield to their urgent entreaties. The story of her short reign of ten days is
well known. On the 27th of July, 1553, she was
sent back a prisoner to that fortress, which she had
so lately entered as an envied Queen ; and on the
13th of November,—together with her husband,
Lord Guildford Dudley, Archbishop Cranmer, and
Lords Ambrose and Henry Dudley,—she was

escorted from the Tower by a guard of four hundred men, to take her trial at Guildhall, for high
treason. As she stood at the bar, on that solemn
occasion, her youth and loveliness, and the fame
which had gone abroad of her extraordinary learning and the sweetness of her disposition, rendered
her the object of universal pity. Throughout the
long and tedious day, her voice never faltered,
neither did her countenance change; and even
while she listened to the awful sentence which
doomed her to a cruel and untimely death, although
every other eye was moist in that crowded assem-
bly, the roses never for a moment faded from her
cheeks.

It has been already mentioned, that Sir Thomas
Wyatt's insurrection sealed the fate of Lady Jane
Grey. On the 5th of February, 1554, Feckenham,
the Queen's Confessor, was admitted into Lady
Jane's apartment at the Tower, and informed her
that she must be prepared to die the following day.
Professing a tender zeal for the welfare of her soul,
he used every argument to induce her to renounce
the reformed religion; and subsequently obtained
for her a respite of three days, during which period
he constantly insisted on intruding himself on her
privacy, and harassing her with religious dispu-
tations. Lady Jane, however, remained constant
to the faith in which she had been educated. At
their last interview in the Tower, Feckenham,
alluding to the improbability of their meeting in
another world, observed, " Madam, I am sorry for

you; for I am now sure that we shall never meet."
" It is true, sir," replied the gentle disputant, "we
shall never meet, except God turn your heart; for
I am assured, unless you repent and turn to God,
you are in a sad and desperate case; and I pray
God, of His infinite mercy, to send you His Holy
Spirit; for He has given you His great gift of utterance, if it please Him also to open the eyes of
your heart."

The short space of time which remained to her
in this world, was passed by the Lady Jane in preparing herself for death, and in writing some tender
letters to those who were near and dear to her. To
her father she wrote affectionately; forgiving him
for the share which he had in bringing her to the
block, and fervently recommending him to the care
of the Almighty. "My death," she concludes,
"although to you it may seem woeful, yet to me
there is nothing that can be more welcome, than
from this vale of misery to aspire to that heavenly
throne of all joy and pleasure, with my Christ and
Saviour; in whose steadfast faith, (if it be lawful
for the daughter so to write to the father,) the
Lord that hath hitherto strengthened you, so continue to keep you, that at the last we may meet in
Heaven." A short time before her death, the
Lieutenant of the Tower, who appears to have
taken a deep interest in his beautiful prisoner, approached her with the touching request, that she
would write a short sentence in his manual of devotions, by which he might remember her. She ac-

cordingly took up her pen, and addressed to him,
"as a friend," a solemn admonition, in which she ad-
vised him of the importance of religion, and con-
jured him so to live, that by death he might in-
herit eternal life : the short homily concluded, "As
the preacher sayeth, there is a time to be born, and
a time to die ; and the day of death is better than
the day of our birth.   Your's, as the Lord knoweth,
as a friend, JANE DUDLEY."   About the same time,
while her hand-maidens were weeping in an adjoining apartment, she took up a Greek Testament,
and, in the Greek language, wrote an affectionate
letter in the blank pages to her sister Lady Catherine, which she enjoined one of her attendants to
deliver, with the book, to the beloved person to
whom it was addressed.   This interesting relic is
said to be still in existence.

It had been originally intended that Lady Jane
and her husband, Lord Guildford Dudley, should be
executed together on the same scaffold on Tower
Hill ; but the Privy-Council, dreading that the
murderous death of two persons, so young and
innocent, would inconveniently excite the compassion of the multitude, determined that Lady Jane
should be executed within the precincts of the
Tower.   Lord Guildford, on hearing that they
were to die separately, expressed a strong desire
to be allowed a last interview with his young wife.
Lady Jane, however, fearing that the scene might
unnerve them both, had strength of mind enough
to refuse his last request.   "Tell him," she said

touchingly, "that our separation is but momentary, and that we shall soon meet in Heaven, where our love will know no interruption, and where our joys and felicities will be for ever and ever."

Lord Guildford, a gallant youth of eighteen, was the first led forth to execution. One would willingly be able to point out the window in the Tower, at which the Lady Jane stood, and waved her hand as a parting adieu to her young husband as he passed to the scaffold on Tower Hill; the window on which the latter fixed his last look of unalterable affection. At the outer gate he shook hands affectionately with Sir Anthony Brown and others, and having requested their prayers, proceeded with a modest dignity to the scaffold. Having ascended the fatal steps, he prayed, for a short time, calmly and fervently, and then as calmly laid his head upon the block.

It must have been a trying interval, between the moment in which Lady Jane fixed her eyes for the last time on her beloved husband, and that on which she herself was summoned to her fate. It is not improbable, that she dreaded lest the frightful apparatus of the scaffold might have unnerved his step, or blanched his cheek, for when she was told with what serenity he had met his fate: " Oh, Guildford, Guildford!" she exclaimed, "the ante-repast is not so bitter that thou hast tasted, and which I shall soon taste, as to make my flesh tremble; it is nothing compared to the feast of which we shall partake this day in Heaven." The fact is a painful one to contemplate, that, as she was standing at the window, the cart, bearing the headless body of her husband, passed by.

Almost at the same moment, Sir John Gage, the Lieutenant of the Tower, came to summon her to the scaffold. She rose cheerfully from her seat, and presenting him with her hand, was led by him to the green in front of the chapel, the spot on which Anne Boleyn and Catherine Howard had previously bared their slender necks to the executioner. Even on the scaffold, she was still persecuted, by Feckenham the Roman Catholic Confessor of Queen Mary. This person appears to have been the only divine who was permitted to attend her; and his indecent importunities were almost enough to ruffle the angelic patience of the meek sufferer. "God will requite you, good sir," she said, "for your humanity, though your discourses give me more uneasiness than all the terrors of my approaching death."

Having addressed a short speech to the people, and concluded her devotions, she submitted herself to her female attendants, who proceeded to unrobe her. "Her gloves and handkerchief," says Fox, "she gave to her maiden, Mistress Ellen, and her book to Master Bridges, the Lieutenant's brother-in-law; and, as she began to untie her gown, the executioner attempted to assist her, but she requested him to let her alone, and turned to her two gentlewomen, who helped her off therewith, giving her a fair handkerchief to bind about her eyes." The executioner then knelt down and asked her forgiveness, which she cheerfully granted. After this, with a steady and serene countenance, she knelt down on the straw, and tied over her eyes the handkerchief, which her ladies had given her. She then stretched out her hands towards the block, but not feeling it, she exclaimed, "What shall I do? where is it, where is it?" One of the bystanders having directed her towards it, she calmly laid her neck upon it, and, while fervently pronouncing the words, " Lord, into thy hands I commend my spirit," the executioner at one blow severed her head from her body.

On the 17th of February, five days after his daughter's death, the Duke of Suffolk was arraigned before his peers for high treason, in Westminster Hall. Having been found guilty, he was re-conducted to the Tower, and, on the 21st, was led forth to execution. As his rashness and ambition had been the cause of so much bloodshed, and especially as it had occasioned the untimely end of his beautiful daughter, he met with but little commiseration. On the scaffold he addressed the multitude in a few words, in which he acknowledged the justice of his punishment, repudiated the "trumpery" of the old religion, acknowledged himself a sincere member of the Protestant faith, and concluded by beseeching the by-standers to pray to God to receive his soul. Then, kneeling down, and devoutly lifting up his hands and eyes to Heaven, he repeated the psalm

" Miserere mei, Domine." Among the last words which he uttered were those which his daughter had used on a like melancholy occasion. "Lord, into thy hands I commend my spirit." The executioner kneeling down to request his forgiveness, " God forgive thee," he said, " as I do; and when thou doest thine office, I pray thee do it quickly, and God have mercy on thee." Then, having repeated the Lord's Prayer, he tied a handkerchief over his eyes, and calling upon Christ for mercy, submitted himself to the stroke of the executioner.

Sir Thomas Wyatt, whose rash enterprise had proved so fatal to Lady Jane Grey and her husband, having been captured by Sir Maurice Berkeley, near Temple Bar, was sent a prisoner to the Tower. From thence he was conducted to his trial at Westminster, where, having pleaded guilty to the charge of high treason, he was sentenced to be hanged, drawn, and quartered. This sentence was afterwards commuted to decapitation, which was accordingly carried into effect on Tower Hill, on the 11th of April, 1554; and his body having been dismembered, his head was stuck on a gallows on Hay Hill, near Berkeley Square, and his quarters exposed in different parts of the metropolis. The suppression of Wyatt's rebellion filled the Tower with a crowd of miserable prisoners, and it is frightful to think of the horrors which followed. In two days, alone,— the 14th and 15th of February,— as many as fifty of the rebels were hanged: altogether, four hundred persons are computed to have suffered death; while four hundred more, having been led before the Queen with halters round their necks, had the good fortune to be dismissed with a pardon. Among the less fortunate was the Duke of Suffolk's brother, Lord Thomas Gray, who was beheaded, on the 27th of April, on Tower Hill.

Among those whom Wyatt's treason very nearly involved in his ruin was the Princess Elizabeth, the future Sovereign of England. After his condemnation, Wyatt, in hopes of saving his life, had given some information which went far to implicate her in his crime, though he afterwards retracted his accusation, and, with his dying breath and on his bended knees, solemnly asserted the innocence of the young Princess. Wyatt's original accusation, however, was sufficient to serve the purpose of her unfeeling sister, and accordingly Elizabeth was committed to the Tower. On the night of her arrest, she was in bed, at her house, at Ashridge, in Hertfordshire, when her chamber was indecently entered by Sir Richard Southwell, and two messengers from the Privy Council, who, with great rudeness, acquainted her with the nature of their errand. The Princess was naturally indignant at this unwarrantable intrusion, and inquired if their orders were so peremptory that they could not wait till the next morning? Their reply was, that their orders were from the Queen, who had commanded them to use no delay, and therefore, " they must take her with them whether quick or dead." All the indulgence which she could obtain, was permission to remain at Ashridge till the next morning, when she was placed in a litter, and conveyed, with as much expedition as possible, to Whitehall, where she found herself placed under close custody.

Elizabeth had remained about a fortnight at Whitehall, when, to her surprise and consternation, she was informed that it was the Queen's pleasure that she should be removed to the Tower, till such time as her guilt or innocence should be satisfactorily established. The idea of being incarcerated in that gloomy fortress,—which, within the last few years, had been crimsoned with the blood of so many persons of royal descent, and where her own unoffending mother had suffered by the axe of the executioner, — struck the Princess, lionhearted as she was, with dismay. She immediately addressed a pathetic letter to her sister, in which she solemnly protested her innocence, and implored that any other place might be substituted as the scene of her imprisonment. Mary, however, turned a deaf ear to her entreaties; and accordingly, on Palm Sunday, when the great mass of the population were attending divine service, she was conducted to the water entrance of the palace, where a barge was in readiness to receive her. How often, in after days,—when, surrounded by the pomp and pageantry of power, she was handed down those steps by the courtly Leicester or her beloved Essex, —must she have recalled the time when she descended them, a friendless and neglected maiden,

on her way to a prison, and in all probability to
an untimely grave. During her passage down the
river, she preserved her usual serenity till she perceived the barge nearing the Traitor's Gate,—that
fatal entrance, through which so few, who had once
entered it as prisoners, had been ever known to return. Her courage for a moment deserted her, and
she expressed a wish to be landed at some other
spot; which, however, was coldly refused. But fear
soon gave way to indignation at the unworthy treatment to which she was subjected; and when one of
the lords, who attended her, offered his cloak to
protect her from the rain, she not only scornfully
rejected it, but, we are told, "put it back with her
hand, with a good dash." As soon as she had set
her foot on the landing-place,—"Here landeth," she
said, "as true a subject, being a prisoner, as ever
landed at these stairs; and before Thee, O God, I
speak it, having none other friends than Thee!"
On entering the fortress, she sat down on a stone,
either to meditate or to rest herself. The Lieutenant of the Tower reminding her that it rained,
and pressing her to rise, — "Better," she said, "to
sit here than in a worse place: for God knoweth
whither you will bring me."

During the time that the high-spirited Princess
remained a prisoner in the Tower, she was subjected to every kind of harshness and indignity.
Her privacy was constantly intruded upon by the
Queen's priests and confessors, who wearied her
with vain importunities to forsake her religion;

during a whole month she was not allowed to
quit her apartment, and when, at length, on her
health failing her, she was permitted to take the
air in the Queen's garden, she was invariably attended by the Lieutenant of the Tower, and a
guard. Even a child, only four years old, who was
in the habit of bringing her flowers, underwent a
strict examination, on suspicion of its being the
channel of communication between the Princess
and the Earl of Devonshire.

Among the illustrious prisoners, who were confined in the Tower during the reign of Queen Mary,
we must not forget to mention the celebrated martyrs, Archbishop Cranmer, and Bishops Ridley and
Latimer, who were for some months incarcerated
here; the fortress being so crowded with prisoners,
that it was found necessary to confine the prelates
together in one room. Among other hardships to
which they were subjected, we find Bishop Latimer,
though a very old man, refused a fire, even when
the frost was on the ground. He bore his misfortunes, however, not only with patience, but with
cheerfulness. "Master Lieutenant," he said, on
one occasion, "I suppose you expect me to be
burnt, but unless you let me have some fire, I am
likely to deceive your expectations, for I shall most
probably die of the cold." Another remark which
he made to his fellow-sufferer, Bishop Ridley, while
the faggots were being piled around them, has been
rendered famous in history,—"Be of good comfort,
master Ridley, and play the man: we shall this

day light such a candle, by God's grace, in England, as I trust shall never be put out." From the Tower, the three prelates were removed to Oxford, where these dauntless champions of the Reformation suffered martyrdom in the flames.

To enumerate the different prisoners, with whom religious persecution and two successive insurrections crowded the dungeons of the Tower during the brief reign of Queen Mary, would occupy more space than we are able to devote to the subject. Numbers there were who fell, almost daily, either on the gibbet or by the axe. Beyond the mere fact, however, of their misfortunes or their crimes, their death or their liberation, there is scarcely an individual whose story presents any feature of particular interest.

Queen Mary died on the 17th of November, 1558; and, to the great joy of the Protestant portion of her subjects, Elizabeth was immediately proclaimed Queen, at Westminster, the Royal Exchange, and other places in the metropolis. She was at Hatfield when her sister's death was announced to her, and from thence she proceeded, after a delay of a few days, to the capital; passing through successive crowds of people, who every where greeted her with enthusiastic shouts of congratulation and joy. The first night was passed by her at the Charter House, and from thence she proceeded to the Tower. "On her entrance into the Tower," says Hume, "she could not forbear reflecting on the great difference between her present fortune and

that which a few years before had attended her,
when she was conducted to that place as a prisoner,
and lay there exposed to all the bigoted malignity
of her enemies. She fell on her knees, and expressed her thanks to Heaven for the deliverance
which the Almighty had granted her from her
bloody persecutors; a deliverance, she said, no less
miraculous than that which Daniel had received
from the den of lions."

Elizabeth continued to keep her court in the
Tower till the commencement of the month of
December, when she removed to Somerset House,
where she remained till her sister's remains were
consigned to the ground. She again returned to
the Tower by water on the 12th of January, and
passed there the three days which preceded her
coronation. On the day appointed for the ceremony, she issued forth from the portals of the
Tower, — a young Queen of twenty-five, — in the
midst of a gorgeous procession. Magnificently
attired, she was seated in an open chariot, superbly
gilt, and of curious workmanship. Before her went
pursuivants and heralds, drums and trumpets;—
surrounding her were "goodly and beautiful ladies,
richly appointed,"—and behind her followed knights
of the garter and peers of the realm, arrayed in the
gorgeous apparel of the age. And, thus, "most
honourably accompanied," she passed under a succession of triumphal arches; along streets hung with
tapestry and damask; and through avenues of the
city Companies, clad in their gaudy liveries of

scarlet and rich furs;—arrested at one moment in
Fenchurch Street by a beautiful child addressing
her in a befitting oration;—pausing at another time
to witness a "goodly pageant," in Gracechurch
Street;—stopped at Cornhill by a representation of
the Cardinal Virtues trampling on Ignorance and
Superstition;—in Fleet Street by a living model
of Deborah sitting in "Parliament robes" under a
palm-tree, prophecying the restoration of the House
of Israel;*—and lastly, at Temple Bar, by a stal-
wart citizen, representing the Giant Gogmagog,—
one of the Penates of Guildhall,—who held in his
hand a scroll in Latin verse, explaining what the
bewildered Queen might or might not have seen
during her fantastic progress. And thus, through
this medley of absurdities,—sharing with Gogmagog and the Cardinal Virtues the applauses of the
populace,—passed the Virgin Queen to her coronation in Westminster Abbey.

Whatever may have been the faults of Queen
Elizabeth, the talent which she displayed in ruling
the destinies of a great country has never been
called in question. An anecdote is related of Edmund Waller, the poet, that, on one occasion when
he was alone with James the Second in his private
closet, that monarch pointed out a portrait to him,
and inquired his opinion of it. "My eyes are dim,
Sir," he said, "and I know not who it is; but it
reminds me, from its likeness, to one of the greatest
princesses in the world." James inquiring of whom

* See Judges, chap. iv. ver. 4.

he alluded? Waller replied that he meant Queen
Elizabeth. "I wonder," said the King, "that you
should think so, but I must confess she had a
wise council."—"And pray, Sir," retorted Waller,
"did you ever know a fool choose a wise one?"
But illustrious as was the reign of Elizabeth, and
happy as she was in the choice of her ministers,
it may be doubted whether her heart was more
feminine, or her disposition more generous, than
those of her detested predecessor. Not even the
unprincipled murderer, Richard the Third; not even
her grandfather, the crafty and cold-blooded Henry
the Seventh, were more jealous of rivals near their
throne, or persecuted them with more deliberate
cruelty. Her treatment of Mary Queen of Scots,
and her persecution of Lady Catherine Grey and
Lady Arabella Stuart, must ever remain dark stains
on her character.

Lady Catherine Grey was the second daughter of
the late Duke of Suffolk, and it is not improbable
that she was as accomplished as she was beautiful,
for it was to her that her sister, Lady Jane, sent her
Greek Testament on the eve of her execution, with
an affectionate letter written in the same language.
Lady Catherine had won the affections of Edward
Seymour, Earl of Hertford, eldest son of the late
Duke of Somerset, and the attachment being
mutual, they were privately married about the year
1560. Although the great granddaughter of Henry
the Seventh, she was not so nearly related to the
sovereign as to render the marriage illegal without

the royal assent. The jealousy of Elizabeth, however, was painfully excited: she committed Lord Hertford and his young wife to separate prisons in the Tower; and was not the less enraged, when she was informed, shortly afterwards, that Lady Catherine had been delivered of a child in the royal fortress.

Eager to behold and embrace the mother of his infant, Hertford subsequently found means to bribe his keepers, who occasionally allowed the lovers to meet in private. The result of these interviews was the birth of a second child; a circumstance which inflamed the anger of Elizabeth beyond all bounds. Warner, the Lieutenant of the Tower, was dismissed from his situation, and Hertford, being summoned before the Star Chamber, was sentenced to pay a fine of fifteen thousand pounds; — five thousand for having corrupted a virgin of the royal blood in the Queen's palace; the same sum for having broken prison; and five thousand more for having repeated his intercourse. The husband and wife never afterwards met again. Lady Catherine died in the Tower, on the 26th of January, 1567, and Lord Hertford was not released till he had paid the large sum imposed upon him, and had suffered an imprisonment of nine years.

The first person of high rank who died on the scaffold in the reign of Elizabeth, was Thomas Howard, fourth Duke of Norfolk, who paid the penalty of his attachment to Mary Queen of Scots, and of his having leagued himself with the desperate

fortunes of that ill-fated Princess. Distinguished
by his high birth and princely fortune, affable, generous, and benevolent, the Duke of Norfolk was, at
this period, the most popular as well as the most
powerful nobleman in England. Endowed with
many virtues, and by nature and education impressed with a strong sense of the duties of religion, he united with these qualities a daring ambition, and a no slight tincture of romance. At the
period when he formed the project of espousing the
beautiful Queen, and restoring her to her throne,
he was still in the prime of life, having only completed his thirty-third year.

It was improbable that the Duke's designs should
long elude the vigilance of Elizabeth and her
ministers; and the Queen, who unquestionably entertained feelings of personal regard for him, more
than once gave him a friendly hint that his designs
were suspected, and of the danger in which he
stood. "Take heed," was, on one occasion, her
significant expression to him "on what pillow you
lay your head." At length, less equivocal information having reached the Queen's ministers, it was
thought requisite to arrest the Duke and to send
him to the Tower. After certain preliminary examinations, on the 16th of January, 1572, he was
brought to trial before an assemblage of twenty-
six peers in Westminster Hall. The charges on
which he was tried were for entering into a treasonable conspiracy to depose and take away the Queen's
life,—for projecting a marriage with the Queen of

Scots, who pretended to be the rightful Queen of
England,—for assisting the Earls of Northumberland and Westmoreland with money during their
recent rebellion,—and, lastly, for proposing to bring
a foreign army into England, and craving aid from
the Pope, the King of Spain, and the Duke of Alva,
in order to set the Queen of Scots at liberty, and to
restore the Popish religion in England. At the
conclusion of the proceedings, the Duke was asked
by the Lord High Steward if he had anything to add
in his defence, to which he replied calmly, " I confide
in the equity of the laws." The peers withdrew for
a short time, and, on their return into Westminster
Hall, brought in an unanimous verdict of " Guilty,"
when the Lord High Steward pronounced sentence
of death on him with the usual formalities. The
Duke listened with a calm dignity to the fearful
words. " Sentence," he said, " has been passed
upon me as upon a traitor, and I have none to trust
to but God and the Queen. I am excluded from
all society, but I hope soon to enjoy the society of
Heaven. I shall fit myself to die. Only this one
thing I crave, that the Queen will be kind to
my poor children and servants, and will take care
that my debts be paid."

From the moment on which sentence was passed
on him, the conduct and demeanour of the Duke
presented a touching picture of manly fortitude and
Christian resignation. From his prison in the
Tower, he addressed the most affectionate letters to
each of his children, in which he pointed out to

them how vain and transitory was human life;
admonishing them of the social duties which they
had to fulfil, and the temptations which they ought
to shun; and pointing out to them that a constant
perusal of the Scriptures, and a strict observance
of their sacred ordinations, formed the only true
road to happiness both in this world and in the
next.

Whether the Queen were really moved by feelings of friendship and commiseration towards the
unfortunate Duke,—or whether she wished that the
world should construe her hesitation in signing his
death-warrant to the feminine compassionateness
of her disposition,—it was not till four months after
Norfolk's trial that she finally decided on sending
him to the block. But this coquetry with justice
and human happiness was no favour to her
unhappy victim. Twice, we are told, she signed
the warrant for his execution, and twice revoked
the fatal sentence; and thus twice did the gallant
and high-minded Norfolk taste the bitterness, and
pass through the valley, of death; thus twice, after
he had composed himself to die, and had bidden
farewell to all who were near and dear to him
on earth, was he in vain recalled to the remembrance that life had still its sweetness, and that the
terrors of the grave might be still far off.

His doom, however, was at length fixed, and on
the 2nd of June, with a firm step and a serene
countenance, — surrounded by a vast crowd of gazing spectators,—he ascended the fatal scaffold on

Tower Hill. In his last speech, though he acknowledged the justice of the sentence by which he died, he solemnly disclaimed any disloyal intentions against the Queen's person or government. His composure never for a moment deserted him. Having concluded his speech, and having affectionately embraced his gallant associate, Sir Henry Leigh, he whispered a few words to his spiritual adviser, Dr. Nowel, Dean of St. Paul's, who repeated their purport to the bystanders. " The Duke," he said, " wishes you all to pray to God to have mercy on him ; and withal to keep silence, that his mind may not be disturbed." One of the attendants offering him a handkerchief to bandage his eyes, he refused it, observing in an unconcerned manner, " I am not in the least afraid of death." He then knelt down to his devotions, and quietly laying his neck on the block, the executioner, at one stroke severed his head from his body.

Whatever difference there may have been between the policy and dispositions of Queen Mary and her sister Elizabeth, it is certain that the Tower was seldom less crowded with prisoners during the reign of the "Virgin Queen," than it had been under the rule of her predecessor. Here, in 1572, was imprisoned, on account of his devotion to the cause of the unfortunate Queen of Scots, the high-minded John Leslie, Bishop of Ross ; and, at the same time, several persons were committed, and two hanged, for a conspiracy to rescue the Duke of Norfolk. In 1581, numbers were incarcerated in the Tower on account of their religious opinions; and the same year, the learned theologian, John Stubbs, was committed for writing and publishing a pamphlet against the Queen's marriage with the Duke of Anjou. Having been found guilty at his trial, he was dragged through the streets to the market-place at Westminster, where his right hand was cut off by the executioner; William Page, the printer of the work, sharing the same fate.

The persons on whom the greatest cruelty was practised during the reign of Elizabeth, were the Jesuits and other missionary priests, whose whole lives and energies were devoted to the interests of their church, and who flocked into England with the enthusiastic hope of rebuilding the ancient faith, or, at least, in the full confidence of obtaining a crown of martyrdom, in the event of their failing in the attempt. The barbarities which were practised upon these unfortunate men were such as have left an indelible stain upon the reign of Elizabeth. It was an age when Puritanism was approaching the zenith of its bigotry, and when even the most enlightened Protestants were inclined to shew little mercy to the agents of that cruel and domineering religion, who, in the last reign, had sent so many of their nearest and dearest relatives to the dungeon, the rack, or the flames. So inhuman, indeed, were the cruelties practised on the Roman Catholic priests within the walls of the Tower, that, in order to stifle the almost universal feeling of indignation and abhorrence, the government of Elizabeth were compelled to publish an apologetical circular in defence of their measures.

Throughout the reign of Elizabeth we find a fresh tide of unfortunate prisoners constantly flowing into the Tower. In 1583, John Somerville, a gentleman of Elstow, in Warwickshire, and his father-in-law Edward Arden, of an ancient family in Leicestershire, were sent to the Tower on suspicion of plotting against the Queen's life; and, having been found guilty at their trial, were hanged, disembowelled, and quartered at Smithfield, agreeably with the terms of their sentence. The following year, we find five more missionary priests hanged for receiving holy orders from the Church of Rome beyond the seas; and, shortly afterwards, Francis Throckmorton, who had been found guilty of carrying on a treasonable correspondence with Mary Queen of Scots, having been previously racked, was led forth from the Tower to Tyburn, where he was hanged, disembowelled, and quartered.

A prisoner of a different character was Henry Percy, Earl of Northumberland, brother of Thomas, the Seventh Earl, who had been beheaded at an early period of the Queen's reign for raising a rebellion in the north. The former Earl, who was a zealous Roman Catholic, was committed to the Tower in 1584, on a strong suspicion of favouring the cause of the Queen of Scots. The dread of death was less strong in his mind than the prospect of bringing ruin on his family, which must inevitably have followed his attainder; and, accordingly, he

determined to anticipate by suicide the fate which
would otherwise have awaited him. Alluding to
the Queen, he was heard to observe, "The bitch
at least shall not have my estate." Accordingly,
shortly afterwards, the Earl was found dead in his
bed in the Tower, the door of his apartment being
locked in the inside, and a pistol lying by his
bedside. He had shot himself through the heart.

Among other persons of importance who were
prisoners in the Tower in this reign, may be mentioned the unfortunate Earl of Essex, to whose fate
we shall hereafter have to refer;—William Parry,
a lawyer of great eminence and learning, who
suffered in 1585, in Old Palace Yard, for conspiring
against the Queen's life;—Secretary Davison, whom
his cold-blooded mistress, Elizabeth, condemned to
a long and cruel imprisonment, on the unjust accusation that he had hurried on the execution of the
Queen of Scots;—and lastly, the gallant soldier and
accomplished statesman and courtier, Sir John Perrot,—presumed to be a natural son of King Henry
the Eighth, and, consequently, half brother to
Queen Elizabeth, — who was committed to the
Tower on charges of high treason, in 1592.

That Sir John Perrot was at one period a great
favourite with Elizabeth, is proved by the following
anecdote, which is curiously illustrative of the manners of the time. In 1571, being then President of
Munster, he was recalled from Ireland to take command of a squadron which lay in the Thames, and
which was intended to act against the King of

Spain. Previous to his departure, his barge, —
"attended by fifty men in orange-cloaks, many of
them gentlemen of birth and quality,"—happened to
pass by the palace at Greenwich, where the Queen
was holding her court. Sir John, we are told, bidding the rowers stop, " sent one of his gentlemen
ashore with a diamond, as a token unto his mistress,
Blanche Parry, willing him to tell her, that a diamond, coming unlooked for, did always bring good
luck with it. The Queen, hearing of this, sent Sir
John Perrot a fair jewel hanged by a white cypress,
signifying withal, that so long as he wore that for
her sake, she did believe, with God's help, he should
have no harm. Which message and jewel Sir John
Perrot received joyfully, and he returned answer
unto the Queen, that he would wear that for his
sovereign's sake, and doubted not, with God's favour,
to restore her ships in safety, and either to bring
the Spaniards as prisoners, or else to sink them in
the seas. So, as Sir John Perrot passed by in his
barge, the Queen looked out at a window, shaking
her fan, and put out her hand towards him, who,
making a low obeisance, put the scarf and jewel
about his neck, which the Queen had sent him."

At his trial, Sir John Perrot was found guilty and
condemned to death. His sentence having once
passed, he declared that he was now reckless of life:
" My name and blood," he said, "are corrupted, and
woe be to me that am the first of my house and
name that ever was attainted or suspected." On
being brought back to the Tower, he exclaimed, in

a passion of rage, to the Lieutenant, and with many
oaths, " What ! will the Queen suffer her brother to
be offered up as a sacrifice to the envy of his strutting
adversaries ? "   Elizabeth, however, seems from the
first to have been fully convinced of his innocence,
and, when pressed to sign his death-warrant, she
positively refused her assent.   Nevertheless, she
allowed him to remain in the Tower, where he died,
—as was supposed, of a broken heart,—in September, 1592, a few months after his trial.

Not the least interesting prisoners in the Tower,
in the reign of Elizabeth, were that accomplished
and enthusiastic band of youths, —headed by Anthony Babington,—who, united by the ties of a tender, if not sublime, friendship, had devoted themselves
to the cause of the beautiful Queen of Scots, and had
sworn either to restore her to liberty, or to perish
in the attempt.   Their designs, however, were soon
discovered by the subtle Walsingham, and, in 1586,
they were arrested and sent to the Tower.   The
appearance presented by these noble-minded youths,
at the bar of justice, is described in a very interesting paper by Mr. D'Israeli, in his " Curiosities
of Literature."   " When this romantic band of
friends," he says, " were called on for their defence,
the most pathetic instances of domestic affection
appeared.   One had engaged in this plot solely to
try to save his friend ; for he had no hopes of it,
nor any wish for its success ; he had observed to his
friend, that the haughty and ambitious mind of
Anthony Babington would be the destruction of

himself and his friends; nevertheless he was willing to die with them! Another, to withdraw, if possible, one of those noble youths from the conspiracy, although he had broken up housekeeping, said, to employ his own language, 'I called back my servants again together, and began to keep house again more freshly than ever I did, only because I was weary to see Tom Salisbury's straggling, and willing to keep him about home.' Having attempted to secrete his friend, this gentleman observed, 'I am condemned, because I suffered Salisbury to escape, when I knew he was one of the conspirators. My case is hard and lamentable; either to betray my friend, whom I love as myself, and to discover Thomas Salisbury, the best man in my country, or else to break my allegiance to my sovereign, and to undo myself and my posterity for ever.' Whatever the political casuist may determine on this case, the social being carries his own manual in the heart. The principle of the greatest of republics was to suffer nothing to exist in competition with its own ambition; but the Roman history is a history without fathers and brothers! Another of the conspirators replied, 'For flying away with my friend, I fulfilled the part of a friend.' When the judge observed, that, to perform his friendship, he had broken his allegiance to his sovereign, he bowed his head and confessed, 'Therein I have offended.' Another, when asked why he had fled into the woods, where he was discovered among some of the conspirators, proudly or tenderly replied, 'For company.'"

The appearance of the gallant youths excited a deep commiseration in a crowded court, and the judge himself shewed how affected he was at the fate which awaited so noble-minded a band. The principal promoter of the conspiracy had been the celebrated Jesuit priest, John Ballard, whose crafty and insidious arguments had originally wrought on the enthusiastic mind of Anthony Babington. He now stood at the bar by the side of the ill-fated youths whom he had entrapped into his net. During the trial, the judge, turning towards him, exclaimed, —"Oh, Ballard! Ballard! what hast thou done? A company of brave youths, otherwise adorned with good gifts, by thy inducement hast thou brought to their utter destruction and confusion." Ballard himself appears to have been deeply affected with remorse at the sight of the wreck he had made. He wished, he said, that all the blame could rest on him, if, by the shedding of his blood, he could save Babington's life.

"When the sentence of condemnation had passed," proceeds Mr. D'Israeli, "there broke forth from among this noble band that spirit of honour, which surely had never been witnessed at the bar among so many criminals. Their great minds seem to have reconciled them to the most barbarous of deaths; but as their estates as traitors might be forfeited to the Queen, their sole anxiety was now for their families and their creditors. One, in the most pathetic terms, recommends to her majesty's protection a beloved wife; another a destitute sis-

ter; but not among the least urgent of their sup-
plications, was one that their creditors might not be
injured by their untimely end. The statement of
their affairs is curious and simple. 'If mercy be not
to be had,' exclaimed one, 'I beseech you, my good
lords, this; I owe some sums of money, but not very
much, and I have more owing to me; I beseech
that my debts may be paid with that which is owing
to me.' Another prayed for a pardon; the judge
complimented him, that 'he was one who might
have done good service to his country,' but declares
that he cannot obtain it.—'Then,' said the prisoner,
'I beseech that six angels, which such an one hath
of mine, may be delivered to my brother to pay my
debts.'—'How much are thy debts?' demanded the
judge. He answered,—'The same six angels will
discharge them.'"

Of these illustrious youths, fourteen, besides the
Jesuit Ballard, suffered the last penalty of the law.
Their names were;—Anthony Babington; Edward
Windsor, brother of Lord Windsor; Thomas Salisbury; Charles Tilney; Chidiock Tichburn; Edward Abington; Robert Gage; John Travers;
John Charnock; John Jones; John Savage; R.
Barnwell; Henry Dun; and Jerome Bellarmine.
"That nothing," says Mr. D'Israeli, "might be
wanting to complete the catastrophe of their sad
story, our sympathy must accompany them to their
tragical end, and to their last words. Ballard was
the first executed, and snatched alive from the
gallows to be embowelled: Babington looked on

with an undaunted countenance, steadily gazing on
that variety of tortures, which he himself was in a
moment to pass through; the others averted their
faces, fervently praying.   When the executioner
began his tremendous work   on Babington, the
spirit of this haughty and heroic man cried out
amidst the agony, — '*Parce mihi, Domine Jesu!*'
There were two days of execution; it was on the
first that the noblest of these youths suffered; and
the pity which such criminals had excited among
the spectators evidently weakened the sense of their
political crime; the solemnity, not the barbarity, of
the punishment, affects the populace with right
feelings.   Elizabeth, an enlightened politician, commanded that, on the second day, the odious part of
the sentence should not commence till after death."

The following pathetic copy of verses was composed by one of the conspirators, Chidiock Tichburn, in the Tower, the night before his execution
in Lincoln's Inn Fields.

> My prime of youth is but a frost of cares,
>   My feast of joy is but a dish of pain,
> My crop of corn is but a field of tares,
>   And all my goods is but vain hope of gain.
> The day is fled, and yet I saw no sun,
> And now I live, and now my life is done.
>
> My spring is past, and yet it hath not sprung,
>   The fruit is dead, and yet the leaves are green,
> My youth is past, and yet I am but young,
>   I saw the world, and yet I was not seen;
> My thread is cut, and yet it is not spun,
> And now I live, and now my life is done.
>
> I sought for death, and found it in the womb,
>   I looked for life, and yet it was a shade,
> I trod the ground, and knew it was my tomb,
>   And now I die, and now I am but made,

The glass is full, and yet my glass is run ;
And now I live, and now my life is done !

On the 9th of February, 1601, the Traitor's gate opened to receive, as a prisoner, the young and accomplished Robert Devereux, Earl of Essex. The story of this ill-fated favourite,—his popularity, his taste for literature, the beauty of his person, and his graceful accomplishments,—his chivalrous gallantry on the field of Zutphen,—beneath the walls of Rouen,—and against the Spaniards in the new world,—his military failures in Ireland,—the indignation of the Queen,—his sudden appearance in her bedchamber, spurred, booted, and muddy,— her fitful returns of passionate affection,—her sending him dainties at one moment and signing his death-warrant the next,—all these circumstances are too familiar with every one to require repetition.

The result of the rash attempt of Essex to stir up the citizens of London was such as his friends ought to have anticipated, and was such as his enemies wished. On the 19th of February, he was brought from the Tower, with his friend, the Earl of Southampton, to Westminster Hall, and, having been found guilty of high treason, the Lord High Steward passed on them the solemn sentence of the law. Southampton,—in a modest and becoming speech, which excited general compassion and admiration,—admitted his crime, which he attributed in a great degree to his affection for his friend: he had never harboured a thought, he said, against the Queen's person, and he earnestly entreated the peers to intercede with her majesty on his behalf. The speech of Essex was of a different character. His principal consideration seems to have been for his friend, on whose behalf he implored the peers to intercede with the Queen. For himself, he said, he valued not life; all his desire was to quit the world with the conscience of a true Christian and of a loyal subject; he was loath, indeed, that he should be represented to the Queen as one who despised her clemency, but, at the same time, he believed he should make no cringing submissions for his life. He then begged pardon of certain lords whom he had offended, requested that he might be allowed to receive the holy sacrament before he suffered, and prayed that a particular clergyman, whom he named, might be allowed to attend him in his last moments.

In the interval which elapsed between the condemnation and death of her favourite, the mind of Elizabeth underwent a severe and bitter conflict between resentment and affection, compassion and pride. On the one hand she naturally revolted from sacrificing one whom she had so tenderly loved; while on the other, the arguments of his enemies; indignation at his refusing to sue for pardon; and, moreover, his own voluntary observation in the Tower, that she would never know safety while he lived, went far to overcome the softer and better feelings of her nature. More than once she signed the warrant for his execution; more than once her tenderness returned; and more than once she coun-

termanded his death. But her pride could not long
withstand his continued obstinacy; the warrant for
his execution was at last delivered into the hands
of the secretary of state, and the 25th of February
was fixed upon as the fatal day.

By his own wish, Essex was executed in as private
a manner as possible, within the walls of the Tower;
the scaffold having been erected in the open space in
front of the chapel. Around it were assembled the
Earls of Cumberland and Hertford, Viscount Howard
of Bindon, Lord Howard of Walden, Lord Darcy
of Chiche, Lord Compton, the Aldermen of London,
and several knights and gentlemen. From the day
of his condemnation, Essex had prepared himself
for death with great devoutness, and he now appeared on the scaffold as one who had no care in
this world, and who looked forward to eternal happiness in the next. He appeared on the scaffold,
attended by three divines, dressed in a gown of
wrought velvet, a black satin suit, a black felt hat,
and a small ruff round his neck. Immediately after
he had ascended the fatal stage, he took off his hat,
and addressed himself to the multitude. He had
been guilty, he said, in his youth of many and great
sins, for which, through the merits of his Saviour,
he had most ardently prayed for pardon. He acknowledged the justice of the sentence by which
he died, but denied that he had ever intended any
violence against the Queen's person, for whom he
prayed for long life and happiness; he thanked God
that he had never been led astray by any Papistical

or Atheistical doctrines, but that he had ever fixed
his hopes of salvation solely on the merits of his
Redeemer.   Lastly he prayed God to fortify him
against the terrors of death, and called upon the
bystanders to pray for the welfare of his soul.

Then the executioner, asking his forgiveness,
which he cheerfully granted, he took off his gown
and ruff, and kneeling down before the block, and
lifting up his eyes to Heaven, prayed fervently for
some minutes; repeating the Lord's Prayer, the
Apostles' Creed, and the first verses of the fifty-
first psalm.   He then laid his neck upon the block,
and, while in the act of giving utterance to some
pious ejaculations, the axe of the executioner fell.
The first blow deprived him of sense and motion,
but it was not till the third stroke had descended,
that his head was severed from his body.

Among those whom the rash enterprise of Essex
involved in his fall, and who were fellow-prisoners
with him in the Tower, were the Earl of Southampton, already mentioned, the Earl of Rutland, the
Lords Sands, Cromwell, and Monteagle, Sir Henry
Bromley, Sir Charles Danvers, Sir Christopher Blunt,
Sir Gilley Merrick, and Henry Cuffe.   Of these
persons, only the four last suffered on the scaffold.
Sir Charles Danvers and Sir Christopher Blunt were
beheaded on Tower Hill, where they met their fate
with great fortitude and composure.   Merrick and
Cuffe were hanged and quartered at Tyburn, and
died no less resolutely than their companions.

We will conclude our notices of the Tower in

the reign of Elizabeth, with the description given
of it by the German traveller, Paul Hentzner,
who visited England in 1598. "Upon entering
the Tower of London, we were obliged to leave our
swords at the gate, and deliver them to the guard.
When we were introduced, we were shewn above
an hundred pieces of arms belonging to the crown,
made of gold, silver, and silk; several saddles
covered with velvet of different colours; and an immense quantity of bed-furniture, such as canopies
and the like, some of them richly ornamented with
pearl; some royal dresses, so extremely magnificent
as to raise any one's admiration at the sums they
must have cost. We were next led to the Ar-
moury, in which are these particularities:—spears
out of which you may shoot; shields that will
give fire four times; a great many rich halberds
commonly called partisans, with which the guard
defend the royal person in battle; some lances
covered with red and green velvet, and the suit of
armour of King Henry the Eighth; many very
beautiful arms, as well for men as for horse-fights;
the lance of Charles Brandon, Duke of Suffolk,
three spans thick; two pieces of cannon—the one
fires three, the other seven balls at a time;—two
others made of wood, which the English had at the
siege of Boulogne in France—and by this stratagem, without which they could not have succeeded,
they struck a terror as at the appearance of artillery,
and the town surrendered upon articles; nineteen
cannons of a thicker make than ordinary, and, in a

room apart, thirty-six of a smaller; other cannons
for chain shot, and balls proper to bring down masts
of ships; and cross-bows, and bows and arrows, of
which, to this day, the English make use in their
exercises. But who can relate all that is to be seen
here? Eight or nine men, employed by the year,
are scarce sufficient to keep all the arms bright.

"The mint for coining money, is in the Tower.
It is to be noted that, when any of the nobility are
sent hither, on the charge of high crimes, punish-
able with death, such as murder, &c., they seldom
or never recover their liberty. Here was beheaded
Anne Boleyn, wife of King Henry the Eighth, and lies
buried in the Chapel, but without any inscription;
and Queen Elizabeth was kept prisoner here by her
sister, Queen Mary, at whose death she was enlarged, and by right called to the throne. On coming out of the Tower, we were led to a small house
close by, where are kept a variety of creatures, viz.,
three lionesses, one lion of great size, called Edward the Sixth, from his having been born in that
reign; a tiger, a lynx, a wolf exceedingly old; this
is a very scarce animal in England, so that their
sheep and cattle stray about in great numbers without any danger, though without anybody to keep
them: there is besides a porcupine and an eagle: all
these creatures are kept in a remote place, fitted up
for the purpose, with wooden lattices, at the Queen's
expense."

James the First, after his arrival from Scotland,
kept his court for a short time in the Tower. From

hence, accompanied by his Queen, and Henry, Prince of Wales, he proceeded in great state to Westminster, preparatory to the opening of his first Parliament; and, during his life-time, we find him more than once paying visits to the ancient fortress, for the purpose of witnessing the combats of the wild beasts who were kept in the royal menagery.

In July, 1603, about four months after the King's accession, Henry Brooke Lord Cobham, Thomas Lord Grey of Wilton, and the celebrated Sir Walter Raleigh, and others, were committed prisoners to the Tower, on charges of attempting to restore the Roman Catholic religion, and to place the Lady Arabella Stuart on the throne. All three were tried and condemned to death. George Brooke, a brother of Lord Cobham, and two priests, were executed for their share in the conspiracy; while Lords Grey and Cobham, — after having been cruelly subjected to all the terrors of death,—were reprieved at the last moment, after they had addressed themselves to the multitude, and were preparing themselves for the stroke of the executioner. Both were remanded back to the Tower. Lord Cobham, sometime afterwards, obtained his release, but his estates having been confiscated, he lived in extreme poverty till 1619, when he ended his unprofitable career. Lord Grey, a man of high promise and noble spirit, died a prisoner in 1617.

The fate of the illustrious Sir Walter Raleigh,— that bright ornament of the age in which he lived, —is more familiar to the reader. Having remained a prisoner in the Tower upwards of twelve years, during which period he composed his " History of the World," he obtained his release in 1615, on payment of a considerable sum to the celebrated favourite, George Villiers, Duke of Buckingham. His subsequent unfortunate expedition to Guiana, his re-committal to the Tower, and the infamous manner in which he was condemned to death for a crime of which he had been found guilty fifteen years before, and for which he may be said to have been virtually pardoned,—are facts which are too well known to require repetition.

On the 29th of October, 1618, this great and accomplished man was conducted from the Tower to Old Palace Yard, Westminster, which had been fixed upon as the scene of his execution. "Sir Walter Raleigh,"—says Dr. Townson, Dean of Westminster, who attended him in his last moments,— " was the most fearless of death that ever was known ; and the most resolute and confident, yet with reverence and conscience. After he had received the communion in the morning, he was very cheerful and merry, and hoped, as he said, to persuade the world that he died an innocent man. He was very cheerful that morning he died, eat his breakfast heartily, and took tobacco, making no more of his death than if he had been to take a journey ; and he left a great impression on the minds of those who beheld him." Though suffering from the effects of recent indisposition, he ascended the fatal stage with a resolute step and a serene countenance. Turning to the Lords Arundel and Northampton, and some other persons who were on the scaffold, he said, "I thank God heartily that he hath brought me into the light to die, and hath not suffered me to die in the dark prison in the Tower, where I have suffered a great deal of misery and cruel sickness. And I thank God that my fever hath not taken me at this time, as I prayed God it might not, that I might clear myself of some accusations unjustly laid to my charge, and leave behind me the testimony of a true heart, both to my King and country." He then addressed himself to the multitude, and concluded a long defence of his public conduct, with an earnest entreaty that they would join him in his prayers to Heaven, that his many sins might be forgiven him, and that his soul might be received into everlasting life.

Having concluded his speech, Sir Walter distributed his hat, some money, and other articles, among the persons who were in attendance on him. Then, having taken a last farewell of Lord Arundel, he turned to the executioner, and desired to be shewn the axe. The man, however, still keeping it concealed, "Prithee," he said, "let me see it; dost thou think I am afraid of it?" Having felt its edge, he said smilingly to the sheriff, "This is a sharp medicine; but it is a physician for all diseases." Having once more entreated the multitude to pray for him, he turned to the executioner, who, having requested his forgiveness, inquired which way he would prefer lying upon the block. "So that the heart be right," he replied "it is no matter which way the head lies." Then, kneeling down, with his face towards the east, he gave the signal which he had agreed upon with the executioner, and at two blows his head was severed from his body.

In 1605, the dungeons of the Tower were filled with the conspirators who were engaged in the atrocious Gunpowder Plot. The principal actors in the intended tragedy, were Thomas Winter, Guy Fawkes, and Robert Keyes, gentlemen; Thomas Bates, yeoman; Robert Winter, Esq.; John Grant, Esq.; Ambrose Rookwood, Esq.; and the handsome and accomplished courtier, Sir Everard Digby, father of the celebrated Sir Kenelm Digby. Their trial took place on the 27th of January, 1606, and, on the Thursday following, Sir Everard Digby, Robert Winter, Grant, and Bates, were drawn on hurdles to the west end of St. Paul's church-yard, where they were hanged, and, having been cut down before they were dead, their bowels were taken out and burnt before their eyes, and they were then quartered and beheaded. Anthony Wood relates an extraordinary circumstance,—as being generally believed at the time,—that when the executioner plucked out the heart of Sir Everard Digby, and, according to custom, held it up, saying, " Here is the heart of a traitor," Sir Everard made answer, " Thou liest!" On the day following the execution of their associates, Thomas Winter, Rookwood, Keyes, and Guy Fawkes suffered the same fate in the Old Palace Yard, Westminster.

Among others committed to the Tower, as having
been concerned in the Gunpowder Plot, were that
stout old philosopher, Henry Percy, Earl of Northumberland; Henry Lord Mordaunt, Edward Lord Stourton, and three Jesuit priests, Fathers Garnet, Oldcorn, and Gerrard. Northumberland was fined
thirty thousand pounds, and continued a prisoner in
the Tower nearly sixteen years; Lords Mordaunt
and Stourton were both heavily fined, and remanded
to the Tower during the King's pleasure; Garnet
was dragged on a hurdle to the front of St. Paul's,
where he was hanged and quartered; and Father
Oldcorn, after having been five times tortured on
the rack, shared the same fate at Worcester. Father
Gerrard was also subjected to the most excruciating
agonies which cruelty could invent; but he was
more fortunate than his comrades, for by some
means he contrived to escape from the Tower, and,
after remaining in concealment in England a short
time, made his way to Rome, where he died.

The name of the Lady Arabella Stuart recalls a
tale of sorrow, which has drawn tears from the eyes
of thousands. This fair and gentle lady,—as celebrated for her accomplishments as for her misfortunes,—was first cousin to James the First, being
the daughter of Charles Stuart, fifth Earl of Lennox; brother to Henry Lord Darnley, the King's
father. To Queen Elizabeth, her near alliance to
the throne had rendered her no less an object of
jealousy, than she had now become to James; she
had been prevented accepting more than one eligible

offer of marriage; and, indeed, from her childhood
she had been little more than a prisoner at large.
At last, her affections fell on Sir William Seymour,
afterwards Marquis of Hertford, and Duke of
Somerset,—that gallant man who afterwards became so celebrated for his loyalty and devotion to
the unfortunate Charles the First. The attachment
of the lovers could not long escape the jealous eye
of James, and, in 1609, they were summoned before
the Privy Council, and severely reprimanded. But
neither the reprimand, nor the terrors of the Star
Chamber, had any effect on the lovers, and a short
time afterwards they were privately married. The
fact soon transpired; they were immediately arrested; Seymour was sent to the Tower, and Lady
Arabella to the house of Sir Thomas Parry, at
Lambeth, from whence she was afterwards removed
to Highgate, where she was placed under the charge
of Sir James Croft.

The lovers, however, found means to correspond,
and in due time concerted a plan for their escape,
almost as wild as it was romantic. Having contrived that a vessel should be in waiting for them
in the Thames, on the appointed day, Seymour,—
leaving his servant in his bed to prevent suspicion,
—disguised himself in a black wig and a pair of
black whiskers, and, following a cart that had been
directed to bring fire-wood to his apartment, walked,
without being questioned, out of the western entrance of the Tower. A boat was in waiting for
him at the Tower Wharf, in which he rowed to the

part of the river where he expected to meet his
bride ; but, finding that she had sailed without him,
he hired another vessel, for forty pounds, to convey
him to Calais, where he eventually arrived in safety.

In the mean time, the Lady Arabella,—having
" drawn over her petticoats a pair of large French-
fashioned hose, putting on a man's doublet, a peruke
which covered her hair, a hat, black cloak, russet
boots with red tops, and a rapier by her side,"—
contrived to elude the vigilance of her keepers, and,
attended by a Mr. Markham, set out from Highgate
on her romantic expedition. " She had proceeded
only a mile and a half," says Mr. D'Israeli, in his
' Curiosities of Literature,' " when they stopped at a
poor inn, where one of her confederates was waiting
with horses, yet she was so sick and faint, that the
ostler, who held her stirrup, observed, that ' the
gentleman could hardly hold out to London.' She
recruited her spirits by riding; the blood mantled
in her face; and at six o'clock she reached Black-
wall, where a boat and servants were waiting. The
watermen were at first ordered to Woolwich ; there
they were desired to push on to Gravesend; then
to Tilbury, where, complaining of fatigue, they
landed to refresh themselves; but, tempted by their
freight, reached Lee. At the break of morn, they
discovered a French vessel riding there to receive
the lady ; but, as Seymour had not yet arrived,
Arabella was desirous to lie at anchor for her lord,
conscious that he would not fail to keep his appointment. If, indeed, he had been prevented in

his escape, she herself cared not to preserve the freedom she now possessed; but her attendants, aware
of the danger of being overtaken by a King's ship,
overruled her wishes, and hoisted sail.   Alone and
mournful on the seas," adds Mr. D'Israeli, "implor-
ing her attendants to linger for her Seymour, she
strained her sight to the point of the horizon for
some speck which might give a hope of the approach of the boat freighted with all her love.
Alas! never more was Arabella to cast a single
look on her lover and her husband!"

She was overtaken by a fast-sailing vessel, which
had been sent in pursuit of the fugitives, and,
having been re-conducted to London, was immediately sent to the Tower.   Here she wore out a
miserable existence; describing herself, in one of
her letters, as " the most sorrowful creature living;"
and is even said to have ended her days in madness.

> Where London's towers their turrets shew,
>   So stately by the Thames's side,
> Fair Arabella, child of woe,
>   For many a day had sat and sighed.
> And as she heard the waves arise,
>   And as she heard the bleak winds roar,
> As fast did heave her heartfelt sighs,
>   And still so fast her tears did pour.

Lady Arabella died in the Tower on the 27th of
September, 1615, about four years after her unsuccessful attempt to escape.

Of the many "foul and midnight murders" which
have been committed within the Tower, there have
been none more foul and atrocious than that of the

accomplished courtier and poet, Sir Thomas Overbury. The story of his tragical fate is well known.
He had long been the intimate friend and confidant
of the celebrated favourite, Robert Carr, Earl of
Somerset, whom he had been accustomed to direct
in all his actions ; composing his despatches to the
King, and even his love-letters to his mistresses.
Their friendship continued unimpaired till the weak
favourite fixed his affections on the beautiful and
abandoned Frances Howard, Countess of Essex,
whom he determined to make his wife. Foreseeing
the misery which such a marriage must entail on
his friend, and personally detesting the young
Countess, Overbury, who was naturally of a haughty
and overbearing disposition, presumed, in the strong-
est terms, to malign the character of Lady Essex,
whom, Weldon informs us, he styled a " strumpet,
and her mother and brother, bawds." He pointed
out to Somerset the ruinous course which he was
pursuing ; he told him, that by marrying such a
woman, instead of happiness, he would only entail
on himself the ridicule of the world ; and lastly, he
loudly threatened to separate himself for ever from
the Earl and his interests, if he persisted in prose-
cuting so disgraceful an affair. Irritated at what he
considered the insolence of an inferior, and urged on
by the implacable hatred of Lady Essex, who was
determined to revenge herself by Overbury's death,
Somerset found means to have his friend committed
to the Tower.

Some days previously, Somerset had procured the

appointment of one of his own creatures, Sir Jervis
Elways, to be Lieutenant of the Tower; and now,
leaguing himself with his abandoned wife, and her
uncle, the Earl of Northampton, he entered into
the atrocious project of poisoning his former friend.
The inferior agents in this horrible transaction were
Sir Thomas Monson, two men of the names of
Weston and Franklin, and the well-known Mrs.
Turner, who provided the poisons.   These were
inserted by Monson in every article of food which
was sent to Overbury's table, and sometimes, it
appears, the dishes were sent by Somerset himself. His death is said to have been finally accomplished by a poisoned clyster; though, according to other accounts, the ruffians,—perceiving an
irruption breaking out over his body, and fearing
lest the symptoms might lead to detection,—released him from his sufferings by smothering him in
his bed. His body, which is described as being
covered with sores and ulcers, was then wrapped in
a sheet, and, the same afternoon, without the attendance of a relative or friend, was committed by his
murderers to the earth, in the Tower Chapel.

Sir Thomas Overbury died on the 15th of September, 1613, and, a little more than two years
afterwards, Somerset and his Countess were committed to the same prison, in which their unfortunate victim had breathed his last.

The accomplices of their crime,—Sir Jervis Elways, Weston, Franklin, and Mrs. Turner, —were
shortly afterwards condemned and executed; but

it was not till several months had elapsed, that
the two principal criminals were brought to trial.
The Countess was tried by her peers, in Westminster Hall, on the 25th of May, 1616, and
Somerset on the following day. Both were found
guilty, and sentenced to be hanged like common
criminals. After their condemnation, they were
reconducted to the Tower, where they remained
till the month of January, 1622, when they were
released from confinement, and their lives were
respited at the King's pleasure.

Among other persons of rank who were committed to the Tower in the reign of James the
First, were Gervase, Lord Clifton ; Sir Thomas and
Lady Lake; the Earl and Countess of Suffolk, the
father and mother of the Countess of Somerset;
the great Lord Bacon; and the scarcely less celebrated Sir Edward Coke.

Lord Clifton was committed on the 17th of
December, 1617, for threatening the life of the
Lord Keeper, and shortly afterwards put an end
to his existence; Sir Thomas Lake and his lady
were imprisoned, in February, 1619, for accusing
the Countess of Exeter of witchcraft and incest;
and the Earl and Countess of Suffolk were committed the same year for bribery and corruption.
Another prisoner of note was Thomas, twentieth
Earl of Arundel, a proud and overbearing nobleman, whom Clarendon describes as affecting the character of a man of learning, though extremely illiterate, and thinking "no part of history so con-

siderable as what related to his own family." His
committal to the Tower arose out of a violent dispute which he had with Lord Spencer in the House
of Lords. The particulars are curious, as shewing
the character of the man. Lord Spencer happened,
during a debate, to mention some transactions in
which both their ancestors had been mutually
engaged. " My Lord," interrupted Arundel contemptuously, " when these things were doing, your
ancestors were keeping sheep."—" When my ancestors were keeping sheep," retorted Lord Spencer,
" your ancestors, my Lord, were plotting treason."
The altercation now became so violent that the
House interfered, and Arundel refusing to apologise,
the Lords committed him to the Tower for his
refractory conduct.

It does not appear that the unfortunate Charles
the First was ever a resident in the Tower. Almost
from the period of the Norman conquest it had
been the custom of the Kings of England to pass
the night, previous to their coronation, in the royal
fortress, and from thence to proceed in great state
to Westminster. At the accession of James, in
consequence of the violence with which the plague
was raging in London, this ancient custom was
omitted, and again, at the accession of Charles the
First, it was dispensed with for the same melancholy reason.

Although but little blood was shed on the scaffold during the reign of Charles, the political
troubles of that disastrous period led to numerous

persons,—chiefly members of Parliament,—being
imprisoned in the Tower; but to enumerate them
would amount to little more than inserting a dry
catalogue of names. Among the most distinguished
were the celebrated patriots, Selden, Hollis, and Sir
John Elliot ; John Felton, the assassin of the Duke
of Buckingham ; the infamous Mervin, Earl of Cas-
tlehaven, better known as Lord Audley, who was
executed on Tower Hill, on the 14th of May, 1631 ;
the famous puritan, William Prynne ; Thomas
Wentworth, the great Earl of Strafford ; Laud,
Archbishop of Canterbury ; and the "memorable
simpleton," Philip, Earl of Pembroke. Of these
persons, only four died on the scaffold.

Not the least remarkable of these persons was
the fanatical assassin, John Felton. The circumstances which—

> Gave great Villiers to the assassin's knife

are well known. Having purchased a common
knife at a cutler's shop, on Tower Hill, Felton
proceeded to Portsmouth, where Buckingham was
then preparing for his second expedition to Ro-
chelle. Having contrived to obtain entrance to
the Duke's residence, — a house still standing in
the High Street at Portsmouth, — the assassin
posted himself in a passage, adjoining the room
in which his victim was at breakfast with his suite,
and, at the moment when the Duke was passing under some hangings leading to the passage, he
stabbed him to the heart. Felton afterwards remarked to those about him, that, at the moment

when he struck the blow, he felt as if he had the "force of forty men" in him; and he added the curious fact, that, as his arm descended, he repeated the words, " God have mercy on thy soul." He was almost immediately arrested, and conveyed, under a strong guard, to the Tower.

Though a man distinguished among his associates for his determined character and undaunted courage, Felton, as his end approached, humbled himself in so penitential a manner, as to cause great annoyance to the thousands, who had heretofore almost worshipped him as a hero and a martyr. On his way to the Tower, he was followed by vast crowds, whom he earnestly entreated to pray for him. At his trial, he expressed great contrition for his crime. When the knife, with which he had stabbed his victim, was produced in court, he shed tears; and when asked why sentence of death should not be passed upon him, he held up the hand which had committed the deed, requesting that it might first be cut off, and that he might then suffer death in any manner the court might think fit. He sent a message to the widowed Duchess, earnestly entreating her forgiveness, which she kindly granted; and he further requested that, on the scaffold, he might be clothed in sackcloth, with ashes on his head, and a halter round his neck, as tokens of his unworthiness and sincere penitence. Notwithstanding these signs of weakness,—if such they may be properly called,—Felton's constitutional courage never forsook him, and it was remarked by Philip, Earl of

Pembroke, who attended his examinations, that he
had never seen valour and piety " more temperately
mixed " in the same person.   He was hanged at
Tyburn, from whence his body was removed to
Portsmouth, where it remained suspended for a
considerable time in chains.

On the 22nd of March, 1641, the famous trial-
scene of Thomas Wentworth, the great Earl of
Strafford, commenced in Westminster Hall.   The
trial lasted seventeen days, and, on each day, the
Earl was brought from the Tower to Westminster,
by water, attended by six barges, and guarded by a
hundred soldiers.   Charles, — however sorrowfully
and reluctantly,—having been compelled to sign the
death-warrant of his faithful servant, the accomplished and high-minded Strafford prepared himself
to die with the piety of a Christian, and the dignity
becoming his high character.   Shortly before his
execution, he addressed an affectionate letter of
advice to his young son, and another very beautiful
epistle to his secretary, Guildford Slingsby.   He
had expressed a strong wish to be allowed a last
interview with one for whom he had long entertained an affectionate regard, the venerable Archbishop Laud, who was at this period a fellow-
prisoner with him in the Tower.   This request, however, having been barbarously refused, Strafford sent
a message to the Archbishop, desiring him to remember him in his prayers, and requesting, when
he should pass to his execution on the following
morning, that Laud would present himself at his

grated window, in order that they might have the
melancholy satisfaction of bidding each other a last
farewell. Accordingly, the next morning, having
been informed that Strafford was approaching, the
Archbishop,—who was suffering severely from illness and the infirmities of old age,—was with some
difficulty supported to the window, where these
two great men looked at each other for the last
time. Strafford requested the prayers and blessing
of the Archbishop, on which the venerable prelate
lifted up his trembling hands to Heaven, and
solemnly blessed, and prayed for, his friend. A
moment afterwards, overcome with grief and natural
infirmity, he sank to the ground. On recovering
himself, he expressed much concern lest his weakness should be attributed to dread of his own approaching death. " I hope," he said, " by God's
assistance, and through mine own innocency, that
when I come to my own execution, I shall shew the
world how much more sensible I am of my Lord
Strafford's loss than I am of my own."

In the mean time, Strafford passed from the
Tower to the adjoining hill, less with the air of a condemned criminal than that of a General at the head
of his army. When the Lieutenant of the Tower
recommended him to make use of a coach, lest he
should be torn in pieces by the people ; " No, Mr.
Lieutenant," he said, " I dare look death in the face,
and, I trust, the people too." On the scaffold he
made a brief speech, in which he asserted, that never
at any moment had he entertained a thought op-

posed to the welfare either of the King or people ;
that he bore malice against no man ; that he sin-
cerely forgave his enemies; and that he died firm
in the true faith of the Church of England. Then,
having shaken hands affectionately with the Archbishop of Armagh, the Earl of Cleveland, and with
his brother, Sir George Wentworth, and others who
attended him, he knelt down by the side of his
chaplain, and remained praying for about half an
hour. Having risen up again, he beckoned his
brother towards him, and charged him with his
blessing, and some touching messages, to his wife and
young children. "One stroke more," he said, " will
make my wife husbandless, my dear children father-
less, my poor servants masterless, and will separate
me from my dear brothers and all my friends ; but
let God be to you and to them all in all."

The Earl then took off his doublet. "I thank
God," he said, " that I am no more afraid of death ;
but as cheerfully put off my doublet, at this time, as
ever I did when I went to bed." Having put on a
white cap, he thrust his hair underneath it with his
own hands. Then, having forgiven the executioner,
he knelt down at the block, the Archbishop being
on one side of him, and another clergyman on the
other ; the latter clasping the Earl's hands in his,
while they prayed. Having concluded his devotions,
he told the executioner that he would first make a
trial of the block by laying his head upon it, but
that he was not to strike till he should give him the
signal by stretching out his hands. Shortly after-

wards, placing his head a second time upon the block, he gave the appointed signal, when, at one blow, his head was severed from his body.

Thus, on the 12th of May, 1641, at the age of forty-eight, perished the great Lord Strafford; and on the 10th of January, 1645, the venerable Archbishop Laud was led forth from the Tower amidst the brutal revilings of the populace, to suffer upon the same spot which had witnessed the death of his friend. The old man prepared himself to die with exemplary piety and fortitude. When the appointed day was announced to him, " No one," he said, " can be more ready to send me out of life than I am to go." The night previous to his death was passed by him in a sound sleep, and when he was awakened by the Lieutenant of the Tower on the following morning, it was remarked that his countenance exhibited the same freshness of colour which it had ever worn. He ascended the scaffold with a serene, and even cheerful countenance, and, after delivering a brief speech, turned calmly to the executioner, and, presenting him with some money, desired him to do his work quickly. Kneeling down, he repeated a short prayer, and then, laying his head on the block, and giving the appointed signal to the executioner, by repeating the words, " Lord, receive my soul," the axe fell, and severed his head from his body by a single stroke.

When the sovereignty of the Commons of England sprung up from the ruined fortunes of Charles the

First, we find them, in their turn, exercising
the most despotic power, and filling the dungeons
of the Tower with the devoted adherents of the ill-
fated King. Among the most distinguished we find
Sir John Hotham, and his gallant son, Captain
Hotham; Sir Alexander Carew; the venerable
Lord Montague of Boughton; the Earl of Berk-
shire; Sir William Morton, the gallant defender
of Sudeley Castle; Colonel Monk, afterwards so
celebrated as the Duke of Albemarle; the Marquis of Winchester, captured at the surrender
of Basing House; the Earl of Cleveland; Sir
Lewis Dives; James, Duke of Hamilton; the gay
and gallant Earl of Holland; the profligate George
Goring, Earl of Norwich; the high-minded Lord
Capel; Sir Richard Gurney, Sir John Gayne, and
Sir Abraham Reynardson, successively Lord Mayors
of London; Lords Beauchamp, Bellases, and Chan-
dos; Edward, Lord Howard of Esrick; the Earls
of Crawford, Lauderdale, Kelly, and Rothes, taken
at the battle of Worcester; the famous Scottish
general, General Lesley; and the celebrated Edward, Marquis of Worcester. We have selected
only a few of the most distinguished from a long
and melancholy list of devoted loyalists, all of
whom suffered more or less by fine or imprisonment,—by the ruin of their families, and the desolation of their domestic hearths.

Of the gallant names, too, which we have mentioned, not a few expiated their loyalty on the
scaffold. Among the first who suffered were Sir

John Hotham, and his son, Captain Hotham, for a
design to deliver up the town of Hull to the King.
The son died fearlessly and piously; but the father,
attached to life, and buoyed up to the last with the
hopes of pardon, submitted himself to the stroke of
the executioner, not only with the greatest reluctance, but evidently depressed by a mental agony,
which rendered the tragedy pitiable in the extreme.
These "two unhappy gentlemen," as Lord Clarendon styles them, were both beheaded on Tower Hill,
in 1644, and about the same time, Sir Alexander
Carew, Governor of St. Nicholas Island, near
Plymouth, having returned to his allegiance to his
legitimate sovereign, suffered a like fate on the
same spot.

The next victims were the leaders of the Irish
rebellion, Lord Macquire and Colonel M'Mahon,
who were brought from Dublin to be inmates of
the Tower. These are among the few persons of
whose escape from the fortress there is any record.
Having contrived to cut through the door of their
apartment, they reached the Tower ditch, which
they easily swam, and for some time remained concealed in the house of the agent of the French
government. Their retreat, however, was at last
discovered, and they were hanged and quartered
at Tyburn, conformably with the terms of their
sentence.

A far more interesting prisoner in the Tower
was the high-minded Lord Capel, of whose attempt
to escape from its gloomy walls Lord Clarendon has

left us so graphic an account. "Having a cord and all things conveyed necessary to him, he let himself down out of the window of his chamber, in the night over the wall of the Tower, having been directed through what part of the ditch he might be best able to wade. Whether he found the right place, or whether there was no safer place, he found the water and the mud so deep, that if he had not been by the head taller than other men he must have perished, since the water came up to his chin. But it pleased God, that he got at last to the other side, where his friends expected him, and carried him to a chamber in the Temple. After two or three days, a friend whom he trusted much, and who deserved to be trusted, conceiving that he might be more secure in a place to which there was less resort, had provided a lodging for him in a private house in Lambeth Marsh; and calling upon him in an evening when it was dark, to go thither, they chose rather to take any boat they found ready at the Temple Stairs, than to trust one of that people with the secret; and it was so late that there was only one boat left there. In that the Lord Capel (as well disguised as he thought necessary) and his friend put themselves, and bid the waterman to row them to Lambeth. Whether in their passage thither the other gentleman called him ' My Lord,' as was confidently reported, or the waterman had any jealousy by observing what he thought was a disguise, when they were landed the wicked waterman, undiscerned, followed them, till

he saw into what house they went, and then went
to an officer and demanded ' what he would give
him to bring him to the place where the Lord Capel
lay ?' and the officer promising to give him ten
pounds, he led him presently to the house, where
that excellent person was seized upon, and the next
day carried to the Tower."

There were two other persons, of high hope and
exalted rank, who were conveyed from the Tower
by the same guard, and who were executed on the
same scaffold with Lord Capel. These were James
Duke of Hamilton, the attached friend of his ill-
fated sovereign, and the gay and handsome Henry
Rich, Earl of Holland, the favourite of two monarchs, and the darling of the fair sex. They were
executed on the 9th of March, 1649, less than six
weeks after the murder of the King, on a plat-
form which had been erected in New Palace Yard,
immediately in front of the entrance of Westminster
Hall : but the story of their tragical fate more
properly belongs to the account of the spot on
which they died.

During the administration of Oliver Cromwell,
the intrigues of the Fifth-monarchists, and the frequent attempts against the life and government of
the Protector kept the Tower constantly tenanted
with prisoners. From hence, in 1654, the young
fanatic, Sir John Gerrard, and the famous school-
master, Vowel, were led forth to their fate,—the
one to be beheaded on Tower Hill, and the other
to be hanged at Tyburn. It was here, too, that the

daring assassin, Miles Syndercombe, was found so mysteriously dead in his bed; and from hence the amiable divine, Dr. Hewett, and the gallant cavalier, Sir Henry Slingsby, were dragged mercilessly to their execution. Lastly, during the administration of Cromwell, we find the witty and profligate George Villiers, Duke of Buckingham,—

That life of pleasure, and that soul of whim,—

a denizen of the Tower; and here, also, was committed,—on suspicion of her being a secret agent of her royal lover, Charles the Second,—the famous Lucy Walters, one of the earliest, and perhaps the most beautiful, of the mistresses of the "merry monarch," and the mother of the unfortunate Duke of Monmouth.

Charles the Second appears to have been the last of our sovereigns who have passed a night in the Tower. Adopting the ancient usage of the Kings of England, on the 22nd of April, 1661,—the eve of his coronation,—he embarked at Whitehall, and passing from thence by water to the Tower, he proceeded the next morning with a magnificent procession to Westminster Abbey.

At the commencement of his reign, the Tower, as might naturally be expected, was crowded with a host of regicides, Fifth-monarchy men, and other political and religious enthusiasts. Among them we find several of the most prominent actors in the late disastrous times.   Here were imprisoned the crafty visionary, Sir Henry Vane; the sturdy enthusiast, General Harrison ; the witty and impious

Henry Marten; Edmund Ludlow; the brutal Solicitor-General, John Cook, who conducted the prosecution against Charles the First; Colonel Daniel Axtell, who commanded the guard on the occasion, and who forced the soldiers to shout for "justice and execution;" Colonel Francis Hacker, who commanded the guard on the scaffold; Captain William Hewlet, accused of having been the masked executioner; and lastly, the heartless fanatical preacher, Hugh Peters. Sir Henry Vane was beheaded on Tower Hill; Harrison, Cook, Axtell, Hacker, and Hugh Peters, were hanged, drawn, and quartered; Henry Marten died in Chepstow Castle, after an imprisonment of twenty years; and Edmund Ludlow in exile in Switzerland, nearly half a century after he had put his pen to the death-warrant of his king. Of the fate of Hewlet we are ignorant, but he was unquestionably not the individual who decapitated the King.

In addition to the persons we have mentioned, we find the names of several others who sat in judgment on their sovereign, and who approved the sentence which condemned him to the block. Of these, Colonel Adrian Scrope, Colonel John Jones, Colonel John Okey, Colonel John Barkstead, Gregory Clement, Miles Corbet, and Thomas Corbet, were condemned to death, and were hanged, drawn, and quartered, in pursuance of the terms of their sentence.

Unquestionably the two most interesting prisoners in the Tower, during the reign of Charles the

Second, were the high-minded friends, William
Lord Russell, and Algernon Sidney. The circumstances which led them to the block are familiar to
every one. Lord Russell was the first who suffered.
On the 13th of July, 1683, he was arraigned for
high treason at the bar of the Old Bailey, and,
having been found guilty, was sentenced to death.
In vain did his afflicted wife throw herself at the
King's feet;—in vain did she implore that the services and merits of her father, the good Earl of
Southampton, might plead as some atonement for
the errors of her husband. Charles remained inexorable, and Lord Russell prepared himself for
the last stroke, with a dignity and resolution becoming the high character which he had ever sus-
tained for piety and virtue.

His last parting with his wife was a severe trial,
but that noble-minded woman had collected all
her strength for the occasion, and, by her own
strengthened the resolution of her unfortunate
lord. As he turned from her, " Now," he said,
" the bitterness of death is past." When his friend,
Lord Cavendish, proposed to change clothes with
him, and to remain in the Tower in his room, he
refused to avail himself of a chance of escape,
which might entail danger on one he loved. Again,
when the Duke of Monmouth offered to surrender
himself, in hopes that by this means he might save
his friend's life, " No," he said, " it will be of no
advantage to me to have my friends die with me."
He continued serene, and even cheerful, to the last.

The day before his execution, being seized with a
bleeding at the nose, he observed to Bishop Burnet,
" I shall not let blood to divert this distemper;
that will be done to-morrow." Shortly before the
sheriffs made their appearance to conduct him to
the scaffold, he wound up his watch, " Now," he
said, " I have done with time, and must think
henceforth of eternity."

The execution of Lord Russell took place on
the 21st of July, eight days after his condemnation. The scaffold on which he suffered was erected
in Lincoln's Inn Fields, whither he was conducted
from the Tower through great crowds of people,
who deeply commiserated his fate. Having concluded his devotions, he undressed himself, and,
without the least change of countenance, placed
his neck upon the block, when, at two strokes, the
executioner severed his head from his body.

Algernon Sidney was brought to the Tower on
the 21st of November, and, on the 7th of December following, was beheaded on a scaffold erected on
Tower Hill. The virtuous and unbending republican
passed to the fatal stage on foot; declining the
attendance even of a single friend, and accompanied
only, " for decency," by two footmen of his brother,
the Earl of Leicester, who walked behind him. He
ascended the scaffold with a firm step, a haughty
look, and erect posture, as one who came rather to
command than to suffer. " Englishmen wept not
for him," says Dalrymple, " as they had done for
Lord Russell : their pulses beat high, their hearts

swelled, they felt an unusual grandeur and elevation of mind, whilst they looked upon him." When asked by one of the sheriffs if it was his intention to harangue the people, " I have made my peace with God," he said, " and have nothing to say to man." A moment afterwards, he added, " I am ready to die, and will give you no further trouble." His last prayer was for the " good old cause." Instead of endeavouring to prolong existence by protracted prayers and lingering farewells, he hurried over the melancholy preparations, and, hastening towards the block, as if impatient to die, submitted himself to the stroke of the executioner.

Not the least remarkable event connected with the history of the Tower, in the reign of Charles the Second, was the mysterious and tragical end of Arthur Capel, Earl of Essex, a nobleman possessed of high attainments, of great personal courage, and of many amiable qualities. He had been committed to the Tower for his presumed share in the famous Rye House Plot, but, in the course of Lord Russell's trial, intelligence was received in court, that the Earl had been discovered with his throat cut by a razor. There existed a strong suspicion that he had been murdered. Notwithstanding, however, some suspicious circumstances, there seems to be little doubt that the Earl was the author of his own death. He is known to have been of an hypochondriacal temperament, and, as he had notoriously expressed himself an advocate for suicide, it is far more reasonable to presume that he laid violent hands on

himself, than that the Court should have con-
nived at so foul and unnecessary a crime. Charles,
indeed, is said to have been deeply affected when
the tragical story was communicated to him. Alluding to the execution of the Earl's father, the
great Lord Capel, " My Lord Essex," he said,
" need not have despaired of mercy, for I owed
him a life."

Probably no person ever paid so many visits to
the Tower as a prisoner, as the profligate and ver-
satile George Villiers, Duke of Buckingham. We
have already seen him imprisoned as a state criminal, during the administration of Cromwell, and
it is remarkable that, during the reign of Charles
the Second, he was committed to the Tower no
less than four different times. The first occasion
was in 1666, on account of a quarrel which he had,
in the House of Lords, with Lord Ossory, eldest son
of the Duke of Ormond, whom he first insulted with
his unlicensed wit, and whom he afterwards shewed
a considerable disinclination to meet in the field.
A short time afterwards, the Duke was committed
for a disgraceful squabble which he had with the
Marquis of Dorchester,—during a conference which
took place between the Houses of Lords and Commons,—on which occasion we find him knocking
off the Marquis's hat, and pulling aside his periwig.
Again, in 1667, he was imprisoned in the Tower
for " treasonable and seditious practices:" but
Charles was too fond of the society of his favourite to allow him to remain long in prison, and,

accordingly, three months afterwards, we find him again taking his seat at the Council-board,—

> In the ring
> Of mimic statesmen and their merry king.

Lastly, the frolic Duke was re-committed to the Tower, the same year, for using unconstitutional language during a debate of great importance in the House of Lords.

On the latter occasion was committed to the Tower, together with the Duke, the turbulent and factious incendiary, Anthony Ashley Cooper, Earl of Shaftsbury, whom Dryden, in his " Absalom and Achitophel," has damned to everlasting fame. Buckingham, on making a proper submission, was released from confinement; but Shaftsbury, desirous of being regarded as a political martyr, chose to remain refractory, and consequently remained a prisoner for nearly a year. As the gay Duke, on being liberated from his uncomfortable lodgings, was passing under the windows of Shaftsbury's apartments in the Tower, the stubborn Earl looked out wistfully, " What," he said, " are you going to leave us ? "—" Why, yes," replied Buckingham, " such giddy-headed fellows as I am can never stay long in one place."

The name of George Villiers recalls that of another prisoner as gay, as witty, and as unprincipled, — John Wilmot, Earl of Rochester. He was committed, about the year 1669, for the forcible abduction of Elizabeth Mallett, *la triste héritière* of De Grammont, whom he afterwards married, and who became the mother of his children.

During the brief reign of James the Second, the prisoners in the Tower of the greatest note were James, Duke of Monmouth; the seven Bishops; and the brutal Chancellor, George Lord Jefferies. After the fatal battle of Sedgmoor, the unfortunate Monmouth, having changed clothes with a peasant, wandered about the country during two miserable days and nights, when he was at last discovered in a dry ditch near Holbridge in Dorsetshire, with some peas, his whole stock of provisions, in one pocket, and the George and Garter in the other. When discovered, he trembled violently, and burst into tears. From the spot where he was discovered, Monmouth was conducted by a strong guard of militia to Winchester, and thence to Vauxhall, where he was received by Lord Oxford's regiment, who brought him by water to Whitehall, whence, the same evening, he was carried to the Tower. For some days after his arrest, his fears are described as distressing in the extreme. The gay and gallant Monmouth, who had so often gained renown on the field of battle, was unable to anticipate without shrinking the terrors of the scaffold.

As his end drew near, however, he roused himself from his despondency, and prepared for the last stroke with a fortitude becoming his natural character. On the day before his execution, his wronged and amiable Duchess expressed a strong desire to be admitted to a last interview with him in the Tower. He complied with her request; but his heart was with another, the Lady Henrietta Wentworth, grand-daughter and sole heiress of Thomas, Earl of Cleveland, and afterwards Baroness Wentworth in her own right. Lady Henrietta returned his affection, and died a few months after her ill-fated lover, of a broken heart. Monmouth had always affected to regard her as his wife in the eyes of God; affirming that his almost infantine marriage with his Duchess, in which he had no choice, had absolved him from its unpalatable ties.

According to Evelyn, Monmouth received his Duchess with much coldness. This, however, does not appear to have been the case. We have the authority of an eye-witness, that "he gave her the kindest character that could be, begged her pardon for his many failings and offences to her, and prayed her to continue her kindness and care to her poor children. At this expression she fell down on her knees, with her eyes full of tears, and begged him to pardon her if ever she had done anything to offend and displease him; and embracing his knees, fell into a swoon, out of which they had much ado to raise her up in a good while after. A little before, his children were brought to him, all crying about him; but he acquitted himself of these last adieus with much composure, shewing nothing of weakness or unmanliness."

It may be remarked that on the day on which the news of Monmouth's defeat reached London, the Duchess was herself most unjustly sent to the

Tower with her two young sons. Her imprisonment, however, must have been a brief one, for
we are assured of the singular fact, that, on
the morning of her husband's execution, the King
invited himself to breakfast with her, which he
could scarcely have done had she been a prisoner in
the Tower.

> She had known adversity,
> Though born in such a high degree;
> In pride of power, and beauty's bloom,
> Had wept o'er Monmouth's bloody tomb.
> *Lay of the Last Minstrel.*

On the night before his execution, Monmouth
was attended by the Bishops of Ely, and Bath and
Wells, who prayed with him, and watched while he
slept; and, on the fatal morning, he was also visited
by the pious Tenison, afterwards Archbishop of Canterbury, who has left us an interesting account of
their interview. About ten o'clock, accompanied by
the two Bishops, Monmouth was conducted through
an avenue of soldiers to Tower Hill. He mounted
the scaffold without the least apparent fear, and
amidst the tears of the populace, of whom he was the
idol. To these he addressed a brief farewell. After
observing that he died in the faith of the Church of
England, he turned to the subject nearest his heart,
and spoke of his paramour. She was a person,
he said, of great honour and virtue, "a religious
godly lady." The bishops reminded him of the sin
of adultery. "No," he replied, "for these two
years last past, I have lived in no sin that I know
of; I have wronged no person, and I am sure when

I die I shall go to God; therefore I do not fear death, which you may see in my face." The Bishops then commenced praying for him, and he knelt down and joined them : they concluded with a short prayer for the King, on which he hesitated a moment, but at length said Amen.

To the Lady Henrietta he sent his ring, watch, and tooth-pick case, and to the executioner he gave six guineas; entrusting four more to a byestander, with injunctions to deliver them to the heads-man, in the event of his performing his task with adroitness. While he was undressing himself, the Bishops continued to exhort him with pious ejacu-lations. "God," they said, "accept your repentance; God accept your imperfect repentance; God accept your general repentance!" Then, having refused to have his eyes bandaged, he knelt down, and laying his head upon the block, gave the appointed signal. The executioner, however, either from dismay or pity, struck so feeble a blow, that Monmouth, to the horror of the spectators, raised his head from the block, and looked him, as if reproachfully, in the face; nor was it till after the fifth blow that the executioner completed his bloody work. The Duke's head having been sewn to the body, his re-mains were placed in a coffin, covered with black velvet, and conveyed in a hearse to the Tower Chapel.

On the occasion of the imprisonment of the Seven Bishops, on the 8th of June, 1688, the land-ing-place at the Tower presented a remarkable scene. They were conducted thither by water, and, as they passed down the river, a great part of the population,—inflamed by religious zeal and trembling for their civil liberties, — flowed to the water's edge to behold the affecting spectacle. With loud acclamations, they extolled the constancy and courage of the venerable champions of their religion, who, in their turn, with a lowly and submissive deportment, exhorted the people to remain true to their loyalty, to fear God, and honour the King. As they neared the Tower, many people waded into the water to obtain a share of their benedictions, and, on landing, even the soldiers, partaking of the universal enthusiasm, flung themselves on their knees before the fathers of their Church, and craved the blessing of those criminals whom they were appointed to guard. On entering the Tower, the Bishops immediately proceeded to attend evening service in the Chapel, and it was remarked how apposite was a passage in the second lesson to their peculiar position. (2 Cor. vi.) " Giving no offence in anything, that the ministry be not blamed : but in all things approving ourselves as the ministers of God, in much patience, in afflictions, in distresses, in imprisonments," &c.

On the 12th of December following, Lord Chancellor Jefferies, — that memorable ruffian, who united the cruelty of Caligula with the buffooneries of a Grimaldi,— was committed a prisoner to the Tower. About the time that King James fled from Whitehall, he disguised himself in the habit

of a common sailor, and took up his abode in a
small house at Wapping. It was generally supposed that he had accompanied the King in his
flight; but, one day, as he was looking out of his
window, with a seaman's cap on, he was re-
cognized by a clerk in Chancery, who immediately gave such information as led to his arrest. On his way to the Lord Mayor, it was
with the greatest difficulty that the mob could
be prevented from tearing him to pieces. The
effect whch his presence produced on the Lord
Mayor was very different. So impressed was he
with terror at having to sit in judgment over the
dreaded and inhuman Chancellor, that, during the
examination, he was seized with a fit of apoplexy,
of which he shortly afterwards died. Either overcome by his misfortunes, or willing to drown the
memory of his crimes, Jefferies, while a prisoner in
the Tower, addicted himself more than ever to
intemperate drinking; and this circumstance, added
to the blows and bruises which he had received
from the mob, shortly afterwards threw him into a
fever, of which he died. The warrant for his burial
in the Tower chapel is endorsed, "George Lord
Jefferies, died 19th April, 1689, 35 minutes past
four in the morning."

The principal prisoners in the Tower, in the reign
of William the Third, were the well-known Arthur
Herbert Earl of Torrington, committed in 1690, for
his conduct in the action with the French fleet off
Beechy Head; Richard Viscount Preston, con-

demned to death for high treason, but subsequently
pardoned; John, afterwards the celebrated Duke of
Marlborough; Charles Lord Mohun; and the gallant
and lamented Sir John Fenwick.

It is remarkable that Lord Mohun was twice
committed for murder during this reign. The first
occasion was in 1692, for the murder of the celebrated actor, William Mountford;— the beautiful
actress Mrs. Bracegirdle, being the origin of the
quarrel. He was again committed, in 1699, with
Edward Earl of Warwick, for the murder of Richard
Coote, Esq., but on both occasions was acquitted at
his trial. He subsequently fought his famous duel
with James Duke of Hamilton, in Hyde Park, in
1712, on which occasion both combatants were slain.

Sir John Fenwick, having been found guilty of
high treason, was beheaded on Tower Hill, on the
28th of January, 1697. He died much lamented
for his manly qualities, and it was affirmed that, in
signing the warrant for his execution, King William
was influenced by feelings of personal hostility and
dislike. That a feeling of mutual ill-will existed
between the King and Fenwick there can be no
doubt. It seems to have originated in a severe reprimand, which Fenwick received from William,
then Prince of Orange, at the siege of Maestricht,
which the former repaid by seizing every opportunity of loading the Prince with abuse. So violent,
indeed, were his invectives, that William once observed, that "had he been a private person, he must
have cut Sir John's throat." Much, however, as we

may lament the melancholy fate of a brave man, there can be little question, that, in signing the death-warrant of Sir John Fenwick, William merely followed the strict line marked out for him by both policy and justice.

During the reign of Queen Anne, the Tower presents but slight features of interest. Comparatively but few persons were imprisoned here during her reign, and of these, Sir Robert Walpole, — committed in 1712, "for high breach of trust and notorious corruption,"—is the only individual whose name is familiar to us in history. That he was innocent of the charges preferred against him there can be but little doubt; while the esteem and admiration with which his own party continued to regard him, must have gone far to soften the rigour of imprisonment. So crowded was his apartment in the Tower by persons of the first rank and distinction, that it is said to have far more resembled a splendid levee than the prison of a proscribed man. Among his constant visitors were the great Duke of Marlborough and his beautiful Duchess; the celebrated ministers, Lords Godolphin, Somers, and Sunderland; and the famous Pulteney,—then his most intimate friend, but afterwards his bitterest enemy. The apartment occupied by Walpole in the Tower was subsequently inhabited by the once celebrated poet, George Granville, Lord Lansdown, when, in 1715, that nobleman suffered imprisonment for his attachment to the House of Stuart. Walpole had written

his name on the window, and the circumstance
being pointed out to Lord Lansdown, he inscribed
beneath it the following lines;—

> Good unexpected, evil unforeseen,
> Appear by turns, as fortune shifts the scene ;
> Some, raised aloft, come tumbling down amain,
> And fall so hard, they bound and rise again.

In June, 1715, shortly after the accession of
George the First, Robert Harley, Earl of Oxford,
was arrested for high treason, and committed to
the Tower, whither he was followed by large crowds
of people, who shewed how deeply they sympathised
with the altered fortunes of the once powerful
statesman. He remained in prison about two years,
when, on his own petition, he was brought to trial
before the House of Peers, and was unanimously
acquitted. A fellow-prisoner with the Earl of Oxford in the Tower, was the eloquent and accomplished statesman, Sir William Wyndham, who was
committed, in August, 1715, for his supposed intrigues on behalf of the House of Stuart. He was
never brought to trial, and obtained his release
after a short imprisonment.

The suppression of the Scottish insurrection, in
1715, crowded the Tower with several gallant and
unfortunate prisoners. Among these were James
Radcliffe, Earl of Derwentwater; William Max-
well, Earl of Nithisdale; Robert Dalziel, Earl of
Carnwath; George Seton, Earl of Wintoun; William Gordon, Viscount Kenmure; William Widdrington, Lord Widdrington; and William Murray,
Lord Nairn. Of these devoted adherents to the

House of Stuart, two only, the Earl of Derwentwater and Lord Kenmure, suffered on the scaffold.
The Earl of Nithisdale contrived to escape from the
Tower in female attire, and Lord Wintoun, by saw-
ing through the bars of his prison and inducing his
keepers to connive in his flight.   Lord Nairn was
respited and subsequently pardoned, and the Earl
of Carnwath and Lord Widdrington were released
by the Act of Grace in 1717.

The Earl of Derwentwater and Lord Kenmure
were executed on the same scaffold, on the 24th of
February, 1716.   The gallant Derwentwater was the
first who suffered.   About ten o'clock in the morning he was brought in a coach from the Tower to the
Transport Office on Tower Hill.   After remaining
there a short time, he was led through an avenue of
soldiers to the scaffold, which was erected directly
opposite, and was entirely covered with black.   As
he ascended the fatal steps, he was observed to
turn pale, but his voice remained firm, and he preserved his natural composure.   Having passed about
a quarter of an hour in prayer, he read aloud a
paper to the bystanders, in which he professed the
most unshaken loyalty to the Chevalier St. George,
whom alone he acknowledged as his lawful sovereign.   He then closely examined the block, and
finding a rough place on it, he desired the executioner to chip it off with his axe.   This being done,
he took off his coat and waistcoat, and told the
executioner, who knelt down to receive his forgiveness, that he would find something in the pockets to

reward him for his trouble. Having first of all lain down and fitted his neck to the block, he repeated a short prayer, after which he told the executioner that the sign he should give him to strike would be by repeating three times the words, " Lord Jesus, receive my soul!" and by stretching out his arms. He then once more fitted his neck to the block, and having given the appointed signal, the executioner performed his office at a single blow.

The virtuous and amiable Lord Kenmure was then brought on the scaffold, attended by his son, a few friends, and two clergymen of the Church of England. He mounted the steps with great firmness, and advancing to one side of the scaffold, passed some time in devotion, in which he was heard to pray audibly for the exiled Prince in whose cause he suffered. Having concluded his devotions, he presented the executioner with some money, telling him he should give him no sign, but that, when he had lain down, he was to strike whenever he thought fit. He then knelt down, and having passed a few moments in inward devotion placed his neck upon the block with his arms clasped tightly round it, when the executioner, seizing his opportunity, raised his axe, and at two blows severed his head from his body.

On the 24th of August, 1722, the celebrated Francis Atterbury, Bishop of Rochester, was committed to the Tower, where he was subjected to a series of privations and oppression, which were

disgraceful to the ministry which authorized them,
but which he endured with the piety of a Christian,
and the dignity of a philosopher.

> How pleasing Atterbury's softer hour ;
> How shines his soul unconquered in the Tower.

He remained in the Tower till the 18th of June,
1723, on which day he was conducted on board the
" Aldborough" man-of-war, and bade farewell for
ever to his native country. The Bishop died in
exile in Paris on the 15th of February, 1731.

We would willingly dwell on the melancholy
fate of the " Rebel Lords" who were committed to
the Tower after the fatal battle of Culloden, but
their stories are so familiar to every one, that a repetition would scarcely be considered excusable.
The old Marquis of Tullibardine,—

> High-minded Moray, the exiled, the dear !

died in the Tower a few months after his committal, and Lord Kilmarnock, and the intrepid Lord
Balmerino were beheaded on Tower Hill on the
18th of August.

Charles Radcliffe, brother of the unfortunate Earl
of Derwentwater, was decapitated on the same spot,
on the 8th of December following ; and lastly, the
hoary traitor, Lord Lovat,—after a hearty meal and
with a jest on his lips,—laid down his life on the
scaffold on Tower Hill, on the 7th of April, 1747.
The only other prisoner of note, in the reign of
George the Second, was Laurence, fourth Earl
Ferrers, who was hanged at Tyburn, on the 5th of
May, 1760, for killing his steward, Mr. Johnson.

As we approach nearer to more humane and civilized times, the annals of the Tower naturally present fewer incidents of stirring or romantic interest. Nevertheless, during the reigns of George the Third and Fourth, we find the Tower containing more than one prisoner whose name history has rendered familiar to us. Here, in 1762, the celebrated John Wilkes was committed for his libel on the King, in the forty-fifth number of the "North Briton;" Lord George Gordon was sent to the Tower, in 1780, as the principal of the Protestant riots; Horne Tooke, and his seditious associates, in 1794; Arthur O'Connor, and others, for high treason, in 1798; Sir Francis Burdett, for the same offence, in 1810; and lastly, here were confined, in 1820, Arthur Thistlewood and the other actors in the notorious Cato Street conspiracy.

END OF THE SECOND VOLUME.

LONDON:
Printed by S. & J. BENTLEY, WILSON, and FLEY,
Bangor House, Shoe Lane.